The Last Shah

The Last Shah

AMERICA, IRAN, AND THE FALL
OF THE PAHLAVI DYNASTY

Ray Takeyh

A COUNCIL ON FOREIGN RELATIONS BOOK

Yale UNIVERSITY PRESS

New Haven & London

Published with assistance from the foundation established in memory of James
Wesley Cooper of the Class of 1865, Yale College.

Yale University Press books may be purchased in quantity for educational, business,
or promotional use. For information, please e-mail sales.press@yale.edu
(U.S. office) or sales@yaleup.co.uk (U.K. office).

Set in Adobe Garamond type by IDS Infotech Ltd.
Printed and bound by CPI Group (UK) Ltd, Croydon, CR0 4YY

Library of Congress Control Number: 2020937955
ISBN 978-0-300-21779-7 (hardcover : alk. paper)

ISBN 978-0-300-26465-4 (pbk)

A catalogue record for this book is available from the British Library.

10 9 8 7 6 5 4 3 2 1

THE COUNCIL ON FOREIGN RELATIONS

The Council on Foreign Relations (CFR) is an independent, nonpartisan membership organization, think tank, and publisher dedicated to being a resource for its members, government officials, business executives, journalists, educators and students, civic and religious leaders, and other interested citizens in order to help them better understand the world and the foreign policy choices facing the United States and other countries. Founded in 1921, CFR carries out its mission by maintaining a diverse membership, with special programs to promote interest and develop expertise in the next generation of foreign policy leaders; convening meetings at its headquarters in New York and in Washington, DC, and other cities where senior government officials, members of Congress, global leaders, and prominent thinkers come together with CFR members to discuss and debate major international issues; supporting a Studies Program that fosters independent research, enabling CFR scholars to produce articles, reports, and books and hold roundtables that analyze foreign policy issues and make concrete policy recommendations; publishing *Foreign Affairs,* the preeminent journal on international affairs and U.S. foreign policy; sponsoring Independent Task Forces that produce reports with both findings and policy prescriptions on the most important foreign policy topics; and providing up-to-date information and analysis about world events and American foreign policy on its website, www.cfr.org.

The Council on Foreign Relations takes no institutional position on policy issues and has no affiliation with the U.S. government. All statements of fact and expressions of opinion contained in its publications are the sole responsibility of the author or authors.

I dedicate this book to my parents and all those who suffered at the hands of the revolution.

Contents

Contents

Cast of Characters

Dean Acheson, U.S. secretary of state, 1949–1953, under President Harry S. Truman

Hossein Alā, prime minister of Iran, March 1951–April 1951 and 1955–1957; ambassador of Iran to the United States, 1945–1950

Asadollah Alam, prime minister of Iran, 1962–1964

Ali Amini, prime minister of Iran, 1961–1962

Jamshid Amouzegar, prime minister of Iran, 1977–1978

Hassan Arsanjani, Iran's minister of agriculture, 1961–1962

Clement Attlee, prime minister of the United Kingdom, 1945–1951

Gholam Reza Azhari, chief of staff of the Iranian armed forces, 1971–1978; prime minister of Iran, 1978–1979

Shapour Bakhtiar, prime minister of Iran, January 1979–February 1979

Teymur Bakhtiar, first director of SAVAK, 1957–1961

Abolhassan Banisadr, first president of Iran, 1980–1981

Morteza-Qoli Bayat, prime minister of Iran, 1944–1945

Mehdi Bazargan, prime minister of Iran, February 1979–November 1979

Mohammad Beheshti, chief justice of Iran, 1980–1981

Ernest Bevin, British secretary of state for foreign affairs, 1945–1951; lord privy seal, March 1951–April 1951

Zbigniew Brzezinski, national security adviser, 1977–1981, under President Jimmy Carter

Reader Bullard, British ambassador to Iran, 1942–1946

James Byrnes, U.S. secretary of state, 1945–1947, under President Harry S. Truman

Warren Christopher, U.S. deputy secretary of state, 1977–1981, under President Jimmy Carter; U.S. secretary of state, 1993–1997, under President Bill Clinton

Allen Dulles, director of central intelligence, 1953–1961, under Presidents Dwight D. Eisenhower and John F. Kennedy

John Foster Dulles, U.S. secretary of state, 1953–1959, under President Dwight D. Eisenhower

Anthony Eden, British secretary of state for foreign affairs, 1935–1938, 1940–1945, and 1951–1955; prime minister of the United Kingdom, 1955–1957

Manuchehr Eqbal, prime minister of Iran, 1957–1960

Akbar Etemad, head of the Atomic Energy Organization of Iran, 1974–1978

Hossein Fatemi, Iran's minister of foreign affairs, 1952–1953

Mohammad Ali Foroughi, prime minister of Iran, 1941–1942

Abbas Gharabaghi, Iran's minister of interior, August 1978–January 1979; appointed chief of staff of the Iranian armed forces in January 1979

Henry Grady, U.S. ambassador to Iran, 1950–1951

Averell Harriman, U.S. ambassador to the Soviet Union, 1943–1946, under Presidents Franklin D. Roosevelt and Harry S. Truman; U.S. secretary of commerce, 1946–1948, under President Harry S. Truman; U.S. assistant secretary of state for East Asian and Pacific Affairs, 1961–1963

Richard Helms, director of central intelligence, 1966–1973, under Presidents Lyndon B. Johnson and Richard Nixon; U.S. ambassador to Iran, 1973–1976, under Presidents Richard Nixon and Gerald Ford

Loy Henderson, U.S. ambassador to Iran, 1951–1954, under President Dwight D. Eisenhower

Cordell Hull, U.S. secretary of state, 1933–1944, under President Franklin D. Roosevelt

Robert Huyser, deputy commander of U.S. European Command, 1975–1979; dispatched as military adviser to stabilize Iran in early January 1979 under President Jimmy Carter

Ayatollah Abol-Qassem Kashani, speaker of the Majlis, 1952–1953

Mohammad Khatami, chief of staff of the Iranian air force, 1957–1975

Ahmad Khomeini, son of Ruhollah Khomeini

Ruhollah Khomeini, leader of the Islamic Revolution and first supreme leader of Iran, 1979–1989

Robert Komer, member of the national security staff under U.S. National Security Advisor McGeorge Bundy

Ali Mansur, prime minister of Iran, 1940–1941 and March 1950–June 1950

Hassan Ali Mansur, prime minister of Iran, 1964–1965

George McGhee, U.S. assistant secretary of state for Near Eastern, South Asian, and African Affairs, 1949–1951, under President Harry S. Truman; U.S. under secretary of state for political affairs, 1961–1963, under President John F. Kennedy

Robert McNamara, U.S. secretary of defense, 1961–1968, under Presidents John F. Kennedy and Lyndon B. Johnson

Arthur Millspaugh, adviser to the U.S. State Department Office of Foreign Trade; advised Finance Ministry of Iran, 1922–1927 and 1942–1945

Vyacheslav Molotov, Soviet minister of foreign affairs, 1939–1949, under Josif Stalin

Nasser Moqaddam, director of SAVAK, 1978–1979

Leland Morris, U.S. ambassador to Iran, 1944–1945, under Presidents Franklin D. Roosevelt and Harry S. Truman

Mohammad Mossadeq, prime minister of Iran, 1951–1953

Nematollah Nasiri, director of SAVAK, 1965–1978

Ashraf Pahlavi, Iranian princess, twin sister of Mohammad Reza Shah

Hassan Pakravan, director of SAVAK, 1961–1965

Valiollah Qarani, head of Iranian military intelligence in the 1950s; chief of staff of the Iranian Armed forces, February 1979–March 1979

Ahmad Qavam, prime minister of Iran, June 1921–January 1922, June 1922–February 1923, August 1942–February 1943, January 1946–December 1947, and for six days in July 1952

Ali Razmara, prime minister of Iran, 1950–1951

Kermit Roosevelt Jr., U.S. Central Intelligence Agency officer who played a leading role on the ground in Tehran during Operation TPAJAX in 1953

Dean Rusk, U.S. secretary of state, 1961–1969, under Presidents John F. Kennedy and Lyndon B. Johnson

Mohammad Sa'ed, prime minister of Iran, 1948–1950

Karim Sanjabi, leader of the National Front; Iranian minister of foreign affairs, February 1979–April 1979

Jafar Sharif-Emami, prime minister of Iran, August 1960–May 1961 and August 1978–November 1978

Walter Bedell Smith, U.S. ambassador to the Soviet Union, 1946–1948, under President Harry S. Truman; director of central intelligence, 1950–1953, under Presidents Harry S. Truman and Dwight D. Eisenhower; U.S. under secretary of state, 1953–1954, under President Dwight D. Eisenhower

Ali Soheili, prime minister of Iran, March 1942–August 1942

William Sullivan, U.S. ambassador to Iran, 1977–1979, under President Jimmy Carter

Mahmoud Taleqani, Iranian ayatollah; head of the Revolutionary Council and member of the Assembly of Experts, August 1979–November 1979

Stansfield Turner, director of central intelligence, 1977–1981, under President Jimmy Carter

Cyrus Vance, U.S. secretary of state, 1977–1980, under President Jimmy Carter

Frank Wisner, deputy director of plans at the Central Intelligence Agency, 1951–1958

Ardeshir Zahedi, Iranian minister of foreign affairs, 1966–1971; ambassador of Iran to the United States, 1973–1979

Fazlollah Zahedi, replaced Mohammad Mossadeq as prime minister during the 1953 coup; prime minister of Iran, 1953–1955

The Last Shah

Introduction

THROUGH THE LOOKING GLASS

Why did Iran have a revolution in 1979? The immediate causes can be easily summarized: The economic recession of the mid-1970s had halted the shah's development projects and created expectations that the state could not meet. Pervasive repression was making peaceful protest impossible. The decayed Pahlavi state lacked a sturdy foundation and had become merely a source of patronage to a dwindling elite. The American support that the shah needed as psychological backing had grown unsteady. The massive protest movement that broke out in the late 1970s had revealed that the upper echelons of the Pahlavi state were manned by hesitant functionaries with no real stake in perpetuating the monarchy. No one was willing to die for the shah, and the shah was dying of cancer. And the determined Ayatollah Ruhollah Khomeini had managed to unify the many strands of opposition behind his uncompromising stance even though, at the outset of the revolt, nearly all of the shah's detractors were willing to come to terms with the regime. All of this is true but insufficient. To fully appreciate how a seemingly formidable monarchy collapsed so suddenly, one must trace its evolution from the time the shah first came to power, in 1941.

When Crown Prince Mohammad Reza Pahlavi first took over, he was twenty-one years old. The great powers had recently exiled his father, suspecting him of harboring pro-Nazi sentiments. The world was at war, and Iran was an occupied and impoverished country. The young shah, often depicted as a dilettante who occupied himself with palace pleasures and had little interest in affairs of the state, was instead an ambitious leader who believed that his country could prosper only if it was led by a modernizing autocrat supported by a cadre of technocrats who would discharge his many schemes. Throughout his life, the shah had contempt for democratic rule and believed that great things happen only when a benevolent dictator is in charge.

At first there were too many obstacles in the shah's way, none more significant than the aristocracy. The landlords, merchants, urban notables, and clerics who made up the Iranian elite were tied to the traditions of their class and devoted to preserving their nation's institutions, including the long-established monarchy. They dominated the parliaments and cabinets and had a real feel for the mood of the nation. This was rule by a narrow cast of elites, but the system was not without democratic trappings. The elections were manipulated, but they reflected an attempt to address local concerns. As men whose wealth was often tied to the land, these authorities could sense the peasants' and laborers' grievances and often responded to their distress. Town and country were tied together.

Iran at this point still produced great men who did much to save the country. Prime Minister Mohammad Ali Foroughi persuaded the Allies to respect Iran's sovereignty and withdraw their forces shortly after the war. This was no small achievement for a country whose army had collapsed and whose monarch had been expelled because of his flirtations with Hitler. When Stalin lingered in Azerbaijan and contemplated dismembering Iran, it was another prime minister, Ahmad Qavam, who tricked the world's most menacing remaining despot into meekly giving up his prey. Mohammad Mossadeq, as prime minister, did more than reclaim Iran's oil from foreigners; his National Front Party had an expansive social-welfare agenda that was to bring health care and education to every Iranian. Ali Amini, Iran's last great premier, prophetically warned the shah that monarchs who rule rather than reign end up doing neither.

The shah never saw the value of these men, and from the outset he chipped away at their authority. He was a man in a hurry, and they stood between him and his autocracy. After the war, he steadily increased his powers, dismissing politicians and undermining the parliament by creating an upper chamber that he controlled. The vibrant press was gradually silenced and independent political parties harassed into extinction. The military was to be the basis of his power and the officer corps his most reliable constituency. Soon he would create a secret police whose reputation for brutality belied its incompetence.

It is impossible to consider Iran's political trajectory without assessing the infamous 1953 coup that overthrew Mossadeq's government. Operation TPAJAX has the distinction of being the only Cold War covert action that has penetrated the popular imagination. The Islamic Republic's emissaries never stop mentioning it, despite their contempt for Mossadeq and the National Front's liberalism. And for many American officials, the pathway to smoothing relations with Iran is to apologize for an event that they poorly understand. The history of the coup is an ambiguous one. In the end, it may be impossible to determine with any precision what happened in Tehran on August 19. We do know that it was a time when Iran's political class was still capable of taking the initiative. Mossadeq's mishandling of the oil crisis was ruining the economy, and his creeping dictatorship was threatening too many stakeholders. It was Mossadeq's aristocratic peers who first turned against him and took the most consequential steps to end his tenure.

Despite its notoriety, the 1953 coup did not fundamentally alter Iran's politics. In its aftermath, the prime ministers still wielded authority, the parliament still discharged its functions, and the old elite still pressed against a monarch eager for more power. In 1954, General Fazlollah Zahedi and Ali Amini took command of the most urgent national issue and negotiated an oil agreement that ended the crisis with little help from the shah. And in 1958, when the shah had to deal with another coup—this time a plot against him— he still had to manipulate, cajole, and bargain. The window was closing but had not yet slammed shut.

The early 1960s were the hinge years of Iran's politics. Ali Amini, appointed prime minister in 1961, was Iran's last consequential premier—the last one to stand up to the shah and fill his cabinet with independent-minded actors whom the monarch distrusted. Amini's tenure would last only fourteen months. In 1965 two appointments heralded the new age: Amir Abbas Hoveyda as prime minister and General Nematollah Nasiri as head of the secret police. Both men held on to their positions for over a decade, a rarity in Iranian politics, because they perfected the art of sycophancy. The shah's new men followed orders, grumbled only in private, enriched themselves by dubious means, and seldom took any initiative.

The shah's twenty-year journey toward autocracy reached its climax in the 1960s. The parliament was reduced to a mere rubber stamp for his demands. Venerable political parties like the National Front became shells of their old selves. The press became a mouthpiece. As the old-school politicians faded from the scene, the new technocratic cadre who replaced them understood that the path to prominence was unquestioning acceptance of the shah's mandates. The armed forces that were the mainstay of the Pahlavi state kept expanding, but the officer corps was largely comprised of second-tier men who had been promoted for their blind loyalty. The most important credential for success in the new Iran was a degree from a Western university, not common sense or wisdom.

The shah's autocracy was not without its accomplishments. The monarch had grand ambitions, and his benchmark of success was always the industrial West. He kept insisting that Iran would catch up to Europe and even surpass it in some categories of production. His signature policy, the so-called White Revolution, included a significant effort at land reform that was not just about undermining the landed aristocracy but also a genuine attempt to empower the peasantry. The shah built schools and universities, highways and airports, health clinics and hospitals. He granted women the right to vote and minorities the right to practice their religion. He increased the literacy rate and reduced child mortality. Tehran was transformed from a sleepy town into a major urban center. Corruption was rampant and there was little coherent planning, but everyone's living standards went up.

The shah's management of foreign affairs was nothing short of brilliant. He was a nationalist who relentlessly increased the price of oil. He developed good relations with the Soviet Union while holding tight to his alliance with America, dominated the Persian Gulf while checking the radical republic in Iraq, and had good relations with the Arab monarchies—as well as with Israel—all of whom recognized Iran as a source of regional stability. He expanded trade relations with Europe and Asia. He was a Third World leader who did not bother with the grievances of the non-aligned movement. If he never transformed Iran into a great power, he did make it a responsible stakeholder.

It is one of Iran's paradoxes that the shah was bedeviled by his own success. He built the modern middle class but refused to grant it a voice in national affairs. Iran in the 1970s was a peculiar place, a seemingly dynamic nation filled with sullen people. Perhaps as a way of resisting the shah's infatuations with the West, many Iranians returned to their traditions and reclaimed their religion. The political atmosphere was suffocating, with spies and informers around every corner. The royal court was imperious and the shah seemed remote. He rarely consulted his advisers and seldom engaged with the public. As so often happens in developing countries, his bargain with his people was transactional: their political passivity in exchange for economic benefits. Even if it had not been undermined by the cooling economy of the mid-1970s, this compact was unsustainable. The Iranian masses wanted a say in how their government conducted its affairs. And by then, the shah's dictatorship did not offer even a pretense of consultation. When the revolution came, the system he had been hollowing out for so long simply crumbled.

The shah was not the man to lead the nation through a crisis. Throughout his life, he had retreated from making tough decisions. In 1953 and again during the uprisings a decade later, others had to step in and take command. By 1978, there were no capable leaders left to take charge. Men who could act with resolution and independence had been excised from the system long before. The shah was too humane for massive bloodshed and his army too timid for a crackdown. The monarchy collapsed like the house of cards it had become.

Any history of the Pahlavi dynasty must take into account the outsized role that America played in Iran. For a generation of U.S. policymakers, Iran was a venue for trying out social science postulations. Franklin Roosevelt hoped to make it a model of what American benevolence could achieve in the developing world. He dispatched numerous missions to Iran to train its police and army and straighten out its finances. For their part, the Persian statesmen, the recipients of this supposed largesse, may have wanted American involvement as a means of fending off Soviet encroachment, but they did not always appreciate the advice of U.S. planners.

The first application of Harry Truman's containment policy was in Iran: Washington stood behind Tehran as it evicted Soviet forces from its northern province. And Dwight Eisenhower's enchantment with covert actions injected America into a Persian melodrama, beginning an argument about who actually overthrew Mossadeq that continues today. The fixation with the coup ignores Eisenhower's persistent attempts to get the shah to focus on domestic reforms rather than the accumulation of arms. As he prepared to leave the White House, a frustrated Eisenhower complained to his aides that he wished Iranian liberals would somehow displace the shah. The history of U.S.-Iran relations is not without irony.

John F. Kennedy brought to the White House the mandarins of modernization theory. The professors who staffed his administration believed that the key to defeating the Soviet Union in the vast post-colonial realm was to launch newly independent nations on a trajectory of development that would culminate in capitalism and democracy. For the shah, this meant dealing with an American president who was adamant about reform and about pruning Iran's military expenditures. The Kennedy administration stands as the most successful of all the presidencies in dealing with the shah. It was the only one that got the shah to cut his military budget and make the right noises about reform. Kennedy bluntly told the shah he would get only the arms that his army and economy could absorb. The shah had to shelve his dreams of advanced weapons systems and focus on reforming his society.

Richard Nixon and Henry Kissinger have been described as realists, but at their core they were pessimists about America's fortunes. They saw their task as managing a superpower's decline. The United States needed allies, proxies, and surrogates, and in the critical Middle East region, the shah was the most worthy and astute of America's partners. They asked little of him in terms of reforming his domestic politics and opened America's armory to him. But they were also dealing with a more confident shah who was not about to humor the demands of a superpower mired in Vietnam. Washington needed Tehran, and the shah would no longer brook lectures by well-meaning Americans. Nixon and Kissinger can be legitimately criticized for enabling the shah's profligate autocracy, but we cannot ignore the pressures they faced as leaders of an overburdened America seeking relief from its global obligations.

By the time Jimmy Carter came into power, it was too late. For all of America's meddling, the revolution was truly a Persian affair. Carter and his aides held hundreds of hours of meetings about Iran. Some pressed for a coalition government; others wanted a crackdown. But the Iranians were no longer listening. Khomeini and his radicals were not about to share power, and the shah and his generals had no stomach for bloodshed.

The story of U.S.-Iran relations is one of unsung heroes. Roger Goiran, the CIA station chief in Tehran, opposed the coup in 1953 and was quickly discharged by Allen Dulles. In the 1960s, White House aide Bob "Blowtorch" Komer tried to single-handedly press the bureaucracy into appreciating the shah's faults and how his rule was doomed unless he radically changed course. He had some success convincing John F. Kennedy, but few others. In the 1970s, countless analysts in the U.S. intelligence services cataloged the many deficiencies of the Pahlavi state and issued multiple warnings. They were ignored by Richard Nixon and blamed by Jimmy Carter for "losing Iran." Thus arose the notion of intelligence failure, as politicians blamed their misjudgments on analysts who, cocooned as they were within their various classified domains, could not defend themselves.

The revolution has to be understood not by its slogans but by what actually happened, especially during the first year of the Islamic Republic, when the regime broke every one of its promises. The shah's generals, who had been promised amnesty, were executed. Liberals were cast aside and traditional clergy were forced to comply with the new strictures. Women's rights were curtailed and religious minorities endured persecution. The Iranian people, who had been promised freedom, were soon disillusioned by an unforgiving revolution that devoured not just its own, but many of its lofty pledges as well.

CHAPTER I

Iran under Occupation

At the outset of World War II, Iran was in the midst of a transformation. The Pahlavi autocracy, founded by the formidable Reza Shah, was well entrenched, but problems loomed all around. Reza Shah was a self-made man who had joined the Persian Cossack Brigade at sixteen, steadily rose through the ranks, and eventually commanded the entire force. But his ambitions were not limited to serving as a military officer. In a coup in 1921, he first made himself the prime minister and then deposed Ahmad Shah, ending the Qajar dynasty that had ruled Iran for over a century. Reza Shah was no ordinary Middle Eastern despot at ease with his country's stagnation. He had a vision of changing Iran into a technocratic industrial state. His was a war against Iran's traditions and its class of nobles. In one of the many ironies in the history of Iran, these nobles would later save the Pahlavi monarchy.[1]

Inspired by the example of Mustafa Kemal Atatürk, whose reforms were molding Turkey into a modern secular nation, Reza Shah soon embarked on his own agenda to refashion a contemporary Iran.[2] His industrial and educational reforms were to generate a new cadre, one beholden to the monarchy and sharing its vision of radical change. The army he built marked the first time that Iran moved beyond militias to concentrate power in the hands of the state. He tried to knit Iran together by constructing a railroad system and developing its ports. He even became an unlikely champion of women's emancipation by prohibiting the veil in public. But the traditional classes of landlords,

8

clergy, and merchants did not disappear. They simply waited for the shah to exhaust himself. Two societies lived side by side, awaiting larger events.

The shah had made himself the master of Iran, but had failed to appreciate the genius and charm of the old political class he sought to overturn.[3] Iran's landed gentry maintained ties to the countryside and could sense when the mood of the peasantry soured. Although many lived in the cities, the land-lords were keen observers—far more than any intelligence service—of what was taking place in the rural areas. The merchant class, too, with its elaborate and informal markets and banking system, kept tabs on the economy. And the clergy were reliable allies of the monarchy, which they viewed as an impor-tant pillar of the nation. (They would not rebel until years later.) As guardians of Iran's religious traditions, they may have been displeased by the shah's cul-tural liberalization measures and his war on the veil, but they were still tied to the institution of monarchy.[4] The point the shah missed was that all these actors were interested in preserving his dynasty. They had their disputes with the shah, but they still served crown and country.

The shah's industrialization effort relied heavily on German goods and technicians, particularly for developing communication systems and building railroads. By the 1930s, the two states had evolved a transactional arrange-ment: the Nazi regime wanted to barter its industrial products for Iran's natu-ral resources (instead of paying for these resources with hard currency), and as a country seeking rapid industrialization, Iran was eager for such offers. Still, there were geopolitical considerations. Iran feared Russia and Britain more than Germany, since it was the Allied powers that had traditionally craved Iran's territory and oil.

Some historians have claimed that the shah and many other Iranians were attracted to Nazi ideas and racial theories. The shah himself, they argue, was seeking to create a form of nationalism that would pull an ethnically diverse Iran out of its torpor, a nationalism that would echo themes of racial purity by portraying Persians as the vanguard race. The Iranian elite was certainly impressed by Germany's rapid economic recovery and its willingness to con-front the Allied powers. But the vulgar and toxic anti-Semitism at the heart of National Socialism found only a limited audience in Iran. It was Iran's distrust of Russia and Britain that explains its disastrous flirtation with the Third Reich.

As the war unfolded in Europe, the shah desperately tried to stay neutral, while failing to appreciate how the conflict was limiting his options. He still sought trade with Germany, which was showing increasing interest in the

Middle East and its resources, and he even sought to purchase its arms for his military. He demanded greater oil royalties from Britain, whose depleted treasury was heavily taxed by a war that it was waging alone. In the meantime, Tehran kept Moscow at bay, rebuffing its demands for trade concessions. The shah would soon learn that 1941 was not a year for such machinations.

As Reza Shah contemplated his options, events next door, in Iraq, would add to his misfortune. In May 1941, alarm bells rang in Whitehall when a contingent of Iraqi officers with pro-Nazi sentiments tried to overthrow the monarchy and the reliably pro-British premier, Nuri al-Said. Britain made short work of the coup, quickly restoring the old order and driving the coup's leader, Rashid Ali al-Gaylani, to take refuge in Iran as he sought to make his way to Germany. But from then on, the British saw the German presence in the Middle East as a potential fifth column that could topple their preferred governments.[5] The shah, with his large share of German experts, technicians, and spies, was now in the British crosshairs.

If the coup in Iraq unsettled Britain, the German invasion of Russia a month later probably sealed the shah's fate. On June 23, 1941, the German army put its tactics of speed and devastation to good use in crushing the Soviet defenses. The German forces soon advanced more than five hundred miles into Soviet territory, sprinting toward Moscow. Stalin, the self-proclaimed man of steel, hid for days in his dacha, incapable of making decisions, while Britain feared that if the German advance continued at that pace, Russia would succumb as easily as France had done a year earlier.

The invasion turned Russia into a beleaguered Western ally whose chances of survival were poor. The war made it impossible to supply Russia over land, while the eastern port of Vladivostok was frozen for much of the year. Iran and its transportation network offered a reliable supply route. Iran had to take sides, clearly and unambiguously. But the shah was so impressed by the German blitzkrieg that he could not predict who would win the war. He thought neutrality might shield him from hard choices, but after the attempted coup in Baghdad, this was a dangerous game. The British demanded that he expel all German personnel. The shah responded by deporting some but not all, angering the Germans while failing to propitiate the British. He seemed not to appreciate the gravity of the crisis unfolding in Europe and the existential nature of the war. His halfway measures, and the suspicion that he harbored pro-German sentiments, made the Allies see him as unreliable.

Still, the main catalyst for the Allied invasion of Iran was not unease with the shah but the need for a land corridor to Russia. As British Foreign

Secretary Anthony Eden acknowledged, "For publicity purposes our reasons for action contemplated will initially be confined to the need to eliminate German influence in Persia." But he went on to say, "If subsequent military operations develop on a considerable scale our action could be justified on the grounds that we are keeping open a line of communication with Russia."[6] The need to supply Russia was paramount. Disposing of a monarch whom the British distrusted was a side benefit.

The shah belatedly recognized the seriousness of his predicament. On August 22 he issued a decree expelling all Germans, but it was too late. The Allies invaded Iran three days later.

The assault was swift and decisive. The army on which Reza Shah had lavished so much attention collapsed quickly and ignominiously, with its officers leaving their conscripts behind as they fled. To be fair, the Iranian army had been designed to deal with tribal rebellions and internal insurrections, not a great-power invasion: its defeat was likely inevitable. But the speed of its capitulation surprised the already shell-shocked monarch. The Allies moved fast to secure their essential concerns. The remaining German technicians were expelled, and Iran was split in two, with Russia controlling the north and Britain retaining the south with its oil reserves. The roads and railways were secured as a supply corridor to Russia.[7]

Even in this moment of Allied solidarity, Britain and Russia were wary of each other's ambitions. Britain controlled Iran's considerable oil deposits and was determined to preserve its spoils. Russia's czars and commissars, for their part, had long eyed Iran's northern provinces and its warm-water ports. When Stalin signed the Nazi-Soviet Pact in 1939, he had directed his foreign minister, Vyacheslav Molotov, to ensure that Iran was in the Soviet sphere of influence.[8] Soon after its forces arrived, Moscow let it be known that given its petroleum and fishery needs, it wanted its zone to include the more distant provinces of Gilan and Mazandaran. This raised concerns in Whitehall that the Kremlin's objectives were not limited to ensuring the safe passage of supplies through Iran—and that the Soviets intended their occupation to last past the end of the war.

Hoping to cling to his throne, the shah at first tried to enlist the support of the most disinterested of the Western powers, the United States. He wrote a letter to Franklin Roosevelt and tried to persuade the small U.S. mission in Iran to take up his cause. The United States was still not a combatant, however, and given the isolationist sentiment Roosevelt was battling at home, preserving the shah's monarchy was not his foremost priority.

An answer to the shah's pleas came not from America but from Britain, which launched a vicious assault on his rule through broadcasts by the BBC— the same BBC that had earlier refrained from criticizing him.[9] The monarch who had enforced strict obedience among his subjects now had to face a barrage of criticism regarding his corruption and tyranny. At this point in their history, the Iranians paid close attention to the doings of the great powers, particularly the British. The BBC broadcasts indicated to a restive Iranian elite that the shah's Western benediction had been withdrawn. That the shah was frequently at odds with both Russia and Britain made little difference to his critics.[10]

It is often observed that foreign invasion stimulates nationalism and benefits the incumbent ruler. Iran in 1941 belies that idea. The Allied attack opened a floodgate of criticism against the shah. Far from rallying around the shah's flag, Iranians saw the Allied invasion as an opportunity to get rid of him. Suddenly, politicians, parliamentarians, and even the press mattered. Politics in Iran may have been the realm of the elite, but the notion of constitutional restraint on the monarchy was revived. What is most striking is that the shah's modernization effort did not generate a base of support for him. The Iranian elite seem to have considered him a tool of the British. In their eyes, it was the British who had put him on the throne in the first place, and now they had withdrawn their support. It mattered little that Reza Shah had come to power through his own guile and cruelty, that he had confronted Britain over its share of Iranian oil profits, that he had rebuffed various Russian entreaties, or that he had sought to drag his country into the age of industrialization. The shah's record was hardly untarnished: corruption and autocracy were hallmarks of his rule. But the notion that he was an agent of Britain is false.

Reza Shah's last days in power were difficult. As the Allied troops moved closer to Tehran, he made belated gestures of appeasement. He chose as his premier Mohammad Ali Foroughi, an old-school politician known for his European sympathies who would do much to save the country. Elderly and in poor health, Foroughi had a distinguished record of public service and had even served as president of the League of Nations. Although he had once been purged by the shah, he assumed the premiership determined to preserve the country's core interests. There was even talk of abolishing the monarchy and appointing Foroughi as president, an idea that he firmly rejected.[11] In his moment of desperation, Reza Shah had to rely on an establishment he had once tried to destroy.

The new premier faced a situation where it was not only the Allied powers who wanted to get rid of the shah: his many domestic opponents, too, wanted to use the specter of a foreign invasion to depose a despot who had diminished their influence.[12] The Majlis (Iranian parliament) soon held a secret session with Foroughi in which they discussed abdication.

A month after the invasion, Reza Shah was forced to relinquish his rule and journey to South Africa. He had hoped for a more hospitable location for his exile, such as the United States or Canada, but the decision was no longer his. He would die in Johannesburg on July 26, 1944.

The collapse of Reza Shah's rule eerily foreshadowed the end of his son's reign thirty-eight years later. Reza Shah's modernization drive had failed to create a constituency loyal to his regime. The army he had created quietly disintegrated. The traditional classes that he disdained rose up in defiance. Both Pahlavi kings tried to refashion Iran according to their vision of modernity, but no one mourned the passing of their dynasty. The young shah, it seemed, learned little from his father, and he would repeat many of his mistakes.

Foroughi proved a commendable choice as premier and is one of the unsung heroes of Iranian history. His main challenge was to preserve Iran's sovereign rights while it was under occupation by two powers with a longstanding interest in its resources. To achieve this goal, Foroughi understood that he had to make important changes in Iran's international orientation. The notion of neutrality was soon abandoned in favor of a "defensive alliance." Many of Iran's elite still clung to the idea that neutrality had served Iran well during World War I. Perhaps Reza Shah had tilted too far toward Germany, they argued, but neutrality was still the best way to preserve the country's independence. In mid-1941, moreover, a German victory was hardly out of the question. Many wanted Iran to hedge its bets.

Foroughi's approach was altogether different. The prime minister understood that Iran had to change from an occupied country to an Allied nation if it was to gain British and (hopefully later) American support for its sovereignty. Given the Soviet Union's seeming intent to remain permanently in its northern occupation zone, Iran desperately needed the Western powers' help to offset Moscow's designs. The new government quickly pledged its cooperation with the Allied war effort if they accepted Iran's independence. Given that the Allies wanted to secure their interests on the cheap, they agreed to withdraw their troops "no later than six months after all hostilities between the Allied powers and Germany and her associates have been suspended." They further promised to "safeguard the economic existence of the Iranian people against the privations and difficulties arising as a result of the present war."[13]

In defending the agreement in the parliament, Foroughi candidly admitted that the Allied invasion had resulted from "mistakes which we made in the past . . . and if we had not committed those past mistakes these developments would not have occurred."[14] He insisted that the future of Iran lay in an alliance with the anti-Axis forces, not the German-tilted neutrality that so many Iranians, including Reza Shah, had favored. The Majlis endorsed his views by a vote of 80 to 13.

The next question was what to do with the Pahlavi dynasty. The elder shah's abdication was inevitable because he lacked both domestic and Allied support. The British Foreign Office, averse to the succession of Crown Prince Mohammad Reza Pahlavi, toyed with the idea of restoring the Qajar dynasty. Sir Reader Bullard, Britain's envoy to Iran, who spent much of his time drafting cables about the deficient Persian character, was hostile to the younger Pahlavi. "The Crown Prince," he wrote, "must be ruled out on account of his well-known pro-German sympathies and we cannot regard the Shah's abdication in his favor as anything but a ruse to prolong the anti-Allied policy."[15] It was Foroughi who made the case for retaining the Pahlavi monarchy. He assured Bullard that the crown prince would support the Allied cause and that he and Foroughi could work well together in administering the country. Bullard had great respect for Foroughi and viewed him as a rare Persian statesman in a sea of charlatans. He accepted the new shah.

In the end, both the British and the Soviets agreed to the succession because they saw no realistic alternative. The British wanted a weak government, and Bullard assured the Foreign Office that the shah was "not credited with much strength of character," a deficit that "might suit our present circumstance."[16] That Iran's clever statesmen had lined up behind the crown prince also diminished the appeal of displacing him. The Soviets, for their part, wanted to abolish the monarchy altogether and replace it with a republican government, but this was unacceptable to both the British and the Iranian ruling elite. Given the exigencies of the war, Moscow was also not eager to disrupt the system. The Pahlavi dynasty limped forward.

Just weeks after becoming prime minister, Foroughi had protected the monarchy and ensured Iran's prerogatives during the war—as well as its sovereign rights afterward. This was no small achievement for the leader of a government whose army had collapsed and whose ruler had been expelled because of pro-German loyalties. The establishment that Reza Shah had so disdained rose to safeguard his country and his patrimony.

The first government following Reza Shah's ouster would face monumental challenges. The breakdown of the administrative order invited tribal insurrections as well as secessionist impulses in the northern province of Azerbaijan, turmoil that the Soviets fueled. Food shortages were compounded by Allied appropriations of supplies, a combination that sparked riots throughout the country. The dismal economic situation was made worse when the Allied powers devalued Iran's currency. In the absence of the former rigid but decisive autocracy, an uncertain government headed by a young, untested monarch struggled to deal with these problems. Iran was fortunate to have a capable coterie of politicians to support the new shah during this tumultuous time.

MOHAMMAD REZA PAHLAVI AT THE HELM

Mohammad Reza Pahlavi was twenty-one years old when he became the shah. He was unsure of himself and was seen by his father as too soft to govern the country, despite an upbringing designed to strengthen the young monarch's character and skills. At age eleven, the prince had been dispatched to obtain a modern education at the elite Swiss boarding school Institut Le Rosey, where he instead spent much of his time tending to his social life. Upon his return, his father had tried to toughen him up by sending him to Tehran Military Academy. During this period, he did at times try to be a dutiful crown prince and accompanied his father on some inspection trips. But it is hard to see how anything in his background could have prepared him to take over a nation during one of the most acute crises in its history.

Still, it is wrong to dismiss the shah as a dilettante who left national affairs to the elder statesmen around him. He did have a vision for his country and monarchy. And he was personally courageous. His love of flying, his reckless driving habits, and his survival of many assassination attempts testify to his bravery and fatalism. He was a mystic who believed that God had chosen him for a great mission. "I will frankly confess that God has ordained me to do certain things for the service of my nation, things that perhaps could not be done by anyone else. In whatever I have done and whatever I do in the future, I consider myself as an agent of the will of God."[17] Throughout his life he would speak of his visions and of divine intercessions on his behalf. And yet he lacked the emotional resolution one needs in a crisis. When confronted with great challenges, he would often retreat and even contemplate abandoning his kingship. He once acknowledged that "physically I am not afraid, but mentally you're constantly afraid of something, either by yourself or something that might go wrong with yourself or with your friends or with your allies that you're counting on."[18] He needed a resilient political elite that could take charge when he would fade from the scene. For his monarchy to succeed, it had to share power and responsibility with other stakeholders. The contradiction that eventually destroyed his rule was that he had a taste for absolutism without the character to sustain it.

Upon assuming power, the shah admitted that he was in a "confused and perplexed state of mind."[19] He had no option but to assuage those who were skeptical of his rule. He pledged loyalty to the Allies who had callously exiled his father. To placate domestic actors, the new monarch freed political prisoners, returned the land his father had confiscated from the clergy, and transferred much of his own landholdings to the state. He promised legislators that he respected the constitution and recognized the parliament's importance. The autocracy that had flirted with Nazi Germany was to be no more.

But beneath this veneer of respect for democratic institutions, the shah tried to undermine the constitutional order. He would often summon the foreign envoys and complain about Iran's chaotic politics. He believed that the modernization of Iran demanded a strong government unencumbered by constitutional limitations and administered by a technocratic elite, not the traditional nobility that recent events had once again empowered. He wanted to shift the national focus away from the rural areas to the urban centers, from the narrow elite to a middle class, and from agriculture to industry. Intent on dragging Iran into modernity by force of will, he never believed that democracy was the best form of political organization. Although at the start of the shah's reign his authoritarian convictions were hemmed in by Iran's institutions and foreign occupation, they were ready to emerge at any opportunity.

The revamped Pahlavi monarchy had ceded control of the bureaucracy to the prime ministers, and it lost some of its power of patronage when the shah gave up much of his land inheritance. But the monarchy held tight to the armed forces, increasing their size and budget. Reza Shah had created the Iranian army, and his son was determined to preserve the monarch's role as commander-in-chief. He went on inspection tours and often appeared in public wearing his military uniform. And he became the protector of the officer corps that had failed to defend the nation from foreign invasion. Instead of punishing those who had deserted their posts, he offered them promotions and salary hikes. The army would be the mainstay of his rule.

The nation that the elder Reza Shah left behind exploded in political activity.[20] The veteran politicians purged from power, the parliamentarians who had merely rubber-stamped the shah's mandates, and the clergy who had been locked in their seminaries all found their voices. Iran, a country occupied by foreign troops, with its sovereignty curtailed, was experiencing a surprising political renaissance. After two decades of dictatorship, power was divided among the royal court, the parliament, and the cabinet.

The clergy quickly gravitated back to the shah. Since the 1979 revolution, the Islamic Republic has tried to portray the religious classes as resolute opponents of the Pahlavi dynasty. The historical record, however, suggests that the clergy saw much benefit in preserving the monarchy. The mullahs anguished about the advent of modern education and the appeal of Western ideologies to Iran's youth. But they weren't the only ones worried about the rise of liberal political parties, an enterprising intelligentsia, and modern notions of separating religion from politics: the monarchy shared these concerns. The young shah reached out to the clergy by doing away with his father's ban on the wearing of veils, and by making several trips to the shrine city of Qom to consult with the men of God. These overtures to the ayatollahs contained a good measure of opportunism: the shah's modernizing ideas were contrary to their traditional ways. But for now, an alliance of convenience between the crown and the clergy served both parties' interests.

As the formerly closed system opened rapidly, the country at times appeared on the edge of disorder. In the four years before the war ended, Iran would have eight prime ministers and frequent changes in the cabinet. The boisterous parliament seemed to spend more time debating trivial matters than legislating. Hovering in the background were the great powers, which remained the arbiters of Iran's politics. All of these divisions, however, concealed an elite pluralism that benefited the shah. During riots and disturbances, the parliament and the court often came together, because both appreciated the importance of protecting the traditional institutions against militant actors. The politicians mobilized their constituents and the parliament supported the shah and the military during crises. The forces of radical change were thus isolated, the monarchy buttressed, and the shah himself inoculated against popular backlash by the national coalition standing behind him. In short, the system worked.

The explosion of political activity in the aftermath of Reza Shah's departure shows that his authoritarianism had never penetrated deeply into Iranian society. During the war years, twenty-two political parties, ranging from reactionary to radical, arose in Iran.[21] A similar flowering can be seen in the press. Tehran alone had forty-seven newspapers. Bullard marveled at so many newspapers circulating in a "city of 75,000 inhabitants, the large majority of whom are illiterate."[22] Many of them were likely associated with political parties, but they still offered readers information and perspective.

The elections to the Majlis also showed that the days when the monarch could be sure of a compliant parliament were over. The interaction between Tehran and the local notables made the system somewhat representative. The prominent landlords led the peasants, tribesmen, and laborers into the polls to choose their parliamentary representatives. This may not have been a Jeffersonian democracy, but the system did transmit the concerns of the peasants and the labor force to local leaders, and from there to the ruling class. There was a channel of communication, a means of addressing grievances, and thus a semblance of democratic legitimacy. The center and periphery were tied together by a gilded bond. In an ethnically fragmented nation with a highly illiterate population, there was a political network that benefited all participants. The diffusion of power meant bargaining among stakeholders, elections that mattered, a parliament attuned to local concerns, and national initiatives that were legitimized by a highly imperfect yet functional process of electoral consultation.

The resulting parliaments featured competing parties such as the National Union and the Fatherland and in due time the National Front. The Majlis included intellectuals, clergymen, merchants, and independent politicians of stature unaffiliated with any party. Mohammad Mossadeq, who would lead the charge for oil nationalization in the 1950s, was one such leader. All bills had to be passed by the Majlis, which also chose the premiers and ministers, in discussion with the shah. The rapid rise and fall of prime ministers—they lasted an average of less than eight months—made the system look more unstable than it was. The same elites were always in charge.

The one area of contention between the shah and the Majlis was the armed forces. Like his father, the shah viewed the army as the main pillar of his rule and tried to protect the ministry of war from intervention by prying premiers and parliaments. He paid particular attention to the recruitment and promotion of the officer corps and connected the monarchy closely to the army. But his interest in the armed forces transcended simple political calculation. He was genuinely fascinated by military matters. He spent a great deal of time studying army manuals and was well versed in history of warfare. Even during his student days, he had been drawn to history and biography. He saw himself as a soldier, and the army as the one institution that could protect his rule.

The political class often worried about the shah's close association with the generals. Having endured the shah's father, this assertive elite understood the danger of allowing a monarch to monopolize the instruments of coercion. The parliament continually tried to trim the military budget, claiming other priorities such as health and education. This was hardly an outlandish claim, but the shah, mindful of their ambitions, kept trying to increase the size of the armed forces instead. The struggle would continue until the 1960s, when he finally eviscerated the old elite.

Even in the war years, the shah made clear his contempt for democratic process. He first appealed to the foreign powers to suspend elections for the duration of the war. When this was rejected, he sought to create an upper legislative chamber to dilute the power of the cantankerous Majlis, only to be rebuffed again by the occupying powers. Suspicious of his cabinet officers, he tried to undermine them by appealing directly to the embassies. Bullard reported once that "the Shah would like to see me fairly often alone without the knowledge of the politicians. He said he felt that some of the ministers distorted the truth for their own benefits."[23] Both the British and American envoys usually rejected these requests and conducted their business through official government representatives. The shah was still too weak, and his power too uncertain, to effectively undermine the government.

Hovering over this elite constellation was one of the most effective and sinister political organizations in Iran, the Tudeh Communist Party, which owed its success to the amnesty that followed Reza Shah's departure.[24] The Tudeh's core leaders, the so-called fifty-three, had been imprisoned by Reza Shah but were set free after his abdication. They quickly moved to reconstitute their organization. Shortly after receiving amnesty, the Tudeh prisoners reached out to their Russian patrons. The Soviet embassy reported back to Moscow in December 1941 that "a group of Iranian Communists, former political prisoners, has begun to revive the Communist Party of Iran. They are also requesting prompt agreement to send their delegate to us."[25]

The Tudeh's initial success stemmed from Moscow's demand that it avoid communist dogma. As the Soviet embassy reported:

> We think that the revival of the Iranian Communist Party, which was always a small sectarian group, would hardly make a difference at the present time, but would definitely cause certain difficulties and complications. This will strengthen suspiciousness and dissatisfaction in the ranks of the ruling circles and provide more opportunities for German

agents to frighten the Iranian bourgeoisie with the danger of the Sovietization of Iran, and indeed they make the British themselves suspicious with respect to the Soviet Union, which is supposedly striving to Sovietize Iran.[26]

The communists were advised not to revive their party but to forge relations with other political groups to broaden the appeal of leftist forces. Thus the party's first slogan, "Bread, health and education for all," echoed the ideas of the liberal opposition. It stopped advocating the collectivization of agriculture and large-scale nationalization in favor of social security, the right to form trade unions, free education, and universal health care. These positions, though adopted cynically, gave the party genuine appeal to the industrial labor force and to an intelligentsia whose voice was growing louder as the result of political reforms. Later, when Stalin began to insist that all communist parties mimic his slogans, the Tudeh's subordination to the Soviet Union would undermine its popularity. But at this early stage, the party did have a constituency.

On the surface, the politics of the war years may look unstable, if not chaotic. All the restrictions were lifted, censorship was gone, and politics became a free and at times reckless sport. The attempt to balance pluralism with authority would take time. Such balances are rare even in mature democracies, never mind an occupied nation. This period can be justifiably criticized for its rotating prime ministers, excessive political intrigue, and inability to craft a sustained national agenda. Missing from such an indictment, however, is how the elite held the country together, sustained the monarchy, and, most of all, manipulated the great powers to preserve Iran's sovereignty.

THE GREAT POWERS AND IRAN

On November 28, 1943, Tehran hosted the first great-power summit of the war. Franklin Roosevelt and Josif Stalin met for the first time and were joined by Winston Churchill as the three leaders plotted the course of the conflict. The most momentous issue on the agenda was Stalin's urgent desire for the Allies to alleviate the pressure on his forces by opening a Western front against Germany. Knowing that this was not going to happen for several more months, Roosevelt spent much of the time trying to placate the Russian strongman. Over dinner, Roosevelt and Stalin even bantered about executing fifty thousand German officers, prompting Churchill to warn them against war crimes and walk out of the room. It is hard to imagine that Roosevelt would have condoned such a grisly act, but he saw the summit as an occasion to establish a working relationship with Stalin. His dream of postwar cooperation among the great powers meant assuaging one of history's greatest mass murderers. It would all come to naught as Stalin's paranoia and thirst for land precluded long-term cooperation with liberal democracies, which he disdained as much as he did the invading German troops.[27]

This summit has often been seen as a moment of Iranian humiliation. The Allies chose Tehran without consulting the Iranian government, and even the date of the meeting was not given to the host country in advance. The shah had some perfunctory talks with the Allied leaders but was not invited to any of their high-level discussions. Despite such affronts, Iran did benefit from the summit, because the Allies reaffirmed its sovereignty with a statement: "The Governments of the United States, the U.S.S.R. and the United Kingdom are at one with the Government of Iran in their desire for the maintenance of the independence, sovereignty and territorial integrity of Iran."[28] That Iran had aided the Allies despite the privation their presence caused was rewarded with a formal guarantee, whose violation would later contribute to the onset of the Cold War.

Even at this early stage, there were reasons to doubt the Russian commitment to Iran's independence. Britain was accustomed to sustaining its influence in Iran through informal arrangements. The British interests were limited to access to southern oil fields and preventing unfriendly politicians from gaining too much power. Whitehall had no problem with Iranian sovereignty, because it had found ways of navigating Iran's politics. Even this ingenious practice, however, would prove short lived in the aftermath of the war, as the British oil concession and its manipulation of Iranian politics became sources of nationalistic contention. The exhausted British Empire would find it hard to sustain its imperial outposts.

The question is why, given his ambitions in Iran, Stalin accepted the Tripartite Agreement. It is important to note that Stalin did achieve many of his objectives in the summit. He did not get an immediate second front, but his allies committed to mounting such an assault in short order. (The invasion of Normandy took place the following June.) As a leader attuned to postwar demarcations, Stalin secured an agreement to adjust the Polish border at Germany's expense, and an acknowledgment that the Baltic states and Ukraine would be in the Soviet sphere of influence. Given all these concessions, Stalin was happy to make a declaration he clearly did not take seriously. It was the Western powers and the Iranians who looked upon such professions with gravity. For Stalin, military power, not lofty statements, would determine the disposition of the areas under Soviet occupation. Still, he did promise to honor Iran's sovereignty, and the eventual violation of this pledge would cost him.

Once it entered the war, America's presence in Iran gradually grew. By 1943, thirty thousand U.S. troops were in Iran facilitating the passage of Lend-Lease supplies to Russia. Approximately a quarter of all supplies to the Soviet Union went through the "Persian corridor." Along with U.S. troops came American advisers, technicians, and diplomats. The Americans were the only occupiers the Iranians welcomed; they were seen as a counterweight to the great powers that had long coveted their land. The United States had no history of colonial intervention, seemed uninterested in imperial exploitation, and appeared genuinely benevolent. Roosevelt's Atlantic Charter, with its idealistic call for self-determination, appealed to many Iranians as well as others in the Middle East, who hoped that the United States would restrain the imperial appetites of its partners in the Grand Alliance.

Iran's new strategy was clearly outlined by General Hassan Arfa, chief of staff of the military, who noted, "Our policy was to bring as many Americans as possible to Iran to be witnesses of the Soviet political encroachment and by their presence act as a deterrent for the more open violations of our independence and interference in our internal affairs."[29] Hossein Kay'Ustavan, a member of the parliament, echoed this sentiment, stressing that as the Iranians looked for a "new friend who would protect them against their two neighbors . . . the choice fell on the United States."[30] This was not a new idea. As we have seen, in his moment of despair, Reza Shah had appealed to Roosevelt to save his throne. At that time, America had not yet entered the war but had unequivocally taken Britain's side, and Roosevelt had no intention of rescuing a monarch thought to have pro-Nazi sympathies. But the end of Reza Shah's rule did not end the Iranian desire for American support.

Even during the war, Iran wanted to lure the United States and began to offer Washington commercial opportunities, including oil concessions. Prime Minister Ali Soheili assured the State Department that "he was anxious to have American businessmen enter all Iranian fields of enterprise."[31] The shah promised the U.S. mission that Iran "wanted to create a close commercial relationship with the United States."[32] Tehran hoped that by deepening America's financial commitments in Iran, it could leverage American interests against the other great powers, particularly the Soviet Union. As Tehran tried to entice the United States, the Roosevelt administration itself began to appreciate Iran's importance for its postwar designs.

For American leaders anticipating a global role in the aftermath of the war, the commitments in Iran were yet another recognition of the impracticality of isolationism and the notion that the world could be kept at bay. This was still the age when the sea lanes were the most important pathways for power projection. A country that bordered the Persian Gulf and was close to America's oil interests in Saudi Arabia gained new importance for America's planners. Secretary of State Cordell Hull warned Roosevelt, "From a more directly selfish point of view, it is to our interest that no Great Power be established on the Persian Gulf opposite the important American petroleum development in Saudi Arabia."[33] Hull's advice was buttressed by Roosevelt's close friend Sumner Welles, the under secretary of state, who told the president that it was important for Iran to serve as "an active and willing partner on our side."[34] An Iran that was the master of its own territory would preclude a rival power from establishing itself along a strategically important waterway.

Roosevelt was most concerned about sustaining the Grand Alliance. Though he spoke in lofty terms about the United Nations, at the core his concept of the postwar world order had the United States, Britain, Russia, and China patrolling their respective spheres of influence and ensuring the stability of the international system. Iran was peripheral in this scheme, but Washington feared that British and Russian competition there could contribute to the fracturing of the alliance. The State Department's internal review noted that "the best hope of avoiding trouble in this regard lies in strengthening Iran to a point at which she will be able to stand up on her own feet and in assuring both of the interested Great Powers that neither one need fear the acquisition by the other of a predominant position in Iran."[35] Iran has always played a role on the international scene out of proportion to its actual size and importance. It appears that many influential voices in Washington were now sensing that the cohesion of the Grand Alliance was partly contingent on Iran becoming strong and self-sufficient.

Among those pressing for greater American involvement in Iran were its representatives in Tehran, where the United States had an array of capable diplomats, including some colorful characters. Roosevelt often appointed personal emissaries to handle jobs usually reserved for the diplomatic corps. One such renegade was Patrick Hurley, a Republican whose ignorance of foreign affairs was matched by his flamboyant temperament. Surfacing in Iran in 1943, he became a proponent of deepening America's commitment and thus reinforced the judgment of the professionals he so often angered with his antics.

Unlike most diplomats, whose cables were buried in briefing books that Roosevelt seldom read, Hurley could transmit his ideas directly to the Oval Office. To the extent that he had an ideology, it was fierce anti-communism and a disdain for British imperialism. He sensed that Iran was becoming a bone of contention between Britain and Russia and sent back surprisingly cogent analyses in which he noted, presciently, that after the war ended "there would be open conflict in the Middle East between the forces of the United Nations."[36] Clinging to the Atlantic Charter more resolutely than Roosevelt, Hurley recommended its application to Iran. He called for upgrading the mission in Tehran to a full embassy, ensuring that Iran become a member of the postwar United Nations, and adopting an open-door policy that would convey to both London and Moscow that Washington had real interests in Iran. Setting aside his antipathy toward Britain, he even called for greater Anglo-Saxon collaboration as a means of fending off the Soviet Union.

Roosevelt had become fascinated with Iran's topography during his brief stay there, and in 1944 he found time to write a letter to the shah about "the lack of trees on the mountain slopes and the general aridity of the country which lies above the plains." He suggested that Iran should "test out the possibility of trees which would hold the soil with their roots, and at the same time, hold back floods."[37] His thoughts soon moved beyond reforestation to the notion of helping Iran lift itself up. He wrote to Hull, "I was rather thrilled with the idea of using Iran as an example of what we could do by an unselfish American policy."[38] To Hurley, he wrote, "If we can get the right kind of American experts who will remain loyal to their ideals I feel certain that our policy of aiding Iran will succeed."[39] Thus began the dispatch of American missions to Iran.

The American zeal for reform was obvious. The disciples of the New Deal, like later partisans of modernization theory, saw Iran as a laboratory for social change. The United States launched missions designed to improve Iran's military, police, food supply, and finances, anticipating that these reforms would generate political stability just as Roosevelt's programs had done in America during the Great Depression. The new U.S. embassy assured the White House that the United States would be "the only nation which may be able to render effective assistance to Iran without rousing the fears and opposition of Great Britain or Russia or of the Iranians themselves."[40] As they sought to transform the feudal nation into a modern state, the American advisers saw the traditions of an ancient country as obstacles to overcome. For Iran to prosper and take its place among the free nations, it had to look like America. Into this charged arena stepped Arthur Millspaugh.[41]

This was Millspaugh's second foray into Iran's treasury. His first mission was in 1922 when he straightened out the government's finances by establishing a budgetary system. In that mission he had the advantage of advising an autocrat who had the final say. This time, he landed in a Tehran that was brimming with intrigues. Millspaugh assumed that given the shah's formal approval, he had all the authority that he needed. But this time, in order to succeed, he had to navigate a turbulent political environment, a task at which he proved singularly incompetent. He never seemed to grasp that the Iranian government may have wanted American advisers, but it would make its own judgments about their advice.

Among his first suggestions was the introduction of a progressive income tax that infringed on the prerogatives of the upper classes. The aristocrats in charge of the parliament were skeptical of his tax bill, not just because it expropriated a larger portion of their profits, but also because it disturbed the existing means of revenue collection, which relied on informal deals between the government and local business leaders. His insistence on price controls angered the merchant class and the guilds, which had their own way of pricing. His quest to bring more food to Tehran impoverished the provinces and aroused the ire of the Tudeh and other leftist parties, which organized demonstrations against his reforms. His attempt at currency reform led only to inflation. Millspaugh's imperious manner did not help his cause, nor did his threats to leave every time he met resistance or criticism.

He soon also tangled with the shah over the role of the military. The entire American contingent in Iran wanted a small army capable of efficiently managing internal issues. The shah, however, desired a large force because he saw the military not just as a security organization but also as a devoted constituency. This would be an ongoing debate between the shah and the United States until the Nixon administration opened up America's armory to the spendthrift monarch.

Millspaugh viewed his mission in purely technocratic terms and was frustrated that the Iranians did not quickly implement his various ten-point plans. In fact, he managed to get himself fired by a government desperate for U.S. involvement in its affairs. In 1944 the Majlis voted to terminate his mission, in a move that appears to have been a collaborative effort between Iran and the U.S. embassy. Prime Minister Morteza-Qoli Bayat was assured by Ambassador Leland Morris that "the State Department would not feel irritation if it was the decision of the Iranian Government to dispense with the services of Dr. Millspaugh."[42]

Millspaugh's failure had little effect on U.S.-Iran relations or the American efforts to reform Iran's police and military. In fact, the American generals fared better because they limited themselves to offering suggestions that the Iranians occasionally adopted. The stakes were too high for both parties to let a haughty bureaucrat stand in the way of good relations. And those relations were soon tested by the thorny issue of oil concessions.

Even as the war raged, Iran's oil became a contested issue among the Allies. When the war began, Britain was already in possession of large concessions operated by the Anglo-Iranian Oil Company (AIOC). This did not prevent the British from eyeing new ventures, however, and in 1943, representatives of the Anglo-Dutch firm Shell Oil Company arrived in Tehran seeking their own fortune. In the meantime, at the invitation of the Iranians, two U.S. firms, Standard Vacuum Oil Company and Sinclair Oil Company, sent representatives to Tehran. But the most dramatic arrival was that of Sergey Kavtaradze, the Soviet deputy foreign minister, with a huge delegation demanding concessions in the five northern provinces adjacent to Russia. The request was ominously accompanied by a Soviet propaganda campaign warning the "reactionary" elements in Iran not to interfere with supply routes to Russia.

The Allied oil gambit was a proxy fight among great powers jostling for geopolitical advantage in postwar Iran. The Soviets clearly perceived oil as a means of ensuring a zone of influence in northern Iran, while the British saw the Soviet demands as the latest Stalinist encroachment on their traditional domain. By 1944, Churchill was already trying to arouse the Americans to the danger that the Kremlin posed. The United States was receptive, seeing oil as a means of securing a foothold in a country that it was coming to recognize as strategically important. For their part, the Iranians encouraged U.S. involvement, offering American firms all kinds of oil concessions because they viewed oil as a stand-in for larger issues and feared the designs of both the Soviet Union and Britain.

The parliament seated in 1944 was one of the most important in Iran's history.[43] Nearly 60 percent of its members were new, showing that the election was relatively free by standards of an occupied nation. In deference to the Soviet Union, communists were allowed to compete, and eight of their deputies were seated. It was also a parliament that featured towering figures who began to lead a movement for reclaiming Iran's oil from foreigners. The advent of a well-organized and Soviet-financed Tudeh Party appears to have stimulated the aristocracy to a greater degree of political cohesion. The factionalism that had long bedeviled Iranian politics was set aside to deal with the urgent Soviet threat. Prime Minister Mohammad Sa'ed took the lead and declared shortly after the new parliament was seated: "It is not required and necessary to grant any oil concessions to any foreign company, until such a time that the economic and financial situations of the world are clear and the peace has been established."[44] Sa'ed then worked out a formula with the Majlis whereby all oil negotiations were put aside until the end of the war. The parliament next passed a law to that effect, thwarting Soviet designs in a way that did not seem to single out Moscow for unique punishment.[45]

The parliamentary measure, however, did not end the oil issue. Kavtaradze assured his superiors that "Sa'ed must resign and the embassy will see that he does."[46] In a press conference the day after negotiations were suspended, the Soviet deputy foreign minister deplored the "disloyal and unfriendly position taken up by Premier Sa'ed toward the Soviet Union, excluding the possibility of further collaboration with him."[47] In retaliation, the Soviets instigated a food crisis in Tehran by preventing the shipment of supplies from their zone. Then they launched a vicious media campaign against the premier and the parliament and staged demonstrations in the northern cities that the police were prevented from dispersing.

The Tudeh then did much damage to itself. It followed the Soviet line and agitated for an oil agreement granting Moscow rights to various fields. This position enraged both liberals and nationalists, who saw the U.S.S.R. as infringing on Iran's sovereignty. The Tudeh's embrace of Soviet demands and the demonstrations it had sponsored against the parliamentary decree did much to alienate the public. The party had hoped for a leftist coalition against the conservatives, but its brazen promotion of Soviet interests left it isolated.

The Western response was swift and decisive. Both Britain and the United States accepted the parliamentary measure and implored their ally to do so as well. Bullard protested to the Soviet embassy in Tehran, while the Foreign Office made its feelings known directly to the Kremlin. Morris assured Sa'ed that the United States respected Iran's right to deal with the oil issue as it thought best. The State Department informed Moscow that the U.S. policy was "based on the American Government's recognition of the sovereign right of an independent nation such as Iran, acting in a nondiscriminatory manner, to grant or withhold commercial concessions within its territory."[48] Washington's response was no accident. Both Premier Sa'ed and the shah had been in contact with the embassy, pressing the United States to forcefully rebuff the Soviet demands.

At the start of 1945, despite many assurances that it would respect Iranian sovereignty, and although the war's end was in sight, the Soviet Union began dispatching even more troops to its area of occupation. At this point, the Tudeh began advocating a zone of influence for the Soviets in northern Iran, claiming this was justified by the need to protect the "Motherland of Socialism." In the Tudeh's telling, the Soviet Union was a benign power whose intentions could not be compared with those of rapacious imperial nations such as Great Britain. As the most consequential center of socialism, the Soviet Union adhered to an ideology of equality and justice and could not be seen as a greedy power. The Tudeh's absurdities touted on behalf of Stalin's empire were a catastrophic misjudgment that paved the way for the crisis in Azerbaijan.

The growing anxieties about the Soviet moves in Iran prompted Churchill and Secretary of State Edward Stettinius, who had replaced the ailing Hull, to press for Iran's inclusion on the agenda of the Yalta conference that February. Roosevelt had already declared, in his breezy way, that Iran could be a test case for Allied relations. Churchill took it upon himself to remind his friend of these claims. But for Roosevelt such musings were ephemeral. He seemed to have genuine concerns about Stalin's conduct, not just in Iran but throughout Eastern Europe, yet he would not press Stalin on these issues because he felt it was more important to cooperate with the Soviet Union to stabilize the postwar global order. When Iran did not come up in the plenary meetings among the three leaders, Foreign Secretary Eden stepped into the vacuum.

By now, Eden's diplomats in Tehran were deluging him with reports of Soviet misbehavior, causing him to approach Stalin's deputy Vyacheslav Molotov. The stern and taciturn Molotov, whose absolute devotion to Stalin had allowed him to survive many purges, was in no mood to bother with the claims of Iranian sovereignty. Eden tried to entice him by noting that the issue of oil concessions should be tied to the withdrawal of all foreign troops, only to be curtly dismissed by Molotov. This led Eden to broach the topic directly with Stalin. The Soviet dictator laughed off Molotov's intransigence by noting, "You should never talk to Molotov about Iran. Didn't you realize that he had a resounding diplomatic defeat there?"[49] Stalin gave no ground and merely agreed to study the issue. The conference ended with the Iran question very much unresolved.

During the war, Iran at times seemed like a disorderly nation. Prime ministers, parliaments, and coalitions came and went. But the achievements of the upper class cannot be overstated. The Iranian elite preserved the country's sovereignty and territorial integrity. In the aftermath of Reza Shah's abdication, there was no guarantee that the monarchy would survive, since both Britain and Russia were prepared to dispense with the Pahlavi dynasty. It was the elite that insisted on maintaining the monarchy as the best means of governing the country. Iran was surely an imperfect democracy, but its elections still mattered. It had a lively press and political parties with diverse ideological leanings. The parliament was assertive, and the cabinet officers exercised a measure of autonomy from the royal court. The elections were not without irregularities, the politicians were often parochial, and parliamentary debates were usually inconclusive. Still, the elite adhered to rudiments of democratic rule that, if allowed to mature, could have anchored the monarchy on a more stable foundation.

The essentials of the shah's personality also became apparent during this period. At the height of his power in 1977, the shah was asked by a sympathetic interviewer why, at the outset of his rule, he had "sat back and permitted democracy to work." His response was revealing: he stressed that the "powers of the ruler had been shattered to such an extent during the war and the occupation period that I really was not left with much choice. The power that I have today did not come overnight. It is the fruit of twenty five years of tears and sweat. Actually, behind the scenes I was working like mad, as much as was possible for any human being, offering passive resistance, trying to salvage what I could."[50]

The young shah, though diffident and prone to yield to the elder statesmen, was already demonstrating a preference for authoritarian rule. His vision of reform, shaped in part by admiration of his father's dictatorship, necessitated a centralized government that would draw its power from the armed forces, sidestepping the messy politics of parliaments and politicians. Toward this end, the shah would cleverly use a series of crises facing Iran to gradually assert his prerogatives at the expense of the aristocracy that had served him well.

The West would come to loom large in the shah's imagination. It was perhaps not unusual for a monarch whose country was occupied by the great powers to seek their approval for the measures he wished to institute. But the specter of his father's exile haunted him, and he never fully trusted the Western powers that were responsible for it. Even after he established his absolutist rule, he never quite trusted the leading Western power, the United States. He worried about what American ideas of reform meant for his rule and was dubious of Iranian politicians who found favor in Washington. The shah would deal with numerous U.S. presidents and at times defy the United States, but the combination of envy and suspicion of the West that shaped his views early on never left him.

As the United States entered Iran, it established a pattern that would repeat itself. The Americans believed their country offered a model that others should emulate. With the New Deal, the American government had assumed a greatly expanded role in the economy through ambitious public works programs, progressive taxation, and regulation of the business sector. This is the blueprint that Millspaugh took to Iran, failing to appreciate that the Persian ruling class had its own ideas about how to govern the country. For the next several decades, Iran would continue to serve as a social science laboratory as the Americans tried out their theories on a nation they often poorly understood.

During the war, as the only country occupied by all three Allied powers, Iran was bound to be a place where their varying interests and ambitions came into conflict. It was not as important a battleground as Eastern Europe, where the cohesion of the Grand Alliance was ultimately determined. But whereas the United States and Britain could not stop the Soviets from imposing their system on the hapless Eastern European nations, Iran fared better. Stalin's famous and cynical quip that whoever occupies a territory will determine its political future was tragically true in the ancient seats of European civilization. But in the peripheral nation of Iran, the Western allies would make their strongest stance, and the Soviet dictator would suffer his most consequential defeat.

CHAPTER 2

A Crisis in Azerbaijan

In 1945, as many celebrated the Grand Alliance's triumph over Hitler's armies, there lurked a sense of anxiety. The Soviet Union had emerged as a formidable power on the world stage, and while the Western allies acknowledged that its people had suffered immensely and that its legitimate concerns had to be addressed, they also knew the Soviets had their own ambitions. At wartime summits, Roosevelt had let Russia take a commanding role in Eastern Europe and make territorial adjustments on its Asian frontier. As the influence of Britain waned, the consensus seemed to be that the Soviet Union was bound to be one of the two great world powers with the United States: the only question was how far it intended to go.

Stalin's moves in northern Iran seem to have been motivated more by a desire for oil than by a drive for more land.[1] Iran was not Eastern Europe, where two German invasions in three decades had convinced Russia that it needed a territorial buffer. Even though Russian leaders had long coveted Persia's warm-water ports, Stalin seems to have limited his ambitions to the country's resources. At this point, Iran was producing more oil than any other Middle Eastern country, and petroleum was proving to be the fuel needed to rebuild economies and armies. Britain had already secured its share of Iranian oil, and Moscow knew that Tehran had tried to entice American firms to buy up concessions. Russia wanted its share of the spoils.

Even in the darkest days of the German onslaught, postwar demarcations had never been far from Stalin's mind. Soon after the German invasion of Russia in June 1941, Anthony Eden traveled to Moscow to assess the new alliance's needs, only to be lectured by Stalin about how he intended to keep the territorial gains granted to him by his ill-fated pact with Hitler. Iran was no different. In 1943, the Kremlin had dispatched three hundred geologists to Azerbaijan to determine the scope of its oil deposits. The sadistic Lavrentiy Beria, the head of Stalin's secret police, was put in charge of the Azerbaijan file. The results of the survey so impressed him that he proposed to Stalin that Moscow should negotiate with Tehran "the obtaining of a concession in northern Iran."[2]

The Soviet Union already had a sizeable contingent of troops in Azerbaijan and was determined to use them to impose a local government amenable to its designs. As a communist ideologue ostensibly guiding the march of history, Stalin normally had no time for national identity, which he considered chauvinistic. His typical response to such claims within the Soviet Union was to uproot ethnic minorities and transport them thousands of miles away, at a cost of millions of lives. His disdain for cultural distinction and ethnic autonomy was typical of a leader who hailed from Georgia and spoke Russian with an accent. But in Azerbaijan, where Moscow hoped to shape the politics so as to give it leverage in its dealings with Tehran, Stalin suddenly became a fervent champion of ethnic nationalism.

In July 1945, the Politburo passed a resolution calling on its local communist allies to "organize a separatist movement in southern Azerbaijan and other provinces of northern Iran."[3] Given that the war had not yet ended, Moscow still had to show some deference to its allies' sensibilities. Consequently, the provincial branch of the Tudeh was ordered to disband, and its members to join the newly created Azerbaijan Democratic Party (ADP). The NKVD, Russia's secret police, warned its local allies, "Do not permit the mechanical transformation of Tudeh organizations into committees of the Azerbaijan Democratic Party."[4] Nothing was left to chance; even the name of the party and its program were conceived by the NKVD. The ADP was to appeal to all social classes with a program that emphasized land reform, health care, maintaining tax revenues for local needs, and greater sensitivity to Azeri language and identity in all educational and cultural matters. A militia was created and, to conceal its source of patronage, equipped with non-Soviet arms.

As with most matters entrusted to Beria, violence and bloodshed soon followed. Beria's local henchmen assured him that "twenty-one experienced

NKVD operatives have been selected who are capable of organizing work to liquidate people and organizations interfering with the development of the autonomy movement in Iranian Azerbaijan."[5] The Soviet agents quickly developed a secret police, manned by reliable communists, then launched an assassination campaign targeting Iranian army officers, police chiefs, local officials, and landed gentry. Despite its democratic claims, the ADP resembled other communist parties proliferating in Eastern Europe in that terror was its preferred instrument.

The next task was to choose a leader for the new party. Ja'far Pishehvari seemed an ideal choice. A longtime leftist activist, he had played a prominent role in founding Iran's communist party and was later jailed by Reza Shah. After he was released in the amnesty arrangement that followed the monarch's exile, he began to edit a newspaper and was endorsed by the Tudeh as one of its deputies, only to have his credentials rejected by the parliament because of his separatist stance on Azerbaijan. He might have spent the rest of his life in obscurity had Stalin not selected him as the leader of his new venture.

The new Azeri government soon moved beyond autonomy and began functioning as an independent state. An assembly was chosen, with ample electoral fraud to ensure ADP's domination. The Iranian military garrisons were forced to surrender, and reinforcements were blocked by Soviet troops.[6] A new flag and postage stamps were issued. Monuments to the Pahlavi dynasty were dismantled. A new educational system came into existence overnight, emphasizing Azeri themes, and a propaganda campaign was launched to make the Azeri people aware of how long they had suffered at the hands of the imperious Persians. All this was enforced by Soviet troops, whose numbers kept increasing despite Stalin's pledges to withdraw his troops after the war ended.

There was always something improbable about this enterprise. Tehran did proscribe Azeri language from its official podiums, and the Persian-speaking majority disparaged Azeri traditions. But the Azeri population saw themselves as part of the Iranian nation, and as the largest ethnic minority in Iran, they had their share of leaders and luminaries in the capital. Despite their resentments toward the central government, the Azeris had no affection for Soviet communism. The ADP never dealt with the economic grievances on which it had based its platform, and its heavy-handed methods only diminished its appeal. In essence, the Soviets made the mistake of looking at Iran as a collection of ethnic groups that they could exploit to advance their ambitions. They failed to see how successive Iranian dynasties had knitted together a cohesive nation.

As the Soviets tried to carve away Iran's most populous province, Prime Minister Ebrahim Hakimi found his choices narrowing. The Tudeh was agitating in the streets, and in the parliament various proposals were put forward calling on the government to negotiate with the separatist movement. From the podium of the Majlis, a Tudeh deputy, Mohammad Rudemanesh, denounced his own country for "fighting democracy" and insisted that the Soviet Union had a right to "have a neutral and democratic power" on its side.[7] Such claims were not limited to Soviet stooges, as even the ardent nationalist Mohammad Mossadeq suggested that Azerbaijan be recognized as a "partly autonomous" province within an Iranian federal structure.[8] Hakimi stood his ground, supported by the shah, who did not want his kingdom dismembered, and the parliament rejected all such proposals. In yet another act of defiance, Hakimi made it known that he was prepared to go to the United Nations and file a complaint against the Soviet Union. The Tripartite Agreement was his trump card, but it was premature, because Russia did not have to remove its troops until March 1946. And it was not clear how much support Tehran would get from the Western powers.

In many ways, Azerbaijan was the Cold War's first accidental crisis. The United States had long insisted on Iran's territorial integrity and had withdrawn its forces even before the Tripartite Agreement expired. But America was not necessarily averse to letting Russia have its share of Iranian oil.[9] In 1945, Washington still hoped to sustain the Grand Alliance, and for a Truman administration preoccupied with issues in Europe, Iran was not a priority. Poverty and hunger in the wake of the war were benefiting communist parties all over Western Europe. There was a real fear in Washington that Soviet power could come to countries such as France and Italy, not through invasion but as a result of free elections. Truman confronted not only a nation still under the illusion that once the war ended it could return to its isolationist traditions, but also a parsimonious Congress not eager to appropriate foreign aid. Even his own advisers were divided over what relations with the Soviet Union should be. Truman had enthusiastically echoed Roosevelt in extolling the virtues of the Grand Alliance and its benevolent Soviet leader, "Uncle Joe." It would be hard for America to simply give up on the late president's vision and embark on a confrontational policy whose benefits were uncertain. All this meant that Truman was not looking for a crisis in the distant land of Azerbaijan.

This message was privately conveyed to Iran when its envoy to the United States, Hossein Alā, discreetly approached Secretary of State James Byrnes for support at the United Nations. In a gentle rebuff, he was told that "the United

States has friendly relations with both the Soviet Union and with Iran, and for us to give advance commitment to either side would not be in harmony either with those relations or with the spirit of the United Nations."[10] In a few months, America's position would begin to harden, but at this point Washington was still struggling to find the right balance between sustaining the Grand Alliance and pushing back on Moscow.

Britain's position was even softer than America's. Prodded by Bullard, who perceived that Iran's ethnic composition required decentralized rule, Britain did not object to either a Soviet oil grab or autonomy for Azerbaijan. As an imperial state with its own sphere of influence in southern Iran, Britain was amenable to a separate Soviet zone in the north. Ernest Bevin, the former truck driver and union leader who had taken over the Foreign Office from Eden when the Labour Party unexpectedly ousted the Conservatives, might have earned his reputation chasing communists out of unions, but he was still a leader of a country exhausted by war and hungry for oil and money. Bevin would later distinguish himself as a cold warrior, but at this point his actions were guided more by mercantilism than by anti-communism. He assured the British parliament that "when a small country happens to possess a vital raw material it is for the allies to arrange their business so as not to make the small country the victim of controversy between the big Allies."[11] Bevin went on to propose that the three great powers form a commission to assess the Azerbaijan situation, a ploy designed to bury the issue and avoid a messy fight with the Soviets. Moscow quickly rejected the idea.

While they contemplated the shape of the postwar order, both the United States and Britain were ready to accept Stalin's oil demands, and they hoped he would take up his concession with a measure of circumspection, avoiding the tactics he was increasingly using in Eastern Europe. But Stalin was not given to subtle exercises of power. He knew there was no possibility of gaining access to Persian oil without first bullying the Iranian government, and the Soviet troop presence in Azerbaijan was essential to that strategy of intimidation.

As both London and Washington continued to hope for a solution to these thorny problems with Russia, the goalposts for such a solution were being carried farther down the field by an assertive Soviet Union. In response to Hakimi's complaints, *Pravda* editorialized that "the fuss that the reactionary circles are making over the evacuation of Allied troops has the purpose of diverting attention from the police attacks on the democratic movement in Iranian Azerbaijan."[12] Russia's deputy foreign minister and representative at the United Nations, Andrey Vyshinsky, first denied that Russia had interfered in Iran's internal affairs and then proceeded to justify the intervention. Vyshinsky was well practiced in the art of double-speak. As the grand master of Stalin's show trials, he made certain that old Bolsheviks confessed to fantastic crimes. The former henchman noted that the "presence of Soviet troops in the territory of Iran is quite legitimate in so far as such a right was granted to the Soviet government by the Soviet-Iranian Treaty of 26 February 1921, and the Soviet-British-Iranian treaties of 1942."[13] In an ominous manner, Moscow was justifying its presence not by wartime exigencies that had already ended but by an outdated agreement, one drafted during the Russian civil war to prevent White Russians from attacking the mainland from an Iranian sanctuary.

On December 12, 1945, James Byrnes arrived in Moscow for a foreign ministers conference. A vain and arrogant man, Byrnes had served both as a Supreme Court justice and as a senator from South Carolina. He resented Truman and that Roosevelt had passed him over for the vice presidency in 1944. During the war years, while Truman had loitered in the Senate, Byrnes had been in charge of the Office of Economic Stabilization and War Mobilization that essentially managed America's economy. Given his proximity to Roosevelt and his sharp political skills, he amassed so much power that he was sometimes called "assistant president." Initially an unsure Truman relied on Byrnes and gave him much authority over foreign affairs. It was a deference that Byrnes would abuse, and Truman, kept in the dark on important matters once too often, eventually fired him. Nonetheless, the secretary of state arrived in Russia with more leeway than any of his counterparts.

After a number of typically inconclusive meetings with Molotov, Byrnes finally confronted Stalin with the Iran problem. The question was not so much oil but Russian troops. Byrnes warned Stalin that the issue might be broached at the United Nations, and while America wished to avoid friction with its wartime ally, it could not tolerate a breach of the 1942 agreement. This was the first indication that Washington saw the United Nations as a potential platform for adjudicating the dispute. Stalin once more brandished the absurd argument that Iran posed a danger to the Baku oil fields, because its agents might cross the border and sabotage the refineries. Byrnes retorted that the United States might yet support Iran's petition and that "it would be difficult for the Soviet Union to convince world opinion that the fifteen-hundred man Iranian contingent somehow threatened a Soviet force of thirty thousand."[14] Byrnes was sometimes too eager for peace with Moscow, but on Iran he displayed a measure of toughness. Even so, he left Russia with the issue unresolved.

Prime Minister Hakimi's last act of courage came in January 1946, when he instructed his representatives to file a complaint against the Soviet Union at the United Nations. He then resigned, recognizing how untenable his position had become given Russia's machinations against his rule.

QAVAM TAKES CHARGE

Ahmad Qavam was one of Iran's most enterprising and devious prime ministers. He succeeded Hakimi at age sixty-nine, having held the premiership on three previous occasions. Iran's monarchs appreciated Qavam's talents as much as they distrusted his motives, and they usually turned to him in times of trouble. Like many members of the Iranian elite, he had suffered at the hands of Reza Shah, under whom he had been purged and exiled. The young shah appreciated Qavam's cunning and supported him behind the scenes. Each was suspicious of the other, but they recognized the urgency of the situation.

Qavam was improvisational, opportunistic, often dishonest, and adept at building alliances with potential adversaries without losing sight of his core objectives. He was a scion of the aristocracy and had the confidence of the traditional classes, who viewed him as one of their own. Taking the helm of power once more, he understood that the Azerbaijan crisis would test all of his considerable skills and cement his place in history.

Qavam belonged to the class of Iranian politicians who subscribed to the notion of positive equilibrium, whereby Iran would ensure its autonomy by developing ties with all the great powers and then manipulating their rivalries to its advantage. It was a delicate balance. Qavam let it be known that he was interested in reaching an oil agreement with the Soviet Union. Such a move by a lesser politician might have provoked a backlash, but the shah and Iran's other notables had no choice but to trust Qavam. The British, meanwhile, hoped that the "sly old bird" might yet contrive some kind of solution. Even the United States saw in Qavam's warm embrace of the Soviets an opportunity to resolve the crisis without disrupting great-power relations.

Qavam had observed his predecessor closely and recognized that a confrontational posture would only lead to the fall of his government. He understood that until March 1946, the Soviets had had a plausible excuse for keeping their troops in Iran. His task was to drag out the oil negotiations until the Soviet presence became a violation of its wartime commitments, a strategy he knew could not succeed without Western support. And he understood that Washington and London would accept an oil deal but not necessarily the dismemberment of Iran. If he could make the Soviet troop presence a bone of contention between the great powers and thus secure the withdrawal of Soviet soldiers, he was confident he could dispose of the separatist movement in the north. As a landowner with substantial holdings in Azerbaijan, Qavam knew better than Stalin that the ADP had almost no popular support and could not survive unless backed by Soviet troops. He entered the negotiations with the least leverage and with the most ambitious agenda. His objective was to deny Moscow both its oil and its sphere of influence.

To achieve his primary goal of restoring Iran's sovereignty, Qavam took a carrot-and-stick approach. He tried to reassure the Soviets by easing pressure on the Tudeh and even bringing some of its members into his government. He also insinuated that there was a place in Iran for the ADP as the governing party of an autonomous Azerbaijan region. But he shrewdly noted that given the nationalist uproar the Soviet occupation had provoked, he could not move on any of these matters so long as Iran was occupied by foreign troops. He was willing to ease Stalin out of his predicament while seemingly granting him his key demands.

As Qavam prepared to journey to Moscow for direct talks, the Soviets began a war of nerves. The troops on Iran's periphery were increased and began ominous maneuvers.[15] The Soviet embassy in Tehran issued statements about how it feared for the safety of Russian nationals, thus laying down a pretext for intervention. The Soviet ambassador warned Qavam that Iran's continued complaints at the United Nations "would be regarded as [an] unfriendly and hostile act and would have unfortunate results for Iran."[16] This was hardly an auspicious start to the premier's diplomatic mission.

On February 18, 1946, Qavam arrived in a frigid Moscow to negotiate with Stalin. The disparity between the two sides could not have been greater. Stalin, the victor of World War II, commanded a vast army and a chunk of Iran's territory. Qavam was the premier of an occupied country with an inconsequential military. In their perfunctory first meeting, Stalin warned Qavam about Iran's treachery and said he could no longer trust Tehran. He pointed to the British oil concessions and stressed that Russia deserved similar deference. Stalin further insisted that under the 1921 agreement the Soviet Union had a right to maintain troops in Iran and warned that Azerbaijan's autonomy "is not contrary to Iranian independence."[17] Qavam would hear these themes repeated often during his stay.

In his more detailed negotiations with Molotov, Qavam tried to play the oil card. He explained that Iran had no intention of adopting discriminatory trade practices, and it was only the parliamentary prohibition that prevented the completion of an oil agreement. Once Stalin withdrew the Soviet forces, then "of course the necessary steps for entering economic negotiations between the two countries will be taken."[18] Then he waited for signs of Soviet moderation.

In his next meeting with Molotov, Qavam's hopes quickly faded. The foreign minister's tone was even harsher and his demands more categorical. Accustomed to berating leaders of small nations, Molotov insisted that the "right of the Soviet government to such [oil] concessions is not open to discussion."[19] As for the troops, they were needed to protect Russia's southern flank. Molotov absurdly claimed that "in Iran there are some rather distinguished statesmen that have based their policies on striving to create problems between the U.S.S.R. and other great countries in order to misuse the possible conflict that might occur to conquer Soviet Azerbaijan, Baku and Soviet Turkmenistan."[20] In essence, Molotov was saying that in the absence of Russian troops, Iran's army would invade the Soviet Union.

As he had done throughout this trip, Qavam brandished the parliamentary decree prohibiting oil concessions so long as Iran's territory was occupied. As for Molotov's claims that Iran could threaten the Soviet Union militarily, he portrayed himself as a friend of the Soviets who was willing to deal constructively with both the Tudeh and the provisional government of Azerbaijan. In essence, he was signaling to the Kremlin that he was the Iranian politician most sensitive to its concerns and thus its most suitable interlocutor.

While Qavam was in Russia, Byrnes issued a strong statement that was passed on to Molotov by George Kennan, the embassy's chargé d'affaires. The secretary informed his counterpart that the United States remained committed to the Tripartite Agreement and "expressed the earnest hope that the government of the Soviet Union will do its part by withdrawing immediately all Soviet forces from the territory of Iran."[21] The American messages seemed to have an impact. In a banquet the following night Stalin was noticeably more subdued, no longer just bullying Qavam but, amid endless toasts, pledging to continue the dialogue with Tehran. Molotov then offered the premier a modified offer that still fell short of Qavam's mandate. In more polite language, Molotov stressed that some Soviet troops, perhaps not all, would remain in northern Iran. He insisted rather incongruously that while the situation in Azerbaijan was an internal Iranian issue, the province had to remain autonomous. As for oil, instead of an outright concession, Moscow was willing to settle for a joint venture with Iran in which Russia controlled the majority of shares.

Qavam left Moscow having managed to withstand Soviet browbeating and threats. He had tried to both rebuff and reassure Stalin. Qavam knew that in the international system, power, rather than ideals, would likely determine the outcome. If he hoped to succeed in preserving his country's independence, he had to have American muscle behind his diplomatic gambit.

AMERICA TURNS TO CONTAINMENT

Fortunately for Iran, at that precise moment America was not just considering a more confrontational policy but also beginning to see Iran as a place to take a stand against Russian aggression. A series of speeches and memoranda that month would define the evolving international order.

On February 9, Josif Stalin delivered a speech in the Bolshoi Theater to great fanfare. Ostensibly intended to congratulate the army and the nation for their heroic sacrifices during the war, the speech also called for a significant increase in industrial production—necessary preparation, Stalin declared, for the coming conflict with the West. He noted the incompatibility between communism and capitalism and how the uneven distribution of wealth within the capitalist bloc had caused all past wars. War remained a possibility, the Soviet dictator implied, so long as capitalism persisted as a system of economic organization. Although such crass denunciations of capitalism were common features of Marxist rhetoric, this one, at this time, was particularly ominous. The Soviet Union did not want war, Stalin insisted, but it had to prepare for one.

Stalin's speech set off alarm bells in Washington as perplexed Americans tried to figure out what their erstwhile ally meant. James Forrestal, secretary of the navy, was an early convert to the cause of containing the Soviet threat and had been looking for suitable advice to peddle to his skeptical colleagues.[22] In January 1946, he had commissioned a study by Professor Edward Willett of Smith College that warned Moscow was committed to a "global, violent proletarian revolution" that made conflict between the United States and the Soviet Union inevitable.[23] Somehow the study did not make an impression, and Willett went back to academic obscurity. Forrestal kept looking, and he soon came across George Kennan.

Kennan had been leery of communism since he first witnessed Stalin's murderous show trials and the convulsions of the agricultural collectivization process, which killed millions of peasants by starvation. A devoted student of Russian literature, he sensed that there was something unusual about Stalin's reign, even in a nation whose history was littered with cruel despots. From his perch in Moscow, Kennan "bombarded the lower levels of Washington bureaucracy with analyses of Communist evil." All were ignored: the intelligentsia of the 1930s considered the Soviet Union a laboratory of social reform. There were plenty of excuses for Stalinism, the most enduring being that Stalin's forced industrialization had actually helped the Soviets fend off the Nazi invasion. The Grand Alliance cemented these feelings, causing many to see the Soviet Union as a gallant and important ally. Thus Kennan was surprised in 1946 to receive an urgent request from Washington for an assessment of Moscow's behavior. "They asked for it," he told himself, "now they're going to get it."[24]

In what later became known as the Long Telegram (it ran more than five thousand words), he described a Soviet cosmology in which the world was divided between two blocs without possibility of coexistence or pragmatic adjustment. "We have here a political force committed fanatically to the belief that with U.S. there can be no permanent modus vivendi," stressed Kennan.[25] Russia's traditional anxieties, when married to Marxist pathologies, meant that Soviet leaders required an external enemy to justify their hold on power. Marxism was the "fig leaf of their moral and intellectual respectability. Without it they would stand before history, at best, as only the last of that long succession of cruel and wasteful Russian rulers."[26] In more subtle passages, Kennan described how the Soviet appetite for global dominance was cleverly fed by a strategy of gradual, yet relentless expansion of influence. Unlike Hitler, Stalin would not use force but would advance his objectives through exploitation of all Western vulnerabilities.[27] The implication of Kennan's analysis was ominous. It suggested that gestures of goodwill and acknowledgment of Russia's legitimate concerns were foolhardy. Soviet hostility toward the West was intrinsic, ideologically animated, and unaffected by accommodation.

Unlike most policy advisers, Kennan did not simply outline the problem; he offered an alternative to the existing U.S. approach. The Soviet Union that Kennan described was not impervious to the logic of power. If determinedly confronted, it would retreat. Kennan stressed that Moscow would seek to avoid war but might lapse into one if it misjudged America's determination. In the deformed political order that Stalin had created, however, it was impossible to determine how information was being conveyed or received. A judicious Soviet functionary would likely offer assessments that affirmed his superior's misjudgments rather than challenge them. Unable to rely on traditional diplomatic messaging, American policymakers, in Kennan's view, had to draw clear lines and transmit their decisions directly to Soviet authorities.

Once convinced of such resolution, Stalin would concede, back down, and even adjust his objectives.

Forrestal read Kennan's telegram and dispatched it to the president and other cabinet officers. With its historical insights and elegant style, it soon became compulsory reading across Washington.[28] Then it resurfaced as an anonymous article in the influential journal *Foreign Affairs*. Kennan was summoned back to the United States, where he presented his ideas to a wide range of audiences, including a series of lectures at the National War College.

Among the reasons for the Long Telegram's success is that it affirmed sentiments already percolating in the bureaucracy. High-ranking policymakers like Dean Acheson were exasperated by the Kremlin's obstinacy. As early as the summer of 1944, Acheson compared negotiating with the Soviet Union "to dealing with an old-fashioned penny slot machine—one could sometimes expedite the process by shaking the machine, but it was useless to talk to it."[29] Ambassador Laurence Steinhardt, who had replaced the disreputable Joseph Davies as America's envoy to the Soviet Union in 1939, wrote, "My experience has been that they respond only to force and if force cannot be applied, to straight oriental bartering."[30] The State Department's own assessment echoed Kennan's, noting the precarious nature of the international system and a balance of power that had swung entirely in the Soviets' favor. The Soviet state's aim was "the complete subversion or forcible destruction of the machinery of governments and structure of society in the countries of the non-Soviet world and their replacement by an apparatus subservient to and controlled from the Kremlin."[31] The Soviet Union would exploit all opportunities because "it possesses and is possessed by a world-wide revolutionary movement, because it is the inheritor of Russian imperialism, and because it is a totalitarian dictatorship."[32]

As Washington contemplated its response to Soviet actions in Iran, a call for confrontation came from a world leader of considerable esteem. Winston Churchill had been unexpectedly ousted as prime minister, but he retained the heroic stature he had gained by his early and solitary opposition to Nazi Germany. At Truman's invitation, he spoke at Westminster College in Fulton, Missouri, on March 5, 1946. Although the address would become known as the "Iron Curtain" speech, its original title was "The Sinews of Peace." It was as alarming as it was prophetic. Churchill began cautiously: "Nobody knows what Soviet Russia and its Communist international organization intends to do in the immediate future, or what are the limits, if any, to their expansion and proselytizing tendencies."[33] But he soon moved to the essence of his argument:

From Stettin in the Baltic to Trieste in the Adriatic, an iron curtain has descended across the continent. Beyond that line lie all the capitals of the ancient states of Central and Eastern Europe . . . all these famous cities and the populations that lie around them lie in what I must call the Soviet sphere, and all are subject in one form or another, not only to Soviet influence but to a very high and, in many cases, increasing measure of control from Moscow.³⁴

Churchill quickly pointed to the next arena of conflict. "Persia and Turkey," he said, "are both profoundly alarmed and disturbed at the claims which are being made upon them and at the pressure being exerted by the Moscow government."³⁵ In this sense, Churchill was reinforcing Kennan's telegram, which had similarly pointed to the eastern Mediterranean as the next target of Russian intrigue. Although the ostensible purpose of the speech was a call for an Anglo-American alliance against Soviet aggression, Churchill echoed Kennan in claiming that power alone, not lofty sentiments, would forestall the Soviets.³⁶

The Iron Curtain speech may be acclaimed today, but it was jeered by many luminaries at the time. Walter Lippmann, the dean of American journalism, charged that Churchill believed "it was important to fight the Russians sometime during the next five years."³⁷ Joseph Kennedy, America's former ambassador to Britain, wrote in *Life*, "Russia does not want a major war now nor in the near future."³⁸ A young congressional candidate named Richard Nixon wondered "if he [Churchill] had gone too far."³⁹ James Roosevelt stood with his father's legacy, stressing, "It is up to us and to every peace-loving man and woman in the entire world to stand up now and repudiate the words, the schemes, and the political allies of Churchill."⁴⁰ Despite these discordant voices, the speech had an electrifying effect. One of the two remaining leaders of the Grand Alliance was now repudiating its aspirations for postwar cooperation.

Moscow's reaction was furious and unhinged. In a rare interview with *Pravda*, Stalin castigated Churchill as racist and compared him to Hitler. He was particularly offended that Churchill denounced his empire as totalitarian. Such an accusation was "not only slanderous but vulgarly tasteless"; Stalin pointed out that while Britain was ruled by a single party, all the Eastern European nations enjoyed coalition governments.⁴¹ Nor was his anger confined to Churchill. He complained to America's ambassador, Walter Bedell Smith, about such "an unfriendly act and an unwarranted attack on himself and the U.S.S.R. which, if it had been directed against the United States, would never have been permitted in Russia."[42] But as he geared up for a confrontation over Azerbaijan, Stalin suddenly had to consider the cost of his belligerency.

Truman was at first inclined to sustain Roosevelt's policy of great-power cooperation. Unsure of himself and surrounded by men with superior knowledge of foreign affairs, he was prone to follow the existing path. Whether in deliberations over Poland or dealing with Soviet aid requests, Truman sought to reconcile his call for self-determination in Eastern Europe with his desire to cooperate with the Soviet Union. He was growing increasingly uneasy about his circumstances and was confused about his options, but the gravitational pull was toward the Yalta Accords and their spirit of accommodation.[43]

Truman was fortunate to inherit from his predecessor sober minds such as Dean Acheson, Admiral William Leahy, and Averell Harriman, who gave him steady criticism of Stalin's rule and the impracticality of uncritical engagement. If he needed further motivation for a more aggressive policy, he also received a highly explosive report from his trusted aide Clark Clifford. The report began with the familiar refrain that "the language of military power is the only language which the disciples of power politics understand."[44] The best means of preserving American security, Clifford argued, would be to deter the Soviet Union from absorbing areas vital to U.S. interests. He clearly noted the increasing overlap between Iran and the need to get tough with Russia, commenting that America's "continued access to oil in the Middle East is especially threatened by Soviet penetration into Iran."[45]

The scale of Stalin's aggression and the increasing consensus among Truman's close aides soon changed the president's perspective. As an upright person who believed that politicians should keep their word, he was predisposed to arguments that Moscow be held accountable for its treaty violations. Along the way, the administration's internal studies, and Churchill's powerful oratory, provided intellectual justification for a president uneasy with his current path and searching for a different strategy. Truman told his envoy to Moscow, General Smith, to advise Stalin "that it would be misinterpreting the character of the United States to assume that because we are basically peaceful and deeply interested in world security we are either divided, weak or unwilling to face our responsibilities."[46] America had a new policy: containment.[47]

At the center of the containment doctrine was the idea that the Soviet Union was not bent on war with the militarily and economically superior West—instead Stalin, a ruthless and clever strategist, wanted to consolidate his sphere of influence at minimal cost. Supporting this view was the observation that Moscow had long seemed open to dialogue as a means of lulling the West into a belief that accommodation was possible. The Kremlin sought the improbable: to sustain the Grand Alliance while advancing the frontiers of the Soviet Empire. Stalin had already managed to impose his totalitarian grip on Eastern Europe while using various diplomatic summits to pledge great-power harmony. All this was to end as the United States committed itself to using all of its power to push back on the Soviet Union. This required building up existing alliances, shoring up America's military, and fending off Soviet probes.

As the Truman administration embraced its new strategy, Iran, which had been peripheral to U.S. concerns, suddenly took center stage. Truman now saw Iran as a critical pillar of his containment policy. As he wrote in his memoir, "If the Russians were to control Iran's oil, either directly or indirectly, the raw material balance of the world would undergo a serious loss for the economy of the Western world."[48] Secretary of State Byrnes, emboldened by the consensus in government and eager for the limelight, decided to declare the Cold War on his own and chose Iran as its principal flashpoint. At the Overseas Press Club, the secretary announced that the United States would not remain indifferent if "force or threat of force is used contrary to the purposes and principles of the Charter [of the United Nations]."[49] While Byrnes had often presumed to make declarations without consulting the president, he did not do that here. "Jim, I've read it and like it," Truman noted on a draft of the speech submitted for his approval.[50]

The American delegation at the United Nations now pressed Iran's complaint against the Soviet Union. In collaboration with Iran, the United States lobbied, cajoled, and pressured other delegates to support Iran's claims of sovereignty. As the future secretary of state Dean Rusk recalled, "The Iranian representative at that time in New York was Ambassador Ala and he was closely and well advised by Mr. John Leyland, who was a member of the Washington law firm of Covington and Burling, and the two of them did a brilliant job in handling the Iranian side of the controversy in the Security Council."[51] The battleship USS *Missouri* was dispatched to Istanbul, ostensibly to return the body of the deceased Turkish ambassador but clearly as a show of force. The stage was set for a confrontation between the two superpowers over an issue to which both had once assigned little importance.

As America pivoted to a more aggressive policy, Britain also began to change its stance. Despite Churchill's anti-Soviet oratory, the British policy was conditioned more by commercial considerations than anti-communism. Because of the Anglo-Iranian Oil Company's centrality in London's calculations, the British had been reluctant to challenge Russia's oil claims. Bevin was lukewarm about discussing the Iran issue at the United Nations, and the Foreign Office was wary about exposing Britain's oil interests to international arbitration. In Iran, Britain glimpsed a problem that it would encounter elsewhere in the Middle East as the Cold War unfolded. While it needed America's support in checking Soviet ambitions, it was often pulled in contradictory and self-defeating directions.

The British policy finally stiffened when the Foreign Office began to fear that the Soviet Union would not respect a spheres-of-influence arrangement. The Tudeh Party's Soviet-supported agitation among laborers in the southern oil fields had already provoked strikes and protests, and London became alarmed that a Soviet presence in the north would endanger its financial interests in the south. Bullard now warned that appeasing Stalin would threaten Britain's oil supplies. In a reversal of policy, the Foreign Office advised that "Britain has to face the unpleasant possibility that a government entirely subservient to the Soviet government might soon be operating in Tehran and that government might either cancel the AIOC concession or by stirring up labor riots make the operation of that concession ultimately impossible."[52] Fearing that Soviet power could not be insulated in the north, Britain decided that the entire Soviet enterprise in Iran had to be dismantled, and it joined the United States in its confrontational stance. The two nations' convergence on the issue resulted less from shared convictions than from Britain's desire to sustain its mercantile empire. Their different perspectives would be a source of friction between them throughout the Cold War.[53] Still, by 1946, they had agreed to confront the Soviet Empire. The strategy of containment now had a venue: Iran.

RUSSIA LEAVES

As the Western powers toughened their stance, Qavam understood that he now had all the elements of an effective carrot-and-stick strategy. Opening with carrots, he informed Molotov that "if the Soviet government will accept my position regarding the immediate withdrawal of all Soviet troops from Iran and on the Azerbaijan issue, I will agree to all conditions for the creation of this [joint Soviet-Iranian oil] society and to present an appropriate draft project for confirmation of the parliament."[54] Meanwhile, in his negotiations with Pishehvari, Qavam appeared to concede on most issues. The premier was prepared to accept Azerbaijan's parliament as the assembly, but he insisted that its militia be incorporated into Iran's National Army. The governor of the province would be chosen by Tehran from a list of candidates submitted by the local authorities. The bulk of the taxes collected would stay in Azerbaijan, and Azeri and Persian would both be recognized as the official languages. The Soviets were thus assured that they could obtain oil for themselves and autonomy for their client through negotiations with Qavam rather than by prolonging a transparently illegal occupation.

Qavam's gestures pleased the Kremlin, but its proxies in Azerbaijan were not impressed. Pishehvari proved a better judge of Qavam than Stalin. In a series of desperate messages, he warned his handlers in Moscow that Tehran would ultimately renege on the oil concession and that as soon as the Soviet forces left, it would crush his nascent republic. The NKVD station reported, "In course of the conversation Pishehvari is nervous . . . He thinks that all this is leading only to the liquidation of the democratic movement and everything won by the people."[55] But for Stalin, the ADP was always a bargaining chip to be sacrificed at the right moment. Once assured by Qavam and pressured by Truman, he seemed ready to make his move.

A new Soviet ambassador was dispatched to Tehran with a counteroffer. Ambassador Ivan Sadchikov promised that Moscow would withdraw Soviet forces if Iran signed a letter granting it an oil concession. The final text of the accord was somewhat different. It agreed that the Red Army would begin its departure on March 24, after which an agreement on a joint Iranian-Soviet company would be presented to the Majlis. Azerbaijan was to be treated as an internal matter, although Qavam hinted that he would accept its autonomy.

As a tyrant sensitive to subtle power shifts, Stalin displayed in this crisis a curious mixture of defiance and conciliation. He had effectively consolidated his European realm and was making significant inroads into Asia, acting with impunity given the lingering legacy of the Grand Alliance and seeming American indifference. The sudden Western resolve surprised and perplexed the Soviet dictator. That both the United States and Britain were willing to go to the Security Council over Iran reflected a level of commitment he had not seen before. And Qavam was now letting Stalin believe that all of his essential objectives had already been secured.

The end of the autonomous republic of Azerbaijan came quickly. The shah issued a decree calling for immediate action. "We must perform our patriotic duty now. We therefore command our armed forces to march forward to Azerbaijan to break down the resistance, and to raise the lion and sun standard in every corner of this dear land."⁵⁶ On December 13, the shah flew to Azerbaijan to take personal command of the military operations. He faced only the ragtag militia left behind by the Red Army, but the image of the monarch leading the attack boosted his national standing. For a young leader still struggling under the shadow of his father, this was his first act of command. He took charge and unified Iran.

Pishehvari was one of the more tragic victims of the entire affair. As the Iranian army marched north, he fled to the Soviet Union, resuming his life of exile. It would not be a quiet exile: he complained bitterly about his predicament, earning an unusual rebuke from Stalin. The Soviet leader rarely bothered with his deposed satraps, but Pishehvari must have agitated him. He took the time to chastise Pishehvari in a letter, warning, "You want to meet all revolutionary demands of Azerbaijan right now. But, the existing situation precludes [the] realization of this program." Stalin conveniently blamed Pishehvari for not creating a more sustainable regime and stressed that the only way Azerbaijan's autonomy could have been secured was by maintaining Russian forces. "We could no longer keep them in Iran, mainly because the presence of Soviet troops in Iran undercut the foundation of our liberationist policies in Europe and Asia." He ended the letter with a chilling note. "You, as I found out, say that we first raised you to the skies and then let you down into the precipice and disgraced you. If this is true, it surprises us . . . It is very strange that you think that we could have let you down in disgrace."⁵⁷ Not long after receiving this letter, Pishehvari died in a car accident.

The stage was now set for the parliamentary elections that would determine the fate of Russia's oil concession. With the end of its client regime in Azerbaijan, Russia's tattered Iran policy now rested only on the oil agreement. Ambassador Sadchikov warned Qavam that Moscow would consider Iran a "blood enemy" should the parliament reject the concession, but with the departure of the Red Army, such admonitions had little impact.⁵⁸ The electoral process was marred by an unusual degree of irregularities. Through his control of the government machinery and careful exclusion of rival candidates, Qavam ensured that the majority of seats went to those opposed to the concession. As one of its first acts, the newly convened parliament rejected the Soviet oil agreement by a vote of 102 to 2.⁵⁹

The end of the crisis also spelled the end of Qavam. His machinations had saved the country, but he had alienated too many power brokers. Initially, he hoped that he could extend his tenure as prime minister by launching an impressive reform package. Qavam's party, the Democratic Party of Iran, issued a program calling for economic reforms and the creation of modern health and education systems. Turning suddenly liberal, he even promised to restore power to the provincial assemblies and, like many prime ministers before him, called for a reduction in the military budget. This was bound to estrange the shah and his generals, who hoped to use the crisis to strengthen their position.

It is hard to judge whether Qavam's reform program was just another ploy for consolidating power or whether he really did have a vision for transforming Iran. It all came to naught as he found he had lost his grip on Iran's politics. The Left saw him as a traitor to its cause, while the Right did not forgive his many flirtations with the Tudeh. The shah, always suspicious of powerful prime ministers, was particularly dubious about Qavam. He had watched him closely throughout the negotiations and concluded that his maneuvers were designed to strengthen his premiership at the monarchy's expense. The shah was trying to claim credit as the liberator of Azerbaijan, and Qavam's presence proved inconvenient.

The great powers who were still arbiters of Iran's politics at this time also had their doubts about Qavam. The Soviets detested him and only belatedly recognized how he had outwitted them. The United States and Britain, despite their support of Qavam during the crisis, had never felt that his anticommunism ran very deep, and his clever dislodging of the Soviet Union from Azerbaijan did not fully dissipate their doubts. Qavam was suddenly without a constituency, and in Iran that usually spelled the end of one's tenure. This was not an unusual position for him: he had been in and out of office for decades. He would resume his sporadic exile, only to return to power one last time during the oil nationalization crisis, but without much effect. One of the ironies of the Azerbaijan crisis is that the shah emerged in much better shape than did Qavam, who had done more to evict the Soviet Union.

In the aftermath of Azerbaijan's reclamation, a more confident shah assumed a visible role in national affairs. He expanded the armed forces and devoted greater resources to his hand-picked officer corps. At the 1948 Olympic games, held in London, he met with a variety of leaders and luminaries. No longer a hesitant young monarch deferring to older men, the shah presented himself to both foreign and domestic audiences as Iran's head of state.

A failed assassination attempt did much to enhance the shah's popularity. On February 4, 1949, while stepping out of his limousine during a visit to Tehran University, he was approached by a photographer who pulled out a pistol and shot at him several times at point-blank range. For a minute, he and his assailant stood inches apart, and only by ducking and dodging did the shah manage to avoid most of the bullets. The frightened guards finally stepped in, killed the assassin, and rushed the shah to the hospital. He had been struck only on the lips and cheek and easily recovered, but he soon developed an elaborate conspiracy theory about the incident. The monarch later noted that the assassin "had connections to some religious zealots, and also some evidence of his connections to the dissolved Tudeh Party. It is also interesting that the assassin's girlfriend was the daughter of the gardener at the British embassy."[60] In this elaborate tale, Britain had conspired with Islamists and communists to plot his murder.

The assassination attempt, combined with the shah's role in liberating Azerbaijan, transformed popular perceptions of him. The institution of the monarchy still enjoyed public support, and the young king's good luck in eluding an assassin's bullet led to an outpouring of goodwill. The bonds between the court and the clergy were further strengthened when the foremost cleric of the time, Grand Ayatollah Mohammad Hossein Borujerdi, wrote to the shah, "May God Almighty preserve your kingdom."[61] This message of support was echoed by professions of loyalty from other clerics. The ayatollahs would provide the shah with much help during his early years in power.

As he did with the Azerbaijan situation, the shah used the assassination attempt to grab more power. He had always believed that Iran required a strongman, and that the troublesome parliament and its bickering politicians stood in the way of progress. He had beseeched successive British and American emissaries to endorse his arguments for a powerful king, only to be rebuffed by foreign diplomats who had little confidence in his leadership abilities. The armed forces remained the institution he most cherished, and they did much to protect him from prying politicians. Following the assassination attempt, the shah renewed his quest for control.

This time the obstacles were less formidable. Riding a wave of popularity, the shah convened a constituent assembly to amend the constitution so as to fulfill a previously ignored part of the 1906 constitution: the establishment of an upper legislative chamber. He insisted on the creation of a senate, half of whose members would be appointed by the royal court. He gave himself the right to dissolve the Majlis, whose terms were reduced from four to two years. In a quick succession of moves, the shah diminished the stature and authority of a chamber that had long served as the bastion of aristocratic privilege.

In the coming decades, the shah would often be advised that accumulating power would not serve his interests, because he would be held accountable for all of the nation's problems. One of the most prescient warnings came from the exiled Qavam, who warned the shah in an open letter that his power grab would backfire. The more authority he assumed, Qavam wrote, the more he would be held responsible for Iran's difficulties. The monarch curtly dismissed the advice of his ousted prime minister.

The nobility whose wings the shah was gradually clipping did not unite as a group to resist him. These were men of tradition who were there to serve a monarch who was still popular. At times, they would counsel the shah against his misjudgments but they could not come together as a class to conspire against the institution of monarchy. The shah had the support of the armed forces, the clerical community, and many within the aristocracy. Most politicians tried to advance their fortunes by appealing to the royal court as opposed to plotting against it.

At this point the shah was focused on trying to cement his ties to America. His chance came in November 1949, when he made his first official visit to Washington. As he prepared for the journey, he displayed his usual mixture of confidence and anxiety. He had had a triumphant year, and now he had to persuade the Americans to invest in his ambitions. The trip began a conversation between the two nations that would last for the next three decades. For the Americans, reducing poverty was an attractive means of fending off communism in the developing world. The Marshall Plan had proven to Washington that economic rehabilitation could undermine the appeal of the proliferating communist parties. The degree to which U.S. policymakers pressed their Third World allies to focus on creating viable economies is the underreported story of the Cold War. Poverty, illiteracy, and corruption were seen as instigators of radical change, and alleviating them required strong, reform-minded governments. An array of organizations were created in Washington to provide funds and technical assistance to local rulers. In their work, they paid less attention to developing democratic institutions than to strengthening the economic foundations of stable governments. Once their economies developed, it was thought, these nations could turn their attention to liberalizing their polities.

The American reform agenda was not on the shah's mind. He wanted new weapons systems. This should not have surprised the White House, since its embassy in Tehran had dispatched countless reports about the shah's unhappiness with the size of America's military aid package. During his stay in America, successive policymakers attempted to convince him that the primary threat to his rule was lack of economic development, not the Soviet army. In the Pentagon, U.S. generals and admirals tried to persuade the shah that his military could not absorb the sophisticated arms he wanted. In a gentle rebuke,

Secretary of State Dean Acheson insisted on "the fundamental necessity of giving priority to economic and social development. All nations in the free world face the same problem. If we attempted to build up our military establishments to a level comparable with that of the Soviet Union, we would wreck our economies and leave ourselves so weakened that we would collapse without even being subjected to military attack."[62] The monarch agreed that he needed to rebuild his country's economy and address its rampant corruption and uneven distribution of wealth. Yet he would quickly return to the notion that given the proximity of Soviet forces, he needed more arms. Much like he had ignored Qavam's advice, the shah chose to disregard his American allies' prescient counsel.

At its core, the dispute was over the basic purpose of the armed forces. The United States saw Iran's military in practical terms: it existed to maintain internal order. For the shah, it was a source of domestic power, a constituency he could depend on to counter the array of forces conspiring against his rule. He had little faith in democracy, was suspicious of Iran's political class, and felt he needed the army in order to survive. While successive American administrations insisted that stability would come from economic growth, a rational bureaucracy, and a growing middle class, the shah obsessed about the size of his army. The argument that no armed force, however formidable, could substitute for an actual constituency fell on deaf ears.

A DECADE OF TRANSITIONS

The 1940s was a consequential decade for both the United States and Iran. The Truman administration was the first to see that the Middle East's strategic location and immense oil reserves made its stability critical to America's global containment strategy. The threat that Truman faced in 1946 would prove an unusual one: direct Soviet military intervention. It was Stalin's misfortune that his military foray came at a time when America defined the Soviet moves as part of a larger assault on the remaining outposts of the free world. While it considered Stalin's gains in Eastern Europe irreversible, at least for the moment, Washington was determined to limit Soviet expansionism elsewhere. Truman and his advisers crafted an imaginative middle route between war and appeasement. They mobilized the international community and used the nascent United Nations to good effect.

While Iran was central to America's calculations, it was never critical to Stalin. The Soviet dictator was in many ways a nineteenth-century strategist who remained fixated on Europe and did not always see the opportunities in the vast colonial region. It would fall to his successors to take full advantage of the post-colonial nationalist uproar in Africa and the Middle East. Long accustomed to Roosevelt's benevolence and to perennially misreading American politics, Stalin seems to have been surprised by Truman's determination. For the first time, the Soviet dictator abandoned territory once held by his troops. In less than a decade, the United States twice upheld Iran's independence at the risk of estranging its allies. America would make its share of mistakes in Persia, but its championing of Iran's self-determination should never be forgotten.

The other key to America's success was a reliable—if not ingenious—Iranian ally. Qavam's determination to preserve Iran's sovereignty made American diplomacy much easier. He understood that he could not prevail without U.S. support, and he hoped that Stalin's excesses in Europe would redound to his advantage. The prime minister withstood Soviet threats, provocative troop deployments, and attempts to carve out portions of his country. The crisis might have worked out differently had Tehran been intimidated into accepting the Soviet mandates. Instead, Qavam challenged one of history's most ruthless tyrants at the zenith of his power.

If the United States had the advantage of clever allies, the Soviet Union was saddled with second-tier ideologues. Iranian communists, like other Marxists in the Middle East, often subordinated national concerns to rigid ideological strictures. The Tudeh repeatedly discredited itself by embracing Soviet priorities at the expense of Iran's sovereignty. It forfeited the mantle of nationalism at a time when this was the most important driver of Iranian politics. Pishehvari's rash conduct contributed to the demise of his government. The notion of Azeri autonomy did enjoy support in the province and even in some quarters in Tehran. But Pishehvari's ham-fisted reforms alienated both landlords and peasants. His use of militias and secret police, and his disregard for the central government's concerns, led many to believe that he was pressing for outright independence and not just autonomy. In some ways, he and the ADP were more aggressive than the Soviet Union in their quest to dismember Iran.

During the 1940s, Iran preserved its sovereignty against remarkable odds. While the country was occupied by great powers debating how to apportion its land and oil, a remarkable set of Iranian politicians reclaimed their nation's independence through courage, defiance, and considerable guile. Statesmen born of Iran's cantankerous nobility, still able to take initiative independently of the shah, managed to get one of history's most formidable despots to disgorge his gains. Along the way, Iran's political parties offered platforms of reform that recognized the need for greater distribution of wealth, modern education, health care, and even a measure of representation. This was still rule by aristocracy with some democratic trappings, but Iran's establishment included many landlords who were attuned to the social dynamics of even the most remote provinces. Iran may have looked divided against itself, but foreigners who assumed that they controlled various Iranian politicians were gravely mistaken. As Stalin learned, the strings were often pulled in the other direction.

Since ascending to the throne, the shah had been guided by a combination of insecurities and ambitions that led him to continually reach for greater power. His outlook was forever conditioned by the way that the great powers had plotted with the Iranian elite to dispose of his father. He was given to conspiracy thinking because his father had been a victim of a conspiracy. The shah never appreciated that Iran's establishment had saved the Pahlavi dynasty and preserved Iran's independence. He never understood that the United States and Britain were not perennially seeking to replace him with a more pliable ruler. And he failed to appreciate the advice of men such as Qavam, who warned him that with absolute power comes absolute responsibility. He used every occasion to chip away at Iran's institutions and its experienced patrons. He wanted to emulate his father, but the elder Pahlavi had been made of tougher stuff. In the end, the shah was too soft to govern Iran without the help of clever prime ministers. His greatest tragedy was that he rejected and undermined those he most needed.

In the 1950s Iran would experience another crisis. This time, it was not foreign occupation but an effort to reclaim its oil. The establishment that had evicted the Soviets now focused its ire on Britain, which had tormented and exploited Iran for decades. By the end of the oil nationalization crisis, two of the great powers that had dominated its affairs for decades would be pushed out. In many ways, this would be the Iranian establishment's finest hour, and its last stand.

CHAPTER 3

The Oil Nationalization Crisis

In 1901, the gold speculator and oil entrepreneur William D'Arcy purchased the right to exploit Iran's oil fields. In exchange for the contract, he paid Iran's rulers twenty thousand British pounds and promised them 16 percent of his annual profits. After World War I, the British government, eager to convert its navy from coal to oil, purchased 52.5 percent of the company's shares. A 1933 amendment to the original concession granted Iran additional revenues in exchange for extending the deal for another sixty years. Thus was born the Anglo-Iranian Oil Company (AIOC), which would play a pivotal and controversial role in Iran's politics.

The AIOC's unjust practices were beyond doubt. The company routinely paid more in taxes to Britain than royalties to Iran. By the 1940s, both Venezuela and Mexico had negotiated fifty-fifty profit-sharing arrangements with American oil firms, making the unfairness of AIOC's concession even more glaring. Working conditions for the Iranian laborers were abysmal: many lived in shantytowns without adequate sanitation or access to hospitals or schools. Iranian workers had little chance of being promoted to managerial positions because the British executives derided their skills. In the postwar years, the AIOC's increased profits still did not mean more money for Iran, because the company's austere directors were determined to keep production costs down. By the 1950s, rising post-colonial nationalism had made the inhuman policies of the past simply unacceptable. Iran was determined to reclaim its oil and nationalize a substantial British investment.

The oil nationalization crisis exposed the emerging differences between the American and British approaches to Iran. The Truman administration, seeing the crisis in the context of the Cold War, believed that a quick solution would stabilize Iran and preserve its oil for the free world. At a time when the White House was pressing the shah to reform his economy, it did not need an oil impasse that would starve his budget. This is not to suggest that Truman sought Britain's expulsion from Iran. Britain was critical to America's global containment effort, particularly as the Cold War spread beyond Europe's boundaries and the two sides waged war on the Korean peninsula. But Truman's enterprising aides hoped that, somehow, Britain would come to terms with the new forces of Iranian nationalism and make its presence acceptable to local leaders. The Americans did not yet see the impossibility of reconciling British imperialists and Third World nationalists.

For its part, Britain saw the crisis as a commercial dispute in which greedy Iranians sought to void a good-faith contract and expropriate a British national asset. Should Iran succeed in this scheme, Whitehall feared, it would set a precedent for Britain's other global holdings and further undermine the empire's increasingly wobbly foundations. It is easy to caricature the British officials as imperialists blind to their own rapacity. But these men believed in their empire and honestly thought its mission was essentially benign. They credited themselves with building schools in Africa, the civil service in India, and the world's largest refinery in Iran. Many in the Foreign Office understood that Iranian nationalism was a force that had to be reckoned with, and Foreign Secretary Ernest Bevin did champion their cause in the halls of government. But in the waning days of their empire, British leaders counted the benefits of the empire more than its burdens. During the nationalization crisis, they would lament the Iranians' ingratitude and the Americans' failure to see the region through the prism of their noble experiment.

Iran's effort to nationalize its oil also exposed fissures within its own political establishment. The prime ministers and parliamentarians who had led the country through its recent crises were soon at odds with one another. Mohammad Mossadeq was one of the most esteemed members of that establishment, yet his handling of the crisis led the cantankerous elite to gradually lose confidence in one of its own. Once more, there are many myths to dispel. It is true that Iran's politicians were often self-serving, routinely used foreign embassies to gain domestic advantage, and would purchase crowds and street thugs to intimidate their rivals. This was how politics was practiced in mid-twentieth-century Persia, including by Mossadeq himself. Yet all these men were nationalists who sought to emancipate their country from the British Empire.

THE RISE AND FALL OF RAZMARA

The British were not the only ones who coveted Iran's oil. As we have seen, Qavam had cleverly outmaneuvered Stalin and deprived Soviet Russia of its claims. The parliamentary moves that denied the Soviet request had an impact on the British concession by requiring that the Iranian government reconsider the 1933 agreement. Sensing the changing mood in Tehran, London offered a Supplemental Agreement that would ensure that Iran's revenues did not fall below four million pounds. In the ensuing negotiations, successive Iranian premiers demanded an equal division of profits and a review of the accord every fifteen years to see if it met both parties' interests. This request was rejected by the AIOC, setting the stage for outright nationalization.

Although the Foreign Office functionaries sometimes criticized the AIOC's intransigence, the perspective of the British legation in Tehran meshed well with that of the oil executives. Her Majesty's envoy to Iran, Francis Shepherd, would follow Reader Bullard's precedent and blame Iran's problem on the deficient Persian character. In one early dispatch, he opined that "Persian cynicism and pessimism, combined with a tendency to confess to their own shortcomings, is apparently less a passing phase than a permanent weakness."[1] Like Bullard, Shepherd would spend his unhappy years in Tehran complaining by telegram about the perfidious Iranians.

To a great extent, the British outlook was shaped by one of the most distinguished historians of Iran, Ann Lambton. A longtime professor at University of London, Lambton, known to her friends as Nancy, was an austere patrician who trained a generation of scholars and left an impressive intellectual legacy on such subjects as Persian grammar and land tenure. She had served in Iran as a press attaché during the war and had helped launch the propaganda campaign that contributed to Reza Shah's ouster. An accomplished scholar whose assessments were widely shared in the Foreign Office, Lambton assured her audience that "Iranian instability could partly be attributed to great power rivalry, but more fundamentally the disequilibrium originated with the stupidity, greed and lack of judgement of the ruling classes of Persia."[2] Iran's leaders looked for foreign scapegoats, Lambton reasoned, to deflect attention from their own shortcomings. The problem was not the AIOC, but the Persians themselves. Lambton would go on to be an early and eager proponent of regime change, insisting that Mossadeq could not be dealt with and the only sensible solution was his overthrow.

At the core, the British believed their presence in Iran had served a benevolent purpose. If not for their investment and innovation, the oil would still be in the ground. Instead of indulging in nationalist agitation, the Iranians should be grateful for all that Britain had done for them. The leaders of the Labour Party—who were busy nationalizing British industry in the name of social justice—acknowledged the AIOC's shortcomings but felt that the company's good deeds outweighed its bad habits. Its practices had to reform, but the Iranians should be prepared to honor a contract that had served them well.

The start of the Korean War affected the allies differently. For the United States, the demands of the war in Asia meant that it needed both British assistance and Iranian oil. Britain was a major part of the military coalition that intervened to stop North Korea's invasion of its southern neighbor, and its troops and resources were indispensable to that effort. At the same time, Iran's oil was necessary for lubricating the Western industrial machine. America did not need distractions in the Middle East that divided the alliance and stirred up Third World nationalism. Washington wanted the oil issue resolved quickly.

The Labour government faced a different set of pressures. Mobilizing for the Korean War meant that the government had to rely more heavily on domestic industries. The AIOC was a substantial British investment, a contributor of much tax revenue and a provider of cheap oil to the Royal Navy. As the elections loomed, the AIOC became part of a contentious debate in which Winston Churchill accused Prime Minister Clement Attlee of appeasement in the Persian Gulf. The Tories, with their sentimental attachment to the empire, were quick to denounce any concession contemplated by their political rival. The war, then, paradoxically enhanced the company's leverage over an already hard-pressed Attlee government.

As the British brandished their orientalist shibboleths, new political groupings were surfacing in Iran that would help lead the nationalization movement. The National Front came into existence as the result of the particularly corrupt election that produced the sixteenth Majlis. In a gesture of protest, Mossadeq led a demonstration to the palace and demanded recourse from the monarch. When the shah refused to budge, the old man and a few of his disciples staged a sit-in on the palace grounds. The shah proved a generous host, providing his guests with ample food that soon tempted them out of their hunger strike. Not long after, Mossadeq abandoned his enterprise, returning home to create a new umbrella organization, the National Front.

The Front's original platform called for free elections, social justice, and respect for the constitution. Oil was not high on its agenda at first. In one of his most consequential mistakes, Mossadeq insisted that the National Front act as a coalition of like-minded organizations rather than as a formal party with a disciplined cadre and regional branches. According to his aide Karim Sanjabi, a future National Front leader, Mossadeq avoided a mass party because he believed that as "organizations grow, inevitably they become corrupt."[3] This would prove his undoing, as competing agendas and ambitions inevitably eroded the coalition's solidarity. Still, the Front soon joined forces with elite parties like the Iran Party and various professional associations, including the lawyers' guild and teachers' union. It also looked for support beyond the intelligentsia, from the bazaar and the clergy. Despite this outreach, the National Front remained a middle-class, liberal coalition seeking an accountable government and legislative remedies to various social ills. The National Front remains one of the most important experiments in progressive rule in Iran's modern history.

By 1950, as the oil issue dominated politics, the National Front had a leadership role. This was a natural position for Mossadeq, who had led the parliamentary charge against the Russian concession and had long condemned exploitation of Iran's resources by foreign powers. Many members of the political class were seeking to accommodate the AIOC, but the National Front called for outright nationalization. Prime Minister Ali Mansur tried to temper this sentiment in the Majlis by establishing a parliamentary commission to study the issue—a delaying tactic that backfired when the commission, dominated by National Front deputies, chose Mossadeq as its chairman. From this perch, Mossadeq quickly rebuffed the proposals put forth by the AIOC, such as granting Iran additional revenue or a greater say in the operation of the oil installations. The National Front's maximalist position was well in line with public opinion, which viewed the agreement as a disreputable relic of the colonial age.

The clerical community would play an unusual role in the nationalization crisis. During this period, the primary goal of the clerical elders was to strengthen the seminary and enhance its financial power. The war years had been difficult ones for the clerical estate: Reza Shah's dictatorship and foreign occupation had pressed it to the margins of society. In 1949, Shia Islam's preeminent leader, Ayatollah Borujerdi, summoned approximately two thousand members of the clergy to a conference that passed a resolution forbidding participation in political affairs.[4] Although this injunction has since been brandished to demonstrate clerical indifference to politics, it is hard to see how the mullahs could have stayed on the sidelines during one of the most turbulent times in Iran's history. Moreover, the conference took place at the time of an attempted assassination of the shah, and the order to abjure politics may have been Borujerdi's attempt to distance the clergy from the violent activist group Fada'iyan-e Islam. The Shia tradition of political quietism has not always been the norm in Iran—during this earlier era, the clerics often engaged in politics. Whatever was intended by the resolution, the clerical class would play an active and controversial role as the nationalization crisis unfolded.

Ayatollah Abol-Qassem Kashani would lead the clerical charge during this period. Trained in a seminary in Iraq, he had eagerly backed the Shia revolt against the British in 1920, causing the British to put a bounty on his head. Reza Shah allowed him to return to Iran, but the British deported him during the war on a charge of having pro-German sympathies, the same accusation they used to exile Reza Shah. At the behest of the new shah, Kashani came back to Iran, was elected to the Majlis, and eventually became its speaker. His disdain for Britain made him a natural supporter of the National Front, but it was bound to be a short-lived relationship. Kashani's opportunism and corruption made him an unsteady ally to the more principled Mossadeq.

Kashani was not an accomplished theologian, but he did command street power and influence over Fada'iyan terrorists who stalked Iran with their targeted assassinations. Like Ayatollah Ruhollah Khomeini, who led the 1979 revolution, Kashani had ample support from lower ranks of the clergy. His message of defiance and religious empowerment found an audience among the urban poor, who shared his antipathy toward the British. An adept coalition builder, Kashani could mobilize his many networks to stage a timely riot or have the Fada'iyan conduct a high-profile assassination. He was not above plotting with the royal court or asking American diplomats for bribes. All of his alliances were tactical, but his overall goal remained constant: cleansing Iran of British influence and creating a society where the religious sector played an active role in politics.

The final consequential actor in the oil nationalization melodrama was the shah himself. Despite his fixation on military hardware, he was trying to revive an economy that had yet to recover from the war, and he had just launched a seven-year, $650 million development plan that was contingent on U.S. aid. But Washington was willing to offer only $23 million in military aid and an additional $10 million loan from the World Bank. When the shah visited the White House, Truman informed him that the rest of his development plan had to be paid for by Iran's considerable oil reserves. This imposed contradictory necessities: the shah needed more money from the AIOC but also its continued help in running the oil industry. He also had to accommodate the nationalist surge sweeping his country while avoiding a showdown with Britain that could cripple his economy.

All the personality traits that would frustrate the shah's associates for the next two decades came to the fore. The shah supported the nationalization of Iranian oil but hoped that Britain's concerns could somehow be accommodated. He appreciated the need for a strong prime minister but was reluctant to trust any member of the ruling class. He often commiserated with U.S. and British ambassadors, but was convinced that the great powers might conspire against him. He always wanted more power but not the accountability that came with exercising it.

In 1950, as Mansur's enfeebled premiership approached its inevitable end, the shah had to contemplate a successor. The British and Americans were demanding a decisive leader able to address the oil issue. The British especially were complaining that the revolving door of prime ministers had deprived them of an interlocutor with the confidence and strength to negotiate and implement an agreement. The shah, sensing that he had to search outside the usual coterie of politicians and look to the armed forces for a leader with courage and vision, chose General Ali Razmara.

Razmara's premiership began with much promise. One of Iran's most distinguished generals, he quickly took command of the situation. He had the support of the political class and even the confidence of the monarch, who rarely trusted powerful military men. Razmara belonged to the generation of Iranians who believed that their country's interests were best served by coming to terms with the great powers. These were practical men who did not want to sever their traditional ties to the British Empire. The AIOC was considered a symbol of abuse by many Iranians, but Razmara and his cohort believed that the company could still help Iran. For their part, the Western chancelleries hoped that, in Razmara, they had finally found a man who could put Iran's affairs in order.

An eager reformer, Razmara sought to placate the National Front by appropriating aspects of its agenda. He denounced corruption, introduced a land-reform bill, and more importantly, called for convening the local assemblies as promised by the constitution. He soon received a lesson in Iran's poisonous politics: the Front opposed legislation that it had once advocated. Mossadeq led the charge, denouncing the assemblies as potentially leading to the disintegration of the country, apparently having forgotten that during the Azerbaijan crisis he too had called for the northern province's partial autonomy. The Left rejected decentralized rule even as its supporters were in the streets accusing Razmara of ushering in a dictatorship. In the meantime, the more conservative members of the chamber stalled the land-reform proposals. Iran's politicians were too busy undermining each other to press ahead with needed reforms.

Razmara had even less success with the shah. Like nearly every prime minister, he implored the monarch to reduce the military budget and spend more on social programs. The shah, however, viewed all such suggestions as ploys to weaken his army and undermine his rule. That the idea now came from one of Iran's most distinguished soldiers made little difference. The shah reminded the general that he had been chosen to resolve the oil issue, not to refashion Iran's politics. So Razmara turned to that task.

From the outset, the general confronted two contrasting mandates. On the one hand, the parliamentary complaints against the Supplemental Agreement were cogent and powerful. The deputies objected not only that the modest revenue increases did not match the fifty-fifty profit-sharing accord obtained by Venezuela and Mexico, but also that the AIOC would still not pay taxes to the Iranian government. Even worse, the contract extended the 1933 agreement for another sixty years. This meant that it would not expire until 1993, with no possibility of adjusting its duration. On the other hand, Razmara quietly commissioned a study by two Iranian specialists on the practicality of nationalization. Their report stressed that given the amount of oil on the market and the domination of the Western petroleum giants, it would be difficult for Iran to sell much of its oil. The American companies were unlikely to take over the AIOC's concession, leaving Iran without the assistance it needed to extract, market, and ship its oil.

Armed with such assessments, Razmara confronted a Majlis agitating for outright nationalization. The prime minister held steady, offering practical arguments at a time of frenzied emotion. In a speech to the Majlis, he told the deputies, "I must declare here that under the present conditions, Iran does not possess the industrial capacity to take the oil out and sell it on the world market." To underscore his point, he added, "Gentlemen, you cannot even manage a cement factory with your personnel."[5] This was not what the deputies swept up by the nationalist fervor wanted to hear. There was no denying that the agreement was unfair and had to be changed. But his encounter with the Majlis disabused Razmara of the notion that he could assuage parliamentary sentiment with detailed studies of Iran's technical capabilities followed by stern lectures. He had to approach the AIOC for further concessions.

In his first meeting with the representatives of the AIOC, Razmara rejected superficial changes to the accord and demanded more money. He argued that the AIOC had to start paying the higher rates stipulated in the Supplemental Agreement even before the agreement was ratified by the parliament. He needed the funds, he stressed, to implement the seven-year plan, and the AIOC should be "sufficiently concerned with [the] economic future of Iran as to be more conciliatory and flexible."[6] The company's representatives responded that they had already made generous compromises and insisted that Iran's politicians were conveniently blaming them for the dismal state of their country.

The United States had hoped to stay on the sidelines of this conflict. Truman was happy to have Britain remain the primary Western power in a region whose politics it claimed to have mastered, and the Cold War was supposed to be a burden shared between the allies. The stalemated negotiations, however, compelled the Americans to get involved. Razmara was the type of leader the administration had hoped would come to power in Iran. Ambassador Henry Grady cabled from the embassy in Tehran that Razmara was an "intelligent, reasonable person who realizes oil settlement must be made if he is to proceed with his development program." Acheson took up this theme with Bevin, informing his friend, "We are, of course, disappointed that your Government has not been able to take a different position on the question of the Anglo-Iranian Oil Company's Supplemental Agreement." In some ways, Acheson was preaching to the choir; Bevin and his diplomats already knew that the AIOC would have to make more concessions. Neither American nor British officials embraced Mossadeq's brand of nationalism, but there was a recognition—more in the State Department than in the Foreign Office—that the company had to make adjustments.[7]

The fate of the Supplemental Agreement was sealed in December 1950 when the Arabian-American Oil Company (ARAMCO) offered Saudi Arabia a fifty-fifty profit-sharing agreement. This was the first time that such terms were given to a Middle Eastern nation. The British, who were shocked by the deal, blamed Assistant Secretary of State for Near Eastern Affairs George McGhee, a former Rhodes Scholar and oil man who they suspected wanted to liquidate the British Empire's share to accommodate American oil interests. They called the deal the "McGhee Bombshell."

In the next round of negotiations, Razmara found the British more chastened. They assured him that "the company would be willing to examine a similar arrangement" to the ARAMCO deal.[8] A cheerful Razmara informed his cabinet that "my good news for you is that the oil issue is settled. However, since we are still at the early stage, I will not discuss it until we arrive at a successful conclusion."[9] The question remains why Razmara did not say publicly that he had obtained a fifty-fifty profit-sharing agreement. It appears that the general's perspective had changed during the negotiations, and he now recognized that nationalization was unavoidable. Thus he saw the new profit-sharing scheme as an interim step and continued to nudge the British toward accepting nationalization. Given the sensitivity of the negotiations, he may have thought it wiser not to speak of the deal publicly until he had a more comprehensive agreement. In public he was skeptical of nationalization, but privately he seemed to have contemplated ways that Iran's national imperatives might be reconciled with Britain's continued presence.

On March 7, 1951, a member of the Fada'iyan-e Islam assassinated Razmara in Tehran's central mosque. The killer left little doubt about his motives: he shouted, "Long live Islam, death to the oil company!"[10] The murder soon generated conspiracy tales, including suggestions that the shah was behind it.[11] It is true that the shah—whose father, a hardened army officer, had disposed of an ineffectual Qajar monarch to begin his own dynasty—was suspicious of strongmen and worried about the general's ambitions. But Razmara's list of antagonists was quite long and included conservatives alarmed by his tolerance of the Tudeh as well as leftists concerned about his oil diplomacy.

Further, all the evidence points to Kashani and his Islamist terror group. Razmara's murder was Kashani's way of taking revenge on him. He publicly extolled the assassin as "a national hero" and later sponsored a bill granting him a pardon.[12] But it appears that Mossadeq was also aware of the impending plot. On being informed of the prime minister's death, Mossadeq said, "Well, he should not have made that speech," referring to Razmara's parliamentary address warning about the hazards of nationalization. It seems that the leader of the Fada'iyan, Navvab Safavi, had informed a close Mossadeq aide, Hossein Makki, of his plans with the understanding that they would be passed on to the old man.[13] Given Mossadeq's stature in the National Front, it is inconceivable that Makki would have withheld this information from him. Both the Foreign Office and the CIA confirmed Mossadeq's foreknowledge of the assassination. The Foreign Office reported that three days before Razmara's murder, members of the Fada'iyan "had conferred with Dr Mossadeq and M. Kashani. Both were reported to have stated categorically that the welfare of Persia depended on the disappearance of General Razmara."[14] The CIA concluded that

Mossadeq had "condoned the assassination of Razmara on the grounds that the latter was too lenient with the British."[15] Targeted assassinations were part of Iran's political scene, and the shah and several of his ministers had already been attacked by hired guns. Mossadeq did not instigate Razmara's murder, but he knew it was coming and did nothing to stop it.

Razmara's death did not immediately end the government's effort to slow the nationalization movement. The shah appointed another trusted old-school politician, Hossein Alā, to try to reclaim the initiative, but this proved impossible. In the midst of all this, the AIOC, blinded by arrogance, decided to reduce the housing subsidy it gave its workers and even lay off some of them as a cost-cutting measure. That it was generating record profits did not dissuade it from this disastrous course. The ensuing strike inevitably led to violence, as local officials stepped in and arrested some of the ringleaders. This only enraged the workers and led to additional strikes, crippling the Abadan refinery. The strikes finally ended when the company rescinded its housing cuts and agreed to increase wages. But the damage was done.

The Majlis now began its consideration of the nationalization act, with Mossadeq, as leader of the movement, marshaling the parliamentary forces. With the quixotic approach that would characterize his premiership, he insisted, "I believe more in the moral than economic aspects of nationalization of the oil industry." This may have been a powerful oppositionist slogan, but it would prove a poor governing template. Still, given the temper of the times, it was sufficient for the Majlis to pass the nationalization bill. The shah signed the decree while calling for calm. Hossein Alā, the caretaker prime minister who was largely a bystander in the unfolding melodrama, resigned. Among his last acts was to ruefully confess to the British that "all Persians regard nationalization as a desirable principle."[16]

The next dramatic act was to choose a prime minister who would lead the nationalization. Passage of the nationalization bill did not immediately open a path for Mossadeq, despite his leading role in the movement. The shah preferred Seyyed Zia Tabataba'i, a royalist with close ties to Britain. A plot was concocted whereby the shah's reliable ally Jafar Sharif-Emami would nominate Seyyed Zia and hope that the conservative deputies would simply ram the choice through the chamber. Sharif-Emami was so confident that Mossadeq would not accept the job that, in deference to his age and stature, he first offered him the premiership. Sharif-Emami ostentatiously and almost ritualistically intoned, "Dr. Mossadeq has our confidence because he—unlike many other politicians—comes from one of the oldest and most distinguished families of Iran."[17] To his and the shah's surprise, Mossadeq accepted the post, and a vote offering him the job quickly followed. The monarch had no choice but to concede, recognizing that "at that moment no one could stand against him."[18] Iran's accidental prime minister was now in command of a nation divided against itself and at loggerheads with Britain.

The appeal of nationalization was not lost on the clerics. With Razmara and his agreement both dead, powerful clerics issued a slew of fatwas urging the nationalization of the oil industry. Once the Majlis passed the bill, leading ayatollahs justified the move by invoking the Quranic injunction that Muslims should not be dominated by other religious sects.[19] The clerical order recognized Kashani's critical role in the nationalization movement, and its leading journal called on "all Muslim people of Iran to join him [Kashani] in a Jihad against all unrighteous politicians and injustice."[20] In a manifesto, leading clerical authorities extolled Kashani's leadership and pledged to support him in his struggles. This established a clear line between Kashani and Qom that would persist throughout the crisis.

The Tudeh found ways to further discredit itself. Although the party would take several positions during the crisis, it initially condemned the entire affair as an American conspiracy to displace Britain as the primary Western power in Iran. Once more, the Tudeh subordinated Iran's concerns to Soviet ones. Its leaders knew that Moscow still desired Iran's northern oil fields, and they feared that the nationalization law would make it impossible for their patron to obtain its own concession. Yet the Tudeh still had power in the street. Its newspaper, *Mardom-e Iran*, was widely read, and the party was capable of staging huge rallies in urban areas.

In 1951, Iran nationalized its oil without a plan or a full understanding of the consequences of such a monumental act. This was not a practical move but a rebellion against an empire. For decades, Britain had controlled Iran's oil and deformed its politics. Mossadeq and the National Front were seeking not only to reclaim Iran's natural resource, but also to purge their country of the corrupting influences of a fading imperial power. They would soon learn that even declining empires can strike back.

MOSSADEQ IN POWER

At the time of his appointment, Mohammad Mossadeq was sixty-nine years old and a towering figure in Iran's political establishment. For nearly four decades, he had moved in and out of government service with his integrity intact and his principles on display. As a young man, he had studied law in Europe, and that legal training did much to condition his reverence for the rule of law. He was also a stubborn man who loved defying the great powers. Unlike many members of his class, he had never been prime minister and was not fully aware of the job's pressures. Had Mossadeq never become premier, he would have been remembered as one of Iran's greatest statesmen, but his time in office would both define his legacy and damage his national standing.

The new prime minister's personal style and temperament confounded his many Western interlocutors. He suffered from several ailments, which he often exaggerated. He was adept at playing the fragile old man and experienced convenient fainting spells. He once greeted George McGhee with the mischievous admission that he had fainted only three times that morning. Mossadeq conducted nearly all of his official business from his house because he claimed to fear assassination plots. While seated in his bed wearing gray pajamas, he would entertain foreign dignitaries and government functionaries. As the U.S. negotiators would learn, he seldom spoke in front of his aides and insisted that the most sensitive negotiations take place with no Iranian in the room. All this may have seemed strange to Westerners, but such histrionics have a well-established place in Persian politics, which combined theatrics with bare ambition.

Mossadeq had long been critical of Iran's foreign policy, which sought to play the great powers against one another. Iranian statesmen had tried to fend off Soviet encroachment by tempting Britain, and later the United States, to become more involved in their national affairs. At the same time, they were not above playing the Soviet card to extract concessions from the West. The problem with this approach was that it constantly invited outside meddling. Its proponents argued that given the country's geography and natural resources, Iran would always be subject to external intervention and the task was to manage the great-power competition in a way that protected Iran's interests. The postwar record of premiers such as Foroughi and Qavam tends to validate this stratagem.

Mossadeq emphatically rejected the British presence. It is hard to fault the sincerity of his outrage at the AIOC, which had exploited Iran's oil and corrupted its politics. But Mossadeq could not see the dispute in terms of technical formulas and profit-sharing arrangements. For him, sovereignty meant shelving economic concerns. He and his allies soon coined the slogan "oil less economy," suggesting that Iran could sustain its national life without its principal export commodity. The National Front government showed its poor understanding of international commerce when it assumed that one of the Seven Sisters, the multinational oil companies that dominated the petroleum industry, would step in and displace the nationalized AIOC. None of this would happen—and some of Iran's more sober minds knew it wouldn't.

The shah had a different attitude toward the crisis enveloping his country. As a man prone to conspiracy theories, he appreciated Mossadeq's diabolical portrayal of Britain. Yet he understood early on that "oil less economy" was an empty slogan, and he appreciated that given the ease of finding other sources, the loss of Iranian oil would not much disturb the global economy. Iran's solvency required an agreement that Mossadeq, basking in nationalist glory, probably could not get. The longer the stalemate with the AIOC persisted, the more radicalized Iran's politics would become, until it even began to threaten the monarchy. But with nationalistic fervor sweeping the country, the shah had little choice but to go along with his premier. For the next two years, the monarch with a thirst for absolute power remained on the sidelines.

The British, who nursed their own delusions, approached Mossadeq's premiership by denying the popularity of the nationalization movement. They saw Mossadeq as a reckless fringe figure animated by an irrational hatred of the AIOC. The Foreign Office stressed that Mossadeq represented a "small band of extremists" who had succeeded in "impos[ing] their will on the Majlis and silencing the voices of reason."[21] British officials believed that by applying maximum pressure on Iran, they could empower cooler heads prone to compromise.

The events in Iran had important regional implications for Britain. The AIOC was its largest overseas asset, and its expropriation by Iran was bound to affect the empire's unsteady foundations in the Arab world. Given its expulsion from India and its diminished role in Asia, Britain's remaining claim to great-power status rested on its commanding position in the Middle East. The Foreign Office feared that should Iran succeed in seizing the oil installations, the "Egyptians might be emboldened to take drastic action to end the military treaty and possibly to bring the Suez Canal under Egyptian control." It was believed that a determined British stance in Iran would have a "salutary effect" on the entire region. According to this view, the empire's prestige hinged on developments in Persia.[22]

From the outset, the British entertained fantastic ideas for undoing the nationalization act. Operation Buccaneer, the first such ploy, called for an invasion of southern Iran by as many as seventy thousand troops. The theme of the day in Britain's halls of power was the need to show force. Minister of

Defense Emanuel Shinwell, an ardent advocate of the plan, later wrote that "we must be prepared to show that our tail could not be twisted interminably and that there was a limit to our willingness to have advantage taken of our good nature."[23] In the Foreign Office, the vain and ignorant Herbert Morrison, who had taken over from the ailing Bevin, paid even more attention to the notions of British prestige.[24] While Bevin had hoped to reinvent Britain's presence in the region in a manner acceptable to the emerging forces of nationalism, his successor was more at ease with traditional gunboat diplomacy.

The impending general election in 1951 further pressed a Labour government whose austerity budget had already made it unpopular. Churchill and the Conservatives accused Labour not only of mismanaging the economy, but also of surrendering in the Middle East. Again there were analogies to Munich and warnings of how the irresolution of Western rulers would embolden aggressive regimes. That the Iranians had responded to the AIOC's offer of a fifty-fifty division of profits with outright nationalization further raised pressure for an armed response.

Some in Britain argued that military intervention could provoke a Soviet reaction, while others openly welcomed a new spheres-of-influence arrangement with Moscow. The 1921 Russo-Persian Treaty of Friendship granted Moscow the right to intervene should a hostile power invade Iran, but many influential voices rejected the idea that Soviet Russia might invoke that right.[25] Others hoped that the Russians would be content to take the northern provinces and leave Britain a free hand in the south. Hugh Gaitskell, chancellor of the exchequer, conceded that a partition might "sound bad but I think it might be the best ultimate solution."[26] At the outbreak of the Azerbaijan crisis, many Britons had been prepared to carve Iran into spheres of influence before they lost confidence in Stalin's willingness to abide by such an arrangement. Now those same people seemed to have forgotten their concerns about Stalin's appetite.

The British saber-rattling alarmed the White House. With its army bogged down in Korea, America did not relish another "hot war" in the Middle East. Truman informed Attlee in no uncertain terms: "I am sure you can understand my deep concern that no action should be taken in connection with this dispute which would result in disagreement between Iran and the Free World."[27] This message was reinforced by both Acheson and Secretary of Defense Robert Lovett. The forceful American response tipped the scale in favor of those urging restraint.

Attlee, who had been skeptical of an attack all along, took advantage of Truman's caution to inform the British cabinet, "We cannot afford to break with the United States on an issue of this kind."²⁸ The prime minister had a greater appreciation of the change sweeping the region than many others in his government, and he confessed in his memoirs that "any attempt to coerce the Persian government by the use of force was out of the question. Such action would no doubt have been taken in former times, but would, in the modern world, have outraged opinion at home and abroad."²⁹ The Conservatives would learn the limits of British power in 1956, when Anthony Eden went to war in Egypt without American support, only to witness the collapse of his effort and the liquidation of the British position in the Arab east.

With an outright military attack off the table, Britain moved to the next less aggressive option: regime change. Ann Lambton was once more summoned to the Foreign Office, where she assured her audience that Mossadeq could not be dealt with and it was time to depose him. She recommended sending her wartime colleague, Oxford lecturer Robin Zaehner, to Tehran to "give the Persians confidence and to set the plan in motion."³⁰ Zaehner had served with Lambton in Iran during the war and had showed an uncanny ability to ingratiate himself with the Persian elite. Returning in 1951 as the new press attaché, he quickly made the rounds in Tehran, being manipulated by the Iranians he thought he was influencing. The embassy was soon besieged by appeals from Iranian politicians for strong action to galvanize opposition to Mossadeq.

The primary obstacle to this scheme was the shah himself. The monarch was uneasy about his premier but felt he could not manage the national uproar that would follow his dismissal. This led Embassy Counselor George Middleton to disparage the shah as a "weak and ineffectual little man."³¹ As the crisis unfolded, such accusations would be aired by a succession of Western diplomats and spies. Regime change would remain Britain's preference even as it pursued other diplomatic gambits.

Clement Attlee was one of the few in the British establishment to appreciate that the nationalization act could not be reversed. Having nationalized his share of British companies, he understood the issue all too well. His approach was more subtle, and he conceded that "we must, in the view of the present highly charged atmosphere in Persia and in particular of the emotional stage of the Persian Prime Minister (who appears to be on the lunatic fringe) agree to accept the principle of nationalization."³² Yet he assumed that Britain could somehow maintain control of Iran's oil. The prime minister may not have shared Morrison or Shinwell's desire to bomb the natives into submission, but he suffered from his own misperceptions. To soften up Iran, Britain would take its case to various international legal bodies while launching a campaign to keep Iranian oil off the market.

In May 1951, Britain took its complaint against Iran to the International Court of Justice at The Hague. Its claim was legalistic and procedural and stressed that "the 1933 agreement cannot be legally annulled or altered except by agreement with the Company under conditions provided in the convention."[33] Britain did not contest any nation's right to control its resources; it only claimed that in this specific case, Iran had relinquished that right. Even more brazenly, Britain claimed that Iran was discriminating against it, because Iran had seized only British assets and no other foreign holdings.

Iran's response was to deny that The Hague had discretion over a dispute between a private company and a sovereign nation. Moreover, the agreement lacked authority given that it had been imposed on a dictatorship. This went to the heart of Mossadeq's complaint: he often stressed that the AIOC had contaminated Iran's politics by cultivating a class of politicians who did its bidding. The court now began its prolonged deliberation that was bound to reject Britain's flimsy legal reasoning.

Meanwhile, Britain orchestrated a successful boycott of Iran's oil. The Foreign Office warned that anyone seeking to purchase Iranian oil would be subject to legal action. Given that most oil tankers at the time were operated by Britain and the United States, it would be hard to move Iran's oil without the approval of the two Western powers. The Royal Navy, too, made it known that it would commandeer any ship carrying Iran's oil. This move had no legal basis, because Britain and Iran were not at war and there was no U.N. injunction against Iranian commerce. Still, all the multinational oil firms heeded Britain's warnings, and America cooperated with the prohibition.

The most important attempt to breach the embargo occurred in March 1951, when the Italian company Ente Petrolifero Italia Medio-oriente (EPIM) purchased 400,000 tons of oil from Iran. To test the British ban, it dispatched a ship to carry a cargo of a thousand tons. The Royal Navy quickly intercepted the vessel and diverted it to the port of Aden. After Whitehall claimed that the ship had been carrying contraband, Aden, a British protectorate, surrendered the oil to the AIOC.

As Iran increasingly failed to secure customers for its oil, its vast petroleum infrastructure began to grind to a halt. In the United States, meanwhile, while the crisis in Iran unfolded, the specter of communism haunted policymakers. American intelligence agencies and diplomats did appreciate the Tudeh's limitations, and they knew that Mossadeq's movement was independent. But the

U.S. response was conditioned by the notion that stalemated negotiations could empower radical actors. Had the Americans had access to the Soviets' records, they would have been shocked by their confusion. Moscow initially thought that Mossadeq "enjoyed authority in Iranian bourgeois-nationalist circles and some young people in the university" but did not support "true Soviet-Iranian friendship."[34] Given his history of opposing Russia's quest for oil concessions, he was seen as just another member of a Persian aristocracy that was traditionally suspicious of the Soviet Union. Nor was the Kremlin impressed by Mossadeq's penchant for neutrality in the Cold War, which it saw as a ploy to replace British patronage with American support. All this meant that Moscow would remain largely a bystander as the crisis unfolded.[35]

The United States became involved at Iran's invitation. Shortly after nationalizing Iran's oil, Mossadeq approached Ambassador Grady to ask that the United States "act as an intermediary in bringing together the Iranians and the British on the oil issue."[36] In June 1951, Mossadeq wrote to Truman, asking for arbitration since America was "a strong supporter of freedom and sovereignty of nations—a belief evidenced by the sacrifices of that great-heartfelt nation in the last two world wars."[37] In response, the president dispatched to Iran one of the Democratic Party's ablest troubleshooters, the veteran diplomat Averell Harriman.

From the American perspective, Iran's claims were neither unwarranted nor illegitimate, and they took on added urgency in the context of rising Third World nationalism. But the Americans were not prepared to embrace Mossadeq's demands completely. They sought an arrangement whereby Britain would accept the nationalization act and Iran would allow Britain to manage its oil fields. In announcing Harriman's appointment, Truman outlined the American case: "Since British skill and operating knowledge can contribute so much to the Iranian oil industry, I had hoped—and still hope—that ways could be found to recognize the principle of nationalization and British interests to the benefit of both."[38] In the end, reconciliation would prove impossible.

Mossadeq seemed as much of an oddity to the Americans as to the British. Even when naming him its Man of the Year, *Time* magazine noted that "in his strange way, this strange old man represented one of the most profound problems of his time: Around this dizzy old wizard swirled a crisis of human destiny."[39] The American diplomats were often frustrated in their dealings with Mossadeq. He would cajole then suddenly retreat. A promise he made one day could not always be redeemed the next. Still, Mossadeq was always polite, and he did observe certain decorum. Both Harriman and McGhee—who dealt with him the most—came to respect and even feel some affection for the old man of Persia. But the tantrums and fainting spells that served Mossadeq so well in the Majlis only tried the Americans' patience.

Harriman arrived in Tehran in July 1951 and was quickly greeted with demonstrations organized by the Tudeh and the religious forces. One of Iran's many paradoxes was that during the nationalization saga, the communist activists and religious zealots often cooperated with each other in mobilizing street demonstrations. Mossadeq allowed the protests because he wanted to show Harriman the depth of Iran's anger. But soon the protests began to slip out of control. After twenty people were killed, Mossadeq had to declare martial law to reclaim his capital. It was a weakness of the prime minister's governing style that he repeatedly stimulated forces he had difficulty containing. One of the lasting consequences of the riots was Mossadeq's dismissal of his minister of interior, General Fazlollah Zahedi, for mishandling the situation. Zahedi would soon emerge as the focal point of opposition to Mossadeq and would eventually lead the coup that deposed him.

Harriman's talks with Mossadeq revealed the chasm between the two sides. Arriving at the prime minister's house and being shown into his bedroom, the American envoy was greeted with a rant against the British. "You don't know how crafty they are. You don't know how evil they are," the prime minister told him.[40] Harriman reminded Mossadeq that he had served as an envoy to Britain during the war and found the Iranian's description of the British grossly unfair. During one of the sessions, when Harriman's oil adviser, Walter Levy, tried to explain to Mossadeq some complexities of the oil business, the premier asked him what he thought of the Boston Tea Party. A startled Levy was then asked again how the American revolutionaries would have felt if a Persian mediator had advised them to remain a British colony. Mossadeq brushed aside all of Harriman's detailed studies and rejected any role for Britain in Iran. He was prepared to consider compensation for the AIOC, but not its continued involvement in the oil industry.

Harriman's meeting with the Iranian delegation went better. The Iranian team depicted nationalization as a means of denying Russia an oil concession. The Iranian document passed on to the Americans warned that should nationalization fail, the masses would be receptive to Soviet overtures. Unlike Mossadeq, his advisers did not present the nationalization law in hysterical anti-British terms but as a legitimate requirement of Iran's effort to fight communism. It was hard to tell if Mossadeq's ministers and technocrats actually spoke for him, however, because he insisted on excluding them from the later stages of the negotiations.

The next stop for Harriman was a meeting with Kashani, already a power broker whom Westerners could not ignore. The embassy's background briefings highlighted Kashani's opportunism and corruption. "He can be bribed. He has at least on one occasion made overtures to the American embassy here for financial support in return for which, presumably, he would support United States policies."[41] Kashani did not ask Harriman for a bribe, but he did emphasize that if Mossadeq retreated from outright nationalization, he might meet the same fate as Razmara. The mullah even threatened Harriman, remarking that previous Western emissaries who had infringed on Iran's rights had paid for it with their lives. But Harriman did not scare easily: he reminded the ayatollah of his long service in some of the world's toughest locations. The meeting ended with each man detesting the other.

Throughout his stay, Harriman tried to persuade the Iranians that even a nationalized oil industry would still need the AIOC's technical and managerial support. This line of argument failed to find many adherents in Tehran. In a cable to Acheson, an exasperated Harriman complained that Mossadeq "expects a foreign [oil] staff to work on his terms, foreign oil companies to buy and distribute oil on his terms, and Iran to get all of the profits with compensation only to owners for property taken over. In his dream world, the simple passage of legislation nationalizing the oil industry creates a profitable business and everyone is expected to help Iran on terms that he lays down."[42] Despite his frustrations, Harriman did come away with a greater appreciation of the sheer force of the nationalism sweeping Iran. The American envoy understood that a certain line had been crossed, and that no Iranian politician could defy the popular mood and hope to survive.

Harriman's one concrete achievement was facilitating the arrival of Richard Stokes, the lord privy seal, to commence his own negotiations with Iran. Before Stokes arrived, the idea of direct talks had bogged down as each side insisted on its own preconditions. The British had stressed that Iran had to stop all moves against the AIOC while the talks took place, while Iran had demanded that Britain accept the nationalization act before any negotiations began. Given the American pressure and Attlee's own inclinations, Britain blinked first and recognized the nationalization law. Still, Stokes came on the scene in August 1951 determined to preserve British control under the veneer of nationalization.

Stokes's initial meeting with Mossadeq elicited the prime minister's usual tirade against the history of British exploitation. After attributing Iran's poverty and lack of development to the AIOC's abuse, he tried to score debating points by claiming that Iran would pay compensation to the AIOC along the lines that the British government had offered to domestic industries that it had nationalized. The premier was seemingly open to retaining British technicians as employees of the newly minted National Iranian Oil Company (NIOC). This concession would later be withdrawn, and many subsequent Western offers would collapse because of Mossadeq's insistence that no British personnel be involved in operating the oil fields.

Stokes's proposals reflected Britain's superficial acknowledgment of the nationalization act. He assured the prime minister that the oil belonged to Iran, but it would be of little use without British skill and technology. Therefore, he proposed, a British firm should enter into a long-term contract with Iran whereby it would manage the fields and oversee the sale of oil. This offer was laced with threats: Stokes insisted that without an agreement, Iran would face economic ruin. Neither the offer nor the threats made much of an impression on Mossadeq.

Still, the meeting with Mossadeq went better than Stokes's discussion with Kashani. The ayatollah relished the opportunity to humiliate a leader of a nation that had arrested and exiled him. Kashani condemned Britain for a litany of transgressions, not only against Iran but also against Muslims worldwide. He pointedly dismissed Stokes's attempt to end the meeting: his speech, he declared, was not to be disrupted by his guest's impatience. Finally, the ayatollah let Stokes know who was really in charge in Iran: "Even Dr. Mossadeq who enjoys the unanimous support of the people, if he deviated from the nine article law, risks losing not only his prestige, but also risks suffering the same fate as Razmara."[43] Thus ended one of the few direct negotiations between Britain and Iran during the entire crisis.

Even at this early stage, Mossadeq made misjudgments that would eventually cripple his government and nearly bankrupt his country. He assumed that greed would attract other multinational oil firms to pick over the AIOC's carcass. He thought that Iran's oil was indispensable to the functioning of the global economy and that the British embargo would backfire on London. And he anticipated that as the world teetered on the brink of collapse, America would step in and make Britain sign an agreement. In his memoirs, he insisted, "Regarding oil exports, given that petroleum was not only economically but also strategically a vital product, we anticipated that we would eventually manage to sell our oil and use its proceeds for the good of the country."[44] None of this happened. There was a glut of oil on the market, and the Arab sheikhdoms were more than ready to offset the loss of Iranian oil. Moss-adeq—mistakenly—believed that he could both sustain his nationalistic defi-ance and ensure his country's economic vitality.

Throughout the oil crisis, the threat of communism hung in the air. It was there because Mossadeq and his aides insisted on it. They would often warn the Americans that failure of the nationalization act would only lead to the Tudeh's takeover. At different times, Mossadeq hinted at a barter arrangement with the Soviet Union in which Russian technicians would be hired, and oil would be sold to Eastern bloc countries. All these were dismissed by the Tru-man administration, which proved judicious in its assessment of the Soviet threat. But later, as Iran's economy crumbled and Mossadeq became more isolated, the Eisenhower administration would come to see his communist flirtations in a different light. Mossadeq presented himself as a barrier to com-munist infiltration as well as its instigator. Once more, he was unleashing sentiments he would find hard to contain.

MOSSADEQ COMES TO AMERICA

After shelving its invasion plan and seeing Stokes's negotiations go no-where, Britain in September 1951 filed a complaint against Iran at the U.N. Security Council. This was an unusual move, given that the dispute was hardly a threat to global "peace and security" but was rather an act of nation-alization that Britain had already acknowledged. Moreover, the International Court of Justice had yet to render a judgment on whether it had jurisdiction over this conflict. Mossadeq was delighted by the challenge. The prospect of journeying to America and presenting Iran's case to the assembled dignitaries appealed to his legal training and love of theatrics. As the drama shifted to New York, the nationalization dispute became largely a bilateral affair be-tween Washington and Tehran. Britain, whose property was nationalized and whose army nearly attacked Iran, essentially stopped engaging Mossadeq.

On October 8, 1951, Mossadeq landed in New York with a large delegation that included cabinet ministers and parliamentarians. True to form, he im-mediately checked into a hospital and began conducting business from there. He was determined to make the most of his opportunity at the United Na-tions. An ambulance was on hand in case he should have a conveniently timed health scare. But this time, Mossadeq set aside his usual histrionics and carefully placed Iran's grievances in the context of the colonial world's struggle for dignity. He stressed that the British government had no jurisdiction over a dispute between a private company and an independent nation. In his conclusion, he mischievously noted that Britain had yet to persuade anyone that the "lamb had eaten the wolf" and invited all the member states to rebuff the arrogant empire. His address was short on details, but he evoked larger emotions widely and deeply felt by the representatives of newly independent countries as well as by the American public.

Britain's case was presented by its dour ambassador, Gladwyn Jebb, who had served in Tehran in the 1920s and absorbed all of the British legation's abundant condescension toward the Persians. While Mossadeq had tried to appeal to the delegates' sentiments, Jebb insisted on offering a legalistic brief. The British government, he stressed, was a legitimate party to the dispute because of the AIOC's importance to Britain's national economy. Then, in a magnificent display of snobbery, Jebb told a hall full of representatives of the developing world that the Iranians were too incompetent to operate the oil installations without the AIOC.

When the spectacle ended, it was clear the British resolution would go nowhere. In a face-saving gesture for Britain, France called for a suspension of the deliberations until the International Court of Justice resolved the issue of jurisdiction. Mossadeq had clearly won the day. As Acheson observed, he had done "his job with great skill . . . overnight he became a television star, quite outshining the British representative."[45] It was then that Mossadeq conducted the most serious negotiations during the entire crisis. After his triumph at the United Nations, Mossadeq traveled to Washington, where he—naturally—checked into Walter Reed Hospital, then became one of the first Iranian politicians other than the shah to meet an American president. Before the White House meeting, Acheson briefed Truman that Mossadeq was obsessed with the symbolism of nationalization, to the exclusion of details. He had to be seen as the premier who not only reclaimed Iran's oil, but also ended Britain's manipulation of its politics. Truman, not wishing to get bogged down in details, tried to keep the conversation at a general level. He assured the prime minister that the United States viewed both parties as friends. Mossadeq, in typical fashion, played the communist card, noting that if the crisis continued, it "would gravely endanger the independence of Iran and the preservation of peace."[46] Truman took the bait and agreed that "Russia was sitting like a vulture on the fence waiting to pounce on the oil."[47] When Mossadeq pleaded for more aid, claiming he led an impoverished nation, Acheson quickly reminded him that Iran was sitting on a sea of oil. This was a clear signal that Iran could escape its economic predicament only by coming to terms with Britain. The amicable meeting set the stage for George McGhee to try to sort out the problems.

From early on, the Americans were puzzled at the stagecraft of the meetings. Mossadeq continued his unusual habit of excluding his advisers from the discussions. He also spoke in French, and the only translator he seemed to trust was Colonel Vernon Walters, who would go on to serve as deputy director of the CIA. Iran's fifteen-man delegation, which brimmed with experts, was left in the dark as Mossadeq asked McGhee not to share any details with them. The secrecy testified to Mossadeq's paranoia and his distrust of his own advisers. For a politician insistent on national empowerment, he seemed more at ease with McGhee and Walters than with the Iranians responsible for assisting him.

Still, the basic contours of an agreement seemed in sight. McGhee devised a formula whereby the NIOC would be in charge but it would grant an international firm, such as the Royal Dutch Shell Company, the right to operate the oil fields on its behalf. The AIOC would be offered a generous compensation package including the right to purchase Iranian oil. At one point, Mossadeq even seemed to have agreed that the Abadan refinery could be sold to a non-British firm—one of the promises that he would soon retract. The one condition Mossadeq insisted on was that no British personnel could participate in the management of Iran's oil industry.[48]

Before McGhee could submit the agreed-on principles to the British, Mossadeq had a sudden shift of mood. In their next meeting, the premier informed McGhee that he "could not sign any agreement until he had first submitted it to the parliament and the parliamentary commission for approval."[49] He further stunned McGhee by saying that he "would forward the agreement to the parliament without publicly endorsing it."[50] All along, the Americans had suspected that Mossadeq would not want to assume responsibility for a compromise and that he was more concerned about his domestic political standing than resolving the oil stalemate. This meeting clearly showed that those suspicions were largely correct.

The negotiating landscape became even bleaker on October 28, when the British elections returned the Conservatives to power. The Labour Party's policies in the Middle East had been a major issue during the campaign. Attlee had the misfortune of facing the voters just as Iran broke off diplomatic relations with Britain, and as Egypt abrogated the Anglo-Egyptian Treaty of 1936, which had given Britain the right to station troops at its Suez Canal base. Churchill had already warned Attlee that Iran "was more important than

Korea" and that "the moral case for using force to preserve the Company's property at Abadan was a strong one."[51] Despite clamoring for the nationalization of domestic industries, the British public still wanted the empire's prestige to be maintained and its assets preserved. The Tories who had cleverly exploited this issue to score a narrow victory were in no mood for McGhee's clever formulas.

Acheson conveyed McGhee's ideas to the new foreign secretary, Anthony Eden, when they met on the sidelines of the NATO summit in Paris.[52] Acheson, who harbored his own reservations about British imperialism, warned Eden that Mossadeq was not about to fold. The secretary of state suggested that although the AIOC would have to relinquish control of the facilities, an arrangement could still be worked out whereby Britain had access to Iranian oil. Eden, however, rejected the proposal and was particularly offended by the exclusion of the British personnel from Iran's oil industry. The new British hardliners thought it was time to stop the negotiations and plan Mossadeq's ouster. In his memoirs, Eden recalled, "I did not accept the argument that the only alternative to Mossadeq was communist rule. I thought that if Mossadeq fell, his place might well be taken by a more reasonable Government with which it should be possible to conclude a satisfactory agreement."[53] A rueful Acheson could only conclude that "the new ministers are depressingly out of touch with the world of 1951, and they are being advised by the same officials who have allowed the government to follow the AIOC meekly into disaster."[54]

When informed of Acheson's failure, Mossadeq accepted the verdict with equanimity. His composure impressed McGhee, who did not realize that for Mossadeq the dispute was always political and not economic. The premier confessed to Walters, "Don't you realize, that returning to Iran empty-handed, I return in a much stronger position than if I returned with an agreement which I would have to sell to my fanatics."[55] He was in a quandary of his own making, having unleashed forces that he could neither propitiate nor confront.

The failure of the Washington talks did not stop the diplomacy. This time it was Pakistan's envoy to the United States, Abol Hassan Ispahani, who suggested that perhaps the International Bank for Reconstruction and Development could manage Iran's oil industry while a settlement was being negotiated. This led to a flurry of activity and yet another plan. According to this proposal, the bank would appoint a neutral body to manage the oil installations. The profits from the sale of oil would be divided in equal parts among Iran, the managing company, and an escrow account held for the AIOC. All the details of production and pricing would be worked out with the NIOC.

Mossadeq was first to object: he insisted that the bank's proposal had to conform to Iran's nationalization law. This meant that Iran would oversee the selection of board members and that no British personnel could participate in the arrangement. The bank officials told him that as a neutral body, they could not acknowledge Iran's possession of the oil installations so long as the issue was being adjudicated by international bodies. Nor was the bank prepared to dispense with British technicians given the lack of alternatives. Thus ended the last major U.S. effort to resolve the issue.

At the beginning of the crisis, the American officials were often frustrated by Britain's inability to appreciate that change was coming to its entire colonial realm. The AIOC was obstreperous and stingy, and the Foreign Office too often yielded to its misjudgments. Mossadeq was seen as a quaint nationalist who still wanted the best for his country. As the prime minister turned down successive offers, the White House began to view his position on nationalization not as a legitimate exercise of a sovereign power but as an irrational outburst. To be fair, London also turned down all the same offers. But the British were partners in the Cold War, holding up the pillars of containment in Europe and dying on the battlefields of Korea. Mossadeq's failure was to discount this relationship and think that by invoking the communist threat, he could manipulate America's policy against its indispensable ally.

THINGS FALL APART

By 1952, Iran's economy was in shambles because Mossadeq could not overcome the British embargo and sell Iran's oil. The oil giants stood with the AIOC, while the Royal Navy deterred smaller firms tempted by Iran's offerings. The United States continued to provide modest aid but refused to bail out Iran's economy. The Iranian government had difficulty meeting its payroll, and its various development plans had to be shelved. Mossadeq's concept of an "oil less economy" turned out to be a delusion; Iran relied on the sale of petroleum to meet its basic needs. In a sense, Mossadeq was correct in thinking that the British wanted to overthrow him, and that many in Iran's upper classes were concerned about his stewardship of the country. Yet his response to all this was unconstitutional and illegal. He tried to emasculate the monarchy by attempting to wrest control of the army from the shah, and he tried to tame the parliament by demanding that the chamber grant him special powers. Although he needed an agreement to stabilize his country, his fear of tarnishing his nationalist mantle kept a settlement out of reach.

As Iran's national crisis deepened, some in the political establishment began murmuring about the possibility of displacing Mossadeq. No one was more enterprising and aggressive in promoting such a change than Qavam. The "sly old bird," as the British called him, launched his campaign in his usual devious manner. Although he had already been in touch with the British embassy, he was not content to deal with functionaries and demanded a meeting with Eden.

The foreign secretary demurred, but he did offer up the Tory parliamentarian Julian Amery, one of Churchill's favorites. As a backbencher, Amery had castigated the Attlee government for its seeming passivity in the Middle East and had made the preservation of the Suez base and the AIOC his most urgent preoccupations. Thus began the furtive Amery-Qavam dialogue.

In a meeting in Paris, Qavam told Amery that once in power, he would at first pretend to be anti-British, but his real aim was to end the oil crisis in a manner acceptable to London. It is not clear whether Amery believed this, but he did assure Qavam that Britain would "regard his return to power as a change for the better."[56] Having secured Amery's support for his premiership, Qavam pressed ahead with his other ambition, deposing the Pahlavi monarchy. He told Amery that the shah could not be trusted and it was best for him to be replaced by an exiled Qajar prince, whom he had brought to the meeting. (The relationship between Qavam and the Pahlavis had always been poisonous: they had used him on occasion, then tossed him aside when he proved inconvenient.) But Qavam, in his old age, seemed to have lost his political touch—the Qajars had no real support in Iran, and the prince he proposed was a British subject who spoke no Persian. His idea was soon dismissed by the British, who had considered restoring the Qajars to power in 1941 only to conclude that the defunct dynasty lacked a solid foundation in the country.

Qavam also reached out to the United States. Even while assuring Amery of his loyalty, he informed the U.S. embassy that should he return to power "he would have no dealing with the Russians, and that he would have minimal dealings with the British."[57] The embassy was intrigued, and in due time Washington did support Qavam's aspirations. It is easy to dismiss Qavam's maneuvers as the self-serving schemes of a power-hungry politician. But his well-honed instinct for deception often coincided with a sense of national duty. In mid-twentieth-century Iran, it was not unusual for politicians to use foreign embassies as a means of securing an advantage over their rivals. The great powers had long been the arbiters of Persian politics, and Iran's aristocratic class viewed their manipulation as an essential condition of sovereignty.

At times, scholarly narratives lapse into false dichotomies between national-ists and mercenaries. Qavam was as much of a Persian patriot as Mossadeq, but he believed that Iran's interests required objectionable compromises. Still, he and his class were no less committed to Iran's independence than were the National Front deputies agitating against all things British.

In the meantime, the simmering tensions between Mossadeq and his many detractors played to Qavam's advantage. Once it became clear that neither the shah nor the parliament would grant him additional authority, the prime minister suddenly resigned. The royal court and the Western chancelleries were thrilled, and the contest for Mossadeq's replacement began in earnest. Kashani, who was concerned about Qavam's scheming, was the first to pri-vately contact the Minister of Court Hossein Alā and "after expressing some faint praise for Mossadeq and going through the motions of giving Mossadeq support, . . . [Kashani] indicated that he thought Busheri [Javad Busheri, minister of roads] the best man to succeed Mossadeq."[58] The shah, however, faced pressure from both Britain and America to appoint his nemesis, Qavam. On July 17, he most reluctantly summoned Qavam to the palace and asked him to form a government. This would be Qavam's final tour as prime minis-ter, and it would last just five days.

As he returned to the helm of power, Qavam seemed incapable of handling the political forces arrayed against him. No one trusted him, least of all the shah, who quietly let the political class know that he had appointed Qavam under duress. Sensing that he needed to control the situation, the new prime minister asked the shah to dissolve the parliament. The monarch rejected the idea, leaving in place a chamber full of deputies who knew that Qavam had tried to get rid of them. Qavam next alienated Kashani by denouncing "black reaction" and declaring, "I will not tolerate the mullahs' intervention in poli-tics."[59] Although the two were in secret talks, Qavam did nothing to quash the rumors that the ayatollah might be arrested.

It was the street that proved Qavam's undoing. Though out of power, Mossadeq was still able to conspire against his successor by organizing street protests. He was helped by Kashani, who pressed his bazaar allies to stage their own marches, and by the Tudeh Party, whose members joined the melee and called for nationwide strikes. In a strange tale of tactical alliances, Kashani even appeared at a Tudeh rally, proudly proclaiming, "It was the union of your workers and the Iranian people that brought us victory against British imperialism."[60] The protests quickly grew violent; when Qavam dispatched the army to quell the riots, the soldiers ended up killing sixty-nine people and wounding seven hundred fifty. In the midst of this national uproar, The Hague ruled that it had no authority to resolve the oil dispute, granting Mossadeq a victory over the dreaded British. All this spelled the end of Qavam's and Mossadeq's triumphant return to power.

The events of July 1952 were another ominous turn in Iran's politics. Iran's leading politicians could always summon a timely protest against a rival. These crowds were often purchased from the lower sectors of society and could be used to intimidate and deter. Once unleashed, the crowd would grow in size, attracting both opportunists and idealists. Mossadeq's return to power came partly through the organizational efforts of Kashani and the Tudeh. Although the intelligentsia and the urban middle class were attracted to Mossadeq's reformist message, he increasingly relied on muscle from religious nationalists and Tudeh militants, who could generate street protests and even kill a troublesome actor such as Razmara. The mob, now the mediator of Iran's politics, would go on to devour other victims, including Mossadeq himself.

Upon returning to office, Mossadeq moved quickly to consolidate his power. He appointed himself minister of war, taking control of the armed forces, and prohibited the shah from having direct contact with his officer corps. The defense budget was reduced and the army went through a purge of officers seen as disloyal to the premier. The royal family was warned to stay out of politics, and the shah's feisty sister Ashraf was sent into exile. Mossadeq pushed through the parliament an emergency measure granting him the right to enact reforms without going through the legislative process, a power that he soon demanded to be extended for another year. The shah, intimidated by Mossadeq's street power and his seeming popularity, meekly acquiesced to his many injunctions. The prime minister had successfully reduced the shah to a constitutional monarch and hollowed out both the parliament and the army.

To the extent that Mossadeq had a plan for resolving the oil dispute, it was to play the communist card. He soon warned Washington's tough new ambassador, Loy Henderson, that "unless foreign financial aid was received there will be a revolution within 30 days."[61] Next he announced that he was ready to sell oil to the Soviet bloc countries. The problem with these threats was that the White House did not take them seriously. The CIA dismissed the idea of helping Iran by stressing that emergency "aid on his [Mossadeq's] terms would strengthen his political position, particularly against the conservative opposition, and postpone the necessity of his coming to grips with the oil question."[62] As for his claim that he would sell oil to communist countries, the CIA noted that "it is unlikely that the Soviet bloc could provide enough tankers to move financially significant quantities of oil from Iran." In the end, the agency concluded, "We do not consider it likely that the U.S.S.R. would be willing to give Mossadeq sufficient financial assistance to enable him to stabilize his position."[63]

The CIA was correct to dismiss Mossadeq's histrionics about a communist revolution should he fail to obtain financial assistance, but it was wrong about Soviet willingness to purchase Iran's oil. Since its initial dismissal of Mossadeq as just another reactionary, Moscow had been looking for ways to seize upon the disorder sweeping Iran. In April 1952, Vyacheslav Molotov instructed the embassy to let Mossadeq know that "we sympathize with the position in which Iran finds itself at the present time and are ready to buy Iranian oil, but we would like to receive specific proposals: what kind of oil is meant: crude or refined into petroleum products." The Soviets did note that they were "experiencing difficulties with the oil tanker fleet," but they believed such logistical issues could be resolved.[64] In the end, despite his neutralist tendencies, Mossadeq was deeply skeptical of Russia because of its history of intervention in Iran. For now, he was willing to threaten the sale of oil to the Soviet Union to scare the Americans, but not to actually carry through with such an arrangement. As the crisis grew worse, Mossadeq would turn to the Soviets, but by then Moscow would have second thoughts about bailing him out. Meanwhile, the ploy put him in the worst possible position. His flirtations with the Soviet Union earned the Americans' distrust, yet he was unwilling to rescue his economy by relying on a country he detested as much as Britain.

Truman, armed with the CIA's judgment, denied Mossadeq's request, writing, "I am sure that you will understand that the executive branch of the U.S. government could not justify to the Congress and the American people a loan of the nature which you have requested at a time when Iran has an opportunity of obtaining revenues of a very great magnitude."[65] Mossadeq continued to wave the communist card in nearly every conversation with Henderson, while Iran's economic situation continued to deteriorate, fracturing his coalition and empowering radical forces on both the Left and the Right.

The Mossadeq who reached the pinnacle of power did not always resemble the elder statesman of Iran's politics. He was a man of probity with a genuine commitment to the constitution and the rule of law. His ideal government was a monarchy whose powers were limited by elected officials. His economic vision was egalitarian, and his preferred elite were the well-educated scions of the aristocracy who shared his zeal for modernization. He leaned toward secularism and distrusted religious reaction. And yet the temptations of power made him behave like the politicians he had spent decades chastising—willing to shelve his principles in the service of power and expedience. He forged a tactical relationship with the unscrupulous Kashani and seems to have known of the plot to assassinate one of his predecessors, General Razmara. And when disorder served his interests, Mossadeq did not hesitate to provoke street riots against legitimate authorities.

Talk of a coup was in the air throughout Mossadeq's tenure in office. The various plots were often initiated by the Iranians themselves and gained even more traction after he returned to office following Qavam's brief premiership. Given the prime minister's plenary powers, many Iranians feared that he could no longer be obstructed by parliamentary roadblocks. Meanwhile, increasing numbers of old-school politicians and military officers were being dismissed from their positions, leading them to further resent a prime minister who was ruining the economy.

The first substantial move against Mossadeq was initiated by the shah through Alā, when the shah sought to gauge Henderson's views on discharging the prime minister. As Alā told the ambassador, the shah felt that "steps must be taken in the near future to have Mossadeq replaced." Henderson made no commitment, but he agreed that "given the disagreements between the British and Mossadeq no oil agreement was possible so long as he remained in power."[66] The shah, as he often did, soon retreated from his own initiative, causing Henderson to exclaim, "As I become better acquainted with him, I am becoming more and more convinced that he lacks courage and resolution."[67] Henderson thus joined the long line of Western emissaries who bitterly complained about the monarch.

The name that increasingly circulated in opposition circles as a replacement prospect for Mossadeq was General Zahedi, who had served in Mossadeq's cabinet before falling out with him. Henderson, who was proving a shrewd judge of Persian politics, cabled his superiors that "there is evidence that the leaders in the National Front are increasingly at odds. The major struggle which seems to be developing is between Dr. Mossadeq and Mullah Kashani."[68] Henderson first broached the idea of a coup when describing a conversation, most likely with Zahedi: "An Iranian political leader who has been a member of one of Mossadeq's previous cabinets also called on me yesterday. This leader who has in the past had close relations with Kashani expressed the opinion that Iran could now be saved only by some form of coup."[69] Henderson would prove an enthusiastic backer of such schemes, but for now the White House demurred.

A similar reception awaited Christopher Woodhouse, MI6's top Iran official, who went to Washington to present "Operation Boot" to representatives of the CIA and the State Department. The plan involved provoking tribal uprisings and street protests as a means of ousting Mossadeq. The British seemed to have settled on General Zahedi as the leader of the anti-Mossadeq movement and emphasized the usual themes of a Tudeh takeover. Once more, however, the White House rejected the idea.

On November 1952, the American people elected the victor of World War II, Dwight Eisenhower, to the presidency. Iran and its boiling politics would now be the general's charge.

CHAPTER 4

The Coup

By 1953, the Cold War had conditioned every aspect of U.S. foreign policy. America was committed to containing the Soviet Union in Europe, defeating communism in Asia, and keeping radical actors from coming to power in the Middle East and Latin America. President Dwight Eisenhower would prove a prudent cold warrior who appreciated that the global containment effort had to be waged in a financially sensible manner. While America's priorities remained intact, the means of prosecuting the Cold War had to be economically more judicious than they had been under Truman. In executing its policy, the United States tried to encircle the Soviet Union with regional alliances. The Middle East's geographic proximity to Russia, as well as its ample oil reserves, made it particularly important to the new administration. Like Truman, Eisenhower appreciated the arrival of post-colonial nationalism and the necessity of aligning the United States with the forces of change.

No president's reputation has changed more than Eisenhower's.[1] In the 1950s, the intellectual classes sneered at his garbled syntax and his affinity for golf courses and millionaires. He was derided as an indifferent chief executive, delegating authority to subordinates who rarely bothered to check with him as they embarked on their initiatives. This was an image that Eisenhower delighted in projecting, because he could conveniently blame his subordinates for failed policies while protecting his own reputation. Throughout his life, Eisenhower was a voracious reader who understood the requirements of leadership and knew how to bend the bureaucracy to his will. As the archival record became available, it revealed Eisenhower to be a master politician who made decisions in private.[2] In what the political scientist Fred Greenstein called the "hidden hand presidency," he was always in charge but not always visible.

In the aftermath of the Vietnam War, many historians have also come to appreciate Eisenhower's unwillingness to become ensnared in land wars in Asia. He is seen as a model of prudence, a rare politician who refused to give in to Cold War hysteria. He is sometimes depicted almost as a pacifist who cut defense budgets at the height of the Cold War and warned against the creeping influence of the military-industrial complex. This is a misreading of Eisenhower, whose defense budgets routinely comprised more than 10 percent of the GDP and who was not averse to nuclear brinkmanship. If he did not want to deploy forces in the jungles of Southeast Asia, he was also not about to cede territory to the Soviet Union. Eisenhower used all instruments of American power to wage an aggressive containment strategy.

To manage foreign affairs, Eisenhower preferred to rely on loyal and able subordinates. John Foster Dulles fit that model perfectly.[3] A respected international lawyer and longtime Republican foreign policy hand, Dulles was an obvious choice for secretary of state. He would often present the administration's case to the public, giving the illusion that he was in charge, but the president made the decisions. As Chief of Staff Sherman Adams pointed out, "the secretary of state never made a major move without the president's knowledge and approval."[4]

The relationship that evolved between the two men had Eisenhower serving as the senior partner while Dulles concentrated on everyday management of affairs. They spent considerable time together talking over the trends in the international scene. As Eisenhower recalled, "Not only were our relations close and cordial, but on top of that I always regarded him as an assistant with whom I could talk things out very easily—when finally a decision was made I could count on him to execute them."[5] Some of the administration's most sensitive decisions were made over drinks, when the two met after hours to review urgent matters. This was when they would discuss interference in other nations' internal affairs.

In the era before White House staffers began to infringe on the prerogatives of the State Department, the diplomatic corps still mattered. Secretaries of state—both Acheson and Dulles—were their presidents' primary advisers on foreign affairs. But the Eisenhower administration's decision-making cannot be fully understood without appreciating the arrival of a new bureaucracy, the Central Intelligence Agency.

The 1947 National Security Act was an effort to impose order and organization on U.S. foreign policy by bolstering agencies like the State Department and by creating the CIA. Given that war between the superpowers was considered to be mutual suicide, covert operations became a prime instrument of the Cold War. This was particularly true in Third World countries, where the intelligence agencies of both blocs used a variety of means to influence political developments. Although covert operations were always a feature of U.S. policy, they became a significant tool of national security strategy under Eisenhower, who considered them the most efficient way for the United States to influence events. The administration's affinity for covert operations ensured a prominent role for the CIA in policy implementation.

The new director of the CIA, Allen Dulles, was an enthusiastic backer of covert schemes.[6] The two Dulles brothers could not have been more different. Foster was austere and evangelical, while Allen was colorful and iconoclastic. Allen had been a spy in his own right before switching to practicing law, while Foster always thought of problems as legal briefs. Still, the CIA's institutional power was enhanced by the fact that the two brothers controlled two of the most important government agencies. The 1950s may have been the CIA's golden age, as its crafty Ivy League staff scored successive wins over the often ham-handed KGB. This was before the debacles in Cuba, the quagmire in Vietnam, and the agency's expansion, which stifled its creativity.[7]

Like most new administrations, the Eisenhower team undertook a comprehensive review shortly after Ike took office, and it soon emerged with a policy it christened the New Look. The New Look was not all that new, because it accepted the prevailing Cold War view of the Soviet Union as a predatory global power animated by an ideology that mandated the relentless expansion of its influence. Eisenhower's sole innovation was injecting economics into the containment strategy. He insisted that "we are engaged in defense of a way of life, and the greater danger is that in defending this way of life, we find ourselves restoring to methods that endanger our existence."[8]

By dangerous methods, he meant intrusive government, repression of economic freedoms, and excessive reliance on the military to keep order; instead he favored mobilizing alliance networks, issuing nuclear threats, and unleashing the CIA.

With Europe stabilized, the New Look concerned itself with the vast postcolonial realm. The custodians of the national security state worried that while the Soviet Union remained committed to global domination, its immediate objective was "the elimination of the United States' influence from Eurasia."[9] One of the most searching questions of the Eisenhower tenure was articulated by Henry Cabot Lodge, the new U.S. ambassador to the United Nations, when he asked the cabinet, "The U.S. can win wars, but the question is can we win revolutions?"[10] In the Middle East, Eisenhower would experiment with a series of coups, deploy a large contingent of U.S. troops to Lebanon in 1958, and even try his hand at Arab-Israeli peacemaking to assuage regional sensitivities.[11]

Iran loomed large in the new administration's plans. Initially, the signs coming out of Washington were not necessarily antagonistic to Mossadeq. Even before Eisenhower's inauguration, Mossadeq wrote to the president-elect complaining that the Truman administration had "pursued what appears to the Iranian people to be a policy of supporting the British Government and the AIOC." This was an unfair characterization of an administration that in fact had devised many proposals while rebuffing both British officials and Iranian politicians who clamored for a coup. Still, Eisenhower responded, "I hope our own future relationships will be completely free of any suspicion, but on the contrary will be characterized by confidence and trust inspired by frankness and friendliness."[12]

Although fear that Iran might be absorbed behind the Iron Curtain would come to guide Washington's priorities, oil was very much on the new president's mind. Writing to his longtime friend Swede Hazlett, Eisenhower confessed, "I am concerned primarily, and almost solely, in some scheme or plan that will permit that oil to keep flowing to the westward. We cannot ignore the tremendous importance of 675,000 barrels of oil a day."[13] He appreciated that Mossadeq belonged to a new generation of Third World leaders whose neutralism made him an unlikely ally against the Soviet Union. But if such a leader could provide stability and ensure the flow of oil, that was fine with Eisenhower.

The Dulles brothers took a more skeptical view. Both had been associated with the law firm of Sullivan and Cromwell, which had been a legal adviser to the AIOC, and Allen Dulles had traveled to Iran in 1949 for business. Given their business experience, they were much more concerned about the disruptive force of nationalism. The fear in many corporate boardrooms and law firms was that if Iran set a precedent by expropriating a foreign company, other nations might do the same. Communism and commerce merged in conditioning the brothers' outlook. But this was Eisenhower's government, and he would set the policy.

There was still a joint Anglo-American offer on the table. It was the latest iteration of the same set of principles that had been considered for two years, in which a multinational consortium would operate the oil fields on behalf of the AIOC. Until a final arrangement could be worked out, the United States would purchase a large quantity of Iranian oil and offer $50 million in aid to stabilize Tehran's finances. Possession of the AIOC's nationalized assets would be settled by the International Court of Justice. The latest point of contention was how much compensation Iran would pay the AIOC for the oil company's loss of future profits, given that their contract would be abrogated before its maturation date. As usual, Mossadeq had both a private and a public position. While publicly rejecting such compensation as the latest presumption of a colonial power that had looted Iran for decades, he intimated privately that he would consider a one-time lump-sum payment if it was not too large. This position was quickly endorsed by the State Department, which informed the Foreign Office that it should propose a reasonable sum, or else Mossadeq would claim that "the British had refused to accept any type of settlement which did not imply Iran might be required to pay indefinitely and in amounts beyond her capacity."[14] This sign that the Americans were wavering provoked a quick visit by Eden.

Eisenhower's dovish attitude shocked the foreign secretary. The president said that he was even considering recalling Henderson, given his strained relations with Mossadeq, and might replace him with W. Alton Jones, who had already contemplated ways of breaking the British oil embargo on Iran. Jones's freelancing had caused so much consternation in the Foreign Office that the Truman administration finally had to rein him in. Dulles managed to quash the idea of replacing Henderson, and he was retained for continuity's sake. But the bad news for Britain did not stop there. Eisenhower bluntly told Eden he considered Mossadeq "the only hope for the West in Iran" and that he "would like to give the guy ten million bucks."[15] All this was appalling to Eden; the British government had hoped that the Republican Party, with its rhetoric of rolling back communism, would take a more hawkish approach toward Iran.

Eden repeated to the new American team what he had told their predecessors: instead of looking for an accommodation with Mossadeq, they should seek to replace him. When this line of argument failed, he summarized the diplomatic record of the past two years and warned that continued American catering to Mossadeq could undermine a Conservative government eager to cooperate with the United States in global hotspots. The foreign secretary was too skilled a diplomat to simply resist the new president's advice; instead he focused on extracting a pledge that the offer then on the table would be the last one. Eden was gambling that the old man of Persia would reject a proposal that he knew full well would be unacceptable to the AIOC. This was Eden's most important achievement during his trip. Throughout the nationalization crisis, every time Mossadeq had rejected an offer, it had been followed by another one. Now the foreign secretary obtained a commitment from Washington that the process would have an end point.

Eden's visit is an important milestone in the Iran saga. Afterward, Eisenhower conceded that "we must recognize that their [the British government's] latest proposals, unlike earlier ones to the Iranians, had been wholly reasonable. It was certainly possible for the United States to do what it thought necessary to do in Iran, but we certainly don't want a break with the British."[16] This position was endorsed by one of Eisenhower's most important aides, Walter Bedell Smith. During the war, Smith had been Ike's chief of staff; after serving as director of the CIA under Truman, he became Eisenhower's eyes and ears in the State Department. Smith, who had been dealing with the Iran file from his perch at the agency, warned Eisenhower that he did not believe further concessions should be granted to Tehran.[17] Dulles subsequently instructed the embassies in London and Tehran that "if Mossadeq rejects the present oil proposal we do not intend to make another."[18]

Mossadeq fell into the trap that Eden had laid for him. The premier quickly poisoned the well with the new administration when he summoned Henderson and reneged on his pledge of a one-time payment. Mossadeq had seemingly agreed that the International Court of Justice could determine how much compensation AIOC should receive for the loss of its future profits, but only confidentially, because it was such an explosive issue domestically. Now suddenly he seemed to backtrack. The deterioration of his standing within Iran made him reluctant to commit to even a private understanding for fear that it might be publicized.

Mossadeq took his case to the public. In a vitriolic speech denouncing the existing offer, he insisted that after two years of negotiations, all he had received was a variation of the same attempt to bring the AIOC back to Iran. Once again, he charged, Britain was plotting to control Iran's oil under the guise of a settlement. Apparently oblivious to how Eisenhower would take his rejection of the proposal, Mossadeq seems to have assumed that the existing pattern—whereby he would reject an offer, and then all sides, led by U.S. mediators, would craft yet another proposal—would continue. But the doors of diplomacy were about to shut.

The first three months of Eisenhower's presidency proved critical for U.S.-Iran relations. Ike had come into office prepared to press Britain if he saw signs of pragmatism in Tehran. Mossadeq's rejection of the offer caused him to accept the British complaint that they had made all reasonable concessions. Once he became persuaded that there was no diplomatic option left, America grew more attentive to the long-standing British preference for regime change. To be fair, the Dulles brothers had long been suspicious of Mossadeq, and the idea of a coup had strong support in the CIA. Frank Wisner, head of covert operations, and his expanding bureau were always enthusiastic regime changers. Even before Eisenhower's inauguration, operatives from the CIA and MI6 had begun meeting and refining their ideas. But Eisenhower was not about to yield to his aides just because a bureaucratic consensus had evolved. It was Mossadeq's obduracy that pushed him to the brink. An administration that was determined to wage the Cold War in the developing world began to see Mossadeq not as a barrier to communism but as an enabler of it. All of this would be given more credence as Iran's domestic scene began to shift for the worse.

MOSSADEQ TAKES CHARGE

Mohammad Mossadeq's second term was bound to be lonely. He had essentially given up the idea of a negotiated settlement out of fear that any compromise with Britain would unleash his domestic opponents. He saw enemies and conspiracies everywhere and was beginning to push out some of the elder politicians who had started the National Front with him, in favor of younger and more militant aides who indulged his rash impulses. He was also unable to see the generosity of the offers he was rejecting. He had gained much by being stubborn, but that tactic should always be used sparingly.

During his final months in power, Mossadeq made nearly all the mistakes that Qavam had made during his last, truncated premiership. The prime minister was determined to usher in a new order in which the monarchy was hollowed out, the traditional aristocracy was deprived of its power, and religion was separated from politics. As minister of war, he took revenge on the military, which he suspected of harboring pro-shah sentiments. The army's budget was reduced by 15 percent and about fifteen thousand of its soldiers were transferred to the gendarmerie. He cashiered 136 high-ranking officers and established commissions to investigate corruption in the promotion and procurement processes. These changes did not sit well with many active duty and retired officers, and provided Zahedi with a fresh pool of opponents to Mossadeq.

None of these misjudgments was more glaring than the premier's mishandling of Kashani. This may have been inevitable, since the relationship between the two men had always been tactical. In February, Mossadeq ordered his agencies to ignore requests from Kashani and began to speak of a secular order free from religious shackles. The parliament that Kashani led as speaker hardly functioned, with pro–National Front deputies routinely disrupting business by denying the chamber the necessary quorum. This angered not only Kashani, who was used to the trappings of power, but also the clerical oligarchs in Qom who were already troubled by the rise of modernizing autocrats all over the Middle East.

Kashani had always kept his options open. The ayatollah had held secret meetings with the royal court, foreign legations, and General Zahedi. As his relationship with the prime minister deteriorated, he gradually moved to consolidate his ties with the nascent anti-Mossadeq coalition. That coalition finally had a chance to flex its muscles when a dispute arose between the shah and his premier.

For months, the prime minister had complained to the shah that the royal court was conspiring against his government. In essence, Mossadeq was demanding that the shah and his aides stop participating in political affairs and instead become a ceremonial monarchy that left affairs of the state to the cabinet. The shah, in typical fashion when the going got tough, responded by suggesting that he might need to leave the country soon for a "rest." The premier welcomed the suggestion, and all agreed that the preparations would be made in utmost secrecy until the departure day was officially announced. It is hard to see how any of the parties involved really believed that such explosive news could be kept secret in a Tehran that was buzzing with rumors and gossip. Sure enough, it was soon leaked that the monarch was preparing to leave Iran.

The news galvanized the anti-Mossadeq forces and gave them their first major victory. Kashani was very much the driver of events, but Ayatollah Mohammad Behbahani, an influential Tehran cleric, made his first significant move against Mossadeq by imploring the shah to reverse his plans. Behbahani had strong connections with the upper echelons of the clergy in Qom and was known for his religious erudition. His opposition was an important signal that the most esteemed members of the clerical class were uneasy about the nation's future. Kashani summoned the Majlis back into session and informed its members of the shah's plan to leave the country. He then quickly passed on a note to the royal court: "The news of Your Majesty's unexpected departure has bewildered the populace."[19] A parliamentary delegation was dispatched to the palace to talk the shah out of leaving. But in Iran at this point, formal politics was not enough: the street had to have its say.

As he had done to bring Mossadeq back to power in 1952, Kashani instigated street demonstrations calling on the monarch to stay. In the bazaar, the shops shuttered in protest. Mayhem and disorder once more threatened to set Tehran ablaze. The shah, surprised by his own popularity, informed the crowds gathered outside the palace that he would cancel his trip since "my going out of the country for health reasons does not meet with your approval."[20] The monarchy as an institution was still valued not just by the elites, but also by average Iranians.

The events of that February are important because they show that an anti-Mossadeq coalition had formed between the clergy and the military. The Association of Retired Officers that Zahedi led provided the trucks used to transport protesters, including soldiers and those aroused by Kashani and the mullahs. A Foreign Office report captured the situation correctly when it noted, "It would seem that Kashani, seizing upon the emotions surrounding the departure of the Shah, cleverly managed to couple popular clamor for the Shah remaining with attacks on Mossadeq."[21] The same coalition, augmented and better organized, would be critical to Mossadeq's overthrow. The Western intelligence services created none of this. They did not foster the pro-monarchy attitudes nor incite the army officers and mullahs to join in opposition to the prime minister.

In the midst of all this, before the shah changed his mind and announced he would stay, a bizarre event took place that demonstrates how paranoid Mossadeq had become. He had gone to the palace to say goodbye to the departing monarch, and as lunch was being served, he received a message that Ambassador Henderson wished to see him. Like most foreign envoys in Tehran at the time, Henderson was trying to figure out what was going on. Mossadeq had to cut his meeting short and return to his office. As he was leaving the palace, he was accosted by protestors and had to be spirited away by the guards, first to an American compound, then to the parliament building, before finally arriving at his office. In his memoirs, Mossadeq depicts this event as a plot by Henderson to have him assassinated. He argues that Henderson organized an assassination posse and then pulled him out of his meeting so they could kill him. There is not a shred of evidence in the U.S. archives to support this strange tale, but it reveals a great deal about Mossadeq's state of mind and the distrustful nature of Iranian politics.

By this time, the National Front coalition had begun to fracture, with two of the most important members of the Front coming out against Mossadeq.

Hossein Makki had founded the Iran Party in 1946 and was Mossadeq's long-time ally. He was one of the leaders of the nationalization movement and had stood with Mossadeq in the parliament in opposition to the Supplemental Agreement. Mozaffar Baghai, the other breakaway leader, was the head of Iran's Toilers Party, which professed its own version of socialism, distinct from the Tudeh's. Baghai had joined forces with the National Front while maintaining a discreet relationship with Kashani. Both Makki and Baghai were now worried by Mossadeq's arbitrary conduct and his inability to resolve the oil issue. They supported the nationalization of Iran's oil but also understood the importance of getting some agreement to prevent the economy from collapsing. The departure of these pivotal figures and their parties from the National Front signaled that the establishment was beginning to distance itself from the prime minister's ruinous policies.

Mossadeq's National Front was becoming a shell of its former self. It had arisen as a coalition that not only pushed for oil nationalization but also called for creating a more accountable government. The party's platform had insisted on Iran's sovereign rights, free and fair elections, the rule of law, and support for social welfare provisions. The goal of nationalization had been achieved, but at much cost to the Front's remaining objectives. Mossadeq's creeping authoritarianism was fraying the bonds of the party whose members had hoped that he would usher in an age of liberal politics. The exodus of establishment figures left the party with only its militant members, who kept stressing that Mossadeq had not gone far enough in dismantling traditional institutions, including the monarchy. Mossadeq did not always share the zeal of his remaining disciples, and increasingly he had to rely on figures whose vision of Iran was different from his. As the National Front disintegrated, Mossadeq's opponents organized and plotted.

Some chroniclers of the coup have suggested that the Western intelligence services settled on Zahedi as their choice to oust Mossadeq. This implies that the general was their creation and that he depended on them for his success. This is a misreading of events. Zahedi's bravery and skill were beyond dispute: he had earned his quick promotion through his many military campaigns against internal insurrections. An ambitious officer with exceptional survival skills, he had endured Reza Shah's many purges of the military only to be arrested by the British during the war and exiled for pro-German sympathies. After the war he resurrected his career, serving as chief of police and eventually as interior minister in Mossadeq's cabinet—although Mossadeq later dismissed him and even issued a warrant for his arrest on a charge of anti-government agitation. By early 1953 Zahedi had emerged as the leader of the opposition largely through his own efforts. As head of the Association of Retired Officers, he could reach out to many senior commanders. He was clever enough to establish good relations with Kashani and even promised him a say in forming his post-coup government. Given that both men were estranged from Mossadeq, they became convenient allies.

A host of colonels and middle-ranking officers had also gravitated to the opposition, independent of Zahedi. The Iranian army was riddled with opposition groups, many with overlapping memberships that would quickly unite under Zahedi's leadership. Among the most important of these organizations was the Committee for Saving the Motherland, which comprised about 250 officers. The committee's objective was the overthrow of Mossadeq, and its members were in touch with many senior commanders, including the army chief of staff, General Nader Batmanqelij, who became one of Zahedi's most important lieutenants during the coup. It appears that once the shah canceled his plans to leave Iran, some members of this committee approached him and asked his permission to move against Mossadeq. The shah was noncommittal, but the group remained cohesive and ready to act.

Kashani, meanwhile, was busy organizing the mosques in traditional neighborhoods. Although he still had connections with the Fada'iyan, who were always available for a timely assassination, he wanted to establish a network that could help him mobilize the street, recruit thugs, and disrupt National Front and Tudeh rallies. The battle lines were being drawn and all the actors involved seemed to be readying themselves for a struggle.

Iran's politics became dense with inflammatory accusations and shifting alliances. Mossadeq's erstwhile allies called him the next Hitler, while others compared him to Stalin, a leader who maintained his power through purges. The newspapers supporting the prime minister castigated his critics as cynics willing to destroy Iran's independence to line their own pockets. The nation's institutions largely ceased to function, which seemed fine with Mossadeq, who now preferred to rule by decree.

Throughout his long career, Mossadeq had been a champion of the rule of law and constitutional demarcations of power. All of that faded away as he increasingly behaved like a despot fanning the flames of xenophobia. He was no longer concerned about governmental institutions like the judiciary or the parliament, which he now described as being filled with agents of Britain. He spoke of his primordial bonds to the masses, rarely appeared in the Majlis, and explained himself to his people only via radio. On those broadcasts, he denounced parliamentary debate as subversion, monarchical concern as lust for power, and the aristocratic class and the army as agents of foreigners. Iran was to be ruled by Mossadeq in the name of his people.

The tragedy of Mossadeq is that even in his last days in power, he still hoped to carry out an expansive social agenda that could have alleviated the poverty and inequality that had plagued Iran for so long. He was sincere in his desire for land reform, a redistributive tax system, and a generous welfare state. But the oil dispute had depleted the treasury and deprived him of the funds to carry out his reforms. He had so estranged the parliament and other institutions of government that ordinary legislative bargaining had become impossible. Meanwhile, the masses were being squeezed by the twin evils of inflation and unemployment. Mossadeq dismissed all of this and insisted that his bond with the people would protect him from a disgruntled political class.

Of Mossadeq's many adversaries, the shah seemed to be the least consequential. He did at times entertain participating in various anti-Mossadeq conspiracies that were presented to him, but after the prime minister's return to power, he feared that involvement in such plots could cost him his throne. The shah hoped that somehow Mossadeq would exhaust himself and be overthrown without his direct complicity. While waiting for that day, he issued the self-denunciations that Mossadeq demanded, sent his own relatives into exile, and even gave up control of his army. When Mossadeq mandated that he cease having contact with foreign diplomats, the shah, in yet another act of self-abnegation, accepted this latest infringement of his powers. Sequestered in his palace, he stewed more than he schemed and passed the time with card games and detective novels. He slept with a pistol and frequently changed bedrooms. His wife worried that he might suffer a nervous breakdown, because he seemed incapable of making decisions. The prime minister had managed to bring the monarchy to one of its lowest points.

Since 1951, a stream of Iranian politicians and generals had gone to the U.S. embassy to ask that the Americans help them depose Mossadeq. Sometimes their requests were limited to asking the Americans to pressure the shah to dismiss his premier. By 1953, Henderson was giving a well-rehearsed response: the United States did not take a position on Iran's internal affairs. But the more the ambassador resisted, the more the Iranians pleaded. The British were also pressing the Americans to consider regime change, and the two nations' intelligence agents had even held preliminary discussions. After Iran severed relations with Britain, MI6 turned over its assets to the CIA station in Tehran. The agency seemed unimpressed by the offering.

The U.S. position began to change subtly in the spring of 1953. In a private meeting, the Minister of Court Alā informed Henderson that Zahedi had been in touch with the shah and was eager to assume the reins of government. It was not clear if the shah had dispatched Alā or if the former prime minister was trying to test the American attitude and use it to pressure the monarch into action. Either way, Henderson's response was more ambiguous then his usual flat-out rejection of such entreaties. While reiterating that the "United States government could not be associated with a coup d'état," he went on to note that Washington would be prepared to deal with a new prime minister if the shah appointed one.[22] Henderson also made it clear that he did not believe the oil issue could be resolved while Mossadeq was in power. The United States was finally beginning to contemplate overthrowing him.

None of this was apparent to the prime minister, who responded to his dire economic situation by once more asking the United States for aid while playing the communist card. He summoned Henderson to his office and insisted that unless the United States purchased large quantities of Iranian oil, "there would be a revolution in Iran in thirty days."[23] When this failed to budge Henderson, Mossadeq warned in their next meeting, "If the National Front government should pass out of existence only confusion or the Tudeh would take over."[24] He once more began to talk loudly about selling oil to the Soviet Union and the Eastern bloc countries. These meetings ironically confirmed Washington's fears that without drastic action, Iran could fall to communism.

After failing to obtain sufficient assurances from Henderson, Mossadeq approached Eisenhower directly. In May, he wrote a letter to the president warning him, "If prompt and effective aid is not given this country now, any steps that might be taken tomorrow to compensate for the negligence of today might well be too late."[25] Eisenhower took a month to respond, and when he did, it was to reject Mossadeq's request: "It would not be fair to the American taxpayers for the United States government to extend any considerable amount of economic aid to Iran so long as Iran could have access to funds derived from the sale of its oil and oil products if a reasonable agreement were reached with regard to compensation whereby the large scale marketing of Iranian oil would be resumed."[26] The letter was then promptly publicized, further damaging Mossadeq's domestic standing. Many of his detractors had assumed that he still enjoyed some support in Washington, and this was still the age when the approval of great powers mattered to the Iranian political class. Once it became clear that Mossadeq could not rescue the economy and that he had lost the confidence of the new occupant of the White House, his situation grew dire. Meanwhile, Iran's slide into chaos continued.

In July, the prime minister mismanaged another crisis. The murder of the pro–National Front police chief General Mahmud Afshartous shocked the political establishment. A string of arrests followed, along with accusations that those apprehended had been tortured. Mossadeq's many critics in the parliament used the occasion to propose a vote of no confidence against the government. To forestall this measure, Mossadeq ordered his parliamentary allies to resign, thus depriving the chamber of a quorum. Then came his disastrous move to dissolve the Majlis through a fraudulent plebiscite.

The Majlis was the most cantankerous podium for anti-Mossadeq agitation. The parliament routinely considered no-confidence votes while offering politicians a privileged sanctuary from which to attack the government. The parliamentary tactics of delay and obstruction that Mossadeq deplored were the same ones he had used when he was in the Majlis. It was Mossadeq the parliamentarian who had blocked many previous prime ministers' initiatives. He saw such legislative maneuvers as acceptable practice—that is, until they were used against him. Then the former champion of the parliament proposed a referendum to dissolve this legislative body.

In this latest act of aggrandizement, Mossadeq seems to have taken an accurate measure of the shah. Dismissing the parliament was a prerogative that the shah had reserved for himself: Mossadeq's own interior minister Gholam Hossein Sadiqi had warned him that given the legally dubious nature of his conduct, the shah could turn around and dismiss him. Mossadeq, however, scoffed at such claims and assured Sadiqi that the shah "does not have the guts to do that."[27] Once more the premier was proven right.

On August 3, Mossadeq conducted a transparently fraudulent referendum to decide the fate of the Majlis. There were no secret ballots: the boxes were marked "yes" or "no" and kept in different locations. The ballot stuffing was obvious. The government claimed that among more than two million voters, only 1,207 had disapproved of the measure. In Tehran itself, the vote was said to be 101,400 in favor and only 68 against. Kashani rejected the referendum and declared his intent to "intensify his activities against the government."[28] State radio, however, celebrated the results, claiming that the "people of Iran will no longer allow the government to be dominated by hooligans, criminals, and traitors to Iran."[29] Mossadeq insisted in his memoirs that the "referendum proved that the people agreed with the government and were in favor of the disillusion of the Majlis."[30] This was another sad episode in the history of the venerable National Front, which had originally come into existence to protest electoral fraud.

The July demonstrations to commemorate the one-year anniversary of Mossadeq's return to power are often neglected by those who study the coup, but they had an important effect on American deliberations. The Tudeh used the occasion to showcase its street power. The National Front and the Tudeh decided to stage separate rallies in different parts of Tehran. As *New York Times* correspondent Kennett Love reported, "The National Front in the morning mustered up a straggling assembly of a few thousand demonstrators and idlers. The Tudeh turned out a vibrantly disciplined throng of at least 100,000."[31] A Tudeh activist confidently approached Love and asked him, "Do you think they [the National Front] can refuse our support much longer? You have seen for yourself today how small they are and how big we are."[32] This came at a time when many communist parties had taken power in Eastern Europe by joining and then subverting popular front coalitions. The most apt comment of the day came from the anti-Mossadeq parliamentarian Mehdi Mir-Ashrafi, who lamented, "There goes the coffin of Iranian democracy."[33]

These events on the ground began to change the U.S. assessment, paving the way for the coup. Henderson emerged as the pivotal figure in the Americans' deliberations over what to do, a dramatic change of fortune for an ambassador whom Eisenhower had considered replacing just six months earlier. Henderson cabled his superiors that "there has been a sharp shift in the basis of Mossadeq's support among political leaders. Most elements [of the] original National Front movement now (repeat now) [are] in open or tacit opposition."[34] Mossadeq's disregard of the political establishment and the institutions it nurtured, his inability to resolve the oil dispute, and his reliance on the mob to intimidate his rivals had left him completely isolated. Henderson assured his superiors that "most politicians friendly to the West would welcome secret American intervention."[35] The ambassador's perspective coincided with the CIA's changing view of the Tudeh.

One reason the White House had not plotted against Mossadeq was the intelligence community's assessment that the prime minister still controlled the government and that his opponents, although growing in number, were fragmented. The Tudeh was seen as menacing but not necessarily poised to assume power. The United States had no real assets it could marshal, and the monarch, who could galvanize the opposition into a cohesive force, was seen as tentative. All of these assumptions began to change.

For much of Mossadeq's tenure, the Tudeh had persistently attacked him and denigrated his efforts to come to terms with Britain. The July demonstrations heralded a new communist strategy. The Tudeh was no longer assailing the National Front government but seeking to join forces with it. The CIA grew concerned that as Mossadeq became more isolated, he might turn to the Tudeh with the hope that he could still control the party. The new, more subtle Tudeh strategy would begin with infiltration of the government through some form of partnership, then move on to gradual assumption of power. That the Tudeh already had cells in the military and the bureaucracy further alarmed the agency.

The CIA now advised that "there is also the possibility that a communist seizure of power in Iran may take place imperceptibly over a considerable period of time. Under this contingency, it would be extremely difficult to identify and demonstrate to our allies that specific countermeasures were required to prevent communist infiltration from reaching the point where it would be able to significantly influence the policies of the Iranian government."[36] Mossadeq's brandishing of the communist threat and his flirtations with the Soviet Union further aggravated these concerns.

Soviet archives reveal that Washington fundamentally misread Moscow's policy, which was utterly confused. American intelligence assessments did not consider the impact of Stalin's death, in March 1953, on the Soviet approach to Iran. The collective leadership of Khrushchev, Molotov, and Bulganin was preoccupied with consolidating its power and dispensing with its sadistic rival, Lavrentiy Beria. Molotov was the key person in charge of foreign affairs, which meant that Soviet policy became unimaginative and suspicious of Mossadeq. Consider a year earlier, when Stalin had been prepared to relieve pressure on Iran by agreeing to purchase some of its oil, but Mossadeq demurred. When Mossadeq tried to reengage Moscow on the oil issue in May 1953, Molotov flatly rejected his plea, telling his ambassador in Tehran that "you should not forget that Mossadeq prepared the decision about liquidating British oil concessions at the behest of or after clearing it with the United States so as to remove from the world market the strongest competitors of American oil monopoly."[37] Molotov seemed to have based this absurd analysis on the KGB's similarly ridiculous claim that Mossadeq was determined to "smash the national liberation movement and suppress opposition elements around the Shah in order to create the conditions for further collusion with [the] American monopolies."[38] Soviet officialdom apparently thought that Mossadeq was an agent of the United States and its oil conglomerates, and that the entire nationalization movement was a scheme concocted by the two sides to take over AIOC's concession. It is perhaps to Mossadeq's credit that each superpower suspected he was an agent of the other. At any rate, the paralysis in the Soviet hierarchy and its fantastic misapprehensions kept Moscow on the sidelines.

Not until 1957, when Molotov was cast aside as foreign minister, did the Soviet Union reassess its policy. The Politburo belatedly chastised Molotov and noted:

> Because of the rigid and un-Leninist policy pursued by Comrade Molotov, who was then minister of foreign affairs, in relation to Iran, these opportunities were not exploited. Comrade Molotov mistakenly saw the conflict surrounding the Anglo-Iranian Oil Company not as a conflict between Iran and the colonizers of the West, but as a conflict between oil companies of England and of the USA, fighting with each other for Iranian oil. As a result of this improper position Soviet diplomacy missed favorable opportunities to improve our relations with the Iranian state.[39]

It would take another two years, until 1959, for the Soviet Union to reclassify Mossadeq's movement as a "revolution of national liberation." By that time, Mossadeq had been out of power for six years, languishing in internal exile.

Given the confusion in Moscow, it is difficult to explain why the Tudeh did what it did. The party was a pliable agent of the Soviet Union and would mimic Moscow's line even to the detriment of its national standing. The Tudeh had rejected nationalization because it feared that it would foreclose the possibility of Russia's obtaining its own oil concession. The party suffered from internal divisions and had strained relations with the National Front. In its report to Moscow after the coup, the Tudeh confessed, "On the day of the fascist rebellion we had a lot of opportunities [on our hands] but we lacked mutual trust, we feared them and they feared us."[40] During Iran's most consequential summer, the Soviet Union and its proxy seemed too bewildered to play a meaningful role in the final outcome of the crisis.[41] None of this was apparent to Washington, as the Eisenhower administration authorized a coup to topple Mohammad Mossadeq.[42]

A TALE OF TWO COUPS

The U.S. intelligence services were not new to Iran. During the war, the United States had deployed nearly thirty thousand troops there and operated a variety of missions to train its police and army. The Americans had also launched efforts to streamline Iran's finances and develop a coherent tax structure. In addition they created an intelligence apparatus, although it shrank dramatically after the war. During the late 1940s, the CIA launched a new operation, TPBEDAMN, that carried out propaganda campaigns aimed at the Tudeh and its Soviet patron.[43] As part of this operation, CIA specialists would write stories critical of the Tudeh for placement in Iran's many competitive and partisan local papers. TPBEDAMN also sought to arm tribal militias should the Soviet Union actually invade Iran, though this aspect of the operation seems to have been less developed than the effort to defame the Tudeh.

The CIA and MI6 had talked about a potential operation against Mossadeq as early as March. This was probably just contingency planning, but it had the support of Frank Wisner, the head of the agency's covert branch. These conversations were made necessary when the severance of diplomatic relations between Britain and Iran led to the United States inheriting Britain's network of assets. The British had long been active in Iranian politics, and their embassy had been the scene of much intrigue. Many Iranian parliamentarians, politicians, newspaper editors, mullahs, and military men had ties to the embassy. Again, it is hard to see who was manipulating whom, because all of these actors had their own motivations. Being anti-Mossadeq should not be equated with being anti-nationalist or mercenary. Still, Britain's most trusted contacts were the Rashidiyan brothers, particularly Asadollah. They controlled the butcher, baker, and other guilds in the bazaar, which enabled them to deploy street toughs to stage demonstrations or attack National Front rallies or government offices. The brothers were as attracted to Britain as they were devoted to the royal family, even though Reza Shah had once sent their father to prison.

By the end of May, meeting secretively in Nicosia, Cyprus, the operatives from the CIA and MI6 finalized their plan, code-named TPAJAX. The core of the operation, which would prove one of the most contentious in CIA history, was remarkably simple. Zahedi was identified as the key player, which seemed obvious given that he was already plotting against Mossadeq and had emerged as the leader of the opposition. A propaganda campaign would be launched to help shape public opinion against Mossadeq—though given that Iran was already simmering, with plenty of opposition newspapers and politicians denouncing everything Mossadeq did, it is hard to see how the CIA's art department would have had much impact. A second prong of the operation would involve the Iranian armed forces.[44] A third part of the operation, getting the shah to dismiss his prime minister, would turn out to be the agency's most important contribution to the coup, because it entailed sending a series of emissaries to the shah to persuade him to act. One million dollars was appropriated for the operation, although much of it remained unspent.[45] In the Eisenhower era of fiscal prudence, even covert operations had to come in under budget.

On June 25, 1953, the CIA-MI6 plan was formally discussed at a meeting chaired by John Foster Dulles. Other key figures present at the meeting were Secretary of Defense Charles Wilson, Walter Bedell Smith, Under Secretary Robert Murphy, Ambassador Loy Henderson, and Allen Dulles. The most important voice in the meeting belonged to Henderson, who assured his colleagues that Mossadeq was a lost cause and had no intention of resolving the oil issue. The ambassador insisted that most Iranian politicians would welcome American help in toppling the premier. There were discordant voices as well: the CIA station chief in Tehran, Roger Goiran, decried the coup as "putting U.S. support behind Anglo-French colonialism."[46] He was soon replaced by Joe Goodwin, a former Associated Press correspondent, who proved more agreeable. In the end, the twenty-two-page document that was to decide Iran's future was endorsed with surprisingly little discussion. Eisenhower quickly gave the plan his formal approval.

The person chosen to lead the coup was Kermit Roosevelt, a scion of one of America's most illustrious families. Roosevelt had all the right connections and credentials. He was the grandson of Theodore Roosevelt and a distant cousin of Franklin Roosevelt. He had been personally recruited to the Office of Strategic Services, the CIA's predecessor agency, by its legendary founder, Bill Donovan. Apparently Donovan admired Roosevelt's dissertation on the propaganda techniques used in England during the Glorious Revolution. During the war, Roosevelt had been dispatched to the Middle East, where he visited Iran. Afterward, he had a brief stint as an academic and wrote for the *Saturday Evening Post*. He traveled extensively in the region and published a book, *Arabs, Oil and History: The Story of the Middle East*, which seemed skeptical of British colonialism. Once the CIA got up and running, Roosevelt joined the organization as head of its Middle East desk.

The CIA had few links to the Iranian army, which was already mobilizing against Mossadeq. As late as May, the agency noted that "it did not possess any military assets."[47] This seems unusual, given that Zahedi and his allies had already approached Henderson several times, and that Zahedi's son Ardeshir, who served as his father's key adviser, had good relations with the embassy's naval attaché, Eric Pollard. The two would occasionally meet, sometimes joined by Kashani's son. The problem was that whenever any Iranians approached the embassy with a scheme to overthrow Mossadeq, the standard American response had been that the United States did not take a position on Iran's internal affairs. It is difficult to recruit assets or develop networks with a policy of non-involvement. Not until July was George Carroll, a CIA paramilitary expert with experience in Korea, dispatched to Tehran to figure out the coup's military dimensions.

Whatever the scale of the American planning, Zahedi and his cohort were already moving on their own. The general had pulled together a military secretariat from existing opposition networks in the armed forces. The group included teams in critical sectors of the army and the ministry of war, all of whom were in touch with Zahedi through trusted liaisons. In addition to Batmanqelij, the group's more important members were Colonel Teymur Bakhtiar, the military commander of Kermanshah; Colonel Hassan Akhavi, who had a large network within the military, particularly in the counter-intelligence bureau where he had served; and General Ali Akbar Derakhshani, the assistant police chief. It appears that Zahedi was establishing military cells not only in Tehran but also in the provinces. Units from outside the capital were considered necessary because the plotters feared that Mossadeq's purges had ensured the loyalty of Tehran's garrisons. As it turned out, Mossadeq's government collapsed so quickly that most of these military contingents were not needed.

It was America's good fortune that it soon established contact with this group. Various coup narratives suggest that the United States was responsible for organizing Iran's armed forces against Mossadeq. This ignores the fact that there was already a substantial network within the military making its own plans. The royalist version of events is equally misleading: it denies any connection between Zahedi and the American conspirators. Most royalists argue that there was no real military dimension to the plan and that the "coup" was really a spontaneous uprising. Again, the military officers who plotted with the Americans believed their country was endangered by the prime minister's recklessness and that the chaos swirling around Tehran would only benefit the Tudeh. Like many members of the Iranian political class, they appealed to foreign embassies, particularly those of Britain and the United States. These men were nationalists who considered it their duty to save the country from a dangerous premier. They did not subordinate Iran's interests to that of a foreign power, as the Tudeh did, but were open to colluding with the Westerners to secure their nation's interests.

Once Eisenhower authorized the operation, the CIA began aggressively churning out propaganda messages against Mossadeq. The Americans planted stories in the press accusing him of being power-hungry, an agent of the Soviet Union, and an enemy of religion. At times, the propaganda took a strange turn, as when Mossadeq was said to have Jewish ancestry. At any rate, given the cacophony of voices already denouncing the prime minister, it is hard to see how these operations made much difference.

In assessing the propaganda wars, it is important to note that there were also plenty of pro-Mossadeq newspapers. The government, moreover, controlled the national radio, through which most Iranians got their news. Iran was, after all, a nation with more than 90 percent illiteracy. All sides had some advantages in the contest for message distribution.

Subsequent studies of the Iranian press at the time have shown a high degree of self-selection in newspaper readership. Those who agreed with Mossadeq read pro–National Front papers, while those inclined toward the monarchy turned to publications aligned with the shah. Given this degree of segmentation, the CIA-generated stories mostly reached those already opposed to Mossadeq, so the CIA propaganda machine probably had little impact. Radio was still the best means of distributing messages to a large swath of the Iranian people, and radio remained in the government's hands until the very end.

Kermit Roosevelt arrived in Iran on July 19, 1953. If his account is to be believed, he oversaw a gentlemen's coup. He moved into a fellow agent's home in a fashionable neighborhood of Tehran, and when not plotting a coup, he drank ample amounts of whiskey, sunned himself by the pool, and played tennis. He spoke no Persian, his agency lacked a reliable network of agents, and the lynchpin of his operation was a monarch famed for his indecision. But none of that seems to have gotten in the way of Roosevelt's considerable leisure.

Recruiting the shah took center stage. The embassy had assessed that "if the Shah were to give the word, probably more than 99% of the officers would comply with his orders with a sense of relief and with the hope of attaining a state of stability."[48] But the shah was still haunted by events of the previous July, when he had accepted Mossadeq's resignation only to recall him after the street riots. Mossadeq had taken revenge for that indiscretion by demanding control of the army as a price for accepting his old job. The shah feared that another botched attempt to oust Mossadeq could end his dynasty.

To stiffen his spine, the CIA arranged for a series of emissaries to visit the palace. First in line was the shah's gutsy sister Ashraf, who was enjoying a pleasant exile on the French Riviera. After being contacted by American and British agents, Ashraf returned to Tehran to urge her brother to rid himself of the troublesome premier. The news of her arrival prompted an irate Mossadeq to demand that the palace renounce her visit and send her back into exile. The shah dolefully obeyed and issued a statement stressing, "The Imperial Court of Iran hereby announces that Princess Ashraf had entered the country without prior permission and approval from the Shah. She has been requested to leave the country immediately after attending to some personal business."[49] Ashraf lingered in Tehran for a few days and eventually managed to sneak in a visit to her brother, but her lobbying did little to nudge the shah in the right direction.

The next visitor was General Norman Schwarzkopf Sr., who had trained Iran's police force in the 1940s and had a good relationship with the shah. He was ostensibly touring the Middle East on private business, a story that convinced no one. The results were the same: the shah insisted he could not move against Mossadeq and hoped that the prime minister would somehow fall on his own. Given that the parliament had already been disbanded, it is hard to see how Mossadeq could have been legally dislodged without the shah's participation. But the monarch preferred to dither and evade responsibility.

One of the Iranian coup plotters, Colonel Akhavi, now found his way into the palace and, unlike his predecessors, managed to make an impression. Akhavi showed the shah a list of forty-one senior commanders who pledged to support the coup, and gave him an unsigned resignation letter from Zahedi assuring the shah that he could dismiss him as prime minister at any time. The shah seemed intrigued; he had always distrusted ambitious officers such as Zahedi. But he remained unconvinced. Roosevelt would have to make his own journey to the palace.

In their meeting, the shah confessed that he was "not an adventurer, and hence, could not take the chance of one."[50] Roosevelt insisted that there was no other choice, and that if he continued to hesitate, the coup might go forward without him. This may have been a bluff, since the shah was indispensable to the coup's success. He was the only one with the legal authority to discharge Mossadeq, and he still had the support of the officer corps and the public. At this point, the shah suggested to Roosevelt that he could give the officers plotting the coup verbal support, retreat to his summer palace, and "let the army act without his official knowledge."[51] When Roosevelt flatly rejected this idea, the shah demanded some tangible sign of Eisenhower's personal support for the plot. This Roosevelt could do. He arranged for Eisenhower to declare, in an August 5 speech, that the United States would not allow Iran to fall to communism. This declaration finally did the trick. The shah retreated to his palace by the Caspian Sea and signed two decrees, one sacking Mossadeq and the other appointing Zahedi as his replacement. The coup was set to begin on August 15.

That the coup was coming was the worst-kept secret in Iran. The chattering classes of Tehran had been anticipating some kind of action for a long time. The pro-Mossadeq press was openly reporting that "the suspicious activities in Tehran of foreign agents during the past two weeks together with their internal counterparts show that a secret organization is hopelessly working against Dr. Mossadeq's government, and the American and British imperialists have not lost faith in the use of their last card."[52] Radio Moscow's Persian-language service warned that "the United States' military advisors and British agents have recently been very active in Iran."[53] The Tudeh-affiliated newspaper *Shojat* was even more specific, alerting the government in its August 13 edition that it must be ready to fend off a coup. The day before the operation, *Shojat* again warned that elements of the armed forces had joined in the plot with the shah and Kashani.[54] But the Tudeh did not just rely on its newspaper: its cells within the armed forces forwarded the details of the coup directly to the prime minister's office. And if Mossadeq did not believe the communists, he was also directly contacted by Mohammad Ashitiyani, a former official with ties to the royal court, who told him about the coup. It appears that everyone in Tehran was aware of Roosevelt's plot.

On the night of August 15, Colonel Nematollah Nasiri, commander of the Imperial Guards, attempted to deliver the decrees dismissing Mossadeq to his residence. Mossadeq, however, was waiting for Nasiri and had him arrested by officers still loyal to the government. Upon hearing of the arrest, the shah fled, going first to Iraq and then to Rome. The coup had failed.

Washington received this news with a combination of resignation and panic. The State Department acknowledged that the "operation has been tried and failed."[55] The National Intelligence Assessment, which pulls together the collective judgment of all U.S. intelligence services, declared on August 17 that "Mossadeq's numerous non-Communist opponents have been dealt an almost crippling blow and may never again be in a position to make a serious attempt to overthrow him."[56] Armed with this judgment, the CIA informed the station in Tehran, "We should not participate in any operation against Mossadeq which could be traced back to us and further compromise our relations with him which may become [the] only course of action left open to us."[57] It was left to General Smith, Eisenhower's crusty aide, to deliver the bad news to the president. Smith—who as Eisenhower's chief of staff during the

war was accustomed to giving him difficult news in an unvarnished fashion—
told him that the coup had failed and that "we now have to take a whole new
look at the Iranian situation and probably have to snuggle up to Mossadeq if
we are going to save anything there."[58] But the collapse of the coup did not
end the efforts to displace Mossadeq. For the Iranians, who were now the main
instigators of events, the struggle went on.

All the discussion of coup and countercoup should not obscure the fact
that the shah had the authority to dismiss his prime minister, and now that
he had done so, Mossadeq's premiership was illegal. The first issue that the
newly empowered Mossadeq had to address, then, was how to deal with the
shah's decree. At first, he wanted to inform the public of his dismissal and ask
them to take to the streets in his support. But after much back and forth with
his aides, he was persuaded, particularly by Foreign Minister Hossein Fatemi,
that he should not even acknowledge the monarchical command. In his trial
after his overthrow, Mossadeq took a different approach: he claimed that he
believed the decree to be a forgery and so not valid. At any rate, the subsequent radio announcement stated only that a coup had failed and all the
perpetrators had been arrested.

Roosevelt and the CIA station in Tehran suddenly found themselves in a
situation they did not fully understand. The station reported back to Washington that "the project was not quite dead since General Zahedi, the Rashidian
brothers and Colonel [ ] were still determined to press [for] action."[59] Roosevelt's principal contribution to the second coup was to organize a meeting
between Ardeshir Zahedi, Kennett Love of the *New York Times*, and Don
Schwind of the Associated Press. Roosevelt hoped that if the shah's decrees were
reported in the foreign press, they would get picked up by the local media.
Zahedi met the two reporters—who had been given copies of the decrees—and
assured them that his father was safe and was Iran's legal prime minister. The
plan worked: many Iranian newspapers such as *Kayhan* and *Mellat-e Iran* carried the story. Soon everyone in Tehran was talking about the shah's orders.
This hardly constitutes a nefarious plot. The CIA simply let reporters know
that the shah had dismissed his premier. The station and the Iranian plotters
understood that the monarchy still had appeal and that the dissemination of
the shah's command would galvanize the public on his behalf.

After the failure of the coup, the National Front and the Tudeh made a
series of mistakes that ensured the government's collapse. The question for
Mossadeq was what to do with a dynasty whose leader had fled the country.
Too often in the literature about the coup, the disorder sweeping Tehran is

blamed on the Tudeh's overzealousness or on CIA-sponsored gangs seeking
to provoke a conservative backlash. But the National Front must bear some
of the blame, since the radical slogans that now permeated Tehran were very
much its creation. Mossadeq hardly treated the failure of the coup with equanimity. Many royalist parliamentarians were arrested, and the Imperial Guards,
the force most loyal to the shah, were ordered to disband. The National Front
staged rallies with fiery speeches by the likes of Foreign Minister Fatemi, who
called for disbanding the monarchy. In response, the crowds yelled "Death to
the treacherous shah" or, less aggressively, "We don't want the shah."[60]

The newspapers affiliated with the National Front also took up the republican theme. *Mardom-e Iran* unequivocally supported a republican government. *Bakhtar-e Emruz,* which was edited by Fatemi, minced no words. One
of its editorials read, "O traitor Shah, you shameless person, you have com-
pleted the criminal history of the Pahlavi reign. The people . . . want to drag
you from behind your desk to the gallows."[61] And the Third Force, a political
party still affiliated with the National Front, had its newspapers publish articles calling for a different type of government.

The anti-monarchical displays and the calls for a republic may not have
been Mossadeq's idea, but the fate of the shah was very much in question. The
morning after the failed coup, Mossadeq met with his cabinet members at his
home to determine the national course. The surge of events was clearly pushing the prime minister away from his long-held preference for a constitutional
monarchy. By the meeting's end, he had endorsed a regency council that
would spell the end of the Pahlavi dynasty. Mossadeq informed his interior
minister that since the shah had fled Iran, it was necessary to form a regency
council. Traditionally, appointing such a council was the shah's prerogative,
but Mossadeq opted for another plebiscite. The local governors were told to
ready their provinces for another referendum. During those heady August
days, Mossadeq was being pushed by his supporters toward a radical position.

The Tudeh added to the disorder with its own blunders, which further undermined the National Front's appeal. On August 18, the party's high command
ordered its cadres to take to the streets and demand a "democratic republic." This
resembled scenes from Eastern Europe, where communist parties had come to
power under such banners. The Tudeh also released a communiqué: "The issue
of removing the monarchy and creating the Democratic Republic must be put
to a referendum, and a Majlis-e Mo'assesan, convened through a free and fair
election, should have the goal of modifying and completing the constitution."[62]
The disciplined Tudeh members then staged massive demonstrations, waving

red flags, tearing down statues of the shah, and getting into scuffles with shop-keepers and bystanders.

This leftist agitation was bound to provoke a counter-reaction in a nation still attached to its traditional institutions. Supporters of the monarchy now took to the streets, leading to repeated confrontations between the contend-ing camps. Too often in the literature on the coup, the violence is said only to come from CIA-purchased roughnecks from athletic clubs, even though the shah's supporters, such as Kashani and the Rashidiyan brothers, did mobilize their network of guilds and street toughs. But once the marches began, they took a life of their own, mushrooming in size and scale.

Crowds always played an important role in twentieth-century Persian poli-tics. The leading parties and personalities often used them to assert their power. The pro-shah demonstrations have been condemned because they helped re-store a monarchy of which the intellectual classes disapproved. But the scope and the intensity of the pro-shah protests surprised even those who were plot-ting to oust Mossadeq. Henderson offered the most useful assessment, noting (in typical telegraphic style) that "the demonstrations began in small way in bazaar area but initial small flame found amazingly large amount of combus-tible material and was soon a roaring blaze which during [the] course of the day swept through [the] entire city."[63] In its own assessment, the British Foreign Office noted, "The crowd grew as time went on and a large number of well-to-do people, who resented Mossadeq's government and specially his recent pro-Tudeh policy, joined the demonstrators."[64] Although Ardeshir Zahedi's partisan memoir has to be read with skepticism, in an intriguing passage he confesses that "an event took place that we did not foresee and had not anticipated. On Tuesday afternoon, throngs of people who were either concerned about the future of the country or ordered by the clerics started to battle the Tudeh in the streets."[65] The best that can be said is that the departure of the shah, the wide-spread distribution of his decree dismissing Mossadeq, and the militancy of the Left all came together to spark an apparently genuine expression of support for the monarchy.

The clerical estate played an important role in mobilizing crowds on the shah's behalf. The mosque became a venue for anti-Mossadeq agitation as prayer leaders exhorted the masses into action. The CIA station reported that "religious leaders [are] now desperate. Will attempt anything. Will try [to] save Islam and the Shah of Iran."[66] Kashani and Behbahani had already devel-oped a network to bring their supporters to the streets, and they now put it to good use. Many historians believe that the more esteemed members of the clergy, led by the venerable Grand Ayatollah Borujerdi, kept their distance from the politicized mullahs. The Islamic Republic has certainly promoted this view: its sanitized version largely exempts the clergy from complicity in the coup. But again, this is a simplification of a complex set of events.

It is true that Borujerdi did not issue a formal statement in support of the royalist insurrection, but that does not mean that the senior ranks of the clergy disapproved of the coup. The subtle ways of the clerical order at that time precluded such official declarations of allegiance. Mehdi Haeri Yazdi, the son of one of the founders of the Qom seminary, who himself interacted with high-ranking mullahs at that time, notes that Borujerdi believed that one "always had to have a positive relationship with the government" and that he would express his views and grievances indirectly, usually through trusted emissaries.[67] During the 1950s, the most important issues for Borujerdi and the upper echelons of the clergy were the Tudeh and the Bahá'í religious sect, which they viewed as heretical. The shah was more than willing to accommodate the clergy on both of these concerns in a way that Mossadeq, to his credit, was not. The monarch had made the prosecution of the Tudeh a high priority, while Mossadeq was prepared to tolerate its political activities. Two years after the coup, the shah launched a campaign to persecute the Bahá'ís that included attacks on their businesses and places of worship. It is inconceivable that Mossadeq would have allowed such acts of religious bigotry. The clergy lined up behind the shah because they were comfortable with a monarch who was deferential to their concerns and would do their bidding.

As important as the demonstrations were, it was the armed forces that finally ended Mossadeq's tenure. The army was dispatched to the streets by Mossadeq's orders, leading to much speculation about why the prime minister had authorized such a deployment. Given that Mossadeq considered himself the legitimate leader of the nation, it was not unreasonable for him to restore order. The coup had failed and it was time for Iran to get back to business. But the mood of the street may also have affected the prime minister's decision. By August 19, the street was beginning to swing toward the shah, leading Mossadeq to try to clamp down on protests that could have endangered his rule. His misfortune was that he chose a royalist army to suppress an increasingly royalist population.

Throughout this time, Zahedi was in his various hiding places, directing army units into action and alerting his sleeper cells throughout the military. Again, this action took place largely independent of the CIA station, whose crisp report back to Washington confessed that "as of night of August 13 CIA cut out of military preparations by Batmanqelij and Zahedi."[68] Many of the commanders who were ordered into the streets to suppress the demonstrations were part of the coup network, and their soldiers quickly sided with the protestors. As Tehran fell into Zahedi's hands, the interior minister informed Mossadeq that "the city is not good. The officers and soldiers are siding with the people."[69] The nationalist regime's tenure ended when rebel soldiers finally captured the radio station and broadcast news of the government's collapse.

Mossadeq initially went into hiding, but he was too much an establishmentarian to remain on the run. He surrendered himself to Zahedi's men and was treated with respect, as the Persian traditions at that time still mandated. Zahedi even advised the shah to pardon Mossadeq as a gesture of national reconciliation.[70] But that was not the monarch's way. Mossadeq was eventually charged with treason, and the prosecutors asked for the death penalty. Given his advanced age and his long service to the country, including the nationalization of the oil industry, his sentence was commuted to three years in solitary confinement, followed by permanent exile in his home village.

Mossadeq lived out the rest of his life in modesty and defiance. He even published a memoir that vigorously defended his conduct and policies. Although forbidden to see anyone but family members, he did at times correspond with his former aides as they sought to resurrect the National Front. By the time Mossadeq died, on March 5, 1967, the shah's despotism had long since escaped the constitutional limits he had tried so hard to impose on the monarchy.

It may be difficult for Americans, raised on a Hollywood diet of nefarious CIA intrigue, to appreciate how humble the agency was in its assessments of the coup. The CIA's internal study noted that the "flight of [the] Shah brought home to the populace in a dramatic way how far Mossadeq had gone, and galvanized the people into an irate pro-Shah force."[71] Richard Helms, then the deputy director of covert operations, noted, "My impression is that bringing the Shah back and putting General Zahedi in as Prime Minister were generally popular in Iran. It is also my impression that the crowds that came into the street in support of this measure came there wanting to see this outcome."[72] Earnest Oney, the chief Iran analyst at the agency, also stressed that "the operation channeled a support for the monarchy that was already there."[73]

Kermit Roosevelt may be the person most responsible for fostering the impression that America single-handedly imposed the shah on Iran. His unreliable 1979 book, *Countercoup: The Struggle for Control of Iran,* is debunked by the declassified record, but it still shapes popular imagination.[74] Eisenhower best captured the entire affair when, after sitting through a briefing by Roosevelt, he shrugged his shoulders and murmured that the whole thing sounded "more like a dime novel than an historical fact."[75]

AN ARGUMENT WITH NO END

The eminent historian Ervand Abrahamian once observed that "Mossadeq had come to power by the streets; he continued to remain in office similarly."[76] And it was the streets that eventually devoured him. Mossadeq's premiership exhausted a public that was hungry for stability. Since 1941, Iran had seen one crisis after another: the Allied occupation, separatism in Azerbaijan, and finally the oil nationalization movement. All the Iranians wanted was to reclaim their oil from foreigners, but given their financial stress, they were eager for an agreement. Mossadeq certainly commanded popular support at the beginning of his tenure, but his obduracy proved his undoing. The public goodwill is a perishable asset, and Mossadeq proved a reckless custodian of it.

The question that has haunted Iran since 1953 is what would have happened if there had been no coup. Counterfactual history is always hazardous because contingency and circumstance do much to shape events, but given the forces arrayed against Mossadeq, it is hard to see how he could have survived. What would have been the result of his planned referendum on the future of the monarchy in a nation that still respected that institution? Would the vote have been rigged, like the one that dissolved the parliament? It is hard to imagine the army, the clergy, and the nobility passively watching their national institutions disintegrate. To the contrary, as the Left grew louder and more strident, the guardians of tradition became more imaginative and daring. Many accounts of the second coup avoid mentioning that it was very much an Iranian initiative. A political class that had preserved the nation's sovereignty through foreign occupation and reclaimed Azerbaijan from Stalin now stepped forward and dispensed with one of its own.

Still, the coup did change Iran's politics. It gradually transformed the shah from a hesitant monarch into a despot who would gradually eviscerate the establishment that had served him so well. He never recognized that the reason he retained a measure of popularity was that he was willing to share power. The legislative initiatives of the parliament, the scrutiny of Tehran's lively press, and the prudence of the old-school politicians were not impediments to his power but the ingredients of a resilient system. A toxic combination of insecurity and lust for power would now drive the shah toward destruction.

Today, the precise events of August 1953 matter less than one's perspective on the nature of U.S.-Iran relations. The strained relations between America and the Islamic Republic have invited mutual blame. For many, the original sin was the most consequential one, and America's complicity in the events of 1953 means that Iranian grievances must be propitiated. Thus the mounting evidence of the complexity of the coup has to be set aside. Perhaps the argument over what exactly took place on August 19 will never end, but the balance of evidence suggests that it was more an Iranian plot than an American one. Unlike the first coup, the second attempt featured too many actors, too much improvisation, and too many unpredictable variables to have been controlled by a single entity. The second coup succeeded because the monarchy had ample support, and because both the political class and the public were fed up with Mossadeq's rule. The men who conspired against him were all nationalists trying to save their country and preserve its institutions. They had more at stake and more to lose than the Americans. And they would have moved against the premier even if Kermit Roosevelt had never set foot in Iran.

CHAPTER 5

The Shah's Emerging Autocracy

When he returned from exile, the shah was determined to start his dynasty anew. His sense of mysticism was on full display. "Once again," he noted, "the mysterious divine power came to my rescue, made my people revolt against Mossadeq and his forces, overthrew him, brought me to my country and restored to me my crown and Kingdom."[1] Upon hearing of the coup's success while in exile, he had exclaimed, "I knew my people loved me!"[2] God and the people had reclaimed his throne for him.

The monarch was now a man with a mission. Many years later, when asked whether the Mossadeq interlude had changed his character, he responded, "Yes, that is a fact; I was not going to tolerate any nonsense any more from any quarter."[3] He was going to rule Iran. The elder statesmen who served him issued their warnings, but their influence gradually waned. A few conspired against the monarch, but most were either cashiered or tried to adjust to the new order's demands for compliance and sycophancy.

The shah wanted power not for its own sake, but to realize his vision for modernizing Iran. He wanted to industrialize his country and redistribute land to the peasants. This task required a technocratic cadre with mastery of new models of development. The price for participation in the shah's march forward was blind loyalty. It was a steep price, but many were willing to become yes-men out of an ambition to serve Iran.

The problem for the shah was that the autocracy created by his father, which he now sought to emulate, was ill-suited for his personality. Ambition and hubris would drive him toward absolute power, but his inability to rise to the occasion in a crisis meant that others repeatedly had to step in. This clash of impulses eventually doomed his rule. He became, in a sense, a dictator with a dangerously passive streak.

All this would take time, because he still faced considerable obstacles. The aristocratic class that had executed the coup remained. More importantly, the Americans were skeptical of monarchical absolutism. The shah relied on America for protection from the Soviet Union, financial aid to revive his economy, and arms to build up his military. Many of the presidents the shah dealt with tried to persuade him that the best way to preserve his dynasty was to reform his economy and broaden his political base. America's record in Iran is hardly unblemished, but to blame Washington for enabling the shah's autocracy is to mischaracterize a complex relationship.

IRAN ON THE BRINK

After the coup, Iran was in shambles. Mossadeq had emptied the treasury and left the economy at a standstill. The parliament had been disbanded, and no one was sure when it would reconvene. Seeing clearly that the bureaucracy and the military had been penetrated by the Tudeh, the shah began a massive purge of both institutions. The National Front had been evicted from power, but many of its leaders were at large and still popular. The oil issue remained unresolved, and Iran's economy would soon collapse without a quick agreement. The United States was offering an emergency aid package of $45 million, but it had no intention of subsidizing Iran's economy for long.

In his first meeting with Ambassador Loy Henderson, the shah revealed an unusual set of priorities for a monarch whose country faced economic disaster. Henderson had sent numerous cables from Tehran decrying the shah's tentativeness and unwillingness to assume responsibility. But when the shah returned after the coup, Henderson reported that he seemed self-assured and strong-willed. In particular, the shah was grateful for Eisenhower's private message of support but proceeded to tell Henderson that he had foreseen his own return. He criticized the new cast of ministers and pointedly asked if Washington had advised on their selection. The meeting ended with the shah telling Henderson that he distrusted the political elite and wanted to empower younger technocrats. The army would be his, and he would no longer let any politician come between the palace and the officer corps. Henderson, while encouraged that the diffident monarch was finally ready to take command, tried to steer him toward resolving his country's mounting problems.

The shah was bound to clash with his prime minister. Zahedi had seen him flee in a crisis while the premier remained in Tehran and calmly guided the royal restoration. In Persian politics, such acts of courage and generosity are rarely rewarded. Nor did it sit well with a ruler seeking adulation from his subordinates that the general usually referred to the shah as "the boy" behind his back. But the most important issue was whether the shah should reign or rule, a subject on which he had clashed with nearly all of his premiers. Under Mossadeq the pendulum had swung too far in the direction of the prime minister, and the question now was how far it would swing back. The general tried to persuade the shah that cabinets and prime ministers were useful buffers who could take the blame for Iran's problems while shielding the monarchy. "One government will go," Zahedi told him, "and another government will be appointed and the crown will remain immune to any intrigues against it."[4] This was sound advice that the shah was bound to reject.

Zahedi did not limit himself to offering guidance to the shah. He had his own relationship with the Americans, having been among the legions of Iranians who had pleaded for the embassy's help in toppling Mossadeq. As the leader of the coup, he had impressed the White House with his daring and determination. Unlike the ousted premier, who had played up his ties to the Soviets, Zahedi informed Henderson that he had responded to Soviet complaints with a firm answer that so long as Moscow did not interfere in Iran's internal affairs, the two neighbors would have normal relations. He assured Washington that he wanted to resolve the oil issue quickly and was determined to put Iran back on track.

All this made the shah even more concerned. Barely a month after returning from exile, he summoned Henderson to the palace and told him it would be better "if Zahedi would realize that he had nothing to do with the army."[5] The general was not the shah's only target: he also expressed concern about the Majlis given the impending election. The conversation took a disturbing turn when the monarch allowed that if he had a reliable army, he would not hesitate to produce a "good Majlis" or dissolve the parliament altogether and rule as a dictator "until his programs prepared the atmosphere for a second round of elections."[6] It was still not clear to the Americans whether the shah had the courage to execute such bold plans, but their mere mention amid Iran's state of disorder set off alarm bells in the United States.

The message from Washington was that the shah should concentrate on the oil issue, not on palace intrigue or political maneuvers. The CIA warned the White House that despite "the removal of Mossadeq, the situation there is still fraught with danger and we cannot afford to divert our attention from the very serious problems confronting the regime."[7] Prodded by the analysis from his brother's agency, Secretary Dulles told Henderson that it was "essential that the Shah have no doubt regarding [the] firmness [of the] United States' support [for] Zahedi and our deep concern at indications [that] the Shah may be considering change [of] government."[8] Henderson, more than happy to deliver this message, told the shah that the United States still had confidence in Zahedi. After its tragic encounter with Mossadeq, the Eisenhower administration was not about to dispense with a prime minister who seemed both resolute and pragmatic. The shah realized that so long as the oil issue remained unresolved, Washington would stand by Zahedi.

Meanwhile, old problems lingered. Britain, which had pressed for regime change in Iran for two years, now took a somber view of its prospects. The British had been expelled from Iran and had their main overseas asset nationalized; now they were being forced to rely on American mediation that they did not fully trust. Then came a message from Eisenhower to Churchill: "I am impressed by the new approach of the Shah and Zahedi and I believe that if we can respond with something which involves a new look without abandoning basic principles, there is a good chance for a resumption of the old cordial relationship which used to exist between Persia and your country and mine."[9] Anthony Eden had preferred to move slowly on the oil issue, beginning first with the resumption of diplomatic relations and only then tackling the complicated oil dispute. The Foreign Office's concerns were only aggravated by the signals coming out of Tehran.

Despite Mossadeq's ouster, public opinion in Iran remained relentlessly hostile to Britain. The political class, which had always been attuned to shifting power balances, seemed to gravitate toward America and away from the diminished British Empire. Zahedi understood that national feelings were still raw, and he wanted some sign of goodwill from Britain before resuming relations. Declining empires too often view such gestures as a sign of weakness, and the always sensitive Winston Churchill was not about to pay to open an embassy that the Iranians had shuttered. Still, Britain needed its embassy if it hoped to reclaim the oil negotiations from the United States. By 1953, America was already mediating the dispute between Britain and Egypt over Britain's military installations in the Suez Canal. Now the Iranian oil issue was in American hands as well. London was concerned that Washington was using these crises to supplant it in the Middle East. Such anxieties may be natural to a junior partner unaccustomed to its new status, but there is no evidence of U.S. scheming against its Cold War partner. Henderson was spending most of his time prodding the Iranians to resume relations with Britain.

Washington understood that an oil agreement was linked to the resumption of diplomatic relations, and that the sooner the British officials returned to Tehran the better the prospects of an accord. The United States did not want Iran's financial difficulties to get worse and felt that stability depended on the resumption of oil sales. The State Department knew that it would be politically difficult for Whitehall to make any concessions so long as it was locked out of Iran. Henderson appreciated Iran's grievances against Britain but insisted to Zahedi that the priority was to stabilize his country, not to yield to the emotions of the street. This was what had undone Mossadeq. Zahedi seemed to understand, but he insisted on one condition before agreeing to open the embassy: no one who had served in Tehran before the coup could come back. Eden reluctantly agreed, and in December 1953 the two nations resumed official relations.

The United States focused on resolving the oil dispute. Dulles appointed Herbert Hoover Jr. as his special emissary to the talks. Apparently the Eisenhower administration felt that if the grandson of a president could restore Iran's dynasty, the son of another could apportion its oil. Hoover knew that the best way to get Iran's oil back to the market was to involve the leading petroleum giants, and he quickly resurrected the idea of a consortium. This meant that Iran would split the profits of its oil sales with a collection of Western firms. Even though the idea had been around for a while, it was received with suspicion in both London and Tehran.

Initially, the Foreign Office hoped to restore the AIOC's monopoly in full. This was an impractical idea pushed by the austere and tone-deaf chairman of the AIOC, William Fraser. Eden confessed that he did not want to be seen as "hustling the Persians unduly," but nonetheless thought it was important to see if the old imperial preference could be reclaimed.[10] The Foreign Office issued to its chargé d'affaires, Denis Wright, fantastic instructions: to inform his new hosts that given AIOC's experience, it was the company best suited to operate Iran's oil fields. Wright, who would go on to serve as Britain's ambassador to Iran in the 1960s, proved a judicious observer of the political scene. He quickly informed his superiors that "with the exception of the Pakistani chargé d'affaires who is not particularly bright," no one thought the AIOC could retrieve its monopoly.[11]

To be fair, the British government was often frustrated with the AIOC's maximalist approach, and the Americans were pressuring the Foreign Office for a quick agreement. London's need for Washington's support and the necessity of presenting a common front to the Iranians meant jettisoning some of Fraser's unrealistic demands.

The Iranians also harbored unrealistic expectations. Mossadeq was gone, but the spirit of nationalism he had unleashed remained very much alive. The Iranians insisted that any agreement had to conform to their nationalization law, which meant that the National Iranian Oil Company (NIOC) would take full control, with some technical assistance from the oil giants. The issue of compensation for AIOC's seized assets would presumably be settled along the lines Mossadeq had envisioned. The Iranian team even privately approached foreign technical consultants about how much oil the NIOC could bring to the market without a consortium. When the answer came back "as much as you can carry in your hat," they began to appreciate their technical limits and thus the need to come to terms with the Westerners.[12] After some wrangling, all sides agreed to a consortium. The real issues were how much compensation the group would receive and how it would interact with the NIOC.

Iran's negotiating team was led by the capable Ali Amini, the minister of economic affairs who had served in both Qavam's and Mossadeq's cabinets. The shah stayed away from the talks because he knew the final agreement was bound to be controversial. The nationalization movement had failed, but it did implant the idea that the AIOC was the root of all Iran's problems. The monarch was happy to leave the negotiations to Zahedi and Amini, who would presumably take the blame while he reaped the benefits of a revived economy.

The first question that all the parties had to address was AIOC's share of the consortium. Eden pressed for at least 51 percent, a notion that both Washington and Tehran rejected out of hand. The resumption of diplomatic relations between Britain and Iran ironically worked to the AIOC's disadvantage: as Wright quickly informed Eden, London had to rebuild its ties to Tehran and "a reasonable settlement will do more than any words."[13] For his part, Zahedi wanted to exclude the AIOC altogether—a position that Amini rejected as impossible.

The final composition of the consortium did not live up to Britain's expectations. The AIOC received 40 percent of the shares, and the U.S. companies —Standard Oil of California, Standard Oil of New Jersey, Standard Oil of New York, Texaco, and Gulf Oil—got 8 percent each, for a total of 40 percent. The Royal Dutch Shell Oil Company received 14 percent of the shares, and the French firm Française des Pétroles got the final 6 percent. After much haggling, it was agreed that all the participating companies would pay the AIOC a total of $600 million for their shares of the consortium.

The next issue was how much compensation the AIOC would receive from Iran. The company's demand of 100 million pounds was rejected by both Hoover and Amini, as well as Britain's own diplomats. The newly arrived British ambassador, Roger Stevens, warned Eden that "nationalist principles remain sacred" and that Zahedi "cannot afford an agreement which does not look presentable."[14] The final figure was 25 million pounds, to be paid over a ten-year period. Then the participants turned their attention to how the consortium would make its decisions, and here Amini had little choice but to accept that production and marketing would be managed by the foreign oil companies, with little say from Iran. In the end, Britain came back to Iran's oil fields, albeit in a much diminished capacity, while Western oil firms retained a great deal of control over Iran's natural resource. The final arrangement fell well short of the original nationalization law.

In presenting the agreement to the Majlis, Amini sounded much like Razmara, when he had warned the parliament that given Iran's technical limitations, it had to compromise with the West. Amini assured the deputies, "We do not claim to have found the ideal solution to the problem of oil, or that the sales agreement we have reached is what our nation wished . . . We can reach the ideal solution only when we achieve the power, wealth, and technological means that give us the ability to compete with countries that are big and powerful."[15] This honest appraisal met with much hostility. The shah tried to blame Zahedi and Amini for negotiating a weak deal and let it be known he was displeased with the accord. Kashani, embittered by his exclusion from power, privately warned Amini, "Don't do this as you endanger your life and reputation."[16] Given Razmara's fate, this was no idle threat, yet Amini courageously chose to ignore it. The National Front mustered some demonstrations, and there were protests at Tehran University. But the Iranian public was too exhausted and too wary of politicians promising defiance to be summoned to another crusade. The Majlis endorsed the agreement by a vote of 113 to 5.

Despite the complaints, the agreement did serve the interests of all parties. The United States stabilized Iran's finances and pried open its oil market. The AIOC, which was despised across the political spectrum, was allowed to maintain a share of Iran's oil production. Tehran obtained an accord much like the one that ARAMCO had offered Saudi Arabia, and more importantly, it finally restarted its oil sales and began retrieving the market share it had lost during the embargo. By the late 1950s, the NIOC was moving beyond the consortium and transacting agreements with smaller firms to develop fields that the original accord did not cover. In these arrangements, Iran obtained up to 75 percent of the profits. The consortium agreement would be revised once more and then terminated in 1973, when Iran nationalized its oil for good.

With the oil issue behind him, the shah resumed his quest for power. He proved a melancholy dictator, confessing to a friend, "You know, there is no more lonely and unhappy life for a man than when he decides to rule instead of reign." The shah had made up his mind to "rule."[17] It took some time to stage-manage Zahedi's ouster, because the general refused to take the many hints sent his way. Zahedi could not understand why, after all he had done for the shah, the monarch was so eager to push him aside. The rumors of Zahedi's corruption, surely instigated by the shah's coteries, were a clear sign of monarchical displeasure. But the essential difference between the two men was that the shah wanted a pliable prime minister, not one who protected his own prerogatives. In 1955, Zahedi took the high road and accepted an ambassadorship to Italy, beginning a life of exile. As he left Iran, he is rumored to have told his friends, "poor Dr. Mossadeq was right after all."[18] Ironically, Zahedi's son, Ardeshir, remained a confidant of the shah, even marrying and later divorcing one of his daughters. Theirs was a friendship capable of surviving many family spats.

Amini was the next to be shipped abroad, after being given a more impressive ambassadorship to the United States. His aristocratic lineage, his ties to formidable prime ministers like Qavam and Zahedi, and his propensity to act independently had always aroused the shah's suspicions. Before leaving, he offered the monarch some sage advice: "You are a national asset. At this age you have gained experience and seen much of the world. You can serve as a national guide. Your interference in government will cause all of its shortcomings to be reflected on you."[19] The shah once more rejected this counsel and further displayed his lack of judgment by sending Amini to Washington, where he cultivated good relations with many American luminaries, including a young senator named John F. Kennedy.

Alā resumed his usual role as caretaker prime minister while the shah contemplated his choices. The British embassy reported that Alā was a perfect choice for the shah: he was "well over seventy years old" and "could not work for more than one or two hours a day."[20] His principal achievement as premier was to survive an assassination attempt that allowed the royal court to finally solve its Kashani problem. Since the coup, Kashani had been a cantankerous critic of the regime, issuing threats and calling for demonstrations against the oil agreement. The Fada'iyan-e Islam's failed attempt on Alā's life led to the execution of its imprisoned leader, Navvab Safavi. Whether or not he had advance knowledge of the attempt, Kashani also paid a price. He was briefly imprisoned and had to endorse the execution of Safavi before being released. Yet he would not relent on his intrigues. He even wrote a letter to Eisenhower complaining about the shah's emerging despotism. But his influence had waned; he could no longer marshal support from the clerical elders or the merchant class, who were still content with the shah. He died in 1962, just when clerical opposition to the Pahlavi state was beginning to emerge over the issues of land reform and female suffrage.

Zahedi's departure heralded the next stage in the shah's evolving autocracy. The shah had always had the constitutional authority to dominate Iran's institutions and was now using those powers to put his own people in critical posts. He would dictate the choice of ministers, once the prerogative of prime ministers and parliaments. The planning commission, which made critical economic recommendations and had been a bone of contention between the shah and Zahedi, would now report to the palace. The shah also took control of the two most important national priorities, foreign affairs and oil policy. The functionaries at the ministry of foreign affairs often knew little of what the shah was doing, and the oil ministers now carried out his demands without question. To be fair, the shah proved to be a shrewd student of international relations and the global petroleum market. He brilliantly managed both portfolios and did much to make Iran an important actor on the global stage.

In 1957, the shah finally settled on Manuchehr Eqbal as his prime minister. A French-trained physician and a former chancellor of Tehran University, Eqbal initially hoped to restore the cabinet's authority. He soon gave up on that idea and confided to the U.S. embassy that his biggest challenge was "maintaining the confidence of the Shah."[21] He achieved this through cringing displays of loyalty and by publicly calling himself the shah's servant. He did not impress the Americans; the embassy thought of him as "an extremely vain man who is apparently more interested in becoming prime minister than [in] struggling with conscience."[22] But the shah welcomed Eqbal's self-abasement and proudly noted that he "was bold enough to admit at the beginning of his term that he was head of the government only as the executor of royal programs and policies."[23] Eqbal epitomized the new type of politician in Iran: ambitious and concerned primarily with catering to the monarch's mandates.

The atmosphere of repression became even more acute with the creation of the secret police, Sazman-e Ettela'at va Amniyat-e Keshvar (SAVAK), in

1957. SAVAK's origins had much to do with Washington's concerns that the intelligence apparatus was too dispersed among the police, the army, and the gendarmerie to deal effectively with the Tudeh and other oppositionist elements. As early as 1955, the embassy stressed "that the Iranian Government [should] be encouraged to strengthen its police-type forces, particularly their capabilities for detecting and coping with subversion, and to improve coordination among all internal security forces."[24]

Both the United States and Israel were intimately involved in creating the organization, providing technical assistance, and training its personnel. SAVAK was eventually divided into nine departments and took on both internal security and foreign intelligence collection. It was the Third Bureau that dealt with the regime's opponents and would be charged with torture. SAVAK ostensibly reported to the prime minister, but over the years the shah became its primary, if not exclusive, client. The shah met with the head of SAVAK twice a week to go over all aspects of its operations. SAVAK was never as ruthless or effective as its critics claimed, but its creation signaled that dissent in Iran was increasingly equated with treason.

SAVAK's first director was General Teymur Bakhtiar, a ruthless and ambitious officer who was promoted rapidly after his participation in the 1953 coup. His principal mission was to dismantle the Tudeh apparatus that had so effectively penetrated the armed forces. By the Tudeh's estimate, approximately one out of every ten officers was a party member.[25] SAVAK, then, not only purged Tudeh members from the military but decimated the party altogether. Ironically, the National Front was given more leniency. The party attempted to revive itself with new leaders such as Allahyar Saleh and Karim Sanjabi, but it limited itself to advocating reforms and generally kept a low profile. It would regroup in 1960 and take advantage of the brief liberal interlude to once more enter electoral politics, but its internal divisions kept it from any meaningful role in national affairs.

The political order emerging in Iran caused concern in both Washington and London. One National Intelligence Estimate noted that the "regime has been unsuccessful in developing a solid basis of popular support and in fact has actually lost ground in this regard since the events of 1953." The report warned that "because of the Shah's assumption of responsibility for government policy, future opposition and reform movements are likely to include him as a target and to take on a more revolutionary cast than in the past."[26] In London, the venerable Ann Lambton, buoyed by her early prediction that Mossadeq could not be dealt with, was summoned to the Foreign Office.

There she offered a scathing view of the shah. "Persia is adrift," she insisted, and the shah could not rule, but "will not let anyone else do it." In essence, he was a "dictator who could not dictate."[27] Both the United States and Britain decided to stick with him for the time being, and to pressure him to implement the necessary reforms. Meanwhile, Middle East politics offered him an opportunity to enhance his stature both at home and abroad.

POSITIVE NATIONALISM

Since his ascension to the throne, the shah had pleaded with America's presidents, secretaries of state, and ambassadors for weapons. If the military was to be the essential pillar of his rule, it had to be expanded and heavily armed. Successive U.S. administrations had denied many of his requests and advised him to concentrate on internal reforms. America did offer military packages, but they were always too modest for the shah. In the aftermath of the coup, as he contemplated dispensing with the existing elite, his need for a robust army became even more urgent. Eisenhower's attempt to build up regional defense networks along the periphery of the Soviet Union offered the shah another avenue for asking for arms. The monarch's embrace of anti-communism had as much to do with his fears of the Soviet Union as with his attempt to fortify his domestic standing.

For decades, Iran's statesmen had tried to manipulate great-power rivalries to their advantage. Mossadeq had rejected this model: his notion of negative equilibrium called for Iran to exempt itself from the Cold War competition altogether. He insisted that neutralism was the best way of ensuring Iran's independence. After the coup, the shah revamped Iran's international orientation with his idea of "positive nationalism." Iran had to take sides in the Cold War, and for the shah that meant embracing the United States. He castigated the Soviet Union as the source of "the new imperialism—the new totalitarian imperialism—that the world's less developed countries today have most to fear."[28]

The tilt toward America was not just about ensuring Iran's territorial integrity. It also had much to do with the shah's expansive definition of security. While Iran was threatened by a Soviet invasion, his regime was endangered by the Tudeh. The party had gained a foothold in his army and appealed to the intelligentsia and the emerging middle class. For a leader who sought to modernize his country, America offered a much more appealing model than Soviet communism. The containment of Russia and the destruction of the Tudeh thus went hand-in-hand. In a bipolar global environment, Iran could no longer stand aside and play the great powers off each other as Persian statesmen had done in the past. The shah saw Stalin's attempt to carve out the northern province of Azerbaijan in 1946 as an act of treachery, and he would often remind Soviet diplomats of it. His anti-communism and his desire to make the army the foundation of his power required a steady superpower patron.

Iran's new foreign policy became evident when the shah agitated to join the Baghdad Pact. The pact was the brainchild of an Eisenhower administration that was trying to encircle the Soviet Union with pro-Western alliances. The fiscally prudent president wanted to tap into the local manpower as a way of containing the Soviets while keeping the U.S. military budget under control, a goal that became more urgent when Khrushchev made appealing to the Third World a high priority. These alliances, created in Asia, Latin America, and the Middle East, were all modeled on NATO but were less successful. The Middle Eastern offshoot, created in 1955, soon became embroiled in the toxic politics of the Arab world. In the 1950s, the United States was still seeking to come to terms with Egypt's dynamic new leader, Gamal Abdel Nasser, whose pan-Arabism was seen as critical to deflating the appeal of communism in the Middle East. As we have seen, the Eisenhower team sought to channel post-colonial nationalism in a direction conducive to containment. Nasser, however, had no intention of joining the pact, and he tried to keep other Arab states out of it as well. To placate him, Washington limited the alliance to the northern tier countries of Iraq, Turkey, and Pakistan. Iran was seen as an important link in that chain but too weak to make a meaningful contribution. The shah, however, refused to be left behind. He began a campaign to join, because it could give him access to the U.S. armory.

The shah's eagerness to join the alliance created some tense moments in U.S.-Iran relations. He told Eisenhower that "in abandoning a negative and sterile policy, the Iranian Government and Parliament have made the conscious decision to turn their backs on this form of isolationism and join hands with the leading nations of the Free World."[29] Eisenhower demurred: he hoped the shah would focus on building his power through domestic reforms. Although his administration would be accused of "pactomania" by its critics, Eisenhower hesitated to accept Iran's request. The State Department stressed that Iran's acceptance into the pact might impose "an undue burden on its national economy." Dulles felt that such a move was "too soon after their troubles."[30]

In the end, America had no choice but to grant Iran's demand. The curious aspect of the American and Iranian deliberations over the pact is how little they had to do with containment of the Soviet Union. The shah viewed membership as yet another step in cementing his relationship with the United States and disabusing the Americans of the notion that they could do without him, while the Eisenhower administration felt compelled to accept Iran for "psychological reasons," irrespective of its concerns about its capabilities. After Zahedi's departure, the shah was seen as the linchpin of Iran's stability, and his moods and ambitions had to be considered. Allen Dulles warned his brother, "Iranian political and popular opinion would tend to interpret the Shah's failure to obtain satisfaction from the U.S. on the military aid issue as an indication that U.S. interest in the future of Iran and U.S. support for the Shah himself were diminishing. This would encourage the revival of anti-regime elements and might facilitate the eventual emergence of another Mossadeq-type government backed by fanatical nationalist elements and the Communists."[31]

Worried about neutralist trends in the developing world, the United States felt it needed to encourage the shah's move away from Mossadeq's negative equilibrium. The shah often complained to U.S. officials that Nasser's Egypt, which had proclaimed non-alignment, was getting generous assistance from both the United States and the Soviet Union while his dedicated anti-communism was not being rewarded. He had, after all, taken a decisive step toward the United States. Vice President Richard Nixon visited Tehran and came back with a positive impression, suggesting, "I think the Shah is beginning to have guts . . . if the Shah would lead, things would be enhanced."[32] Hoover, who became Dulles's deputy after his successful mediation of the oil dispute, echoed Nixon's assessment and warned that "the Shah had burned his bridges and come firmly to the side of the U.S. . . . whether Iran stays active on the side of the Free World or reverts to its traditional posture of neutralism depends a great deal on military programs and military development."[33] The administration knew that Iran was in no position to divert resources to the defense pact, but the need to lift the shah's morale meant they had to humor his imprudent request.

The shah and his American ally never agreed about the role of the armed forces. The Eisenhower administration did not see how Iran's army could be sufficiently strengthened to withstand a Soviet attack, and thought the shah's best option was to rely on U.S. guarantees. He should focus on developing an efficient military that dealt with internal threats and leave containment of the Soviet Union to the United States. The advent of the Eisenhower Doctrine in 1957, whereby the United States essentially took over the burden of safeguarding the Middle East after the Suez War discredited the British presence, was

seen as a further sign of American commitment to the conservative monarchies. Foster Dulles told the cabinet that he hoped the doctrine would signal
to the Iranians that "they do not need military forces on the scale that they
have hitherto been insisting they required."[34] To a monarch who never fully
trusted the great powers and saw the army as his most reliable constituency,
these arguments made little sense. Even after Iran joined the Baghdad Pact,
the two sides still argued about the scale of U.S. military assistance.

The attempt to gain membership to the Western alliance was not the
shah's only move. He also began to deepen his ties to Israel. On July 24, 1959,
while on a state visit to India, he announced Iran's de facto recognition of the
Jewish state. In the 1950s, an Arab Cold War descended on the Middle East,
with the radical republics led by Egypt pressing against the conservative order.
These inter-Arab conflicts offered the Soviet Union a path for entering the
Middle East, and it soon became the militant states' patron. Many in the region thought that radical Arab nationalism was the wave of the future and
that conservative monarchies would soon be swept aside by the tide of history. Israeli Prime Minister David Ben-Gurion tried to escape his country's
isolation by forging ties with non-Arab actors such as Iran and Turkey. The
shah seemed receptive, but he never fully embraced relations with Israel. He
often paid lip service to the Palestinian cause and usually voted against Israel
at the United Nations. Still, both countries were disturbed about the rise of
radical Arab states and obsessed with Nasser and his conspiracies. In a disorderly Middle East, the two states' ties were bound to grow.

Not long after a coup that nearly toppled his dynasty, the shah had compiled an impressive international record. He had forced his way into an
American-led alliance even though Eisenhower doubted that Iran could contribute much to the containment effort. Over American protests, he had increased his army from 120,000 to 200,000 men while nearly doubling its
budget. He had forged good relations with an Israeli state that was soon to be
a regional powerhouse. He had secured an oil agreement that was rapidly re-
plenishing his coffers. On the domestic front, however, the shah was about to
face some of his most vexing challenges.

ANOTHER COUP

The late 1950s was a time of transition, and the institution that perhaps
suffered the most from the shah's refashioning of Iranian politics was the Majlis. He diluted the power of the legislative branch by establishing a senate,

half of whose members were hand-picked by the royal court, and by expanding membership in the Majlis from 136 to 200 deputies as a way of attenuating its cohesion. The number of parliamentarians required for a quorum was reduced, basically ending the ability of minority parties to obstruct legislation by denying the chamber a valid vote. The venerable assembly was gradually being reduced to an exalted debate forum. Meanwhile, the elder politicians who believed in parliaments and cabinets were being replaced by a younger cadre intent on placating the monarch. These were not always incompetent men, although as the decades wore on they often lacked both caliber and judgment. Many were technocrats with little feel for the nation's politics; some were corrupt court jesters padding their foreign bank accounts. They all understood that to get ahead in the new Iran, one had to cater to the shah's whims. The scheming and backbiting that were endemic to Persian politics became even more intense as Iran became a conglomeration of personalities rather than a nation of institutions.

These shifting politics were bound to provoke concern in Washington. The United States had always urged the shah to undertake reforms and rely on a modern middle class as the best means of fending off communist subversion. His refusal to implement such changes and his obsessive focus on armaments led the National Security Council (NSC) to conclude, "If the present regime is to succeed it must capture the nation's imagination and confidence by providing in tangible ways its ability to cope with Iran's age-old weaknesses."[35] Given the lack of alternatives, the Eisenhower administration decided to keep supporting the shah but send him an unmistakable sign of displeasure. Relying on ambassadors to nudge him in the right direction was not enough. It was time for the CIA to get involved.

The shah was always concerned about American press coverage, and he assumed that the newspapers reflected White House sentiments. He often summoned U.S. ambassadors and asked whether messages were being passed on to him through the press. At times, too, he would use media reports to his advantage. When some negative stories appeared about Zahedi, the shah asked Henderson whether they signaled that Washington had lost confidence in the prime minister and it was time to dismiss him. The CIA decided to exploit the shah's sensitivity by planting stories in the New York Times warning of instability in Iran that could endanger the monarchy.

Beginning in January 1957, Sam Pope Brewer of the New York Times published a number of articles that jolted the shah. The first report noted that "Iran is in a state of discontent that is dangerous to her internal security and to the stability of the Middle East."[36] Brewer revealed that he had secretly met with opposition leaders, who told him that the "Shah was ignoring widespread corruption extending even to members of his own family."[37] In a signal to the palace that he was talking with U.S. officials, Brewer claimed, "Foreign observers in Tehran are alarmed about the danger of internal friction if the Shah does not find the means of reasonable compromise with the non-Communist opposition."[38] The CIA gave information to SAVAK hinting at its role behind the critical articles. The shah, who always viewed the *Times* as an official organ of the U.S. government, understood the need for some gesture. But his idea of reform proved superficial and self-defeating.

In spring 1957, with much fanfare, the shah authorized the creation of two parties, one liberal and one conservative, that he thought mimicked the American two-party system. Both parties were led by his loyalists, with Eqbal heading the National Party and Asadollah Alam leading the People's Party. Alam, a major landowner and a childhood friend of the shah, at times would distinguish himself by taking on hard tasks that the monarch preferred to avoid. It was widely understood that the two parties would not interfere in foreign affairs or military matters, which the shah had carved out for himself. Nor did the parties tackle corruption or political reform. In Tehran, they soon became known as the "yes" and the "yes sir" parties.[39] None of this was lost on the embassy, which reported that "almost everyone will admit that the two parties are phonies and rather than aiding the regime by serving as the first steps in developing a democratic government, their very transparency as window-dressing serves to feed the dissatisfaction of many politically sophisticated Iranians."[40]

The deteriorating situation once more led many disgruntled Iranians to bring their qualms and criticisms to the United States. This was not just the usual liberal agitation, as conservative politicians also told the embassy that the shah's current path would irreparably damage the monarchy. Even more ominously for the shah, some of the grumblings were coming out of his own army. The embassy now informed Washington, "More recently rumors have been circulating in military circles concerning [the] possibility of a coup."[41] The American diplomats were not just picking up gossip: the United States soon became implicated in another coup—this time against the shah.[42]

General Valiollah Qarani was the head of the military intelligence, and unlike previous rebellious officers he had no links to the Tudeh. He came from a devout middle-class background, and like most officers who stayed loyal to the shah in 1953, he was rapidly promoted. The shah, who seems to have been fond of Qarani, extended his portfolio beyond military affairs to take on domestic political issues. Qarani was not a typical product of the system and seems to have had doubts about the shah's emerging dictatorship and its tendency toward corruption and nepotism. He was influenced by his friend, the lawyer and journalist Hassan Arsanjani, and his reformist intellectual circle. Arsanjani had been active in politics for many years, serving in various Qavam governments and editing a crusading newspaper. He had close ties to Amini, who would also be caught up in the coup. Qarani felt that Iran's problems could best be addressed if the shah adhered to constitutional limits. His thinking mirrored that of the Eisenhower administration, which kept issuing reports and assessments on how the shah's despotism was endangering Iran's stability.

Qarani initially did not seek to depose the shah, only to prevent one-man rule. He hoped to force the appointment of a new cabinet headed by Amini, with himself serving as minister of interior. Arsanjani would presumably be the deputy prime minister in this new government, and the rest of the cabinet would be drawn from his list of contacts in progressive circles. In this new formation, the shah would once more be a constitutional monarch. But given that no one really believed the shah could adjust to such a diminished role, the question was whether these limited steps would inevitably culminate in the overthrow of the monarchy. In earlier years, Mossadeq had also started out pressing for recession of monarchical powers, only to end up organizing a referendum that would do away with the Pahlavi dynasty.

John Foster Dulles's plan to visit Tehran in January 1958 seemed to have triggered Qarani's approach to the Americans. The first meeting between the general and embassy officials was arranged by the CIA asset Esfandiar Bozorgmehr at his house. At that meeting, Qarani told the U.S. officials that "the present government has no popular support and is despised by the masses of Iranian people, particularly by the professional and intellectual groups." Playing on the Americans' Cold War obsessions, he advised: "it is urgent that a change in government be brought about now by a pro-Western group rather than waiting for the Soviets to take advantage of the present unrest and the discontent of the people." Bozorgmehr interjected that Qarani had "an intellectual group of 2,000 Iranians, 1,200 of whom were educated in the United States and the balance attended the American University of Tehran." The plotters insisted that the "Shah should reign and not rule," and it was important for Dulles to press this point to the monarch. When asked what else the United States could do, Qarani answered that "this meeting was enough for the present, and that additional contacts will be requested at a later date."[43]

The cumbersome declassification rules make it difficult to fully sketch out the coup, but there appear to have been additional meetings between the plotters and the Americans. The Dulles trip that was supposed to be the focal point of Qarani's effort seems to have passed uneventfully. But in early February, Bozorgmehr met with Assistant Secretary of State for Near East Affairs William Rountree in Athens and once more told him that the shah's current course would benefit only the Soviet Union. Bozorgmehr asked that the American and British ambassadors approach the shah and tell him directly that he "should reign and not rule." In addition, the "Majlis should adopt [the] necessary reforms required for Iran and take steps to see that they are implemented." The record of the meeting between the two sides is heavily redacted as are most of the documents pertaining to this affair. It does appear that there was at least one more meeting between Qarani and embassy officials in Tehran. The embassy informed the State Department that "it seems highly desirable to keep abreast of their plans and activities." The embassy also stipulated that "at the same time, every precaution will be taken to avoid involvement with them." Still, the succession of meetings and the involvement of high-ranking officials could have signaled to the Iranians that the United States approved of their plans.[44]

It is hard to see how Qarani thought he could succeed, given that part of his mission involved conspiring with a wide range of political figures, Majlis deputies, and even newspaper editors. SAVAK was bound to get wind of it. Qarani seems to have thought he could conceal his true intention by telling the shah he was pretending to plot against him in order to expose the true subversives. This probably worked for a while, but the meetings with the U.S. officials, particularly the one in Athens, were bound to arouse the monarch's suspicion. At any rate, on February 27, Qarani and thirty-eight of his accomplices were finally arrested. (The general's strange story did not end there: he was given a three-year sentence, after which he operated a construction business for a while, only to be arrested again in the mid-1960s for anti-government activities. Qarani next resurfaced after the revolution, serving as the Islamic Republic's army chief of staff, only to be assassinated on April 23, 1979, by a radical Islamist group that targeted many of the regime's officials.)

An even more intriguing subplot is Amini's role in the coup. Qarani had hoped that Amini would lead the post-coup government. And Arsanjani, who was close to Amini, spent a few weeks in prison for his part in the plot. In his various testimonials after the revolution, Amini conceded that Arsanjani may have been implicated in the coup but denied his own complicity.[45] At any rate, the shah, who always distrusted Amini, believed he was involved in the plot. Recalling the incident to SAVAK's deputy director, General Hassan Alavi-Kia, the shah, who seemed to have had a soft spot for Qarani, mused, "Is the ministry of interior really worth conspiring with foreigners and Amini?"[46] Three years after the coup, Amini would return to government as prime minister while Arsanjani became the architect of the land-reform program.

Although the 1953 coup has captured the popular imagination, hardly anyone recalls the 1958 conspiracy against the shah. Given the available documentary evidence, it can be said that the United States was certainly aware of it and did nothing to stop it. The U.S. officials who met with the plotters did not dissuade them from their plan, nor did they tell the shah about the coup. In 1958, the Eisenhower administration was certainly frustrated with the shah and had instigated a propaganda campaign against him through the *New York Times*. How far Washington would have gone if the coup was not aborted is hard to say. Still, its legacy haunted both America and Iran as they sought to pick up the pieces.

After the scheme was exposed, there was much concern in Washington that the affair would damage relations with the shah. Dulles chastised his own embassy: "The Department [has a] serious concern that the nature of contacts with opposition elements which have come to the attention of [the] Shah, and [the] manner of [their] confirmation by [the] Ambassador, may have raised serious doubts in minds of [the] Shah and GOI [Government of Iran] regarding the intentions of U.S. toward [the] present government."[47] It was unfair for Dulles to cast all the blame on the embassy, since there is no way Rountree would have met with the plotters in Athens without the secretary's authorization. The diplomats had kept the department fully informed of their actions: this was no rogue operation.

Relations with the shah were indeed harmed. The monarch, determined to exact revenge, summoned Ambassador Selden Chapin and demanded that his embassy cease all contact "with any dissident or even opposition elements of the Majlis."[48] To his credit, Chapin rejected this demand, which helped shorten his tenure in Tehran. The next U.S. ambassador, Edward Wailes, decided to placate the shah by telling him he had instructed his staff to "avoid all contact with dissidents and doubtful characters."[49] The CIA station seems to have kept dealing with intellectuals and the media, but the United States was gradually cutting itself off from valuable sources of information.

Throughout his tenure, the shah was concerned that the Americans would plot against him as the great powers had plotted against his father. He now had what he considered conclusive proof of U.S. involvement in a conspiracy to unseat him. The coup would make him even more obsessed with America; signs of displeasure from Washington would darken his mood while indications of approval would lift him up. The episode also sharpened his increasing thirst for absolute power; he began to demand complete loyalty from his subordinates, which meant relying on second-tier functionaries. The shah wanted officials who had neither the daring nor the imagination to conspire with foreigners. The problem was that such lackluster people were precisely the wrong sort to manage an ambitious modernization plan.

The institution that suffered most was the armed forces. The military that the shah was building may have looked formidable, but it was a sluggish force increasingly commanded by mediocre men. The army was structured to prevent a coup: The service chiefs could not communicate directly with each other and had to go through the palace. No officer could visit Tehran without first asking for the royal court's permission. The shah had to approve all military flights. The mechanisms of control were suffocating, with overlapping intelligence services monitoring the officers' activities while the shah encouraged infighting among his senior generals. Insecurity permeated the ranks. The type of leadership that Zahedi and those around him had displayed in 1953 was inconceivable to the emerging officer class. The shah had made himself so central to the functioning of the armed forces that it was not clear the military could discharge its tasks if the monarch lost his will, as he did in 1979.[50]

DANCING WITH KHRUSHCHEV

The year 1958 was difficult for the shah. Having survived a coup, he awoke on July 14 to the news that a group of officers had assumed power in Iraq and decapitated the monarchy. The grisly scenes of the mutilated bodies of Iraqi royal family members being dragged through the streets of Baghdad were shocking and frightening to him. Tehran went on high alert, and the security around the royal palace was beefed up. The occasion was not without its comic moments. CIA station chief Colonel Gratian Yatsevitch recalled that after the events in Iraq, "Ardeshir Zahedi decided to sleep outside the Shah's door to protect him in the event of a coup."[51] In his moment of distress, the shah even summoned the elder Zahedi to resume the premiership, but the exiled general refused.

The demise of the Iraqi monarchy had lasting implications for Iran. The tense relations between the two states began in earnest with the rise of the radical regime in Iraq. The two monarchies had gotten along well and had managed to mediate their differences. Now, instead of standing together in a pro-Western alliance, the Baghdad Pact was deprived of its seat and limped along with its remaining members—Iran, Pakistan, and Turkey. Over the next two decades, the shah and the Ba'ath Party ideologues who ruled Iraq would provide sanctuary to each other's opponents, contest their countries' common border, and even fight military skirmishes. After the revolution, when the vengeful mullahs decimated Iran's officer corps, another Iraqi strongman saw his chance to finally humble the Persians. Saddam Hussein's folly would provoke the longest war in the history of the modern Middle East.

The events in Iraq also jolted Washington and raised questions about the shah's durability. The White House commissioned a series of studies by the intelligence community that greatly distressed the president and his senior advisers. One National Intelligence Estimate concluded that if "there are no substantial reforms of the Iranian political, economic and social structures, we think the overthrow of the monarchy is likely."[52] American diplomats once more pressed the shah to broaden his government and institute important changes, particularly in land reform and taxation. So soon after the coup, this was hardly the reassurance the shah wanted from his ally.

Given the intelligence services' dire assessments, another NSC meeting was convened to determine whether the United States should look for alternatives to the shah. A somber atmosphere permeated the meeting with General Charles Cabell, the deputy CIA director who five years earlier had informed Eisenhower of Mossadeq's overthrow, flatly informing the assembled officials that "he could not discern at this time any strong character on the Iranian scene who could replace the Shah." Christian Herter, Dulles's deputy, agreed that the "Shah was the only rallying point to which the U.S. could look for the moment." Perhaps the most discerning comment was made by George Allen, director of the U.S. Information Agency and one-time ambassador to Iran, who stressed that while the shah would never institute the necessary reforms, he had no recommendations on how to fix the problem. For now, the Eisenhower administration decided to stick with the shah. The monarch, however, was not above sending his own message to the United States by courting Khrushchev.[53]

Following the Iraqi coup, the shah had been subject to a relentless propaganda campaign from Moscow, frequently led by Khrushchev himself. Having failed to dissuade Iran from joining the Baghdad Pact, Moscow finally saw its chance to unsettle the monarch. Khrushchev led the charge, claiming, "He [the shah] is none too sure, apparently, of the solidity of his throne and for this reason he keeps his private capital in Britain, and not in Iran."[54] What was most troubling about Khrushchev's indictment was that much of it was true. The shah seemed to be in both superpowers' crosshairs.

In 1959, the shah opened a secret channel to the Soviets, looking for a non-aggression pact. He had made a successful state visit to Moscow in 1956 that scored symbolic points despite achieving nothing substantive. As always, Khrushchev's inflammatory rhetoric concealed a pragmatic streak: he too was looking for an opening to Iran. He scolded the Politburo, asking, "What did we do in Iran? We put our troops there and started to boss them around. And when the smell of gunpowder was in the air and we had either to fight or leave, Stalin said we must leave before it's too late, and we left. We poisoned the Persians' mood."[55] The cagey Soviet leader, no doubt sensing strains in U.S.-Iran relations, may have thought that he could pull the shah away from the American containment network.

For Tehran, the talks with the Soviets offered an opportunity to annul the dreaded 1921 Russo-Persian Treaty, which Moscow had often used to threaten military intervention in Iran. Article 6 of the treaty gave the Kremlin "the right to advance her troops into the Persian interior" should Russia be threatened by a hostile power from Iran's territory.[56] Moscow had last invoked the treaty during the Azerbaijan crisis, to keep Soviet troops in Iran past the end of World War II. For his part, Khrushchev was not looking for an alliance with Iran, only its neutrality in the Cold War. He told the shah's envoy that "Iran would obtain more money from both the U.S. and U.S.S.R. by pursuing neutralist policies than the present policies."[57] The Soviet Union demanded that Iran leave the Baghdad Pact, or at least not sign the bilateral defense agreement that Tehran and Washington were then contemplating.

The shah's game was ironically similar to that of Mossadeq when he had hinted at rapprochement with the Soviets in order to coax concessions from the United States. The shah now summoned Denis Wright of the British embassy and complained about U.S. complicity in the coup against him. His participation in the pact, he said, had not gotten him the level of arms that America was providing Turkey or Pakistan, and he was dubious of American security assurances. He concluded the meeting with Wright by saying that the Americans were treating him as a "concubine and not as a wife."[58] The shah knew full well that Wright would pass on all these protests to the U.S. embassy. But given his well-founded fears of the Soviet Union and his obsession with all things Western, the shah was not about to leave the alliance. His problem was that the Americans knew this.

The shah's maneuvers made little headway in the United States. Wailes cabled the State Department that the embassy "believed [the] Shah's motive in entering the negotiations with U.S.S.R. was primarily [to] blackmail for more U.S. aid."[59] Eisenhower's famous temper exploded, and he told Dulles he would never give in to such threats. In a letter to the shah, he warned that "the principal objective of the Soviet Union in Iran remains unchanged and that objective is inconsistent with Iran's independence and integrity and with the security and stability of Your Majesty's regime." The president made his point clear when he told the shah that "almost regardless of the actual terms of any new treaty with the Soviet Union, the impact on your friends would be unhappy."[60] Instead of offering more military aid, Eisenhower reminded the shah that America always took Iran's concerns into consideration, but disagreed "about the size of the military program that should be maintained, and could be supported, without grave jeopardy to the Iranian economy."[61] Like Mossadeq's gambit, the shah's attempt to wheedle concessions out of Eisenhower by playing the Soviet card failed.

The shah's next step was to disappoint the other superpower leader. Khrushchev let it be known that he was prepared to drop his demand that Iran leave the Baghdad Pact and was ready to nullify the offending provisions of the 1921 treaty. His only request was that the shah not sign a defense agreement with the United States. The shah sought to resolve his predicament by informing the Western envoys that he wanted to sign agreements with both superpowers, a position that was unacceptable to both sides. He had come to a fork in the road and had to choose between the two great powers. He chose America.

Having failed to intimidate Eisenhower, the shah once more tried his hand at liberalization. To fend off American concerns about popular discontent, he announced that the 1960 parliamentary election would be free and fair. The two official parties were told to run energetic campaigns. More importantly, independent politicians and even some of the shah's detractors, such as Amini, were allowed to run for office. A revamped National Front entered the political fray after one of its new leaders, Karim Sanjabi, assured the shah, "We do not oppose the monarchy. We are constitutionalists and if His Majesty agrees to free elections, he will benefit the most from it."[62] The religious intellectual Mehdi Bazargan and Ayatollah Mahmoud Taleqani, both of whom would play an important role in the revolution, formed their own party, the Liberation Movement. The shah's mistake was that he refused to recognize that his critics still believed in the monarchy and thought the best way to preserve it was for him to yield some control.

Like the previous attempts at liberalization, the election was marked by massive fraud, including ballot stuffing by SAVAK. Protests once more rocked the capital, and the police were called in to repress student demonstrations at Tehran University. The shah tried to calm the situation by nullifying the election results and promising a clean poll in the near future. Eqbal was offered up as a sacrifice and he tendered his resignation, even though he was not the only one responsible for the election fiasco. The shah now turned to one of his reliable cronies, Jafar Sharif-Emami, whose knowledge of economics was limited to dismantling the planning commission and offering civil servants pay raises that the government could ill afford.

Ironically, while the shah was desperately shoring up his power, the head of SAVAK was privately complaining to the Americans. General Bakhtiar warned Wailes that the "present policies of [the] Shah and [the] Government are leading Iran toward [a] revolution."[63] Bakhtiar proposed a solution: he informed the Americans that he "favors a constitutional monarchy with the Shah's half-brother Gholam Reza as the most suitable successor."[64] Barely two years after the Qarani affair, however, Washington was not about to engage another scheming Iranian general. Bakhtiar would later resurface with more plots and conspiracies, which eventually led to his exile and finally to his assassination. Under Eisenhower, the United States had given Iran $567 million in economic aid and another $450 million in military assistance, yet the country was still coming undone.

As Eisenhower prepared to turn over the presidency to his youthful successor, John F. Kennedy, he was despondent about Iran. Giving additional funds to a government that would not reform seemed to him like giving money to "a juvenile delinquent to buy a 'hot rod' that might kill someone." In a remarkable confession, the president who had authorized Iran's 1953 coup admitted that "the situation there might be improved if the liberals could succeed in deposing the Shah and taking over the government."[65] The history of U.S.-Iran relations is not without its share of irony.

CHAPTER 6

The Age of Reform

In the 1960 presidential election, the American people turned to a young, charismatic senator who promised to "get the country moving again." The Eisenhower years seemed stale and stagnant and America was ready for a touch of glamour. Although John F. Kennedy's martyrdom has generated its share of mythologies, historians have come to respect him as an intellectually curious politician who was genuinely impressed by the power of ideas. Washington during his time seemed to dazzle, as the capital celebrated authors and cultural icons while offering room for professors eager to put their paradigms into practice.[1]

Kennedy inherited a Cold War that was rapidly moving beyond its familiar European terrain. As a senator, he had traveled widely and appreciated the Third World's importance in the struggle against Soviet communism. He also sometimes strained the Atlantic alliance with his critique of the French colonial wars in Algeria and Indochina. As for the Middle East, Kennedy believed that Eisenhower had wrongly tied America's fortunes to unpopular and ultimately unsustainable autocracies, a charge that was not always fair.

Kennedy's presidency would be consumed by the crisis in Berlin, the nuclear standoff in Cuba, and the simmering conflict in Vietnam. In the Middle East, the administration took its turn at peacemaking between Israel and its Arab neighbors and tried to settle the civil war in Yemen that was threatening to engulf the region. Iran, too, would present the new president with its own set of challenges and his intellectuals with an opportunity to test their ideas.

In the 1950s, many prominent American social scientists undertook the study of development. This was a Cold War–generated preoccupation as the post-colonial realm became the new epicenter of the superpower rivalry. These scholars surmised that the newly independent nations were vulnerable to communist insurgencies and thus their internal structures had to be strengthened. The task was to guide these nations toward the highest stage of development, as represented by Western capitalism and democracy. It was assumed that many of these countries were still trying to grow out of their traditional stage, and once they were moved to a takeoff point, their developmental trajectory would be immune from Soviet manipulation. Moreover, so the theory went, these societies could be elevated to that point only with American aid and expertise. The disciples of modernization assumed that America could diagnose a post-colonial nation's precise stage of development, then guide it onto the preferred path.[2]

This view of modernization found its most hospitable home at the Massachusetts Institute of Technology, and one of its most ardent proponents was the economic historian Walt Whitman Rostow. Rostow was nothing if not ambitious. While still an undergraduate at Yale, he had made it his mission to refute Karl Marx's presumptions about mastering history. His most important work, *The Stages of Economic Growth: A Non-Communist Manifesto,* nicely summarized the modernization creed. Rostow was not the only architect of this theory, but he was the one who brought it into the Oval Office. At the State Department and the White House, he insisted that reality conform to his paradigms. Modernization's most constructive application was the Alliance for Progress, a program of economic and technical assistance to Latin America, and the establishment of the U.S. Agency for International Development. Like many postulates coming out of the academy during the Cold War, it was eventually buried in the jungles of Vietnam. Still, the Kennedy administration seemed infatuated with the idea.[3]

Modernization would define the contours of the administration's strategy in Iran and even play a role in its advocacy of reform. While Rostow dealt with high politics, the official in the White House most responsible for the nuts and bolts of Iran policy was Robert Komer, a longtime CIA official who had also worked at Eisenhower's NSC and had seen firsthand that administration's frustrations with the shah.[4] He earned the nickname "Blowtorch" because of his aggressive approach to bureaucratic roadblocks, and he quickly impressed the president and his new national security adviser, McGeorge Bundy, with his crisp intellect and ability to get things done. An early and persistent critic of the shah, Komer would relentlessly pressure the administration to push the monarch toward structural reforms. In the annals of U.S.-Iran relations, he stands out as the most impressive official who ever dealt with the Iran issue. His analysis was always sharp, his understanding of Iran's murky politics was unusually comprehensive, and his projections were prophetic. Kennedy's would be the last U.S. administration to press the shah for judicious reforms, and Komer deserves much of the credit for this important episode in U.S. diplomacy.[5]

The shah did not lack advocates in the new administration, because the ever-cautious secretary of state, Dean Rusk, believed that only gentle nudges would work with the temperamental monarch. Recalling that time years later, Rusk said, "I was developing a resistance to these eager beavers who wanted to tell everybody else how to run their own business."[6] The eager beaver he had in mind was clearly Komer. Under Rusk, successive U.S. ambassadors to Tehran made assuaging the shah's sensibilities their foremost concern and essentially behaved as advocates of the Persian court in Washington. Loy Henderson was the last American envoy who had no illusions about the shah until William Sullivan arrived in Tehran in 1977.

A number of individuals outside the formal bureaucratic structure, however, had no hesitation in telling Kennedy all that was wrong with the shah. Supreme Court Justice William O. Douglas had traveled widely in Iran and had grown fond of Mossadeq, even giving him a tour of the Court during his visit to Washington. As he recalled, "I talked to Jack frequently about conditions in Iran and the corruption that was rampant."[7] Attorney General Robert Kennedy, his brother's closest confidant, had talked with Iranian students in America and had learned from them the many inadequacies of the Pahlavi state. Both men were strong proponents of pushing the shah toward change, if not off the stage altogether. Many of Kennedy's old senate colleagues also took a dim view of the shah. Frank Church, the Idaho senator who would gain fame in the 1970s for exposing CIA secrets, insisted, "All I know about history says he [the shah] is not long for this world, nor is his system. And when he goes down, boom, we go down with him." Hubert Humphrey, then a senator from Minnesota, echoed this assessment, stressing, "They are out. It is just a matter of time."[8] Senate Foreign Relations Committee Chair William Fulbright of Arkansas—Kennedy's first choice for secretary of state, who was ultimately ruled out because of his segregationist background—had his own doubts about the shah.[9]

The situation in Iran, meanwhile, continued to deteriorate even though its oil revenues had risen from $36 million when the consortium was first established in 1954 to $262 million by the end of the decade. But it was not enough. Iran relied on deficit spending and aid from the United States to sustain itself. The government was quickly depleting its foreign reserves while inflation eroded living standards. Strikes became a common feature of life: some twenty major work stoppages occurred between 1957 and 1960. Poor harvests, rampant corruption, and excess spending on the armed forces further stressed the national budget.

In Tehran, the shah was anxious about the new American crowd and its intellectual dispensations. He had hoped that his friend Richard Nixon would win the presidency and was deeply disappointed when he did not. He badgered Ambassador Wailes for an invitation to Washington, only to be told that the White House was not yet ready to entertain guests. He sent a letter to Kennedy with his usual complaints about lack of U.S. aid and arms. Komer, shown the letter by Bundy, exclaimed, "I would not give him a bloody nickel. His problems are internal more than external. He has always seen the Soviets and Nasser as about eight times larger than they really are."[10] Kennedy's response—drafted by Komer—did not ease the monarch's concerns but instead urged the shah to focus on internal reforms and on expanding his political base. In response, the shah decided to dispatch the head of his secret police to Washington for a firsthand assessment of the situation.

Bakhtiar was an unusual choice as the shah's emissary, given his history of scheming against the monarch, but he seems to have discharged his task with an unusual degree of responsibility. Perhaps the general was trying to get his own sense of the new administration, with an eye toward approaching the Americans at some point with his latest plot. His mission was twofold: to figure out what the new team was thinking, and to pass on the shah's grievances. The general insisted to Rusk that Iran was threatened not only by the Soviet Union but also by its neighbors Iraq and Afghanistan, and to remain secure it needed both military and economic aid. Rusk dismissed the notion that Iran was seriously challenged by its two neighbors and again stressed America's commitment to defend Iran against the Soviets. He told Bakhtiar that "an effective defense against Communism must rest not only on military strength but on the positive loyalty and confidence which depends on social and economic progress."[11] Bakhtiar's subsequent meeting with Kennedy yielded only a promise to dispatch his "ambassador-at-large," Averell Harriman, to Iran to lift the shah's spirits.

Harriman had not visited Iran on official business since 1951, when he had tried to convince Mossadeq to accept an oil deal. His return trip a decade later, in advance of the 1961 summit meeting between Kennedy and Khrush-chev, began more auspiciously: he was not greeted by protestors calling for his death. He assured the shah that the new administration would not sacrifice Iran's interests during the summit. Still, Kennedy's roving ambassador was not just on a mission to reassure; he informed the king that the new crowd in Washington was serious about internal reforms. For all his experience, Harri-man still fell into the shah's trap. After the meeting, he advised his superiors that if the United States gave the monarch the arms he wanted, "we should be able to convince him that he should concentrate more on his economic and social problems."[12]

In the spring of 1961, Kennedy had many other preoccupations. In April, the disastrous invasion of the Bay of Pigs tarnished his presidency. Then in June, he went off to Vienna, where he was browbeaten by Khrushchev. In the midst of all of this, the Iran issue somehow resurfaced. Khrushchev, still smart-ing from the shah's rebuff of his non-aggression treaty, taunted Kennedy that Iran would fall without his "moving a finger . . . It was going to collapse be-cause of corruption and inefficiency of its own government."[13] Kennedy could only mumble that "if the Shah did not improve conditions for the people, change would be inevitable."[14] All these conflicting signals meant that a task force was needed to thoroughly study the Iran issue.

The task force that was assembled was headed by Assistant Secretary for the Near East Phillips Talbot, but Komer was its driving force. The group's conclusions could not have pleased the shah. The task force recommended that the "U.S. while supporting the Monarchy as the symbol of unity and a stabilizing influence in Iran, more actively encourage the Shah to move to-ward a more constitutional role." It stressed the need for land reform, a more rational tax collection system, and better budgetary practices. The task force did not limit itself to economics, calling for the United States to "encourage the formation and growth of broadly based political parties in Iran." It also insisted that "the U.S. must actively seek to widen its contacts with National-ists and encourage those who give promise of providing firm and reasonable leadership against those who have developed extremist, anti-Western tenden-cies." These recommendations became the guideposts of Kennedy's policy toward Iran. It was time for the shah to respond.[15]

AMINI AT THE HELM

Strikes had become common in Iran, but the teacher strike of 1961 was on a different scale. Teaching was an exalted profession in Persia, where learning and academic achievement were prized. Yet inflation had been particularly devastating for teachers. The average teacher's salary, between forty and sixty-five dollars a month, had not kept pace with inflation, leading to strikes and demonstrations. The government had chosen to deal with the protests by sending the army into the streets, causing the death of one high-school teacher and injuring three others.

Nearly fifty thousand angry teachers gathered in front of the parliament building, demanding dismissal of the government. This soon triggered protests by other segments of society, with the bazaar closing and students shutting down Tehran University in expressions of solidarity. The shah relented, agreeing to wage increases and a health-care provision, but the protesters' anger had overflowed its proximate cause. Sharif-Emami became the shah's latest sacrificial lamb: his government resigned. Amid all his troubles with Washington, the shah was now without a prime minister.

The shah recognized that his choice of premier would be closely watched by the White House. There had even been murmurs out of Washington that he should reach out to the more moderate members of the National Front. This he found completely unacceptable. He had barely survived the Mossadeq interlude and still harbored grievances against the old man and his party. But neither could the shah summon another politician from his coterie of sycophants. His next prime minister had to have independent stature, possess a reputation as a reformer, and be held in high regard in Washington. The shah reached out once more to his nemesis Ali Amini.

The selection of Amini has generated its own controversy. Whose idea was it to bring him back to the government? Many have speculated that the choice was dictated by the Kennedy administration, and it was certainly unusual for the shah to rehabilitate a politician whom he not only disliked but also thought was complicit in a coup against him. Amini had gained a good reputation in Washington from his deft handling of the oil negotiations in 1954 and his later stint as ambassador to the United States. But much of the loose talk about Amini's appointment was generated by the shah himself. In 1974, at the height of his power and arrogance, the shah confided to Alam, "That idiot Kennedy once told me that Dr. Amini was the only hope for Iran."[16] Still later, in the bitterness of exile, the shah returned to the theme of Amini's selection, claiming, "The U.S. wanted him [Sharif-Emami] out and its own man in as Prime

Minister. This man was Ali Amini, and in time the pressure became too strong for me to resist, especially after John F. Kennedy was elected president."[17] The White House certainly wanted a reformer in that position, but the actual choice of Amini seems to have been the shah's. Given Iran's dire economic situation and its unsettled political scene, the monarch may have thought that Amini could mollify both his domestic detractors and the Americans.

Amini's premiership was in many ways Iran's last chance to preserve its constitutional order. He had served in several cabinets, and with his French doctorates in economics and law, he was finally ready to put his ideas into practice. He had long believed in the importance of instituting land reforms, dealing with corruption, and pruning excess spending—especially military spending. He represented the old political class but was attuned to the reformist impulses that permeated Tehran's intellectual circles. His tenure, however, would prove turbulent, his time in office too short, and the challenges in front of him too great.

Amini's negotiations with the shah about the scope of his responsibilities demonstrated the two men's differing ambitions. Having seen so many prime ministers fall, Amini asked for a clear understanding of how much autonomy he would have. The shah quickly retorted, "I will either rule or leave." To which Amini prophetically responded, "If you rule, you will leave."[18] The monarch kept the ministries of war, interior, and foreign affairs to himself. Amini insisted on dissolving the Majlis, because he wanted to tackle the contentious issue of land reform without legislative bickering. The remainder of Amini's cabinet would be an eclectic mix of traditional politicians, a repentant communist, and even a leader of the teachers' protests that had brought down the previous government. The most essential member was Hassan Arsanjani, who was put in charge of the all-important land-reform policy.

In Washington, the administration hoped it had finally found its man. Komer said to Kennedy, "Iran [is] now pretty far down the road to chaos, we had better do everything feasible to give the Amini 'experiment' a fighting chance, helping to protect him against pressures from both the Shah and the left."[19] Bobby Kennedy insisted to one of the shah's officials, "We believe in Dr. Amini's government, and as long as Amini is prime minister we will do whatever is necessary to help him."[20] This confronted the shah with a unique dilemma, because he wanted to undermine Amini while ensuring the success of the prime minister's land-reform measure. The shah still held some traces of idealism, and he understood that the redistribution of land was necessary for creating a modern society. He had started a land-reform program himself in the early 1950s, when he had distributed 500,000 acres of the crown's holdings to the peasants.[21] As a leader who wanted to get rid of the existing political class, he was tempted by the prospect of being the peasantry's champion and marshaling that force against his foes. Given that the peasantry then constituted three-quarters of the population, the shah was not averse to land reform. He was merely against Amini getting credit for it.

Amini established a number of goals for his government: dealing with corruption, distributing land, and reaching out to the National Front. The question of corruption was both endemic to and emblematic of the Pahlavi state. Most developing countries that come into sudden wealth suffer some degree of corruption, but in Iran a large dose of cynicism accompanied the age-old problem of graft. The shah tolerated corruption among his senior staff because it gave him leverage over them. SAVAK was notorious for collecting incriminating information about the shah's subordinates in case the palace needed to dispense with a troublesome official. On the rare occasions when a general or a minister was actually tried for corruption, the public understood this to indicate that somehow that official had lost the shah's confidence. The corrosive cynicism that permeated Iranian society would only get worse over the coming decades, as national revenues went up, budgets increased, and government contracts enriched those connected to the royal court.

Amini seemed serious about dealing with corruption. He dismissed over a thousand civil servants, had the former ministers of finance and interior arrested, and cashiered thirty-three generals and 270 colonels from the armed forces.[22] The purges, dismissals, and arrests continued and one year after commencing his campaign, Amini confidently told the *New York Times* that he had "cut down high-level corruption by 60 percent."[23] But graft did not end. The shah's Iran would be drowning in corruption for years to come.

In many ways, Amini was an unusual choice as an advocate of land reform, since his own family owned an estate nearly the size of Massachusetts. But he understood that failing to deal with the inequalities in the countryside might provoke violent change. He warned his fellow landowners, "Divide your land or face revolution—or death."[24] Despite previous attempts at reform, in the early 1960s nearly 70 percent of Iran's arable land was still owned by absentee owners, who often lived in urban areas and mingled in politics and commerce while bailiffs managed their villages. The peasants who tilled the land often saw little profit from their labor.[25]

The political implications of land reform were not lost on the major estate owners. The landed gentry and the clerical class had often mediated between the government and the peasants. They influenced the selection of candidates to the parliament and manned the various cabinets. The religious foundations, with their vast tracts of land, financed the seminary and its charitable activities. Land reform put both groups at risk of losing their revenue streams and thus their political influence. The system that had provided the Persian countryside with a measure of representation was now threatened by an unusual intrusion of state power in its financial prerogatives.

The government had introduced a land-reform bill in 1960, only to have it languish in the parliament. The landowning class that dominated the chamber resented being charged with feudalism and insisted that the peasants were not ready to take control of their own land. Any redistributive measure, they charged, would only reduce agricultural production and thus provoke migration to the cities. The idea that illiterate peasants could use modern agricultural implements, deal with the credits and commerce of agribusiness, and figure out the best means of cultivating the land was seen as absurd. The bill died amid legislative maneuvering.

The new minister of agriculture would have none of this. Arsanjani had championed land reform for decades and had used his newspaper to propose various means of distributing land, including radical measures such as expropriating all land belonging to absentee owners. In 1951, he had called on the shah to set an example for large landowners by giving away his own holdings. Perhaps to his surprise, the shah did so, issuing a royal decree giving many of his villages to the peasants. This may have been a symbolic gesture, but it did implant the idea that rural inequalities had to be addressed. The shah called on his fellow landlords to emulate his example, but few did.

Once in power, Arsanjani launched his reforms with energy and determination. Azerbaijan, with a large concentration of absentee landlords, was the first province chosen for implementing the new law. The existing land-reform bill had measured property by acreage, but the traditional means of assessing the scope of a landowner's holding was by how many villages it contained. In the first phase of Arsanjani's multi-phase plan, each landlord was limited to one village, and the rest was to be taken over by the government and then sold to the peasants already tilling the fields. To calculate the owner's compensation, the value of the land would be determined by its most recent tax assessment. Arsanjani also established rural cooperatives where the newly franchised farmers could band together into units large enough to obtain credit and loans from the government. The cooperatives were designed to wrestle the management of rural affairs away from the landlords.

The peasants who bought the redistributed land from the government could make payments over fifteen years; these were usually collected at harvest time to make things easier. The arrangement seemed fair, but some peasants whose families had worked the land for generations grumbled about paying anything at all. The cooperatives, which all the peasants had to join in order to get their land, would help with financial credits, marketing of the crops, and furnishing agricultural tools. All this constituted the first phase of the program, which affected about 14,000 of Iran's 53,000 villages and some 30 percent of the rural population.[26] In the next phase of the program, Arsanjani aimed to tackle the villages not already addressed.

There were some legitimate criticisms: the reforms were moving too fast, not enough time was spent on irrigation, and the financing issues were often confused. The reforms were not limited to large estates but sometimes affected medium-sized landowners who were hardly absent from their villages. The newly empowered farmers did not always know how to use the modern machinery and reverted to their old practices, which reduced production and so meant that some of the new independent farms were difficult to sustain financially. In some cases, government bureaucrats replaced the previous owners as the new overlords of the rural areas. In his public presentations, Arsanjani frequently castigated the landlords as bloodsuckers known for "drink and drugs and for beating and torturing the peasants."[27] Such incendiary language was not always fair and did not ease the reforms. By this time some of the landowners understood the need for change, and they might have been more supportive if Arsanjani had not insulted them at every turn. Still, this was the first time in Iran's history in which large tracts of land were distributed to the peasants.

Amini had power but no real constituency. The CIA correctly diagnosed his strategy as creating a "union between moderate Mossadeqists and moderate conservatives under a Shah with reduced powers."[28] By the early 1960s, the National Front was reviving itself. It resumed publication of its newspaper, it held a rally that drew perhaps as many as eighty thousand people, and it was once more appealing to university students, bazaar guilds, and the industrial working class. To cement his position, Amini reached out to the leaders of the National Front and assured them of his sincerity in fighting corruption and pursuing land reform. If he failed, he told them, it would be detrimental to all those seeking progressive change. It was a persuasive case that the Front could not accept because of its own internal divisions and its lingering resentment of Amini for having abandoned Mossadeq when the prime minister ran afoul of the shah. The dismissal of the Majlis was also too bitter a pill for the

Front leaders to swallow, even though Amini sought to explain that a recon-
stituted parliament would have throttled his reforms. Sanjabi bluntly told
Amini, "Your closure of the Majlis is a violation of the constitution. If you
understood the constitution, you would know that there have to be elections
three months after the Majlis is dissolved."[29]

The National Front's internal fragmentation diminished its influence. Its
more moderate faction might have been inclined to cooperate with Amini despite the limitations of his reform agenda, but some of its younger cadre, such
as Shapour Bakhtiar, who would later be the shah's last prime minister, favored
a more confrontational approach. That Bazargan's Liberation Movement had
split with the Front and articulated its own vision of religious modernism
further divided the nationalist opposition. To some extent these divisions were
always there, but Mossadeq's prestige and stature had managed to sustain the
coalition. Although the old man was still alive and in occasional contact with
his disciples, he could not exercise the leadership needed to prevent the movement from splintering. Amini would receive no respite from the Left, because
the Front could not allow itself to be seen as less progressive than the shah's
premier. To refurbish its credentials, the Front decided to tarnish his.[30]

In January 1962 there was another student protest, with chants of "resign
Amini." The student movement was led by the younger members of the
National Front, such as Bakhtiar, but it also had some support from the clergy
and from members of the bazaar who were concerned about Amini's agenda.
The students not only decried the land-reform measures as inadequate, but also
called for free elections and neutrality in the Cold War. In response, the army
and SAVAK personnel raided the university, bashing heads and destroying dor-
mitories, classrooms, and libraries. The esteemed chancellor of Tehran University, Ahmad Farhad, resigned and issued a blistering statement, "I have never
seen or heard so much cruelty, sadism, atrocity and vandalism on the part of
government forces. Some of the girls in the classrooms were criminally attacked
by the soldiers. When we inspected the university buildings we were faced with
the same situation as if an army of barbarians had invaded an enemy territory."[31]
At a time when the economy was still spluttering, the university riots further
damaged Amini's reputation and ended his flirtation with the Left. Many leaders of the National Front were now imprisoned, removing them from the scene
during the tumultuous protests that were still to come. But one constructive
result of these events was that they gave Amini the opportunity to remove General Teymur Bakhtiar as the head of SAVAK for his heavy-handed response to
the riots and his incompetence in failing to anticipate them.

Bakhtiar, still the same restless, scheming officer who thought running SAVAK was too small a job for him, now targeted Amini, who was proving vulnerable on all fronts. Bakhtiar had begun soliciting support from his fellow officers and had even approached leading landowners and clerics like Behbahani who were concerned about Amini's reforms. For now, the only thing this nascent coalition could agree on was its distaste for Amini and his enterprising minister of agriculture. Everyone understood that the shah was likely to scapegoat an official for mishandling the university protests—the only question was who would be offered up. Amini and Bakhtiar each viewed the occasion as an opportune time to dispense with his rival. It is here that the United States may have played a role, because it is difficult to believe that Bakhtiar would not have approached the Americans with his latest plot.

The U.S. documents from this period are filled with references to rejected coup offers, with hints that they came from Bakhtiar. In summer 1961, a National Intelligence Report noted, "The United States has not favored any Iranian military coup group. It has gone even further and, to the extent possible, has informed potential plotters that it does not favor such action, and intends to support the legal government of Prime Minister Amini."[32] Komer also reported to Kennedy that the administration must "forestall any military coup against Amini (e.g. from General Bakhtiar)."[33] Given America's declared commitment to Amini, Bakhtiar seems to have changed his tune, as yet another CIA report indicates: "Bakhtiar asserts that he intends to support Amini but will continue with his 'contingency planning' to be ready to act on short notice if the Amini government fails."[34] The university riots were certainly a sign of such failure, but it appears that the general still did not receive a green light from the administration.

The shah certainly had no reason to trust Bakhtiar, given his corruption and ambition. The monarch was campaigning to secure a state visit to America and was not about to remove Amini from power until he had gauged the mood in Washington. The shah was determined to prove to the new team that he was a true reformer with his own progressive agenda. Someone therefore had to pay for the brutal assault on the university, and that meant Bakhtiar. After sufficient prodding from Amini, the shah summoned the general and informed him that he had to leave the country. He seems to have left the door ajar for Bakhtiar to return to Iran at some point, but the general was not propitiated. Bakhtiar became the latest Iranian official to be exiled, but a quiet life in Europe was not for him: he began concocting plots with anyone who would listen, a list that at various times included the government of Iraq, the Tudeh Party, and disgruntled clerics. He was finally assassinated in Iraq in 1970 by a SAVAK agent.

The shah appointed General Hassan Pakravan as the new head of SAVAK. The appointment triggered a remarkable change in the organization, because Pakravan was an erudite, humane man known in intellectual circles for his love of poetry and Western literature. He informed the shah that Iran's problem was militants who embodied the "frustrated nationalism and reformist aspirations of the urban middle class."[35] At a time when the shah was entertaining conspiracy theories of all kinds and SAVAK was nurturing an obsession with the Tudeh, Pakravan was a voice of reason. The early 1960s were the high point of bureaucratic reform in Iran, with Amini in the office of prime minister and Pakravan in charge of SAVAK. Both men understood that the nation's problems were not limited to communist subversion, and that any further concentration of power in the monarchy would endanger the entire system.

THE SHAH COMES TO AMERICA

The year 1962 began with the shah once more agitating for an official visit to America. The monarch needed arms and wanted to make his case directly to Kennedy. In a meeting with the new U.S. ambassador, Julius Holmes, he even threatened to abdicate if he could not command a large army. He insisted that "the only real stability lay in him and [the] armed forces; that in order for Iran to succeed he required a loyal army with good morale."[36] Holmes, who was as sensitive as his predecessor to the shah's shifting moods, supported his request. The threat of abdication seems to have done the trick, and the shah was invited to visit Washington in April 1962.

For much of the year, the State Department had been issuing reports about the lingering problems in Iran. The Iran Task Force had met at regular intervals and called for supporting Amini and his reforms. In a typically trenchant memorandum to Kennedy, Komer insisted, "I still believe we are going to hell in a hack in Iran, and that our policy *is not* sufficient unto the need." The economy was getting better, but it was still hobbled by deficits and inflation. It was time, Komer warned, to decide "whether we will continue along this road or whether we will at long last make a determined effort to force the Shah to face up to the fact that his real problems are internal, not external, and that if he doesn't do more about them, his days are indeed numbered." Blowtorch was willing to sign off on a state visit because he believed that "only JFK will be able both to tell the Shah the home truths which [the] Ambassador obviously will not and to reassure him (with the Kennedy flair) of our unflagging determination to defend Iran."[37] The policy debate in Washington now focused on the issue of military assistance to Iran.[38] During its initial review, the Kennedy administration had accepted that Iran could maintain an army of 200,000 men. Upon further reflection, Bundy and Komer began pushing for a reduction to 150,000, with the savings to be used to help the economy. Holmes naturally opposed all this, because he was already being besieged by the shah for more arms. To placate the monarch, it was decided to combine the request for troop cuts with an offer of "glamor" weapons systems.

As he embarked on his third state visit to Washington, the shah had his own objectives. Once more, he hoped to impress upon the Americans how his country was being menaced by the Soviet Union and its many Arab proxies. His latest obsession was Nasser's Egypt, which he accused of funding his domestic opponents while seeking to colonize the Persian Gulf region. But because this was still the age of reform, the shah had an additional burden: he had to convince the Kennedy team not only that he was a reformer, but also that change in Iran could come only through the monarchy. He succeeded to a remarkable degree.

Given that the invitation was partly designed to lift the shah's morale, the trip was to be high on symbolism and pageantry. The White House pressed the reluctant Senate majority leader, Mike Mansfield, to have the shah address a joint session of Congress. He was also to give a speech at the National Press Club and meet with business delegations. But the trip was not without controversy; the shah was heckled by Iranian students at every stop.[39] He would encounter this problem on all of his future trips to America and Europe. The Iranian embassy implored the United States to deport the protesting students, a request that Bobby Kennedy's Justice Department summarily rejected.

At their first Oval Office meeting, Kennedy tried to express support for Amini in a manner that would not disturb the shah. The president complimented the shah on the "strong Government in Iran, including a distinguished Foreign Minister and an effective Prime Minister."[40] Given his chronic budget deficits, the shah wanted direct financial assistance, a position that was inconsistent with the Kennedy administration's new aid policy, which emphasized funding specific projects over budgetary support. Kennedy tried to convince the shah that the "development projects were aimed at achieving more sustained improvements in living conditions and therefore . . . political stability in the long term."[41] When the question of military aid inevitably came up,

Kennedy stressed to the shah that "no military build-up in Iran would allow Iran to stop a Soviet attack"; thus "a very large Iranian army was not needed."[42] The shah, pulling out his favorite trope for the occasion, insisted that America "treats Turkey as a wife and Iran as a concubine." The administration was well prepared for this line: General Maxwell Taylor, chairman of the Joint Chiefs of Staff, had already prepared a study stressing that Turkey got more arms because "It is a member of both NATO and CENTO, which gives us a double return on our assistance. It stands astride three traditional routes from Russia to the Middle East . . . It has much larger and more effective armed forces than Iran, which can absorb considerable equipment."[43] Kennedy casually dismissed the shah's request, telling him that he believed that "the main problem in Iran was internal."[44] The actual nuts and bolts of how much Iran's army was to be pruned were left to Secretary of Defense Robert McNamara to lay out when he hosted the monarch at the Pentagon.

McNamara, who was already gaining fame for his abstruse statistical computations and system analysis modeling, told the shah, "We believe it would be wise to reduce manpower levels by about 25 percent." With proper modernization of equipment, he added, a slimmed-down army could be even more effective. The United States was prepared to "undertake a five-year program for the supply of necessary equipment, if Iran would agree to so reduce the size of its armed forces."[45] The five-year military aid package would amount to $300 million. Once more the shah engaged in some haggling, and it was finally agreed that a commission from the Joint Chiefs of Staff would travel to Iran for a firsthand assessment. In due course, the commission conducted its survey and came up with a figure of 160,000 as the right force contingent for Iran. By the end of the Kennedy administration, Iran's army stood at 185,000 men, which in practice meant a reduction of 15,000 troops. This was not as deep a cut as Kennedy wanted, but it was the last time an American president succeeded in getting the shah to reduce his army. The monarch seems to have appreciated the zeal of the new American team, and he spent the remainder of his trip touting his commitment to reform.

The shah unveiled his new theme in his address to Congress when he told the assembled legislators, "We have framed a law for the limitation of landownership and the regulation of the relationship between farmer and landowner which compares very favorably with those of the most progressive countries."[46] In his speech to the National Press Club, he again insisted that he was committed to providing every one of his subjects with "free education, free health care, decent housing, adequate clothing and adequate food."[47]

These professions of reform seemed to have softened up Kennedy. The shah may not have been considered the agent of Iran's liberalization, but he was no longer seen as the main obstacle to its transformation. In their last Oval Office meeting, the shah tried to impress upon Kennedy the virtues of authoritarian-style reforms. He assured the president that he had a robust reform agenda in mind, one, he said, that was likely to alienate important power brokers like the landowning class and the clergy. The shah assured Kennedy that "he is not by nature a dictator. But if Iran is to succeed, its government would have to act firmly for a time, and he knew that the United States would not insist that Iran do everything in an absolutely legal way." Kennedy conceded that "there are always special factors that have to be taken into account in different countries."[48]

This was an important change in U.S. policy. Initially the administration had combined its focus on economic development with calls for greater political participation and had even discussed bringing the more moderate elements of the National Front into the government. But hearing the shah claim a commitment to economic reforms and a willingness to cut the size of his army, the administration shelved all talk of political liberalization. This was a mistake, for the shah's natural inclination was to create a docile authoritarian state. He must have walked away from the White House thinking that economics trumps all other considerations. To be fair, in the spring of 1962, Iran was not a high priority for Kennedy, who was dealing with an impetuous Soviet leader, a simmering crisis in Cuba, and civil wars in Southeast Asia. From Kennedy's perspective, the Iran problem, though not solved, had perhaps been put on the right track.

Once the shah returned from Washington, Amini's days were numbered. Despite his best intentions, his premiership was a troubled one, due in part to some headwinds of his own making. As the controversial land-reform measures got going, he focused on fiscal discipline and the anti-corruption campaign. He had the misfortune of being in office during a global economic recession that reduced the market for Iranian oil. He exacerbated this problem by publicly declaring that the government was nearly bankrupt and corruption was a disease that evaded a cure. This set off a panic, particularly among the merchant class. Amini's anti-corruption crusade had increased his popularity, but he lacked a solid constituency or a political party to buttress his power at a time when the shah was waiting to pounce on any mistake.

Amini next took a page out of his predecessor's playbook and implored the shah to reduce military spending. But the shah was not about to agree to further cuts. Amini's appeal to the United States for emergency funds, too, went against the administration's aid policy. As he was running out of allies on all fronts, Komer kept a watchful eye on Amini's fortunes, making one last effort to persuade Kennedy: "I urge as strongly as I know how that we base our policy on saving Amini if possible . . . he's the only good PM Iran has had in the last several years and the only one anybody knows of who can carry Iran where we want it to go."[49] But by this time, both Iran and Amini had become less urgent priorities for the president.

Amini seemed to sense that the end was coming. He confessed, "I must not stay around and wait to be thrown out, and the best for me is to go on my own."[50] On July 19, 1962, he submitted his resignation, which the shah accepted with alacrity and enthusiasm. Amini would linger in Tehran, holding his salons, lamenting Iran's mounting problems, and being closely watched by SAVAK, which compiled a huge file on him that the Islamic Republic later published.[51]

The shah appointed one of his confidants, Asadollah Alam, as the new prime minister. Alam could be counted on to offer the usual self-abnegations in the shah's presence, but his posthumously published diaries show that privately he had a more nuanced understanding of Iran's problems. He would not breach the shah's confidence or offer up solutions to the problems that he himself acknowledged were real, but he could be counted on to deal with tough situations that the monarch preferred to avoid. In many ways, Alam was a rarity in Persian politics: a sycophant with guts. The first issue he had to deal with was what to do with Arsanjani. The "trouble," he confessed, "is if we keep Arsanjani out, the foreigners will think we have given up on land reform."[52] Arsanjani was kept around for another six months before being shipped off to Italy to serve as ambassador.

The shah's dismissal of Amini did not provoke howls of protest from Washington: the administration was focused instead on ensuring that the shah carried out his pledged reforms. An NSC study concluded that with "Amini out of the picture, the Shah is the principal bastion of pro-Western strength. It is now even more essential that we reclaim his confidence and goodwill."[53] So Kennedy wrote to him, "I was sorry to hear of the resignation of your able Prime Minister, who had been laboring so diligently to advance Your Majesty's program of progress and reform . . . I feel certain, however, that with Your Majesty's support the new Cabinet will be able to make similar progress, utilizing the accomplishments of its predecessors."[54] He then decided to dispatch Vice President Lyndon Johnson to Tehran to bolster the shah while emphasizing, again, the message of reform.

Johnson, whose dislike of the Kennedy clan was more than reciprocated, treated the trip like a political campaign journey of old. He dashed into crowds, handed out pictures of himself, and seemed to genuinely impress the Iranian people with his curiosity and warmth. Komer accompanied Johnson on the trip, but the embassy had concocted a scheme to keep him out of the capital as much as possible by insisting that he go to witness the military's campaign against tribal insurgents in the south.

Still, Johnson had come to Tehran to reiterate the need for reform in light of Amini's departure. The Johnson "treatment," whereby he would press, cajole, and compliment reluctant senators to see things his way, had less influence on the shah, who felt he was finally in control of the situation. And Johnson could hardly wrap an arm around the shah's shoulder, poke a finger in his chest, lean in close, and refuse to let the smaller man go until he agreed to what Johnson wanted. The vice president did tell the shah that "the ultimate strength, prosperity and independence of Iran would lie in the progress made in the fields of economic well-being of the population and in social justice."[55] The shah seemed to agree and made all the right promises. Indeed, Johnson and the shah did end up establishing an easy rapport. Perhaps they found common cause in their mutual dislike of the Kennedys, particularly Bobby. For the shah, Johnson was the type of anti-communist politician he could do business with, even if they were not entirely on the same page about domestic change.

The shah would have been delighted with the message Johnson took back to the White House. The vice president informed his colleagues, "In Iran we must accept the Shah, with his shortcomings, as a valuable asset. We must cooperate with him and influence him as best we can, since we have no acceptable alternative."[56] Johnson neglected to mention that the reason the United States lacked an alternative to the shah was that the monarch was creating a political system where he was the only option.

THE WHITE REVOLUTION AND ITS DISCONTENTS

Amini's dismissal allowed the shah to dominate Iran's politics, a position he would not abandon until his final departure in 1979. This time, however, the shah came back to the scene as a revolutionary avenger on behalf of the masses. "If there is to be a revolution in this country, I will be the one to lead it," he insisted.[57] This was to be a transformation guided by the shah on behalf of his people—a "White Revolution," so called to differentiate the shah's controlled rebellion from communist red or reactionary black. The old structures had to be dismantled and the old elite retired. The land-reform efforts were to be incorporated in a new set of initiatives that included female suffrage, establishment of health and literary corps, and rapid industrialization. The shah would be at the helm of a dynamic state, manned by a new technocratic elite pursuing his agenda of change.

The White Revolution signaled a transformation of Iran's political order.[58] Since his ascension to the throne, the shah had relied on a conservative coalition of landed gentry, clerical elders, and army officers to sustain his rule. This was essentially the partnership that had preserved the monarchy in 1953. He now signaled that he wanted not to be another feudal monarch but instead the ruler of a modernized country. He was dispensing with his old alliances to usher in a new coalition of the urban middle class and the peasantry. The army and the SAVAK were to be the sentries of this new order. But in Iran's modern history, the peasantry rarely played a consequential political role, while the urban middle class wanted a representative government that the shah refused to deliver. In his moment of triumph, the shah and his American patrons failed to appreciate that the monarch was adrift, crafting a state without a reliable constituency.

The spirit of reform coming out of the Pahlavi state was bound to disturb the clerical community. The religious foundations, with their own tracts of land, subsidized the seminaries and provided upkeep for the mosques. While the land-reform law carved out some exceptions for the religious foundations, they were not entirely immune from its mandates. The shah's reforms threatened not only the clerics' purse but their overall influence. He wanted to expand state schools, establish more universities, and create a judicial system with secular civil codes. This would be a significant change: in rural areas, the courts were still largely clerical institutions that settled the disputes between the faithful, and religious schools were the main providers of elementary education.

The clergy were concerned about not just the government's infringement on their prerogatives, but also the overall direction of national affairs. The mullahs were at ease with a Pahlavi regime that defended their concerns and was traditional in style. The emerging autocracy, with its concentration of power, distressed them as much as it distressed other sectors of society. Their opposition to land reform was not just about self-interest; it also had much to do with the Islamic canons protecting private property. The secular pretensions of the shah's modernization drive, his membership in America's Cold War alliance, and his emerging ties with Israel were a source of anguish for those concerned about Western cultural influence. While the clergy and the court shared an opposition to Soviet communism and its domestic enablers, they parted ways over Iran's absorption into America's containment network. And the displacement of Palestinian Muslims in the Holy Land was something the mullahs often denounced from their pulpits.

The shah's reforms coincided with important changes in the seminary that occurred after the death of Ayatollah Borujerdi in 1961. As Iran's most revered and authoritative religious leader, Borujerdi had ensured that the clergy spoke with one voice, and all the other ayatollahs submitted to his direction. The fragmentation of the clerical order after his death led to a range of approaches to state power. Some esteemed members of the community, such as Grand Ayatollah Qasim al-Khoei in Najaf, stood apart from politics and focused on training the next generation of theologians. It was no surprise that after Borujerdi's death, the shah directed his condolences to Khoi, a traditional way for the monarch to indicate his preference among potential successors. The more moderate camp, led by Ayatollah Kazem Shariatmadari and Ayatollah Mohammad Hadi Milani, may have been concerned about the modernization program but still preferred to influence the shah through quiet lobbying. These men believed in the institution of monarchy and hoped to restrain the shah through dialogue and persuasion. At the far end of the spectrum stood Ayatollah Ruhollah Khomeini, who took a much more confrontational approach. He would soon reject the monarchy altogether in favor of an order where religion defined the national course.

Khomeini was politically savvier than many of his contemporaries, and he benefited from the changing complexion of the clerical community in the 1960s. The modest life of the seminary was increasingly being challenged by the temptations of the modern economy and the sprawling urban centers. The scions of the wealthy, rather than enter the religious orders, were opting for the prestige and rewards of the universities and the civil service. The new class of seminarians, largely from the lower classes, were parochial in their outlook and radical in their politics. They were predisposed to oppose a monarchy bent on modernization, which often meant appropriating Western cultural symbols, and offended by gender integration and the retreat from religious dogma. These men became Khomeini's disciples and would provide the ayatollah's main connection to Iran after his exile.

On January 9, 1963, in an address to the National Congress of the Farmers of Iran, the shah formally unveiled the six-point reform plan that constituted his White Revolution. He called for land reform, profit-sharing for factory workers, a literacy corps, and female franchise. The original six proposals would later be augmented by an additional six that focused on establishing health and job corps, state courts for the countryside, and nationalization of the waterways. Some of these measures had already been enacted by monarchical decree, but the entire plan would now be subject to a referendum. Even though Iran's experience with referendums was not happy, the shah decided that national acclamation was necessary for his proposals' credibility.

The second and third phases of land reform now got going. The Alam government's approach was more conservative than Arsanjani's and more attuned to the concerns of the wealthy. In this next phase, landowners whose property had not already been affected were offered several options for apportioning their excess holdings. They could sell the land to the peasants at prices set by the government; they could rent or lease it to them for thirty years; or they could form a joint partnership with the peasants to operate the fields. By the time it ended, in 1971, the land-reform program had achieved impressive results. Even the Islamic Republic has acknowledged that some two million peasants received land through the shah's reforms.[59]

Land reform was accompanied by an attempt at rapid industrialization with a new five-year plan. The state invested a great deal in the national infrastructure, knitting the country together with expanded rail service, new port facilities, and many more paved roads. Entrepreneurial activity was encouraged with low-interest loans from government banks. The state's investment in primary and secondary schools succeeded in raising the literacy rate from 14.6 percent of the population in the mid-1950s to 47.5 percent on the eve of the revolution. Improved health-care facilities led to a population increase, while the famines that had historically plagued Iran essentially came to an end.

To celebrate his achievements, the shah even published a book on the White Revolution, written with his typical mixture of arrogance and self-pity:

> Today, my people and I have a strong mutual bond, both sentimental and spiritual—there has probably never been such a bond in any place of the world. The root of his bond is not limited to my own firm will to devote my existence to the progress and flourishing of my country, nor to the trust which the thankful and noble people of Iran have put in the sovereign who has for twenty-six years suffered so many trials and tribulation, but this bond is based mainly on the nature and the spirituality of the royal function and the person of the Shah in Iran, an institution that goes back to very ancient traditions.[60]

The country seemed to be moving again, just as it was about to experience one of its most dramatic political convulsions.

There was much debate within the clerical community about how best to oppose the White Revolution.[61] The clerics feared that land reform and the health and educational measures would gain popular support. Some of the more hot-tempered mullahs denounced the shah's program in its entirety from their pulpits. Khomeini, who was as offended by female suffrage and land redistribution as his colleagues, demonstrated his political acumen by arguing, "We must not attack these bills, for they will use these slogans to turn the farmers and people against us."[62] It was best to focus on the unconstitutional nature of the referendum, the shah's emerging dictatorship, and his ties to America and Israel. The ayatollah was already looking beyond the seminary and seeking allies among disaffected leftists and nationalists. In the end, the clerical leaders came together and called for a boycott of the referendum.

To deter clerical agitation, the shah initially took a tough stance. He ordered his security forces to be ready for action and traveled throughout the country displaying his religious devotion by recounting the number of times that divine intercession had saved his life. He went to Qom and personally granted parcels of land to the peasants there. In a speech, he made clear his animosities: "They were always a stupid, reactionary bunch whose brains have not moved . . . Black reaction understands nothing . . . its brain has not moved in a thousand years."[63] The black reaction became his new favorite euphemism for his clerical detractors. The referendum, held on January 26, 1963, predictably received 99.5 percent approval.[64] It is entirely possible that the majority of Iranians endorsed the shah's program, but it is hard to believe that out of nearly six million votes cast, only five thousand were against it.

Ruhollah Khomeini was not a man to back away from a fight. Senior ayatollahs tried to defuse tensions by sending a parade of emissaries to Tehran to appeal for some compromise, but Khomeini scoffed at such gestures: "These gentlemen are not ready for a struggle, I'm afraid."[65] He was a rarity in the clerical culture, maximalist in his objectives and indifferent to the loss of human life. He implored his followers to take to the streets and protest the referendum.

The rivalry between the ayatollah and the shah finally turned violent in March, when the regime's security forces attacked a prayer congregation at Feyziyeh mosque in Qom. Commandos ransacked the venerable seat of Shia learning, killing at least three people. As would often happen during the revolution, the event soon gave rise to exaggerated stories and inflated casualty figures. But there was no gainsaying that the regime had violated the boundaries of the seminary and deliberately tried to humiliate the ayatollahs.

At a time when most of the leaders of the National Front were languishing in prison and clerical elders were looking for a truce, Khomeini emerged as the leader of the opposition. He quickly escalated the crisis by calling for the overthrow of the monarchy. "With this crime, the regime has revealed itself as the successor to Genghiz Khan and has made its defeat and destruction inevitable . . . The son of Reza Khan has dug his own grave and disgraced himself."[66]

In the ensuing propaganda battle, the regime's media outlets called the protestors mere reactionaries who opposed progress. Khomeini, whose speeches were being tape recorded and disseminated throughout the country by his followers, insisted that the referendum was a fraud and the shah was an agent of Israel who did not want Iran to live according to Islamic principles.

The monarchy's troubles were compounded by the advent of the month when Shiites mourn Imam Hossein's martyrdom. The processions through the streets and the sermons in the mosques all invoked the theme of pious resistance to the injustices of the infidels. In this charged atmosphere, a confrontation between a cleric and a monarch was bound to be subsumed in Shia rituals. Khomeini returned to Feyziyeh and once more denounced the shah in contemptuous terms. "You wretched, miserable man, forty-five years of your life have passed. Isn't it time for you to think and reflect a little, to ponder about where all this is leading you, to learn a lesson from the experience of your father?"[67] In the early hours of June 5, Khomeini was finally arrested, setting off riots throughout the country. And then the shah lost his nerve.

Although everyone had anticipated a reaction, the scale of the protests overwhelmed the government. Tehran was particularly hard hit, with marchers threatening to sack the parliament building and the radio station. The Ministry of the Interior was attacked, and symbols of Western decadence such as cinemas and bars were set ablaze. Some rioters even made it to the shah's Marble Palace only to be beaten back by guards. The royal family, having relocated to their summer residence away from the city center, were spared the sight of rampaging crowds attacking their home. The bazaars closed. Most ominously for the regime, the crowds reflected a cross-section of the society, not just traditional elements.

Despite his tough talk before the uprising, the shah reverted to form and seemed incapable of making decisions. When the cabinet met to decide its course, Alam had to take charge. The prime minister summoned the generals and told them to quell the riots, but they balked and insisted that they would take orders only from their commander in chief, not from a cabinet officer. Alam was in a difficult spot. The country was veering out of control, and the shah was not prepared to take responsibility for the violence necessary to restore order. In a dramatic gesture, Alam tried to impress the generals by placing a direct call to the shah and informing him that it was time to send the troops into the streets. In his book *Majestic Failure,* Marvin Zonis relates the resulting conversation:

> SHAH. You mean open fire?
> ALAM. That is the only way, Your Imperial Majesty.
> SHAH. But Mr. Alam, many people might be killed.
> ALAM. Yes, Your Imperial Majesty, but there is no other way to restore order.
> SHAH. Mr. Prime Minister, if that is your judgement and you are prepared to take the consequences of your judgement, you may proceed.[68]

As the regime confronted its most serious crisis since 1953, the old shah resurfaced, quickly abdicating his obligations and handing the issue over to Alam. This was a remarkable dispensation for a monarch who had resolutely refused any mediation between himself and his army. It was his good fortune that someone was there to accept the charge and execute the monarchical deed. In the end, 125 people were killed before order was restored.[69]

Alam would often remind the shah of this moment when he rescued the Pahlavi state. In 1973, as he and the shah reminisced about old times, Alam took the occasion to say to the monarch, "Remember, I said, how I told Your Majesty that I would hit them where it hurts, and how you laughed when I said I would give them the screwing they'd been asking for." The shah could only respond, "Oh yes, I remember it well enough. I shall never forget the service you rendered."[70] Both men thought the age of clerical dissent was behind them.

After his arrest, Khomeini spent two months in an army barrack and another six months under house arrest in Tehran, where he was treated with deference. Other clerics interceded on his behalf to ask that his life be spared, but there was little chance that the regime would kill an ayatollah whose martyrdom would spark massive riots. There appears to have been some loose talk in SAVAK about executing Khomeini, which Pakravan flatly rejected. Pakravan and Khomeini often met for lunch and discussed religion, philosophy, and affairs of the day. This was a humane gesture that Khomeini would repay by making sure that Pakravan was one of the first people executed after the revolution. Khomeini was finally set free in March 1964.

In Washington, the mayhem was ironically seen as an indication of the shah's stability. The embassy predicted after Khomeini's arrest that "should the disorder be repressed, religion as an active political force in Iran will have been dealt a mortal blow."[71] A month later, the embassy assured Washington, "Nothing can stop the 'White Revolution' now and certainly no reactionary groups can succeed."[72] Komer, a discordant voice, stressed that this was just a lull in the storm and that Iran would likely experience more turbulence. "I can't help but feel that we're paying too much attention to the tail and not enough to the dog," he warned in his usual vernacular.[73] His concern carried little weight. By then, Lyndon Johnson was in charge, and his administration had settled on the shah as its agent of change and dismissed his opponents as conservative relics who would soon be swept aside by his reforms.

The launch of the White Revolution did much to enhance the shah's confidence. Though he had needed Alam to salvage his fortunes, he was the driving force behind the reforms that launched Iran on its path of modernization and rapid growth. Yet the Pahlavi dictatorship made peaceful expressions of dissent nearly impossible. As he was being dispatched to prison in 1964, Bazargan offered his own warning to the shah: "We are the last to rise up to fight with constitutional means. We expect the president of this court to bring this point to the notice of authorities."[74] Such prescient advice no longer made any impression on the monarch.

A DENOUEMENT

After the year's disturbances, the shah did some housecleaning and decided it was time for a new prime minister. Alam remained very much in his good graces and would soon be appointed minister of court, but the shah wanted a younger man to shepherd his White Revolution. Hassan Ali Mansur seemed to have all the right credentials. He was the son of a former prime minister and had served in the foreign ministry, where he had always been on the lookout for a quick promotion. This was an era when Tehran had many discussion circles where ambitious young men would gather and wrestle with the world's problems. Mansur had set up his own group, called the progressive circle, which had attracted the shah's favorable attention. The monarch had even blessed the circle in an official proclamation and christened it the

Special Bureau of Economic Studies.[75] As a tool of self-promotion, the ploy worked brilliantly, and in March 1964, Mansur was appointed prime minister while still in his thirties.

Mansur's first task on the job was to deal with an imperious American demand. In March 1962, the United States had submitted what seemed like a routine request to the Iranian government. The note suggested that Iran pledge to offer immunity from prosecution to all Americans serving in Iran and their dependents. There had been a number of car accidents involving U.S. personnel, and the embassy wanted to provide all Americans with blanket protection. This essentially meant that all Americans in Iran would be exempt from prosecution under Iranian law for any infraction they committed. Amini, in his day, had the good sense to see the explosive nature of this request and had quietly shelved it. But when Washington raised the issue again with Mansur, the young prime minister lacked the judgment to avoid this trap and submitted the request to the Majlis.

The parliamentary bill immediately ran into problems even in a Majlis that had been hand-picked by the shah and was known for its docility. The Americans' demand was too reminiscent of the capitulation laws that foreigners had imposed on Iran, but the shah's father had abrogated. That Iran was at the time negotiating a $200 million credit for military purchases made it seem that the shah had traded the country's honor for a fistful of dollars. After a raucous debate, the Majlis approved the bill by a narrow margin of 74 to 61. All parties blamed each other. The State Department and the embassy, both of which had insisted on the blanket protections, blamed the Iranian government. The shah blamed his premier. And Mansur blamed the frightened parliamentarians. In another misjudgment, everyone assumed that with the passage of the bill, the issue was laid to rest.

The immunity bill was a ready-made issue for Khomeini because it insulted the average Iranian's nationalistic sensitivities. Many Iranians saw the bill not as part of a military agreement but as a claim by the United States that Iran's judicial system was too primitive to pass judgment on Americans. To a nation obsessed with symbols of independence, this smacked of the arrogant colonialism of the past. Khomeini was quick with his condemnations: "If a servant or a cook of an American citizen kills or pummels under his feet your *marja-e taqlid* in the middle of the bazaar the Iranian police cannot arrest him; the Iranian courts would have no jurisdiction. His file is to be forwarded to the United States so as to be adjudicated by the masters there."[76] The rebellious cleric seemed hardly chastened by his previous imprisonment.

More than any of his counterparts, Khomeini appreciated that the clerical order had to compete with leftist intellectuals for the allegiance of the youth and the modern middle class. Seeking to dispel the popular notion that the mullahs were the enablers of monarchical absolutism, he had broadened his attacks to include corruption, disparity of wealth, and Iran's ties to America and Israel—all of which were already sources of contention in the universities. Khomeini was ecstatic about the opportunity that the immunity bill offered him. "They can no longer call us reactionary," he exclaimed. "The point is that we are fighting against America. All the world's freedom fighters will support us on this issue."[77] To be sure, he did not abandon his retrogressive views on female franchise or land reform, but he could now emphasize different themes. The ayatollah had learned how to appeal to traditional elements as well as leftist activists, disgruntled students, and the middle class.

The regime's response was tough and unyielding. Khomeini was apprehended in the middle of the night and exiled first to Turkey and then to Iraq. His expulsion was followed by restrictions on the activities of even moderate clerics such as Shariatmadari. In an act of royalist vengeance, seminary students were made subject to the draft, and martial law was imposed on Qom and other cities. There were some protests but nothing like the uprising of June 1963. The lesson the monarchy drew from the crises of 1963–1964 was that its soldiers were willing to shoot at crowds. And these crowds were made up not of privileged university students whom the draftees from modest backgrounds may have relished repressing, but of devout men motivated by religion. After his previous hesitations, the shah grew confident in the coercive power of the state and more willing than ever before to rely on its security organs to maintain order.

On January 26, 1965, Mansur paid the price for Khomeini's exile. He was gunned down outside the parliament building. The assassins, members of the Fada'iyan-e Islam, had ties to Khomeini's circle. The shah responded by appointing another colorless functionary, Amir Abbas Hoveyda, as the new prime minister while General Nematollah Nasiri became the head of SAVAK. This marked a turning point in the history of the Pahlavi dynasty. During the first twenty-four years of his rule, the shah had appointed twenty-six prime ministers, an average of one every eleven months. Hoveyda, by contrast, would keep the job for thirteen years. He did so by perfecting the art of sycophancy and by deliberately exempting himself from sensitive affairs of the state. Nasiri was a corrupt and unintelligent man who made SAVAK as notorious in reputation as it was incompetent in practice. He too would hold his job for over a decade. The shah chose these men not for their ability but for their limitations.

Throughout the many layers of the Pahlavi state, a new technocratic class was coming to power. These were often relatively young men, usually in their mid-forties, who differed in background from the likes of Mossadeq and Amini. They were not bound to the landed aristocracy, which despite its limitations had cleverly gauged the nation's political temperature. Unlike the National Front leaders, who pressed for reform, they lacked a liberal temperament. This was a generation that viewed Western training as the main qualification for leadership. They had little time for the religious classes, because they saw Iran's traditions as a barrier to progress. They submitted to the shah and seldom questioned his choices or challenged his misjudgments.

In 1967, the shah held a coronation ceremony for himself and professed himself the legitimate representative of the Iranian people. "For myself, I am delighted and proud that today my people and I are joined by an unbreakable bond of mutual loyalty and love, marching hand in hand on a path of progress, happiness, and greatness," intoned the shah.[78] Over the next decade, Iran appeared to be a country on the move led by a modernizing monarch. The economy grew, the bureaucracy enlarged, new industries were created, and the middle class expanded. Oil revenues steadily increased, giving the regime ample financial cushion. The shah seemed to have finally tamed Iran. The institutions of the state, such as the Majlis and the cabinets, were shadows of their former selves, incapable of challenging monarchical fiat or mediating between the palace and the public. The landed gentry was dispossessed, while the Tudeh and the National Front were near extinction. The shah had stared down the clerical estate and dispatched one of its most esteemed members to exile with little protest from his peers. Yet beneath the veneer of stable progress there were signs of discontent. The growing middle class had no avenue for channeling its grievances or asserting its claims. Corruption was becoming endemic. A spirit of cynicism and alienation was descending on Iran, particularly on the universities, which became hotbeds of agitation. The shah had loyalists but few who truly believed in the system. The paradox of Iran was that it was a dynamic country that few wanted to live in.

CHAPTER 7

Master of the Universe

The shah was accustomed to giving illuminating titles to his foreign policy doctrines. In the 1950s he conjured up "positive nationalism," the notion that Iran's interests lay in holding tight to the American alliance. By the 1960s, positive nationalism had been overwhelmed by the changes in the global order and in the Middle East itself. The Soviet Union did not seem all that menacing, and the United States was not entirely reliable. Arab radicals were tamed by Israeli armor in 1967, and a year later, Britain announced its decision to leave the Middle East. The shah wanted to become the hegemon of the Persian Gulf but sensed he could not do so as America's client. It was time for what he dubbed "independent international policy." In the last decade of his rule, he spiked up oil prices, cozied up to the Soviet Union, cemented his ties with America on his terms, and obtained grudging accommodation from the Arab sheikhdoms. This was the shah at his most brilliant, demonstrating skills and acumen that he rarely displayed when managing domestic affairs.

The shah found Leonid Brezhnev to be a more agreeable leader than the erratic and unpredictable Khrushchev. Brezhnev's Soviet Union was beset by competition from China and burdened by militant Arab allies suffering from misfortunes of their own making.[1] In this environment, Moscow wanted better relations with nationalist leaders like the shah despite their unwillingness to embrace its ideological mandates. After decades of strife, Russia wanted stability on its southern frontier. The shah was willing to play his part and pledged that he would not accept U.S. missile bases on his territory. This was a cheap promise, because the United States had no plans to put missile fortifications in Iran, but symbolic gestures have their uses. The two sides soon began discussing various commercial ventures.

Amid much fanfare, the shah had a successful visit to the Soviet Union in 1965. While his last flirtation with the Kremlin had provoked a stern rebuke from Eisenhower, this time he confidently asserted that "things have changed since the time of Stalin. The new idea is, if we live as neighbors, why not live in friendship instead of animosity."[2] Shortly after his trip, the two sides agreed that Russia would build a massive steel mill in Isfahan. Domestic production of steel was not always practical, and Iran could have obtained better technology from Japan or Europe, but the deal was more about politics than economics. Then came a natural gas accord requiring the construction of a 650-mile pipeline that could eventually export a billion cubic meters of Iranian gas to Russia per year. Both deals involved complex arrangements for financing and technical assistance, paving the way for an expanded relationship between the two neighbors.

This was the core of the independent national policy: the shah was willing to improve ties with the Soviet Union without abandoning his alliance with America. He did not trust Moscow—there was too much historical baggage for such lofty sentiments—but he was prepared to pursue a transactional relationship. So long as Brezhnev could accept that Iran would remain in the American containment network, the shah was ready to reward him with commercial contracts. Even within the communist bloc, the shah proved a cagey player: he soon forged good ties with China and the more independent-minded Eastern European states such as Romania. His approach was conditioned by a pragmatic assessment of Iran's national interests and shrewd judgment about shifts in the global balance of power. In essence, the shah was cleverly trying to create a situation where both superpowers were invested in his rule.

In one of the paradoxes of history, it was a war in South Asia that made the shah both skeptical of America and more reliant on its arms. In 1965, India and Pakistan began fighting yet again, and the Johnson administration tried to calm the situation by curtailing military aid to Karachi. It was not lost on the shah that in applying this pressure, the United States had cut off military assistance to a member of its own alliance organization, the Central Treaty Organization (CENTO). "We see now what CENTO really is," the shah remarked. "It is a device to protect the West only."[3] Iran would have to take care of its own security needs, but at this stage it could not do so without American arms. Military purchases had been a source of contention between the shah and every president he dealt with. As he prepared for another visit to Washington, the question was bound to come up again.

Before his trip, the shah sent Washington an unmistakable signal by purchasing $110 million worth of arms from the Soviet Union, making Iran the first member of CENTO to buy weapons from America's Cold War rival. All sides reassured themselves that this was a one-time transaction and was limited to basic items such as trucks, artillery pieces, and anti-aircraft guns. The CIA, however, feared that more sophisticated arms sales might follow, deepening defense ties between the two states while Soviet spies dressed up as technicians flooded into Iran.

By this time, the Pahlavi state was developing a chorus of American supporters who would mimic its grievances and press its claims. This strategy had not yet reached the crescendo it would achieve in the 1970s, when influential voices in the White House and in the business community became ardent advocates of a monarch who was becoming unhinged. But even in the mid-1960s, the shah had a constituency. Ambassador Armin Meyer, following the well-trodden path of his predecessors, acted as the shah's spokesperson in Washington, warning his superiors that the monarch resented our "papa knows best attitude." Kermit Roosevelt, having abandoned spycraft for a vice presidency at Gulf Oil, resurfaced and contacted another veteran of the 1953 coup, George Carroll, who was working for Vice President Humphrey, and stressed that the shah was "tired of being treated like a schoolboy."[4] This bit of lobbying seems to have worked. Humphrey forgot his own previous warnings about the probable collapse of the shah's regime and advised that the monarch be treated more sympathetically.

The Johnson administration had not completely abandoned Kennedy's notion that the shah should focus on his country's economic development and not spend so much on arms. Even with the trend toward greater accommodation of the shah, the administration's top policymakers tried to hold the line. Rostow informed Johnson that "most of us believe that the Shah is foolish to spend his money this way . . . but since he is determined to buy arms somewhere, the best we can do is to lean on the brakes."[5] The perennially cautious Rusk was more charitable, noting that the shah's outlook was "changing as the country's financial position is improving."[6] McNamara remained adamant: "The Shah is not going to get a nickel's worth of military equipment from me. Kennedy knew how to handle this; he shouldn't have any military equipment."[7]

But by the late 1960s, besides being more confident, the shah had greater leverage with the United States. By every statistical measure, his White Revolution was working; Iran was no longer even receiving U.S. aid. The shah was one of the few leaders of the developing world to back the Vietnam War, a gesture much appreciated by the beleaguered Lyndon Johnson, who was looking for support wherever he could find it. The breakdown of relations between the United States and Pakistan, too, meant that the CIA had to move its listening posts, and Iran's long border with the Soviet Union provided an ideal location. CIA Director Richard Helms lobbied hard on the shah's behalf and informed a skeptical McNamara that "the Shah has been comparatively cooperative in permitting us to expand exclusively United States facilities in Iran."[8] Those intelligence installations were becoming even more critical in the age of arms control, because they gave the United States a way to monitor the Soviet nuclear arsenal. The shah was coming into his own, and America had to take notice. The pendulum was gradually shifting and it was increasingly Washington that needed things from Tehran.

The shah's 1967 trip to America reflected how things had changed. All the background memorandums and briefing books prepared for the trip contain little talk of political reform. The shah was seen as a successful modernizer, even a model for other developing nations. At one point, Johnson mused about whether the lessons of Iran could be applied to Vietnam. The United States accepted the shah's dealings with the Soviets and began treating the monarch more like a partner than an unsteady ruler it had to keep an eye on. The intelligence community kept on chronicling the Pahlavi autocracy's deficiencies, but its reports were largely ignored by senior policymakers.

The shah's visits to America increasingly followed a predictable script, with much pageantry and effusive toasts marred by protesting Iranian students. And once the two sides got down to actual talks, their conversations were dominated by the issue of arms. At the outset, the Johnson team tried to sustain the Kennedy parameters and limit arms sales to $50 million a year. But this had already changed, as Washington had previously agreed to an increase of $200 million in sales for the period between 1965 and 1969. McNamara still insisted that every year a survey be done to make sure that the arms sales did not adversely impact Iran's economy. General Hamilton Twitchell, the head of the Military Advisory Group in Iran, also stressed that the shah should not be allowed to purchase hardware that his army could not absorb: thus the procurement and training schedules had to be properly aligned. The shah not only wanted to dispense with these conditions; he sought more weapons. While he did not get everything he wanted, he did chip away at the prohibitions. Johnson agreed to increase the arms sales by an additional $200 million a year, but the Pentagon's conditions remained in place. Meanwhile, the Middle East was changing in a way that made the assertion of Iranian power much easier.

In the history of the modern Middle East, the 1960s stand as a watershed, after which things changed dramatically. For much of the decade, Nasser loomed large in the shah's imagination. Pan-Arabism was still a force to be reckoned with, even though Nasser's unity schemes all failed amid competing nationalisms. Nasser's intervention in Yemen's civil war alarmed the shah even though it was an unmitigated disaster: no matter how many troops Nasser sent into the desert, the Egyptian army could not defeat a tribal militia. All of this eluded the shah, who feared a hostile force on his periphery, irrespective of its tragic predicament.

Iran's sizeable Arab population in the province of Khuzestan, near all of its major oil fields, worried the shah as much as it did his Islamist successors. At various points, all of the radical Arab states—Egypt, Syria, and especially Iraq—have clumsily appealed to Khuzestan to join the larger Arab body. But this was agitation without impact as the citizens of the province remained unmoved. Iran has had difficulties at times in Azerbaijan and with its Kurdish population, but rarely with the Arabs of the south. Still, Persian rulers had always been sensitive to the Arab states' blandishments and subversions.

The shah's concerns about Nasser were surely exaggerated, but that did not stop the two sides from waging a relentless propaganda war. Nasser's Radio Cairo, best known for electrifying Arab public opinion, also targeted the shah, castigating him as a corrupt, reactionary ruler in collusion with the forces of Zionism. And in 1965, the shah and Saudi ruler King Faisal bin Abdulaziz Al Saud tried to deflate Nasser's regional pretensions by creating the Organization for the Islamic Conference. At a time when Nasser was challenging the legitimacy of the monarchical order, they looked for ways to assert their authenticity and push back against a secular republic that they claimed relied on imported ideologies.

On June 5, 1967, Israel launched a devastating attack against Egypt, Jordan, and Syria. Nasser's army was shattered, his economy was left in shambles, and his horizons were finally limited. The lion of Arab nationalism belatedly learned the cost of his militancy. In the aftermath of the Six-Day War, not only did Nasser change; so, too, did his country. Nasser became suspicious of the radicals in his camp and more pragmatic in his dealings with the conservative monarchies he had once relentlessly attacked. To obtain the

Saudi petrodollars he desperately needed to rebuild his economy, he ended his Yemeni misadventure. His next step was to concede to U.N. Resolution 242, which called for the exchange of land for peace with Israel. Nasser died in 1970, but he set the stage for the fundamental change in Egypt's foreign policy that occurred under his successor, Anwar Sadat.

The shah approached all of this with a degree of magnanimity. He declared three days of mourning after Nasser's death and dispatched Hoveyda to the funeral. Apparently appreciating that he was one of the beneficiaries of Israel's triumph, he soon forged close ties with Sadat. The death of one of his most consequential rivals was soon followed by a surprising announcement from Britain that was greeted with much joy in Tehran.

Britain had been patrolling the Persian Gulf since the late nineteenth century, when it had offered a series of treaties to the sheikhdoms in which it provided protection while they tended their own internal affairs. By the 1960s, there was little justification for Britain's presence. India had long been independent, and Britain had been expelled from the Arab east in the aftermath of the Suez War of 1956. Still, the fear of Soviet encroachment, the reality of Egyptian meddling in Yemen, and Iraq's territorial revisionism provided some justification for those in Whitehall who insisted that Britain was still a global actor. This soon came to an end. On January 16, 1968, Prime Minister Harold Wilson of the Labour government declared Britain's intention to leave the Persian Gulf by 1971. The ostensible cause was economic difficulty and the various currency devaluations that were undermining Britain's fiscal health. As early as 1966, a Defence Policy Paper had stipulated that if Britain wanted to protect the sheikhdoms, it had to replace its aging aircraft carriers—but the cost was prohibitive even after the panicked Gulf rulers offered to subsidize the British presence. Wilson's Labour Party could not be seen cutting domestic programs while spending lavishly on imperial holdings. He promised his colleagues that although he was "prepared to withdraw and reduce the number of troops East of Suez, he would never deny Britain the role of a world power."[9] This stance implied that the only way Britain could sustain its global role was to dispense with unnecessary commitments. The British public seemed ambivalent, and the Conservative Party leader, Edward Heath, promised to reverse Labour's decision should his party come to power. When it did in 1970, he quickly reneged on that pledge.[10]

The question that preoccupied the Western chancelleries was what to do with the Persian Gulf. The British had been a stabilizing presence, with London mediating disputes between quarrelsome sheikhdoms and keeping the larger powers at bay. Despite talk of a federation among the Gulf principalities, no one had a clear idea what would happen next. The conventional wisdom was that Iran and Saudi Arabia would emerge as the major regional powers provided they could keep their competitive impulses in check. The one certain outcome, which the Foreign Office was at pains to deny, was that Britain's announcement had set off a scramble for influence in the critical waterways.

The Middle East rarely offers much respite to Westerners wishing to be relieved of their troubles. The Six-Day War, coming on the heels of Egypt's closure of the Suez Canal, further aggravated Britain's currency crisis and forced it to accelerate its defense cuts. The disciples of Ernest Bevin gave way to a generation of Labour politicians who were more focused on Britain's European future than its imperial past.

In the late 1960s, Europe was beckoning Britain. The Labour government was once more seeking to leapfrog over Charles de Gaulle's objections and join the Common Market. Roy Jenkins, chancellor of the exchequer, noted that rejoining Europe was "the only way to make sure that Britain retained a place at the top table."[11] Although France would not yield until de Gaulle left the presidency, the wall separating Britain from Europe was beginning to crumble. Whitehall's evolving strategic conception left little room for the Gulf sheikhdoms. And given the unpopularity of the Vietnam War among the Labourites, no one in the party was willing to shoulder the Arab burden for Lyndon Johnson's sake.

Johnson spent the last years of his presidency routinely lashing out at his enemies, real or imagined. Support for his war became the litmus test of reliability and Harold Wilson never measured up to his vision of a trusted ally. It did the special relationship little good when Johnson castigated the British prime minister as a "little creep camping on my doorstep."[12] Undeterred, Wilson kept lecturing Johnson about the war, prompting the president at one point to snap, "Why don't you run Malaysia and let me run Vietnam?"[13] As it turned out, Wilson did not want to run Malaysia either. He abandoned Britain's imperial ramparts in Southeast Asia as fast as those in the Gulf. America had to devise a new Gulf policy at a time when it had neither the desire nor the means to deploy its own forces.[14]

Eugene Rostow, serving in the State Department, took up the challenge of coming up with a solution to America's dilemma. His ideas about the Middle East were as impractical as his brother Walter's ideas had been for Vietnam. Eugene Rostow dug up the Eisenhower-era notion of a regional security network, this time featuring Iran, Pakistan, Turkey, Saudi Arabia, and Kuwait—a proposal that had the distinction of being unacceptable to every relevant party. The Gulf rulers had no interest in letting Pakistan and Turkey meddle in their affairs. Iran and Saudi Arabia were both offended by the idea that they should rely on Turks and Pakistanis to safeguard their neighborhood. Nor was it obvious that Ankara and Karachi were willing to undertake such commitments. After an uproar, the Rostow plan was quickly shelved, leaving Washington without a strategy for coping with Britain's withdrawal.

The shah, for much of his tenure, had focused on great-power machinations and on dealing with the challenge of radical Arab states. This began to change once he understood that Iran's moment had come and the goal of hegemony was well within his reach. His gaze became focused on the Gulf, in contradistinction to his Islamist successors and their expansive regional mission. As he began to assert his claim, he cleverly insisted that no superpower replace the departing Britain. "We do not intend to invite anyone, either British, Russian, or Americans," he stressed. "In fact, we would like to make the Persian Gulf a close[d] area."[15] The last thing he wanted was another great power patrolling the Gulf and restricting his options. But he was also trying to keep the Gulf out of the Cold War. He understood that in a zero-sum game, if one superpower deployed its forces in a sensitive area, the other was bound to follow. By keeping the American armada out of the Gulf and steadily improving relations with Moscow, he hoped to prevent Russia from eyeing the region and further strengthening his Iraqi rival. His hegemonic claims were thus presented as confidence-building measures. Iran would safeguard the free flow of oil and ensure the stability of the Gulf by checking revisionist states such as Iraq. To a remarkable degree, this proved acceptable to both the United States and the Soviet Union.

A year before the arrival of the Nixon administration and its doctrine of empowering local surrogates, the Johnson team was already moving in that direction. This policy was a consequence of the Vietnam War: an exhausted America, with half a million troops stuck in the jungle, could not undertake additional commitments. The public was too divided, and Congress was too wary of such ventures, for the White House to ease its way into another region. Rusk therefore acknowledged that "Iran was the keystone of American plans." Saudi cooperation was surely important, but it was understood that "Iran was clearly the stronger partner, progressive and developing."[16] This became the essence of Nixon's "twin pillar" policy, with one pillar bearing most of the weight.

It shows the success of the shah's diplomacy that the Soviet Union essentially endorsed his position. Moscow would sign a treaty of friendship with Iraq in 1972 and sell it large consignments of arms, but it was skeptical of the Ba'ath Party and its ever-changing cast of leaders. Brezhnev's Soviet Union was dubious of regimes that combined chaotic domestic politics with territorial ambitions that could spark war. The shah offered stability and a means of keeping the United States out of the Gulf. After one of the shah's visits to Moscow, the two sides even issued a joint communiqué stressing that "the Soviet Union and Iran expressed the firm conviction that questions relating to the Persian Gulf security zone should be resolved, in accordance with the principles of the U.N. Charter, by the states of this region themselves without outside interference."[17] As the shah's independent international policy had envisioned, both superpowers were comfortable with Iran's projection of power.

The security of the Gulf in the aftermath of the British departure would prove a difficult balancing act. This was as much about politics as defense imperatives. Any security arrangement had to be informal, because the sheikhdoms were unlikely to join an organization dominated by an aspiring Persian hegemon. It also had to have Western support, but only indirectly. The lesson of the Baghdad Pact was that too close an association with the West could expose Arab regimes to the charge of enabling occidental imperialism. Thus the evolving regional order had to feature Iran without seeming to concede to its pretensions. It had to be aimed at containing Iraq without appearing to do so. And it had to be fortified by America without too visible traces of its sponsorship. This is essentially the structure that the shah created.

As the shah put the pieces of his strategy together, he needed money to finance his schemes. This meant he had to sell more oil at higher prices.

OIL GIANT

The shah hated the consortium that controlled Iranian oil, and the idea that a collection of foreign oil companies could dictate his essential production and pricing decisions. Iran could not be a great power while its most valuable natural asset was controlled by Westerners. The shah had previously nibbled at the consortium, contracting with smaller firms to develop oil fields that were outside the scope of the 1954 concession. But by the 1970s, the era of nibbling was over. This was a decade of big appetites. More than Mossadeq or any other Persian statesman, it was the shah who finally reclaimed Iran's oil.[18]

As he had done with military matters, the shah turned himself into a petroleum expert, studying technical manuals and marketing reports and generally mastering the oil business. The fourth development plan, covering the period 1968–1972, called for $11 billion in investment, 80 percent of which was to come from oil revenues. The shah therefore approached the consortium and demanded that it increase its annual payment to one billion dollars. The companies balked, because it meant increasing production at a time when they were not sure how to dispose of the excess supply. Moreover, Iran's demand could trigger a similar move by other oil-producing countries, causing an oil glut. The executives rushed to Tehran to complain, and they were soon joined by both American and British ambassadors who pleaded with the shah to reconsider his move. The shah held firm: "What I say is absolutely clear. I say this is our oil—pump it. If not we pump it ourselves."[19] The consortium folded, increasing its payment to $950 million with the remainder to be made up by an interest-free loan. This only whetted the shah's appetite. As he told Alam, he was done haggling with the consortium. "We should take the oil in our own hand and sell it ourselves. The companies should be our clients. Then we should not have to fight any longer."[20]

The shah soon took his campaign public, hinting at his displeasure with the consortium even as he continuously renegotiated the contract. In an interview with the *New York Times,* he stressed, "When we signed the agreement it was the best we could get at the time. One of the terms of the agreement was that the operating companies would protect Iran's interest in the best manner possible. We have evidence that this has not been the case."[21] On January 23, 1973, in a speech commemorating the tenth anniversary of the White Revolution, the shah stressed that the consortium could await the expiration of its contract in 1979 and then become just another buyer, or it could nullify the concession in exchange for becoming a privileged customer at discounted prices. Given little choice, the oil giants accepted the collapse of their original arrangement. The move was widely celebrated in Iran as the final act of the nationalization saga. For the first time in its history, Iran was in control of its oil.

But this was only the beginning. The shah also needed higher prices to finance his development plans. In 1960, the leading oil producing countries had come together and formed the Organization of the Petroleum Exporting Countries (OPEC) to challenge the so-called majors. The shah initially did not like joining states like Iraq against the West, nor was he thrilled with another mechanism that could limit his ambitions. But he appreciated that there was safety in numbers and that it was time for the global south to assert itself against the imperious north. Not only did Iran become a member of OPEC; the shah also soon emerged as one of its most zealous price hawks.

The shah's man for dealing with OPEC was his minister of finance, Jamshid Amouzegar, who proved a cagey negotiator. (He would later falter as prime minister, a job requiring a political touch that the shah's technocrats usually lacked.) Amouzegar pushed his colleagues for price increases, and in January 1971 he presented a NIOC study that suggested oil was underpriced at $1.80 per barrel and that its price could be increased by as much as 40 percent. Soon it shot up to $2.81 and then to $5.10 per barrel.

Iran seemed always to benefit when Arabs and Israelis went to war, and this was as true in 1973 as it had been in 1967. On October 6, 1973, Egypt and Syria launched an attack on Israel that caught both Jerusalem and Washington by surprise. In solidarity with the invading parties, the Gulf states announced that they would cut their oil production by 5 percent, followed by an additional 5 percent every month until Israel returned to the pre-1967 boundaries.[22] King Faisal, whose anti-Semitism drove his deep animosity toward Israel, went even further and stopped all oil sales to the United States. The shah, however, refused to join the embargo and openly bragged about selling oil to Israel. He also shook the oil markets by successfully pressing for a price increase to $11.65 per barrel. "The industrial world," he declared, "will have to realize that the era of their terrific progress and even more terrific income and wealth based on cheap oil is finished."[23]

The money poured in. Iran's oil income shot up from $885 million in 1971 to $17.8 billion in 1975. Its GDP skyrocketed from $4 billion in 1961 to $54 billion in 1976, and during the same period, industrial output increased by an annual rate of 20 percent. The shah's fifth development plan, which originally set an investment goal of $36 billion, was nearly doubled to $63 billion. Throughout Tehran, hotels and high-rises went up at a record pace. Trade delegations arrived from around the world, selling every imaginable gadget. Despite all the corruption and mismanagement, everyone seemed to benefit. Having humbled the oil giants, the Persian monarch now turned his gaze to the Middle East.

MASTERING THE MIDDLE EAST

In 1967, Richard Nixon embarked on one of his world tours and wanted to visit Iran. The former vice president was thought to be finished politically after losing the presidency in 1960 and the gubernatorial race in California two years later. The shah initially demurred because he did not want to be seen as meddling in U.S. politics. His relations with the Kennedy clan were already, he felt, poisoned by allegations that he had made secret financial donations to Nixon's presidential campaign. But Alam and Zahedi, who was now foreign minister, persuaded him to grant Nixon an audience. By this point, the shah was accustomed to holding court and offering geopolitical dispensations to visiting dignitaries. The experience with Nixon, however, was altogether different, as the two awkward men rekindled their friendship. The shah wanted to be the policeman of the Gulf, and the Vietnam War had convinced Nixon that America needed reliable surrogates for this task.

There was a time when running for president involved brandishing one's intellectual credentials by writing articles on weighty matters. As he contemplated such a run, Nixon published an important article in *Foreign Affairs* that is best remembered for its hints of an opening to China. But the article also stressed, "If another friendly country should be faced with an externally-supported Communist insurrection—whether in Asia, or in Africa, or even in Latin America—there is a serious question whether the American public or the American Congress would now support a unilateral American intervention, even at the request of the host government."[24] In the age of retrenchment, relying on the shah was no longer a choice; it was a necessity.[25]

In 1968, when Nixon won the presidency, America had no real strategy for extricating itself from the Vietnam quagmire. Nixon wanted "peace with honor," détente with the Soviet Union, and normalized relations with China. There was no room in this outlook for getting bogged down in Third World disputes. Nixon's America would be a prudent power, using diplomacy to mitigate superpower tensions and employing proxies to patrol vast regions of the world.

Upon arriving in the White House, the Nixon team conducted elaborate studies on the Middle East that essentially confirmed its predecessor's policy. Lyndon Johnson had already decided that America was not going to replace Britain and that the local actors had to maintain stability in the Gulf. The new national security adviser, Henry Kissinger, replaced most of the NSC staff but retained Johnson's senior aide Harold Saunders, who had been the top adviser on the Middle East. In its study of the area, National Security Decision Memorandum 92, the new administration paid the usual lip service to the twin pillars, Saudi Arabia and Iran, but it was understood that the shah would be guardian of the Gulf. The memorandum concluded that it would be in America's interest to promote "cooperation between Iran and Saudi Arabia as the desirable basis for maintaining stability in the Persian Gulf while recognizing the preponderance of Iranian power and developing [a] direct U.S. relationship with the separate political entities of the area."[26] The administration recognized that the sheikhdoms were not keen on Persian hegemony, but the logic of power meant they had to make the necessary adjustments.

On one level, Iran was the beneficiary of Saudi Arabia's strategic reticence. The kingdom under Faisal had recovered from the ruinous financial practices of his predecessor Saud bin Abdulaziz Al Saud, but it was still too mindful of Arab sensitivities to serve as America's policeman in the Gulf. The Saudis preferred to deal in subtleties, using their ample petrodollars to pay off their opponents. Moreover, there was a real concern in the U.S. national security bureaucracy about the longevity of the House of Saud, making reliance on Riyadh questionable at best. In 1973, in a gesture that in retrospect can only be considered ironic, Kissinger even crafted a secret deal with the shah that should the Saudi monarchy collapse, Iran would intervene and secure its oil fields.

The one place where the Nixon administration differed from its predecessor was in its evaluation of the shah's rule. Both Kennedy and, to a lesser extent, Johnson had been concerned that the shah's regional ambitions and military expenditures could undermine domestic reform efforts. They never stopped badgering the shah about internal reforms, with Komer and McNamara taking the lead in questioning his priorities. By the time Nixon took office, the shah had greater control of his society, and his White Revolution was clearly producing results, but the CIA was still documenting ample signs of discontent. This was Nixon and Kissinger's biggest failure: they persistently ignored mounting evidence that the shah's regime might be less stable than they assumed. The real tragedy of this period was that Nixon's was the last U.S. government that could have saved the shah's throne. By the time Jimmy Carter came to power, the situation was no longer salvageable.

Nixon first hinted at his new doctrine in a meeting in Guam with the South Vietnamese leader Nguyen Van Thieu, telling the assembled reporters that "the United States is going to encourage and has a right to expect that this problem will be increasingly handled by, and the responsibility for it taken by, the Asian nations themselves."[27] Although Nixon was speaking about East Asia and the war in Vietnam, the same sentiment would apply elsewhere, including the Middle East.

If the United States was to rely on proxies, they would have to be heavily armed. The shah, who had argued with every American president about needing more weaponry, found the new U.S. administration to be a more sympathetic partner. As he began his fourth decade in power, his ideas about his armed forces were changing. Throughout his reign he had looked at his army as an indispensable constituency that would protect his regime from domestic detractors. As long as an assertive elite had been able to muster massive demonstrations, a reliable army was essential. But by the 1970s, the shah increasingly perceived that he no longer needed the army to protect his dynasty. The feeble opposition could perhaps engage in targeted assassinations but nothing more. Terrorism, after all, is the weapon of the weak. Mossadeq was dead, Khomeini was exiled, and the Tudeh and National Front were shadows of their old selves. Whatever dissent still existed, SAVAK could easily handle. The military had to be repurposed to project power abroad as opposed to preserving order at home. Thus while the shah would spend lavishly on all branches of the armed forces, at this point he paid particular attention to his air force and navy. The shah was creating not just a hollowed-out officer corps, but also one with little appetite or capacity for handling a national uprising.

In October 1969, coming to Washington for a firsthand assessment of the new administration, the shah was in a mood to lecture. He told Secretary of State William Rogers that the root cause of America's problem in Vietnam was the coup against Ngo Dinh Diem in 1963 that had led to his assassination. At dinner with Kissinger, he extolled the virtues of one-man rule and claimed that Soviet policy was much more predictable under Stalin than under the collective leadership that took over the Politburo after his death. Dictatorships have their uses, he stressed, and America should always stick with its friends. This message resonated in the Nixon White House.

The issue of arms sales was going to be tricky for the shah, because he had just signed a multi-year agreement with the Johnson administration. Even though Nixon intended to concentrate power in the White House, he hit a wall of bureaucratic resistance to the idea of increased arms sales to Iran. It is important to note that throughout the 1960s and 1970s, every U.S. secretary of defense—including Robert McNamara, Melvin Laird, James Schlesinger, and Donald Rumsfeld—opposed heavily arming the shah. The Pentagon was concerned not just about the impact of military expenditures on Iran's economy, but also that the weapons systems the shah demanded were so sophisticated his army could not absorb them in a timely manner. Sometimes the shah wanted fighter jets that had yet to come off the assembly line. Many in the Pentagon thought Iran would be better off if it focused its limited pool of technicians and engineers on civilian needs rather than military logistics.

Melvin Laird was more than a match for Kissinger at bureaucratic games-manship. As a former congressman with well-honed political skills, he had the fortune of heading an institution that, unlike the State Department, could not be easily sidestepped. Kissinger's NSC staff could replicate some State Department functions, but there was no way they could get around the leviathan that is the Pentagon. Early in the administration, to resist the White House's relaxed attitude toward the shah, Laird commissioned a National Intelligence Assessment that claimed the Soviet Union had little desire to in-tervene in the Gulf and Iraq was no match for Iran. At Laird's instigation, Chairman of the Joint Chiefs of Staff Earle Wheeler warned that Iran "would have trouble digesting all of the equipment they have in mind."[28] The Penta-gon used every trick in its bag, such as insisting that any additional sales had to await the conclusion of its various survey missions. Given that Congress had to approve all arms sales, the White House could not just dismiss the Pentagon's concerns.

Not everyone in Iran approved of the shah's appetite for weaponry, but the system he had created kept such skeptical voices from reaching him. When informed of the amounts the shah planned to spend, Hoveyda tried to get the new U.S. ambassador, Douglas MacArthur II, to dissuade the monarch. When MacArthur asked why the prime minister himself did not do so, the hapless Hoveyda could only respond, "You know, Doug, His Majesty doesn't like to have negative views from any member of his cabinet."[29] General Mohammad Khatami, commander of the air force, confided to Alam that "we are ordering more planes than we can possibly use. We simply haven't got the pilots, or the facilities to train more." As Alam ruefully noted, "Yet, despite being his brother-in-law, the Commander dares not draw the matter to HIM's [the shah's] atten-tion."[30] Nor did Alam, who understood that the shah's pet projects were not to be questioned. Still, during much of Nixon's first term, the Pentagon bureau-cracy managed to prevent a massive increase in arms sales.

This all changed in 1972, when after a triumphant summit with Brezhnev, Nixon made a short visit to Tehran. He was greeted with four separate terror-ist attacks, which should have made him question the stability of the country he was relying on as America's surrogate in the Gulf. This was the famous occasion when Nixon implored the shah to "protect me." The price of that protection would be arms transfers—the so-called blank check. Kissinger soon codified this gesture in an official policy directive, stating, "With regard to the question of arms sales to Iran, the President's policy is to encourage purchase of U.S. equipment. Decisions as to the desirability of equipment acquisition should be left in the hands of the Iranian Government and the U.S. should not undertake to discourage on economic grounds."[31] The shah was ecstatic, claiming, "Nixon gave me everything I had asked for."[32]

Still, the idea of a blank check is exaggerated. Nixon's outburst did not stop the Pentagon from evaluating Iran's arms requests: the bureaucracy still went through its processes. But it was understood that the requests had to be given sympathetic hearing. The notion that military sales should be evaluated in light of their impact on Iran's economy was set aside, partly because the country's soaring oil revenues convinced many in Washington that the shah could afford both guns and butter. As James Schlesinger, who took over for Laird, recalled, "I understood that we were supposed, in general, to support the Shah—because I resisted certain arms sales, certain commitments by the United States which I did not think were in our interest, and sometimes were not in the Shah's interest, and on some of them I just got overruled."[33] Over the next four years, the shah would spend approximately $17 billion on arms, devoting more than one-third of his annual budget to military hardware.

In 1971, Britain's long shadow in the Middle East finally receded. The shah tried to ease the simmering tensions in the Gulf by presenting himself as an agent of stability. His principal objective was to protect Iran's vast oil installations and defend its navigational routes. The Persian Gulf was then, as it is today, Iran's major link to global oil markets and thus the lifeblood of its economy. The shah, however, presented his ambitions as a service to the international community. This was his way of becoming a global player and of keeping the superpowers out of the Gulf. If they wanted unimpeded commercial traffic, then he would provide it, for the common good.[34]

Before becoming the benign protector of the Gulf, however, the shah had to settle Iran's contentious claim over Bahrain. Shah Abbas, of the Safavid dynasty, had expelled the Portuguese from Bahrain and taken over the archipelago. That ended in 1783, when the Al Khalifa family made Bahrain a British protectorate. Successive Persian rulers, however, never acknowledged that reality. Even when Mossadeq nationalized Iran's oil, he included the Bahrain Petroleum Company on the list of assets that Iran was to seize. In 1957, the shah submitted a bill to the parliament that designated Bahrain as Iran's fourteenth province, a claim the foreign ministry defended by noting that Iran's rights went back to the eighteenth century and that "our Arab brothers should know that Bahrain is part of our body and the question of Bahrain is of vital interest to Iran."[35] The shah understood that the Bahrain issue was damaging his hegemonic ambitions, but many centuries of Persian chauvinism stood in his way. History and pragmatism now collided, and he had to find a way out of his predicament.

As was his habit by now, the shah was more forthcoming with Western envoys than with his own officials. He confessed to British Ambassador Denis Wright that in Bahrain "the pearls have run out. The oil is running out. It is no good to me. I must have some face saving formula."[36] The shah suggested a stage-managed way of resolving the issue by holding a referendum in Bahrain. Once the Bahrainis had rejected Iran's claims, the shah would magnanimously forfeit his inheritance. The idea came to naught, however, because the Sunni royals of Bahrain, who ruled over a Shia majority, were fearful of any democratic gesture.

The Foreign Office next considered adding Bahrain to the confederation of sheikhdoms that it was creating, which already featured the Trucial states and Qatar. This was acceptable to Bahrain but raised concerns in Tehran. The final arrangement that seemed acceptable to all the parties was for the United Nations to dispatch a mission to Bahrain to determine the opinion of its inhabitants. Wright informed the shah that the purpose of the exercise was "to affirm the 'Arabism' of Bahrain but in such a way as to get the Iranian government off the hook. It would thus amount to a prearranged public relations exercise."[37] The shah played along and announced, "If the people of Bahrain do not want to join my country first of all, it is against our principle to use force in order to reattach this land of ours."[38] The U.N. commission duly conducted its survey in the spring of 1970 and, as expected, reported that an overwhelming majority of Bahrainis favored independence over being annexed by Iran.[39] The shah accepted the verdict and arranged for a parliamentary vote that endorsed the U.N. mandate.

Although he acted with restraint over Bahrain, the shah was uncompromising on another issue, one he considered vital. The three islands of Abu Musa and Greater and Lesser Tunbs sit at the mouth of the Strait of Hormuz. This is the choke point of Iran's commerce, and the occupation of those islands by a hostile power could endanger its trade. Iran had a historic claim over the islands that it had rarely asserted, but on November 1971 it seized them by force. Despite having just rejected the use of force in the Gulf, the shah had little compunction about deploying his navy and marines here. This would not be his only military intervention: next he rescued the monarchy of Oman.

Relations between Oman and Iran began tentatively, with the shah taking three months to recognize the new regime. The sultan of Oman, Qaboos bin Said, had come to power the old-fashioned way: in 1970 he had launched a coup against his aging father. The elder ruler had used draconian measures to try to isolate his nation from all external influences, only to witness a growing Marxist insurgency in the province of Dhofar. On a state visit to Iran, Qaboos pleaded with the shah for military aid to help him defeat the rebellion. The shah initially hesitated as he had too many other issues in the Gulf to sort out.

By 1973, this had begun to change as the conflict in Oman reached a stalemate. The royalist forces could not defeat the insurgents, and the British, who had long aided Oman's military, were unwilling to step up their assistance. Meanwhile, the rebellion enjoyed the support of Russia, China, Iraq, and Yemen. The rebels claimed that "freeing Dhofar is only the first step in our campaign to free all of the Persian Gulf from imperialism."[40] As the guardian of the Gulf, the shah could not tolerate a militant rebellion, particularly one aided by his Iraqi nemesis. Iran's intervention began gradually, but eventually the shah dispatched four thousand troops supported by naval and air assets. Because the shah viewed the occasion as a chance to give his army combat experience, he rotated his troops out every three months, compromising their operational efficiency. Still, Iran's forces seem to have performed well, and their new weapons systems passed their first real test.

Two years after Iran's intervention, the insurgency petered out and Qaboos secured his position. Two hundred Iranians were lost in putting down the rebellion. The sultan would remain grateful to Iran, and even after the collapse of the monarchy he would establish good relations with the Islamic Republic.

The year 1975 was one of the shah's best: he not only defeated a radical rebellion in Oman but also humiliated Iraq's new ruler, Saddam Hussein. The shah habitually exaggerated threats to his country, but the challenge of Iraq was real. The officers and Ba'athists who ruled Iraq after the monarchy's overthrow aspired to lead the Arab world. Saddam Hussein was one such leader whose brutality and ambition would unsettle the Middle East for decades to come. The core of the problem between the two states was the 1937 Treaty of Saadabad, negotiated under British auspices, which essentially gave Iraq control over the Shatt al-Arab waterway so Baghdad could have an outlet for its oil exports. To be sure, the treaty called for further negotiations over the joint management of the river, which also passed near Iran's major oil installations, but somehow those talks never took place. In 1969, the shah renounced the treaty as a legacy of colonialism, and insisted on shared custody of the river. Iraq saw this renunciation as a breach of its sovereignty.

The ethnic composition of Iraq offered the shah an opportunity for mischief. The Kurds had spent their time in the modern state of Iraq rebelling against and then signing various truce agreements with Baghdad. The Ba'ath Party's more rigid policies invited yet another Kurdish uprising, which the shah was happy to support. The monarch was never a champion of independence for Iran's own sizeable Kurdish population. In 1946, the Soviet Union had made him even more cautious of ethnic minorities by setting up a short-lived autonomous Kurdish republic in northern Iran. This made the shah cautious of ethnic separatism even as he inflamed it next door. He did not want the Kurds to succeed, just to make the Iraqi army bleed. Once he had the Ba'athist regime trapped in a stalemate, he would offer to cease his aid in exchange for territorial concessions.

Given that Iraq is now one of the central dilemmas of America's Middle East policy, it strains the imagination to think that during much of the Cold War, it was a peripheral concern. Eisenhower had quietly shelved the calls for U.S. intervention that followed the 1958 coup, and Washington was bewildered by the ever-changing cast of characters who had run Baghdad since then, seemingly in a continuous series of plots against each other. That Iraq kept selling oil to the West despite its occasional flirtations with the Soviet Union lessened the urgency. The Kennedy administration, in its perennial search for authentic Arab nationalists, attempted to improve relations with Iraq, only to abandon the idea. America stood aside from Iraq's internal squabbles despite the pleas of the conservative monarchies. Nor did Israel's support for the Kurds whet the American appetite. The Nixon administration took a different approach not for some compelling strategic reason but simply to placate the shah. If Iran was to be America's surrogate, its adventures had to be supported.

By the 1970s, the Iraqi Kurds were once more battling the central government for greater autonomy and looking to outsiders for help. For the shah, this was an ideal opportunity to impose on Iraq an agreement regarding the sharing of Shatt al-Arab. The monarch was always clear with his American interlocutors about his objectives. On one of his many visits to Washington, he informed Kissinger that "the Kurds must remain within the Iraqi state and seek a solution there. But our only lever over the Iraqi government is the Kurds."[41] Kissinger meekly replied, "As for the Kurds, we will do what can be absorbed."[42] The U.S. aid to the Kurds that was channeled through the CIA was always modest because Washington sought to keep its participation secret. The shah was the main actor. At the height of the conflict, Iran gave the Kurds more than $30 million a year.

The Kurds never trusted the shah and understood his ploy. They were drawn to Tehran because of their desperation and American involvement, and they wrongly assumed that the United States would not callously with-draw its support once the shah's scheme had been carried out. Kurdish leader Mustafa Barzani later confessed, "Without American promises we wouldn't have acted the way we did."[43] Nixon and Kissinger fully implicated the United States in this cynical power play in a country they poorly understood. In a rare gesture of modesty, Kissinger even confessed, "We did not know much about Kurds . . . we thought they were some kind of hill tribe."[44]

By 1974, a series of events had pressed both Tehran and Baghdad toward a negotiated settlement. The simmering conflict was proving too embarrass-ing for a Ba'ath Party that took pride in its revolutionary élan. The Iraqi army was now fully deployed to defeat the insurgency. While mobilizing his army, Saddam also sent word to the shah that he was prepared for constructive talks. The shah, meanwhile, had begun to fear the loss of his leverage should the Iraqi assault succeed. And on August 9, 1974, Richard Nixon resigned the presidency to avoid impeachment for crimes arising from the Watergate scan-dal. The shah, who assumed that dark forces led by big business and the CIA were behind Nixon's ouster, began to doubt America's resolve. All roads led to a settlement that would betray the Kurds.

A quick series of diplomatic encounters paved the way for an agreement with obvious outlines. After a meeting of foreign ministers, it was agreed that the shah and Saddam would directly tackle the issue at the next OPEC meeting, to be held in Algiers in March. By this time, the shah was concerned that keep-ing the Kurdish resistance alive might require direct Iranian intervention—a step he was not prepared to take. The same wish to avoid a military clash also propelled Saddam toward a compromise.

On March 5, 1975, the fate of the Kurds was sealed. Saddam told the shah that his "unsparing sword cut down the flower of Iraqi youth."[45] The shah, who had arrived at Algiers with little concern for the Kurds, told Alam that the notion of Kurdish autonomy was "moonshine from the word go."[46] Each side agreed to respect the other's sovereignty, which meant cutting off the Kurds and dividing the Shatt al-Arab in the middle.

In Washington, the new president, Gerald Ford, received the following report as part of an intelligence briefing: "The withdrawal of Iranian forces from Iraq suggests that the Shah has given Baghdad a free hand to pursue a military solution to the Kurdish problem to a conclusion in return for Iraq's acceptance of the Iranian position on border demarcation."[47] CIA Director William Colby followed this up by informing the White House, "The funda-mental premise of our past commitments has been that all aid to Kurds must be indirect via the Iranians, and in the new situation we believe direct aid by us would be even less defensible than in the past."[48] The United States thus also terminated its assistance to the Kurds. Saddam's armies moved in and ended the Kurdish insurgency.

By the mid-1970s, the shah was the most consequential ruler in the Middle East. In the Arab east, he had good relations with both Egypt and Israel. He meddled a bit in the politics of Lebanon but its complex confessional makeup seemed to have eluded him. He had seamlessly displaced Britain in the Persian Gulf and checked radical actors in both Oman and Iraq. He had abandoned a useless claim over Bahrain while taking over the strategically important islands at the mouth of the Strait of Hormuz. His army kept watch over the world's oil supply and patrolled the region's all-important waterways. The great civilization that the shah wanted to create now began eyeing nuclear science.

CHASING THE ATOM

The United States supported the shah's regional ambitions because it saw his assertions of power as consistent with American interests. Not so with his atomic program. Successive administrations stood in the way of the shah's attempt to develop a sophisticated nuclear infrastructure. One of the enduring myths of our time is that the United States enabled the shah's nuclear program and developed qualms about Iranian proliferation only after the Islamic Republic came to power. But even Gerald Ford, who favored intimate ties with Iran, rejected the shah's pleas for nuclear technologies.

Iran's nuclear program began in the late 1950s when it participated in Eisenhower's lofty dream of using atoms for peace.[49] In 1957, with American assistance, Iran obtained a research reactor for Tehran University that was to rely on enriched uranium from abroad. Under the terms of the contract, Iran agreed that its nascent nuclear program would "not be used for atomic weapons or for research on or for development of atomic weapons, or for any other military purposes."[50] The reactor, the ultimate white elephant gift, sat unused for a decade. In the 1960s, the shah made all the right noises and signed the Nuclear Non-Proliferation Treaty (NPT).

In March 1974, the shah let the world know about his latest determination. "We shall, as fast as we can, enter the age of using the atom and other sources of energy in order to save oil for production of chemical and petrochemical products," he declared.[51] Like every other aspect of life in Iran during the 1970s, this was to be a crash program. Akbar Etemad, the person chosen to head the new Atomic Energy Organization of Iran (AEOI), had long lobbied for harnessing atomic energy and was a rarity in Iran: a man with an actual background in nuclear physics.[52] He had jump-started the dormant reactor in Tehran University and headed the newly inaugurated Institute for Research and Planning for Science and Education. Although he was given the title of deputy prime minister, it was understood that he would report to the shah and not Hoveyda. The prime minister had doubts about the program—doubts that, as usual, he kept to himself. The parliament duly passed a bill authorizing the creation of the agency even though its structure and mission were not entirely clear. But these were no longer questions that the parliament probed. This was, after all, the shah's project.

At first the AEOI was a shell of an organization, but with a budget of a billion dollars a year, things moved quickly. Etemad successfully persuaded about a hundred Iranian scientists to return from abroad and even hired some Argentinian technicians looking for work. By the eve of the revolution, the organization had a staff of over 3,500.[53] The AEOI had little oversight and rarely submitted reports to the parliament. Given that the program was dear to the shah's heart, Etemad's only supervisor was a capricious monarch.

By this point the shah rarely discussed his plans with his Iranian advisers, so it remains unclear why the leader of the world's third-largest oil producer wanted nuclear energy. What we do know is that nuclear science was in vogue, and possession of atomic infrastructure was seen as a mark of modernity. The nuclear club was no longer limited to the West because ambitious nations like India and Japan were well on their way to conquering the atom. Despite all his success, the shah still thought of Iran as a backward country, demeaned its traditions, and seemed almost embarrassed by his own constituents. What better way to impress the world than by joining the exclusive nuclear club? Prestige is usually an overstated motivation for a nuclear program, but for the shah it was an essential factor. The monarch's self-image as a modernizing ruler caused him to obsess over grand projects.

Although he kept his functionaries in the dark about his plans, the shah was unusually chatty with the Western press. In the aftermath of India's 1974 nuclear test, the French magazine *Les Informations* asked the shah if he wanted the bomb and he blurted out "without any doubt and sooner than one would think."[54] This set off a panic in Iran's foreign ministry, which issued a string of denials. A year later, the shah decided to unburden himself to the *New York Times*. While denying that he wanted the bomb, he allowed that "if 20 or 30 ridiculous little countries are going to develop nuclear weapons, then I may have to revise my policies."[55] A few weeks later, he again told the *Times* that he did not want nuclear bombs, but "if small states began building [them] then Iran might have to reconsider its policy."[56] In his own crude way, the shah was hinting at a hedge strategy.

Alam claims in his diaries that the shah had other plans for his nuclear program than energy production. But on this issue, Alam is a poor guide. It was Etemad who spent the most time with the shah discussing his ambitions. Once he was made head of the AEOI, Etemad decided to home-school the monarch on the fundamentals of nuclear science. In one of their tutorial sessions, the shah, in an expansive mood, seemed to reject building the bomb. Given Iran's decisive conventional weapons advantage in the Persian Gulf, he feared that if Iran breached the taboo and introduced nuclear arms to the area, it could trigger a cascade that would cost him his military edge. Saudi Arabia could rely on Pakistan while Iraq was already eyeing nuclear arms. If the genie ever escaped the bottle, it would compromise Iran's hegemony.

Even a self-sufficient civilian nuclear program can be dangerous. The technology such an apparatus requires can easily be converted to military purposes. A nation that has mastered enrichment of uranium or reprocessing of plutonium spent fuel has the basic ingredients for a bomb. The question is whether the shah would have crossed the threshold and actually assembled a weapon. What factors would have propelled him toward such a provocative policy?

The shah's calculations were fundamentally different from those of his Islamist successors. As we have seen, the shah always hedged his bets and sometimes pointed to how regional exigencies determined his atomic choices. But he was also desperate to join the West, and that meant accepting at least some conditions. In the 1970s, non-proliferation was becoming an accepted virtue among the Western nations. The shah's violations of that norm were bound to provoke a reaction and perhaps even cause him to be shunned in America and Europe. He was determined that Iran not become a rogue nation, which is why he was so obsessed with Western news coverage. Even before Jimmy Carter introduced human rights into American foreign policy, the shah tried to clean up SAVAK and eventually opened its prisons for inspection by international organizations. For some peculiar reason, the shah was concerned about what the Western press thought of him, which is why he often confided to foreign journalists. In private, he would deride Western intellectuals and opinion-makers, but he never stopped seeking their approval. Consequently, the values of the

Western club that the shah was so eager to join were bound to influence his decisions. Conversely, the Islamists who displaced him reject the global order as an American conspiracy and are comfortable with violating its standards.

Iran's quick acceptance of membership in the NPT in 1968 reflected all of these influences and priorities. As usual, the Iranian government did not deliberate much about the agreement. This was an important Western proposal and the shah was eager to be one of the first to sign it. Iran was not about to join the chorus of Third World nations condemning the agreement as unfair to the have-nots. The shah's Iran was part of the responsible West, not the impetuous non-aligned movement. At the various NPT review conferences, when the developing nations ritualistically condemned the treaty's so-called inequalities, the shah's diplomats stood aside. As a monarch who routinely pledged to catch up to the industrial West, the shah had a different audience in mind.

Given the shah's deft handling of foreign relations, it is hard to see Iran's strategic picture darkening to a degree that he would have to reach for the bomb. America still provided a security umbrella: even after being humbled in Vietnam, it had no intention of retreating from its global obligations. Moreover, the shah had worked hard to improve his ties to the Soviet Union. The two countries' relationship was no longer guided by the 1921 treaty granting Russia the right to intervene in Iran whenever it chose. They had signed numerous commercial contracts and treated each other with respect.

Nor did regional conditions compel the shah to race to a bomb. Iran had good relations with Israel (which had developed a bomb in the 1960s) as well as with the largest nations of the Middle East—Turkey, Egypt, and Saudi Arabia. Iraq stood out as a potential problem, but Saddam's nuclear odyssey would not become serious until the 1980s. Whether the shah would have tried to thwart Saddam's designs or escalate his own nuclear program in response is hard to answer. At any rate, all these contingencies mandated a strategy of hedging rather than actually crossing the nuclear threshold.

Iran entered the atomic age on the shoulders of others. The shah was in too much of a hurry to gradually build up a scientific foundation and train a cadre. He preferred to acquire technologies and expertise from abroad. At first, hoping to transact his nuclear commerce with the United States, he wrote a letter to President Ford in which he made his plea: "I would therefore very much hope, Mr. President, that your non-proliferation policy would remain flexible enough to allow a fruitful and meaningful cooperation to prevail between our two countries in the field of nuclear energy."[57] This plea would go unanswered.

In the first two decades of the Cold War, the United States did not take the threat of nuclear proliferation all that seriously. The Eisenhower administration's permissive policy was reflected in its Atoms for Peace program, which envisioned exporting nuclear technologies with the presumption that their use would remain peaceful. That changed in 1964, when China detonated a bomb. Once it appeared that atomic weapons might no longer be the domain of Western powers, Lyndon Johnson established a committee under the leadership of Deputy Secretary of Defense Roswell Gilpatric to study the issue. This committee, which would define U.S. non-proliferation policy for decades to come, concluded that nuclear proliferation would not just disturb the existing U.S.-Soviet deterrence structure, but also weaken American influence throughout the world. Its report noted that the "recent Chinese Communist nuclear explosion has reinforced the belief, increasingly prevalent throughout the world, that nuclear weapons are a distinguishing mark of a world leader, are essential to national security, and are feasible even with modest industrial resources."[58] This report paved the way for the NPT, which sought to regulate the spread of nuclear resources.

The shah's atomic explorations came at a particularly inopportune time: India had just jolted the international system with a nuclear test. That India had apparently used plutonium from a reactor it obtained from Canada led to concerns about safeguards. There was much alarm in Congress about the implications of India's test, with various committees conducting hearings and investigations. Within the executive branch, the Pentagon and the Arms Control and Disarmament Agency took the lead in resisting nuclear transfers.

It was in this atmosphere that the United States and Iran began negotiating over a bilateral nuclear agreement. The intelligence community set the stage by stressing, "The Shah is not likely to seek nuclear weapons in the near future, but he will probably attempt to acquire the necessary technology."[59] The Americans set exacting terms: Iran had to forgo enrichment and reprocessing of spent fuel at home and agree to additional safeguards beyond those stipulated in the NPT. At times, the Americans spoke of a multinational nuclear facility, but it was unclear exactly how such an entity would operate. As Etemad recalled, "From the beginning they had the precondition that they should have complete control over our nuclear fuel cycle."[60] Baffled and exasperated, Etemad believed that given the primitive state of Iran's nuclear program, there was no need to give the United States such a veto power.

In the 1970s, the concern about proliferation centered on plutonium, because this was still the path chosen by most nuclear aspirants. Although

America's prohibition of domestic enrichment was clear, much of the discussion between Tehran and Washington focused on preventing Iran from reprocessing spent fuel for military purposes. The NSC memorandum prepared for Gerald Ford emphasized that the administration must reserve the "right to approve where the U.S.-supplied fuel can be reprocessed and the resulting weapons-usable plutonium retained. Our objective is to preclude reprocessing and storage in wholly *national* facilities."[61] The United States sought Iran's commitment that all of the plutonium produced in its reactors would be sent abroad.

Henry Kissinger proved to be the shah's most accommodating listener, because he wanted to encourage all Middle East potentates to go on spending sprees. Kissinger felt that one reason that regional actors could so easily scale back their oil production during the embargo was because their excess capital cushioned them from reduced revenues. If he could get these nations to invest heavily in all sorts of projects, from military hardware to nuclear power plants, they would have a harder time playing the oil card. As Kissinger told Ford, "What we need to do is to preempt the structure of relationships in the area and to develop a flow of benefits which they won't want to lose."[62] In other words, Washington should be prepared to indulge all of the shah's fantasies, however impractical. But with Nixon gone and both Congress and the bureaucracy asserting their power, Kissinger had less room to maneuver. He simply could not overcome the many obstacles in his way.

The shah's May 1975 visit to Washington was designed to offer Ford assurance. It was agreed in the White House that if the shah objected to U.S. demands, the president would merely table the issue for expert discussions. At any rate, the subject did not come up: the shah spent most of his Oval Office visit condemning India's test. This seems to have been his idea of a confidence-building measure.

With the shah soft-pedaling the issue, it was left to Etemad to flatly reject the American terms. In his meeting with U.S. officials, he denounced the idea of a multinational facility as inconsistent with Iran's sovereign rights. The notion of being discriminated against by the United States was brandished by Etemad, who ended the meeting by stressing that "the final decision on [re] processing in Iran must rest with Iran—not [the] U.S."[63] The impasse in the negotiations lasted throughout the Ford presidency. The shah would have better luck in Europe, where both France and West Germany were eager to provide Iran with nuclear technology. The French nuclear industry needed money, and the Germans were looking to expand their trade with Iran in all areas. This caused friction in the transatlantic alliance, as Washington pressed its allies to follow its tough line.

Jimmy Carter's liberal tendencies augured poorly for the shah's nuclear dreams. Carter viewed proliferation as a global problem and established rigid conditions for any nuclear transaction. In 1978, the administration unveiled its Nuclear Non-Proliferation Act, which imposed stringent terms on any nation wanting to access American nuclear technology. But by this time, the Pahlavi state had bigger problems than a parsimonious Carter administration. The revolutionary tremors soon caused the shah to scale back his grandiose projects. The Iranian government tried to deal with the growing economic crisis by reducing state expenditures. The AEOI was transferred to the Department of Energy, and Etemad was let go. Meanwhile, the shah began his descent into an emotional morass that deprived the nuclear program of its most consequential patron, at least until the mullahs took over.

CHAPTER 8

The Revolution

In 1971, the shah decided to celebrate the 2,500-year anniversary of the Achaemenid Empire. This was his way of establishing a mystical connection between his monarchy and the great Persian dynasties. The event, held in the ancient city of Persepolis, featured thousands of soldiers masquerading in traditional uniforms while sixty-eight heads of state lingered in air-conditioned tents. The themes were Persian, but the food was imported from France and almost all the guests were foreigners. SAVAK made sure Iranians were kept away from the festivities, which were estimated to have cost between $200 and $300 million.[1] More bizarre acts were to follow, but none was stranger than the monarch's replacement of the calendar based on the Prophet Mohammad's migration to Medina with one that started with King Cyrus's enthronement. This was the shah's Great Civilization.

In the mid-1960s, the distinguished scholar Marvin Zonis conducted a survey of Iranian elites that demonstrated their sheer cynicism. Over 70 percent of those surveyed believed the system was not working, while 60 percent felt that having the right connections was the only basis for promotion.[2] A corrosive alienation had descended on Iran. By this time, the elder statesmen with the confidence and expertise needed for independent action had all but disappeared. Iran no longer produced great men such as Qavam, Mossadeq, or Amini. In their place were technocrats who were not permitted to make any decisions. No official was indispensable, or even allowed to amass much power. Contradicting the shah usually meant dismissal or at best a transfer to a less important post. Paradoxically, the shah grew contemptuous of those who populated his state machinery. He demanded sycophancy but was put off by those who displayed it.

The bureaucracy, in turn, was hampered by the shah's predilections. By this time, he rarely consulted with his advisers and would make sudden decisions that they had to scramble to understand. The monarch routinely met with his ministers, generals, and heads of SAVAK and NIOC, where he would speak and they would listen. He encouraged not just competition but backstabbing among his elite, a management style that destroyed any solidarity within the system. On matters of international relations, the shah dealt with dignitaries without his foreign minister or diplomats present, and he rarely reported back to them about what had been said. He issued commands and his functionaries were to implement them even if they questioned their wisdom.

In many ways, the shah was a victim of his own success in creating a modern middle class and a vast student population. In a system that rewarded lack of initiative, tolerated corruption, and punished ingenuity, there was little room for those who believed in meritocracy. The members of the new urban middle class wanted participatory politics and a voice in their nation's affairs. But the shah was prepared to offer them only financial compensation, which proved fleeting as Iran's economic miracle turned into a mirage.

The disenchantment was most visible on college campuses. This was troubling for a regime whose modernizing agenda demanded a capable but politically passive cadre. Prime Minister Hoveyda said of the new Pahlavi creed, "The Iranian student must be courageous and willing to sacrifice. He should and can form student unions and organizations. He should not, however, build these into anything political. That is not his business."[3] This was the same compact the shah was offering to the professional classes and the intelligentsia— material rewards in exchange for political quiescence. The students could be part of Iran's march forward, but only if they shed their ideals.

Evidence of social pathology among young Iranians, including drug abuse and high suicide rates for a traditional society, should have alarmed the authorities. Many Iranian students who went abroad chose not to return home. Given the pervasive repression, opposition ideas appeared as novels, plays, and poems with indirect allusions. The shah was not unaware of the turbulence in his universities and complained to Alam that "despite their [students'] access to a wide range of scholarships and other privileges, they are completely uninterested in the progress that this country is making." Alam, who sometimes gave the shah blunt advice, merely responded that it could be "explained by the fact that they are denied any role, either in the university, or in national political affairs." The shah usually dismissed such criticism and blamed the agitation on communist subversives.[4]

The façade of authoritarian stability was disrupted by the advent of urban guerrilla movements. This new class of guerrillas came largely from the universities and took their inspiration from the revolutions of Mao Zedong and Fidel Castro. In time, the North Vietnamese would also assume an iconic place in their imagination. The Fada'iyan-e Khalq used Mao's tactic of starting in the countryside and attacking remote police stations and village officials. The more Islamist Mujahedin-e Khalq took its violence to the urban centers by assaulting government offices, banks, and barracks. They also mounted attacks on American installations—attacks that were underreported by the press because the Iranian government and the U.S. embassy successfully covered them up. The guerrillas were finally defeated in 1977, but their daring and courage impressed many Iranians, including even the shah, who confessed to Alam that the "determination by which they fight is quite unbelievable. Even the women kept battling on to their very last gasp."[5] The guerrilla forces would reconstitute themselves during the revolution and play an important role in the fall of the Pahlavi state.

As Iran's anxious decade unfolded, the shah was creating a social order in which moderate opposition was hemmed in from all sides while, on university campuses, the fallen heroes of the armed struggle were venerated. The old National Front politicians still congregated, under close SAVAK surveillance, but their patient political path was no match for the times. The Tudeh had long been eviscerated, while Bazargan's Liberation Movement limped along with its leaders in and out of prison. The notion that the government could not be reformed and must be taken out root and branch was gaining currency in all sectors of society.

And then came the exodus of the shah's best and brightest, even before the initial murmurs of revolution. Michael Metrinko, one of the more astute political officers in the U.S. embassy, kept asking well-heeled Iranians why they were leaving the country, only to be told that Iran was an awful place to live.[6] The embassy estimated that in 1976 alone, six thousand Iranians purchased houses in London. As the revolution unfolded, the best place to find the Pahlavi elite was in the airport VIP lounge.

The signs of brewing discontent were not lost on U.S. intelligence services. It is the conceit of President Carter and his senior aides that they were blindsided by the political turmoil in Iran. They soon scapegoated the intelligence community and blamed it for their own misjudgments. In fact the CIA and the rest of the intelligence services did a reasonable job of tracking developments in Iran, and they produced many prescient reports that successive White Houses ignored. The intelligence community's record was imperfect, but it is wrong to cast all the blame on the CIA.[7]

As early as 1969, a National Intelligence Estimate stressed that "demands for greater political participation by the educated groups are likely to grow. If such participation is not permitted and if Iran's economic progress should falter, this could pose serious problems for his [the shah's] still narrowly-based regime, particularly if dissent were to find support within the heretofore loyal military ... Over the long term, economic development probably will not provide a satisfactory substitute for greater political participation. Hence in a few years, unrest may again begin to reach significant levels among the politically aware elements."[8]

As for the armed struggle emerging in Iran's streets, a State Department report informed its readers that the "urban guerilla activity has attracted some public sympathy and even admiration because it provides for many a vicarious expression of the resentments which they have but do not dare express."[9] Even Kermit Roosevelt resurfaced and, after a trip to Tehran in 1972, wrote a memorandum for CIA director Richard Helms that was passed on to Kissinger. Many senior Iranian officials, he reported, "expressed concern that the Shah has pressing domestic problems that are not being given enough attention."[10] There is no indication that these assessments made an impression on Nixon and Kissinger, who were determined to make Iran a pillar of their Middle East strategy.

By the mid-1970s, alarm bells were ringing in the CIA. According to an intelligence assessment in May 1975, "Dissent among civil servants in Iran has now reached an alarming degree, even though superficially everything appears normal on the surface ... Students and labor groups have always been sources of discontent, but now this malaise has reached the civil servants." The cause was "corruption among high officials, lack of efficiency in government operations, and the dismay over the establishment of a new political party which will not satisfy the growing urge for greater democracy."[11] Once more Kissinger ignored these reports. As noted earlier, at this time he was conspiring with the shah against Iraq and was more than willing to send large shipments of arms to a country that hardly needed them and increasingly could not afford them.

Meanwhile, beneath the veneer of Westernization, Iran was experiencing a religious revival. Religious books topped the best-seller lists and annual pilgrimages attracted a large segment of the public. Men with beards and women wearing religious attire became common sights in the universities and even in government offices.[12] Anthony Parsons, an unusually incisive British ambassador, recalled in 1976 "a well-informed professor at Aryamehr University [Iran's MIT] telling me that about 65 percent of his students were motivated by Islam and about 20 percent by communism while the neutral remainder would always side with the Islamist groups if it came to trouble."[13] No one, apparently, believed in the shah's mission even at a university that he took so much pride in creating.

Two intellectuals would do much to popularize Islamist themes, although neither lived to see the revolution triumph. Jalal Al-e Ahmad's 1962 book *Gharbzadegi,* loosely translated as *Westoxification,* celebrated indigenous values untouched by occidental intrusion. Born of a religious family, Al-e Ahmad, once a clerical student who later fell under the influence of Marxism, saw Islam as inextricably intertwined with the Iranian identity. For Al-e Ahmad, Islamic history was glorious, while occidental history was a prelude to aggression. The charge of *Westoxification* became an effective gravamen against those who understood that modernization, by definition, meant borrowing ideas from Europe and America. Al-e Ahmad died in 1969, but his critique became the dominant creed in Iran's universities.[14]

Another intellectual, Ali Shariati, electrified Iran's lower- and middle-class youth, increasing numbers of whom were attending universities, with his own equally contentious reading of Islamic history. Shariati came from outside the clerical order and expropriated religion as an ideology of rebellion. He had obtained his doctorate from the Sorbonne in the sociology of religion and was influenced by the turbulent politics of France, especially the Algerian war of liberation and the anti-colonial struggle that strongly influenced a generation of Third World intellectuals already disillusioned with the Soviet Union. Shariati found a hero in Frantz Fanon and translated his seminal work, *The Wretched of the Earth.* Fanon, a new type of revolutionary intellectual, had moved beyond Marxism and sought authenticity in his local culture. In his own quest for a revolutionary creed, Shariati sought to refashion the canons of Shiism as symbols of protest.

Shariati became famous as a lecturer and spoke to packed audiences. With a gift for amalgamating disparate concepts into a seamless narrative, he refashioned Shiism as a religion of dissent led by rebels seeking social justice. In his rendering, the forces of oppression stood in the way of the Prophet Mohammad and his companions because they feared the loss of their privileges. Shariati's Islamic history was certainly confused, but he understood that many of Iran's youth and members of the middle class were looking for a more authentic belief system. He offered his mesmerized listeners a chance to accept modernity while holding fast to their traditions. His message was anti-monarchical, because it implied that the shah's despotism was inconsistent with the Prophet's egalitarian vision. Shariati died in 1977 from a heart attack in Britain, where he had taken exile after much harassment by SAVAK. He died of natural causes, but the revolution needed martyrs, and many soon came to believe that foul play had been involved.

Shariati did much to agitate the leading ayatollahs, who resented his meddling in their domain. A young intellectual who had not spent time in the seminary, he was quick to condemn the esteemed men of religion as purveyors of an ossified Islam. Only one exiled cleric stood above everyone else in terms of courage and charisma: Khomeini, Shariati's ideal ayatollah. Khomeini had been expelled from Iran because he gave no quarter to the shah, and he had spent his years in exile denouncing everything the monarch did. In 1970, he published a series of his lectures as a book, *Islamic Government*, which included the novel idea that the clergy should assume political power. This contravened Shia thought, which emphasized that government belonged to the Hidden Imam and until his return, the guardians of faith should keep their distance from centers of power. Khomeini's contempt for democratic rule and his hatred of religious minorities are evident throughout the text. In the very first pages of his manifesto, he argued that

> From the very beginning, the historical movement of Islam has had to contend with the Jews, for it was they who first established anti-Islamic propaganda and engaged in various stratagems, and as you can see, this activity continues down to the present. Later they were joined by other groups, who were in certain respects, more satanic than they. These new groups began their imperialist penetration of the Muslim countries about three hundred years ago, and they regarded it as necessary to work for the extirpation of Islam in order to attain their ultimate goals.[15]

As the revolution unfolded and his media-savvy advisers sought to sanitize him, *Islamic Government* became a source of controversy. Many officials and academics claimed to be unaware of its existence even though copies of the book were circulated in the West and available at the libraries of the major universities; on December 30, 1978, the *New York Times* even profiled it.[16]

Khomeini had a ready-made network of supporters from his days leading the uprising of 1963–1964. He had an underground operation that would quickly disseminate his writings and, later, the taped recordings of his sermons. His hundreds of students were dispersed throughout the country, and at least some of them maintained their allegiance to his vision. Moreover, as we have seen, the seminary had changed in the 1960s, drawing recruits from villages and small towns who were offended by the changes taking place around them. Khomeini was the only leader to persistently call for the shah's overthrow at a time when most of his contemporaries were willing to accommodate the monarch.

Khomeini's appeal was apparent in June 1975 when riots broke out in the shrine city of Qom on the anniversary of his expulsion from Iran.[17] Seminary students took to the streets chanting his name—which at that time was a criminal offense. The regime had to send troops to put down the riots, eventually arresting some two hundred seminarians. The shah dismissed the demonstrators as "stateless Reds and black reactionaries shouting slogans."[18] He would often return to the theme of Marxist-Islamist collaboration because he never believed that the clerical estate was actually behind the revolt that overthrew him.

Once more the American intelligence services produced timely and incisive reports. The CIA assessed that

> probably no more than 10 percent of the clergy who receive government support can be counted as outright supporters of the Shah. They are probably the least influential of the clergy and are considered by many to be no better than government employees. Probably 50 percent are in outright opposition to the government and are wholly dependent on their popular following for support; this includes nearly every religious leader of any stature. The remaining 40 percent qualify as fence-sitters, maintaining a popular following but avoiding overt attacks on the government.[19]

A National Intelligence Estimate in 1975 stressed that

> prominent in the opposition are the religious leaders and through them the religious establishment. Religion has been a major influence on the urban lower classes and the bazaar merchants. Even the intelligentsia,

who in other circumstances would be scornful of religious establishment[,] now apparently perceive the religious leaders as sharing common grievances against the present system.[20]

A CIA study of the Iranian elite conducted in February 1976 noted, "The clergy would probably not prefer the elimination of the monarchy, but would be happy to see the present Shah go . . . The present generation of religious leaders, moreover, seems to be convinced that the Shah, as his father before him, is determined to destroy Islam in Iran."[21]

Nor had Khomeini's growing stature escaped the notice of Iranian and American officials. As early as 1970, upon the death of the Ayatollah Mohsin al-Hakim, the spiritual leader of the nearly seventy million Shiites, the embassy in Tehran reported that the "leading contender for the leadership among the faithful is Ayatollah Khomeini, who commands considerable respect and popularity in the bazaars of Iran."[22] SAVAK feared that if the aging and popular Ayatollah Abol Qasim al-Khoei should die, "the majority of his followers will go to Khomeini."[23] It appears that there were observers in both systems who appreciated Khomeini's appeal among the vast community of believers.

Once he sensed the popular agitation, Khomeini began to subtly distance himself from his own writings. He never renounced the notion of an Islamic government, but he presented it as offering freedom within a religious context. His comments were a jumble of contradictions, but the frenzied public chose to hear what it wanted to hear. Khomeini's first move was to ignore his core idea that a single cleric should govern. In an interview in 1978, he said that "the religious authorities will not rule by themselves; they will rather supervise and direct executive affairs . . . This government will rely on the people's votes and will be under public control, evaluation and criticism at all times."[24]

As for himself, he insisted, "I do not want to run the government myself. But I will guide the people in choosing the government, and I will announce its terms to [the] people."[25] This would be his persistent theme: the clergy would oversee national affairs but would not participate in day-to-day operations of the government. It is hard to see how clerical supervision could be reconciled with democratic government, but Khomeini proved adept at measured mendacity.

As his country teetered on the brink of full-scale revolt, the shah became a remote presence. His picture was on display everywhere and statues of him went up at a record pace, but his subjects no longer saw him as they had seen him in the 1960s. He traveled the country by air for safety, and the journalists he spoke to were usually Westerners. The risk of yet another assassination attempt is often cited to justify his detachment, but the fact is that the shah always harbored a measure of contempt for his countrymen. Iran, in his mind, was a laboratory for social experimentation as opposed to a complex nation undergoing immense change.

In summer of 1974, the shah was diagnosed with chronic lymphocytic leukemia. This finding was kept hidden: even the queen was not informed until 1977.[26] It is hard to see how the secret was maintained, given that the shah's French medical team made thirty-five visits to Iran between the diagnosis and his departure in 1979. But the always discreet Alam, who suffered from a similar condition, managed to keep things off the books. The question that has bedeviled historians is what impact the cancer had on the shah's management of national affairs at such a turbulent time. He always faded from the scene during a crisis. The uprisings of 1953 and 1963 had been handled by General Zahedi and Alam, respectively, because the shah refused to take responsibility for tough actions. His propensity to vacillate cannot be attributed to his illness, but the cancer did focus his mind on succession. He did not think his young son was up to managing a dictatorship whereby a single individual made all the essential decisions. He therefore had to put Iran's affairs in order before turning things over to the crown prince.

The problem for the shah was that he had spent decades cleansing the system of independent-minded politicians and had emasculated Iran's great national institutions. The technocratic elite had no feel for the country and felt little loyalty to the imperious royal court. Reforming a system based on fear and patronage would be difficult at any time, much less a time when the shah insisted on speed. Still, signs of change subtly started to appear. When Alam finally dared tell the shah that Iranians felt the nation's material gains "had nothing to do with them," the monarch seemed to agree. "I've sensed the same thing myself. We have to put some thought into this," he told a startled Alam.[27]

Yet it was hard for the shah to have a clear idea of what liberalization would entail. He had an authoritarian personality, had long derided democracy as a Western disorder, and thought the Iranian people required a firm and steady hand. He seemingly understood the need to open up the system and revitalize the institutions that he himself had eviscerated, yet even as the buzz of reform filled the air, he remained convinced of his own popularity. He reminded himself that he had lifted millions of Iranians out of poverty. He had given land to the peasants, industrialized the country, and reclaimed its oil from foreigners. Iran was an important actor on the international scene, with the world's statesmen making frequent visits. He had encountered opposition from the landlords, mullahs, and liberals, but the masses, he believed, had always been with him.

The shah's first attempt to mobilize the population demonstrated how hard it is for an authoritarian leader to implement reforms even when he senses the need for change. In 1975, he finally did away with the two docile political parties, which had become something of a joke, and replaced them with a single national entity. Thus began the short, unhappy life of the Rastakhiz (Resurgence) Party. The shah wanted a mass organization that would build up the "self-confidence and self-respect in the people, a belief in our power and ability . . . to fight the tendency of the people, especially the youth, to deny, to denigrate, to reject."[28] Yet he insisted that his White Revolution was beyond reproach, and that he had no intention of engaging his critics in an actual debate. Membership in the organization may have been compulsory, but it failed to excite the masses.

The Rastakhiz would never have the strength of the Soviet Communist Party, but it did signal to the public that the regime was about to intrude further on their lives. The shah wanted a party that would mobilize the nation as it faced a succession crisis, but he simply could not cede control. Perhaps the best description of the party's first congress came from Alam, who said, "The whole thing was excellently stage-managed, but hollow, utterly hollow and false."[29]

The cooling of Iran's economy, too, made the mid-1970s an inauspicious time for tinkering with the political order. The global recession lessened demand for Iran's oil, causing its production to dip from a high of 6 million barrels per day to 3.5 million by 1976. Meanwhile, power outages hampered industrial operation while the government's budget deficit continued to grow. Even the military budget was reduced, for the first time since the 1950s.[30] Inflation reached 24 percent, and the agricultural sector could not keep up with population growth. Iran had to subsidize foodstuffs and rely on imports to meet its basic needs. The cities continued to lure massive numbers of people from the countryside, causing housing shortages and requiring the average family to spend up to 60 percent of its income on rent. By the 1970s, approximately half of Iranians lived in the cities, up from 30 percent who did so in the 1950s. Little urban planning had been done to deal with the influx, and shanty towns began to grow on the edges of cities.

The economic downturn is often said to have sparked a crisis of unfulfilled expectations, fueling the revolutionary fires. But this notion has to be unpacked with great care. There was always income inequality in Iran, but so long as the economy was growing, everyone could hope to get a share. They might grumble about the size of that share, but most Iranians were confident that they would receive some benefits. The recession of the mid-1970s, however, provoked a peculiar psychological reaction. Most assumed that the good economic times were over forever, and they resented being left behind. This sentiment was bound to have political consequences: many Iranians were angry at those who had gotten ahead through their connections to the royal court. This was, after all, still the most reliable path to self-enrichment. Economic anxiety, social envy, and political disenfranchisement became powerful political forces directed against the shah. The good times were thought to be over, and only the shah and his cronies had benefited.

This sense of gloom did not escape the shah as he summoned his trusted Alam. "We're broke," he lamented. "Everything seems doomed to grind to a standstill, and meanwhile many of the programs we had planned must be postponed. Oil exports seem likely to fall by as much as 30 percent, and the recent price rise will do little to compensate."[31] Alam tried to boost the shah's spirits by assuring him that he would be remembered as Persia's greatest modernizer. Yet he harbored darker premonitions and confided to his diary, "I genuinely fear that this may be the first vague rumbling of impending revolution."[32]

It was the shah's misfortune that he entered the most dangerous period of his life without Alam, who succumbed to cancer in 1978. Alam sensed the mood of the country as only a landlord who spent time in villages and distant provinces could. Despite his slavish displays of loyalty, he understood the shah's many limitations. It was Alam who in 1963 had made the tough decisions that quelled the uprising, and it was Alam who had seen through the glitter of the 1970s to the discontent beneath. In one of his last conversations with Hoveyda, whom he despised, he confessed, "The smoldering resentment seems exceptional even allowing for the inadequacy and occasional ineptitude of this government in responding to the public's needs."[33] As Iran came undone, an isolated monarch was left alone to contemplate the future of his creaky dynasty.

LIBERALIZATION GOES ASTRAY

In 1977, the shah decided that the era of liberalization required a new face, and he appointed Jamshid Amouzegar to the premiership. Among the mistakes the shah made that doomed his monarchy, this appointment has to rank high on the list. Amouzegar was a Western-educated technocrat who had performed well as finance minister and understood the intricacies of the oil industry. He epitomized the shah's new elite: a man with no sense of Iran's complexities whose most prominent political role was the leadership of the disastrous Rastakhiz Party. Hoveyda, for all his faults, at least understood the shah's many misjudgments even if he did nothing to correct them. Amouzegar lacked even that basic appreciation: he attributed Iran's problems to bureaucratic inefficiency.

The new prime minister's first charge was to tame inflation and balance the budget. He was comfortable with numbers but lacked the political touch that such a task required. He had no ability to build coalitions, refused to bargain with other stakeholders, and seldom communicated with the public. Like the shah, he was aloof and reticent, and contemptuous of subordinates.

Amouzegar decided to curb inflation by assaulting the bazaar. Even in the era of modernization, the bazaar, with its traders, merchants, artisans, and guilds, could still serve as a platform for political mobilization. In 1953, prominent merchants were the ones who organized the pro-shah rallies that eventually devoured Mossadeq's premiership. By the late 1970s, the bazaar, with its 400,000 or so shops, controlled much of the domestic trade and about 30 percent of all the imports.[34] Such independent financial power made it a critical player in Iranian politics.

In the Pahlavi conception of modern Iran, where all things had to have a Western tinge, the bazaar stood as a relic of the past. The shah and his elite believed the masses would be better off if they avoided the maze of shops with their old ways of haggling. The new Iran should look like Europe, and the new Iranians should shop at European-style stores. Accordingly, the government began setting up its own supermarkets, which essentially took over the distribution of such goods as meat, sugar, and cement. Then came the inflationary pressures, which further damaged the bazaar.

The Amouzegar government compounded these difficulties by imposing price controls and intensifying a vicious anti-profiteering campaign. As inflation surged, the prime minister tried to address the problem by intimidating the shopkeepers. Gangs of students were authorized to roam the bazaars and fine and jail offending merchants. By the state's own admission, 220,000 merchants were punished.[35] Nor did the government limit itself to issuing fines: its agents sought to humiliate those they cited. Once a shop was shuttered, a notice was usually pasted on its door saying the owner was guilty of profiteering. To further shame shop owners, the newspapers were ordered to publish the names of all those who were convicted. It was Amouzegar's anti-profiteering campaign, more than any other factor, that persuaded the merchant class to take collective action against the state. In his first move in power, Amouzegar had managed to alienate an important institution with significant financial power. The men of God and the men of commerce would soon join forces against the shah.

The liberalization program was launched amid this economic turmoil. Hushang Ansary, who held many cabinet posts and had most recently been one of the leaders of the Rastakhiz Party, flamboyantly declared, "Let the pens write and the tongues speak so that the exchange of thoughts and experiences paves the way to the achievement of the aims of the [shah-people's] revolution."[36] Amouzegar's spokesman, Dariush Homayoun, followed this up by claiming, "Henceforth no one should be afraid of criticizing the government."[37] The shah, ever mindful of Western opinion, invited representatives from Amnesty International and the International Commission of Jurists to inspect his prisons and see for themselves that torture had ended. Following their recommendations, he agreed to limit the use of military tribunals and try all political prisoners in civilian courts, where they would have access to their own lawyers.

The first to take advantage of this opening were the National Front leaders Karim Sanjabi, Shapour Bakhtiar, and Dariush Forouhar, who wrote in an open letter,

> The only way to restore national unity and individual rights is to abandon despotism, respect the constitutional laws, observe the Universal Declaration of Human Rights, abolish the one-party system, permit freedom of the press and assembly, release political prisoners, allow exiles to return home, and establish a government that enjoyed public confidence and respected the fundamental laws.[38]

When the authors, to the surprise of many, were not arrested, the floodgates opened. Every imaginable association, from the lawyers' guild to trade unions, issued its own letters. The politicians of the past resurfaced, intellectuals published manifestos, poets read protest poems, professors organized sit-ins, and students tore up their classrooms.

In October 1977, the Goethe Institute, a German cultural society in Tehran, sponsored a series of poetry readings that drew an audience of more than ten thousand. The poems soon yielded to speeches calling for constitutional rule, an end to censorship, and judiciary reform. The police tried to disrupt the meeting, causing the nascent opposition movement to take to the streets—where it would remain throughout the revolution. So far, the protest was led by intellectuals and old-time activists, but soon the clerical community would claim leadership of the revolution.

As the intellectuals and poets garnered all the press attention, Khomeini's vast network sensed an opportunity to flex its muscles. "The recent indulgences on the part of the establishment, which gave the opportunity to the writers to write and the speakers to speak, is a big ruse to absolve the Shah and pretend that there is freedom," Khomeini thundered.[39] His status as the leader of the 1963 rebellion made him attractive to many seeking a legitimate voice of dissent. Soon a shadowy organization called Iran's Militant Clerics surfaced and staged its own protests, which got little media attention. The group's demands were not modest: it rejected reform and called for replacing the monarchy with an Islamic government. The notion of religious rule was still vague enough to appeal to many strands of opposition, but from the beginning, Khomeini and his followers made it clear that they had no tolerance for a constitutional monarchy and preferred a system in which religion informed politics.

On October 23, 1977, Khomeini's eldest son, Mustafa, died of an apparent heart attack. Although there is no indication of foul play, his death was quickly attributed to SAVAK. It appears that in 1970s Iran, no politically prominent person died of natural causes. The commemorations of his death naturally combined religious themes with political provocation. At a time when many dissidents still wanted to come to terms with the shah, Khomeini appeared as a man who had sacrificed much for his unyielding commitment to principle. First he was torn away from his homeland, and now the regime had murdered his son.

Khomeini and his cohort were quick to politicize Mustafa's death. Two of Khomeini's leading disciples, Ayatollahs Morteza Motahhari and Mohammad Reza Mahdavi-Kani, tried to induce as many people as possible to attend the various memorial ceremonies for Mustafa. Khomeini himself used the occasion to attack the regime, writing, "We are facing a great calamity and should not mention personal tragedies."[40] He further insisted that the aim of the liberalization policy was "to cleanse the Shah of his crimes."[41] Khomeini did not attend his own son's funeral, and when told of his death, he merely repeated the Quranic phrase that all who belong to God shall return to him. He always displayed an indifference to human life that was often mistaken for stoic resolution in the face of tragedy.

The Shia ritual calendar is ideal for political manipulation because it is filled with commemorative occasions. A hundred or so days a year can be set aside for some type of religious event. As the revolution gained traction, all such episodes became platforms for denouncing the regime. One such powerful occasion is to mourn the dead forty days after their passing. Mustafa's forty-day remembrance conveniently coincided with the martyrdom of Imam Hossein, usually an occasion of high emotion as believers lament the killing of a just man at the hands of an iniquitous caliph. These religious themes easily played into the hands of the opposition, with Mustafa seen as the martyr and the shah the cruel caliph bent on murder and pillage. The thousands of attendees at the ceremony carried Khomeini's picture and called for an Islamic government.

The shah at this point seems to have been unconcerned with these signs of clerical agitation. The clergy had historically supported the monarchy, and of the leading ayatollahs, only the exiled Khomeini continued to inveigh against the regime. The government missed the increasing segmentation of the clerical order that had taken place since the 1960s. While the senior ayatollahs preoccupied themselves with theological disquisition, the younger, more parochial mullahs were drawn to Khomeini's message of defiance and would eventually push the senior ayatollahs to take more radical positions. It was Khomeini's appeal among the lower strata of the community that allowed him to establish hegemony over the entire clerical estate.

The paradox of Iran would soon become the foremost concern of a one-term governor of Georgia with little knowledge of foreign affairs.[42] In 1976, the shockwaves of Vietnam and Watergate led the American people to entrust the presidency to a man who promised not to lie to them. Jimmy Carter initially sought to transcend the prevailing Cold War orthodoxy that saw the Third World as just another arena of superpower competition. Shortly after assuming the presidency, Carter proclaimed, "We are now free of that inordinate fear of Communism which once led us to embrace any dictator who joined us in that fear."[43] In the aftermath of the Vietnam War, he and many of his aides were skeptical of right-wing dictatorships and predicated their foreign policy on respect for human rights. The shah may have been unsettled by Carter's pieties, but he had grown more inflexible since the early 1960s and was not inclined to acquiesce to another reformer in the White House.

In January 1977, when Carter assumed the presidency, Iran was hardly on his mind. The new administration was focused on transacting arms control agreements with the Soviet Union and completing the normalization of relations with China that Nixon had started. To the extent that the new team had a Middle East policy, it was to settle the conflict between Israel and its Arab neighbors. In the aftermath of the 1973 Yom Kippur War, Henry Kissinger had negotiated a series of armistice agreements that the White House hoped to transform into actual peace accords. Iran was still viewed as an important and reliable ally, however despotic its ruler might be.

One of the Carter administration's first actions on human rights was to defend Iran. The 1977 State Department report on human rights emphasized Iran's social and economic progress. Although political prisoners were mentioned, the department acknowledged the shah's liberalization efforts. "We believe that the Iranian government is committed to prison reform and that prison conditions have indeed improved," the report noted.[44] Iran was moving in the right direction and the shah was committed to reforms.

As was his custom, the shah decided to make his own trip to Washington for a full assessment of the new administration. On November 15, 1977, he arrived at the White House only to be greeted by the same student protests that had dogged all his previous trips to America. It is often reported that some one thousand Iranian students denounced the shah, but these reports neglect to mention that the embassy had arranged for two thousand pro-shah demonstrators to turn out to support him. The inevitable clash between the two sides was poorly handled by Washington's Metropolitan Police, whose use of tear gas caused the shah and President Carter to spend most of the welcoming ceremony wiping tears from their faces. This disastrous public relations display, however, should not distract us from the success of the two leaders' first summit.

Once the shah and Carter got down to business, their discussion was dominated by the usual concerns. The shah complained about arms shipments, particularly his stalled attempt to purchase the highly sophisticated AWACS (Airborne Warning and Control System) surveillance aircraft. (The administration eventually pushed the sale through a reluctant Congress.) The shah also impressed his audience with his mastery of geopolitics. Chief of Staff Hamilton Jordan marveled that he gave "more than a presentation—it was a performance."[45] The changing nature of Arab politics and the fluctuations of the oil markets capped off the topics discussed at the leaders' first official meeting.

The issue of human rights was not on the formal agenda, but Carter raised it with the shah privately. The president's message was hardly radical; he urged the shah to pursue a dialogue with dissidents and ease up on his repressive tactics. The shah answered, "No, there is nothing I can do. I must enforce the Iranian laws, which are designed to combat communism."⁴⁶ Thus ended Jimmy Carter's attempt to pressure the shah of Iran on the issue of human rights. The monarch was rather pleased with his trip and informed one of his subordinates, "Carter is beginning to see sense. He's no longer preaching the same old nonsense that he did during the election."⁴⁷ At least at the beginning, the two sides were on the same track.

If Carter's human rights advocacy did not instigate reforms, it did energize the opposition. Bazargan recalled, "We did not believe the Shah when he started the liberalization policy, but when Carter's human rights drive lifted the hope of the people, all the built-up pressure exploded."⁴⁸ Given the centrality of the United States in the Iranian imagination at that time, the shah's liberalization program was seen by many as an indication that America had lost confidence in its ally. Paradoxically, Carter's first months in office bolstered both the shah and his opponents.

On one of his first world tours, Carter stopped in Tehran to celebrate New Year's Eve, the last night of 1977, at the shah's palace. In a moment of excitement that would haunt him forever, he proclaimed that "Iran, because of the great leadership of the Shah, is an island of stability in one of the more troubled areas of the world."⁴⁹ Carter's aides subsequently tried to rescue his reputation by claiming that he often overreacted on such occasions with exuberant toasts. The shah was certainly impressed. As he noted in a memoir that is otherwise replete with bitter denunciations of America, "I have never heard a foreign statesman speak of me in quite such flattering terms he used that evening."⁵⁰

The Carter administration eventually dispatched an experienced ambassador to Iran, William Sullivan. Sullivan had been ambassador to Laos and the Philippines and was part of Kissinger's delegation at the peace talks with Vietnam. He has the distinction of being blamed by both Carter and the shah for losing Iran. Carter, who later said he regretted not firing him, claims that Sullivan often failed to discharge his instructions.⁵¹ For his part, the shah believed that Sullivan was too enamored of the opposition and was eager to see his dynasty collapse. These charges are unfair. To be sure, Sullivan did himself no favor with his angry memoir, *Mission to Iran*. Yet, reading through his cables, one can see that Sullivan was a capable diplomat who astutely sized up the shah and his ministers. His judgment of them as indecisive men who could not grasp the enormity of the challenge they faced was spot-on. Sullivan was not as good at understanding those whom he did not meet, namely Khomeini and his clerical disciples, and he often confused Bazargan and other moderates with the real leaders of the revolution. His cables thus have an uneven quality. But it must be noted that Sullivan was an honorable professional who never ignored or watered down his instructions as Carter and his national security adviser, Zbigniew Brzezinski, would later charge. Sullivan did his best under extraordinary circumstances and should not be blamed by an Iranian monarch who lost his kingdom and an American president who went on to a landslide defeat of his own.

Two media-savvy Iranians living in the United States, Ebrahim Yazdi and Sadeq Qotbzadeh, understood that Khomeini had a great opportunity to take advantage of the new political opening. But first they had to sanitize the ayatollah and sweep aside his inflammatory opposition to anything but a rigid theocracy. The public relations management of an antediluvian figure straight out of the Old Testament would be difficult, since Khomeini rarely concealed his contempt for liberal norms. Still, in the unusual atmosphere of 1978— when many Iranians were reclaiming their traditions—it was easy to believe in Khomeini's Islamist vision.

Given Khomeini's fulminations, the shah was eager to take on the cantankerous cleric. Having done so much for Iran, he had no intention of letting himself be pilloried by an exiled mullah trapped in an Iraqi seminary. One of the shah's favorite tactics was to use the media to attack his opponents. When the National Front started to revive itself, for instance, stories suddenly appeared in a number of publications attacking Mossadeq. Now Khomeini would receive the same treatment. A defamatory story about his background, the shah thought, would be an ideal means of discrediting him. Thus began one of the shah's worst mistakes.

The article was passed from Hoveyda, now serving in the royal court, to Information Minister Dariush Homayoun, who casually gave it to one of Tehran's largest dailies, *Ettela'at*. The article had reached Homayoun in an official royal envelope and he was not the type to stand in the way of the monarch. The article, titled "Iran and the Red and Black Colonialism," claimed that Khomeini

> was an adventurer, a faithless and ambitious man associated with and subservient to colonial powers. A man with a mysterious past who was attached to the most reactionary colonial elements. Since he failed to acquire a status among the country's most senior clergy—despite all the suspicious support that he had received—he sought an opportunity to make a name for himself by means of inciting a political adventure.[52]

The editor of *Ettela'at* understood immediately that the article would provoke a backlash. Informed of the editor's concerns, Homayoun contacted Amouzegar, who had not read the piece himself but insisted that it was what the shah wanted. The article was published on January 7, 1978, and sparked riots throughout the country.

The shrine city of Qom was the first to explode. The demonstrations were led by young seminary leaders and their students, who not only denounced the shah but also demanded that the senior ayatollahs take a stand. Soon the protests moved beyond the seminary, with some ten thousand people taking to the streets chanting "Death to the Shah." The police responded by firing into the crowds, setting off a dispute over the exact number of casualties that would go on for the rest of the revolution. It appears that four people were killed, but exaggerated numbers were soon reported.

As the young seminarians stood outside their homes calling on them to act, the senior ayatollahs were shamed into supporting one of their own. Ayatollah Mohammad Reza Golpayegani condemned the regime, saying, "They are lying if they claim that we agree with their policy." Ayatollah Kazem Shariatmadari, one of the more esteemed members of the clergy who was in frequent touch with the royal court, shed his inhibitions and told the protesters, "What you are doing is sacred, as you are defending the position of the religious leadership and the clergy." In the past, Shariatmadari could be counted on to call for calm, but now he had no choice but to denounce the government. The respected men of religion may have been dubious of Khomeini's tactics, but they had no option but to line up behind him.[53]

From his perch in exile, Khomeini understood that he had his clerical counterparts exactly where he wanted them, and he was not about to let them off the hook. In an unsparing statement, he pronounced that "only false clerics can agree with the Shah."[54] At a time when the young seminarians were protesting in the streets and facing the shah's police, the senior ayatollahs could not maintain their traditional role as a bridge between Qom and the royal court. The shah's maladroit move and Khomeini's deft reaction were radicalizing the clerical community. Only Khomeini could benefit from such an outcome.[55]

The forty-day commemoration of the dead ensured that the cycle of protest continued. The worst riots took place in Tabriz, where for two days demonstrators attacked banks, offices of the Rastakhiz Party, hotels, and cinemas, leaving six dead and 125 injured. The protests took two days to quell, and the army had to be called in and martial law imposed for the first time since 1963.

Khomeini praised the "struggling people in Tabriz . . . for giving the [regime] a smash in the mouth."[56] Then came the cascade of protests to mourn the most recent dead, this time in the cities of Kerman, Yazd, Qazvin, Mashhad, and Isfahan. There were demonstrations in Tehran itself. For the moment, the scale of protests was such that the local authorities could handle them without calling in the armed forces.

In the 1970s, Iran had 9,000 mosques and a clerical order that comprised 90,000 men, with 50 ayatollahs and perhaps 11,000 seminarians.[57] No secular party could command such a network. This is not to suggest that the mosque was a privileged sanctuary for the revolutionaries. Published SAVAK documents reveal that it kept the mosques under tight surveillance. Dissident mullahs were arrested, exiled, and banished to different parts of the country. But despite the harassment, the mosque was a resilient national institution, and the clergy retained their influence in the urban shanty towns, small cities, and villages across the country. They managed endowments, collected contributions, and adjudicated disputes. The regime could shutter a political party's offices, but it could not easily close down a mosque given its role in the community. Once Khomeini and his allies controlled the vast majority of the mosques, the government was powerless to prevent the dissemination of their message.

The shah, meanwhile, behaved with the inconsistency that had always confounded his allies. He still looked for hidden hands, insisting to Sullivan that "there was no evidence that the mullahs were that well-articulated or capable of pulling such a demonstration together."[58] He was sure that the Iranian people loved him and that these protests were the death throes of the fanatics. He remembered confronting demonstrations after launching the White Revolution and defeating those reactionary forces.

At the same time, the shah offered a series of concessions that made little sense. He dismissed the provincial governor of Azerbaijan for using excessive force in Tabriz—an unusual gesture for a monarch who had briefly lost control of one of his major cities. Next, *Ettela'at* published a rebuttal to its original article by Ayatollah Marashi Najafi, who criticized the newspaper for attacking Khomeini and blamed the riots on the government.[59] The monarch followed this up by sacking his longtime head of SAVAK, General Nasiri, and replacing him with General Nasser Moqaddam, who had good relations with the upper echelons of the clergy. No one in Iran was sure where the shah's red lines were, but it soon became evident that there was little penalty for violating them.

The American bureaucracy once more produced reports that captured the urgency of the situation. Sullivan cabled his superiors, "The greatest potential danger to the Shah is that he may lose control over the religious elements and their adherents, leading to the inherently more dangerous confrontation of secular modernizers against fundamentalist religious leaders—a problem that has been avoided for almost 15 years."[60] Later, Sullivan reported that "Khomeini retains an almost mystic respect of mass of illiterate population and Shariat-madari feels he cannot differ to a significant degree with Khomeini in public."[61] The embassy saw that the moderate divines were reluctant to challenge Khomeini and his hold over the clerical estate.

The State Department's Bureau of Intelligence and Research (INR) also reported, "The recent incidents of violence in Iran are the most serious of their kind in a decade. Though they are not an immediate threat to the Shah's regime, they have put his traditionalist Islamic opponents in their strongest position since 1963." The report also noted that the demonstrators were not just seminarians but a "broad range of traditional dissidents (Islamic conservatives, student progressives, dissatisfied intellectuals and terrorists) and some new and potentially powerful elements (judges, lawyers and businessmen)." The CIA's National Intelligence Daily echoed these concerns: "There appears to be little room for compromise between the Shah and conservative Muslim opponents, who believe that reforms instituted by the Shah and his father threaten the future of Islam in Iran."[62]

Since the Islamic Republic's publication of vast troves of the shah's documents, we have a better understanding of the deliberations within the Pahlavi state. The regime's top military officers and the SAVAK leadership did meet periodically during this time to assess the situation, but they were often hampered by the shah's conspiracy theory about a Marxist-Islamist collaboration. When SAVAK director Moqaddam briefed the high command in summer of 1978, he had to adhere to the story the shah had laid out:

> We notice great solidarity among the mullahs as they use religion for their purposes. These mullahs that we are speaking of are communists in clerical garb and use the pulpit to instigate the masses. There is such unity among the mullahs that even those who support the government are completely silent. For instance, some mullahs who were against the commotion in Qom still remained quiet. Also, in Tabriz and Isfahan, the clerics who support the government have remained passive. The vast majority of the mullahs who started all these disturbances are supporters of Khomeini.[63]

It is hard to believe that Moqaddam, who had many connections in the clerical order, really thought that communists were masquerading as clerics, but he had to humor the monarch's favorite absurdity. The more important point that Moqaddam was trying to convey to the assembled officers was that Khomeini and his allies had taken over the mosques, and even the clerics who were dubious of their tactics were unlikely to challenge their control.

All revolutions ebb and flow. At the start of summer in 1978, there was hope that perhaps the crisis had passed. The cycle of protests had simmered down and the attempt in June to commemorate Khomeini's expulsion had largely fizzled. The liberals appeared intrigued by the shah's reformist moves. Demonstrations still occurred in various cities, but the protest movement seemed to have stalled. Violence returned as the Islamists targeted symbols of Western decadence such as theaters, cinemas, liquor stores, and even restaurants—but none of this unduly disturbed a Pahlavi state that had been dealing with terrorists since it had put down the armed struggle in the early 1970s.

At the palace, the shah and his coterie still thought liberalization would succeed. The shah spoke with unusual confidence and insisted, "Nobody can overthrow me. I have the support of 700,000 troops, all the workers and most of the people. I have the power."[64] He thought that through liberalization, he could isolate the extremists and set off a legitimate dialogue between the court and responsible members of the opposition about how to strengthen the monarchy.

In a more discreet move, the shah allowed Hoveyda to negotiate with Shariatmadari, who was also concerned about the course of events. The Grand Ayatollah, whose base of support was in Azerbaijan, was disturbed about the convulsions in the province's main city of Tabriz. He remained dubious about Khomeini and his radical postulations and wanted the government to leave the religious sector alone and respect the 1906 constitution. The shah was not averse to negotiating, but he wanted Shariatmadari and other moderate divines to take a stand against Khomeini. Both sides were trapped in their inhibitions. The shah was unwilling to yield much power, while Shariatmadari was reluctant to confront Khomeini. The talks would eventually fail, but at the time they gave everyone the impression of progress.

During Iran's most consequential summer, practically everyone left town. Sullivan and Parsons, thinking the situation was under control, both took extended home leave. The shah spent most of the summer on the shores of the Caspian Sea, provoking gossip about his health. The embassy reported that "rumors range from terminal malignancy, Leukemia, simple anemia to having been wounded in the arm or shoulder by General Khatami's son or Princess Ashraf's son."[65] The shah's health in fact did deteriorate, and he was visited by his French medical team late that summer.

On August 5, the shah gave his annual Constitution Day speech, but this time he took a giant step toward advancing his liberalization agenda. He announced, "This is a new chapter in our country and we shall enjoy a maximum of freedoms allowed by the law . . . We shall have freedom of speech and freedom of press according to a new press law that may be adopted from any of the world's freest nations." He assured his listeners that "elections will be a hundred percent free, everyone will have a right to vote and have his vote read." The next parliamentary elections were scheduled for the following June. There would also be a new code of conduct for members of the royal family. The shah was finally responding to all those Iranians who wanted a genuine representative order. Then came the bombing of Rex Cinema in Abadan.[66]

At times, terrorism changes the trajectory of history. The Rex Cinema bombing was one such event. The Islamists had wanted a spectacular act of violence to commemorate the anniversary of the 1953 coup. Cinemas had been targeted before: the revolutionaries had already bombed about thirty. Khomeini detested cinemas: he considered them a source of Western cultural pollution and had openly endorsed their destruction. He once publicly mused, "The Shah's cinema is the center of prostitution and the trainer of mannequins unaware of themselves and even more so of the disorganized state of the country. The Muslim people consider such centers to be against the interests of the country, and think that they ought to be destroyed without the clergy having given any instructions to this effect."[67] The crew selected for this assignment was a motley group of former drug dealers and hardcore militants. They first targeted a different cinema, but after their explosives failed to discharge, they retreated to the desert for a few days to try out their munitions and make sure they would work the next time.

On August 19, the terrorists struck again. The Rex Cinema was packed: it was showing a controversial film called *Deer* that had just been passed by SAVAK's censors. The doors of the theater were slammed shut as the explosives were set off. The perpetrators fled, but it took the fire department more than an hour to respond to the emergency, and by then 479 people had died. This was the most egregious act of arson in Iran's modern history—meticulously planned and designed to provoke national outrage. The perpetrators were soon apprehended in Iraq, and their eventual trial showed them to be Islamists.

The bewildered Pahlavi state, however, found itself blamed for the tragedy. The palace issued its condemnations, the shah pledged to bring the perpetrators to justice, and the government offered compensation to all of the victims. But as the nation mourned, the Queen Mother insisted on going ahead with her annual party commemorating the 1953 coup. The luminaries of the Pahlavi court gathered at Saadabad Palace to celebrate the shah's triumphant return. The monarch himself seemed dejected, even shattered, by the news out of Abadan—yet the orchestra played, champagne flowed, and buffets of imported food were served to the out-of-touch elite. It was a particularly insensitive touch that the garden party was followed by a massive fireworks display. No member of the royal court went to Abadan to console the victims. There is no evidence in the SAVAK files published after the revolution that the government was responsible for the tragedy, but its public relations blunders led many to blame the shah.[68]

Khomeini seemed ready for the moment. After a period of unusual silence, he proclaimed, "This inhuman act is contrary to all the laws of Islam, and therefore, cannot have been committed by the opponents of the Shah, who have risked their lives for the sake of Islam and Iran." He added, "This heart-breaking tragedy is the work of the Shah, his masterpiece, and designed as grist to his vast propaganda mills both at home and abroad."[69] This message was repeated from mosque pulpits across the country and even echoed by the liberal opposition. In the end, Khomeini managed to blame the royal court for a mass murder committed by his own followers.

The Rex Cinema bombing was an inflection point in the history of the revolution. The bombing completely overshadowed the promises the shah had made in his Constitution Day speech. A leader who could set human beings on fire could not be trusted to usher in a liberal order. The sense of outrage also transformed the protest movement. Up to this point, only hardcore opponents of the shah had participated in the demonstrations. Now many fence-sitters began tilting toward the opposition. The size of the marches grew by the thousands as Iran's uprising finally became a popular revolt.

The most immediate victim of the Rex Cinema bombing was Amouzegar, who reluctantly offered his resignation. His premiership had begun with the anti-profiteering campaign and ended with a national insurrection. He left his post nurturing conspiracy theories about how his rivals had caused the mayhem in order to undermine his premiership. It was a mark of the shah's confusion that in the coming months he would often regret dismissing Amouzegar.

NATIONAL RECONCILIATION

On the surface, Jafar Sharif-Emami looked like the wrong man to take the premiership amid a national uprising. He was a fixture in Iranian politics, having served as both prime minister and president of the senate, and had spent his years between government posts enriching himself.

His legendary corruption had earned him the nickname "Mr. Five Percent." He had most recently been head of the Pahlavi Foundation, the depository of the royal family's misbegotten wealth. But he did have ties to the clerical community, and his appointment can best be understood as a product of back-channel negotiations between the royal court and Shariatmadari. The Grand Ayatollah appreciated the shah's Constitution Day address but insisted on a new cabinet. For the post of prime minister he recommended Sharif-Emami or Amini. Given that the shah still despised Amini, Sharif-Emami was the choice.

Sharif-Emami dubbed his government one of national reconciliation. He relaxed censorship, cashiered a number of officers, abolished the cabinet position for women's affairs, closed down bars and liquor stores, and restored the Islamic calendar. In an ironic move, he even announced an anti-corruption campaign. He also offered amnesty to political dissidents, including Khomeini, who could now return to Iran. These steps were necessary, he believed, to jump-start negotiations with Shariatmadari. More importantly, he thought that once all the strands of opposition came to the surface, they would devour each other in internecine conflict, and he could then offer the masses an opportunity to reclaim their religious traditions in the context of a constitutional monarchy.

Sharif-Emami is routinely vilified by the monarchists for taking down the last ramparts of the Pahlavi state. They deride his strategy as an effort at appeasement that only emboldened the opposition. He did resume the negotiations with Shariatmadari, as well as with Bazargan. But the accusations of appeasement are unfair given the unpalatable choices he faced in the fall of 1978. This is not to absolve Sharif-Emami of his misjudgments, especially his failure to see how the clerical estate had changed over the decades. He confidently predicted, "One group, which follows Ayatollah Khomeini, is radical but very small. The other, which follows Shariatmadari, is moderate and very large. A split between them exists in every city and every village."[70] He clearly did not grasp how Khomeini had imposed his hegemony on the clerical order.

It appears that few outside Sharif-Emami's inner circle believed he could mollify the ayatollahs. Hoveyda, the first to pursue this strategy, told Sullivan in early spring that he was confident a compromise could be worked out. But when Sullivan checked with him upon his return in August, a more somber

Hoveyda told him, "It didn't work because the Khomeini people had fright-ened the moderates."[71] This was Hoveyda's last act on the national stage: he was soon dismissed as minister of court and later arrested to propitiate the opposition.

It is unclear when the shah gave up on his regime. At the end of the sum-mer, a mournful monarch returned to Tehran and, as usual, confided only in Westerners. Sullivan, the first to see him, reported that the shah "evinced no conviction that Sharif-Emami would succeed. He felt that Ayatollah Kho-meini, 'that mad man,' is forcing the Islamic pace and that the other Ayatol-lahs are scared to resist him."[72] Parsons was shocked by the shah's appearance, reporting that he "looked shrunken: his face was yellow and he moved slowly. He seemed exhausted and drained of spirit."[73] In a quizzical tone, the shah stunned Parsons by asking him "why it was that the masses had turned against him after all that he had done for them."[74] The ambassador offered assurances, but they failed to assuage the monarch. This was the first of many occasions when the shah would ask foreign envoys to explain his country to him.

The shah had the peculiar habit of revealing himself to Western journal-ists. He seemed to assume that if he shared his secrets with them, they would become his advocates. In September, Joseph Kraft of the New Yorker arrived in Iran for an extended stay. His first interview was naturally with the shah, who appeared depressed and gloomy. When Kraft told him that at least he still had a formidable army, the shah blurted out, "You can't crack down on one block and make the people on the next block behave."[75] By the time this quote was published in the New Yorker, the military government was in power. It appears that by September, the shah was doubtful of a compromise with the mullahs and did not believe a crackdown would work either. His tragedy is that he was right on both counts.

Even though the royal court had given up on Sharif-Emami, his outreach created much consternation in Khomeini's camp. The Imam, as his followers now called him as a way of elevating him above other grand ayatollahs, thun-dered, "We will not make peace at the expense of our martyr's blood . . . No party, front, or movement will or may make peace with this government, for making such a peace is to enslave the people and to commit treason against the nation."[76] Always sensitive to power shifts, Khomeini perceived that the government was vulnerable and that the shah seemed to have lost his bear-ings. It was therefore time to strike even harder. While Iran's other opposition leaders had to be mindful of the regime, Khomeini did not hesitate to call on his followers to take to the streets. By now, his cassettes were pouring into

Iran and his proclamations were being aired by international news media—particularly the BBC Persian Service, which had millions of Iranian listeners.

Sharif-Emami's reckoning came on September 8, which came to be known as Black Friday. The day began when a large crowd gathered in Tehran's Jaleh Square to celebrate the end of Ramadan. The opposition had pledged that the commemoration would be peaceful, but soon protesters began yelling out slogans calling for the shah's ouster and for the establishment of an Islamic government. The poorly trained conscripts sent to deal with the situation opened fire on the crowd, killing eighty-five people. The demonstrations spread beyond the square until the entire city was engulfed in smoke and fire. Bizarre stories began circulating in Tehran that Israeli commandos dressed as Iranian soldiers had killed thousands of protestors. The government accurately reported the casualty figures, but by now the opposition was routinely exaggerating the numbers and the Western press would uncritically repeat its claims.

Black Friday brought a shift in public opinion. The massacre at Jaleh Square evaporated what was left of the regime's tattered legitimacy after the Rex Cinema bombing. Those who could envision the collapse of the Pahlavi state began to outnumber those who insisted on its durability. This may have been a subtle shift, but its impact was real. What was once unthinkable became at least plausible: Iran might actually dispense with a 2,500-year institution of monarchy. No one knew what an Islamic government might look like, but an increasing number of Iranians were willing to find out.

The most consequential victim of Black Friday was the shah himself, who lost what was left of his confidence. Having long been cloistered in his palaces and accustomed to the veneration of sycophantic aides, he understood Iran's economic problems and the corruption of the ruling class but somehow thought the public considered him to be separate from the government they opposed. As he surveyed the wreckage of his capital from a helicopter, he seemed stunned. Returning to his palace, he could only mumble to his puzzled staff, "But what did I do to them . . . have you heard their slogans?"[77]

Always prone to conspiracy thinking, the shah now began to look for the actual culprits behind the disturbances. Ironically, he ruled out the Soviet Union. Even he could not believe that the Tudeh could muster such crowds. Britain came under early suspicion, since Iranian officials had never stopped complaining about how the BBC had given Khomeini a platform. The Labour Party government, led by James Callaghan, assured the shah of its support and correctly stressed that it had no control over the BBC, a claim that few in Iran believed.

Eventually the shah's search for culprits led him to the United States. He summoned Sullivan and bluntly asked him, "Why was the CIA suddenly turning against him? What had he done to deserve this sort of action from the United States?"[78] Sullivan's angry denials failed to mollify him, and his officials now confronted their American counterparts about the CIA's machinations. On the margins of the U.N. General Assembly, Iran's courtly foreign minister, Amir Khosrow Afshar, quizzed Secretary of State Cyrus Vance about stories circulating in Tehran that the United States was collaborating with the opposition. Vance assured him of America's complete support. Ardeshir Zahedi, serving another stint as the shah's ambassador to Washington, approached Deputy Secretary of State Warren Christopher and with some embarrassment asked for assurances that the CIA was not involved so he could calm the shah's nerves. Christopher naturally told him "that the story was totally without foundation."[79] Most of the shah's aides did not share his suspicion, but they still had to indulge his latest theory.

As he had done in 1953, the shah once more contemplated abdication. His basic humanity prevented him from shedding blood. He was devious and cynical, but he was not cruel, and he sincerely believed that a monarch should not kill his subjects.[80] Nor is it clear that an officer corps unaccustomed to making decisions could take command of the situation. On the rare occasions that force had been used, it was on such a small scale that it had outraged the public without inspiring fear of the regime. After the revolution, the Islamic Republic's Martyrs Foundation determined that between October 1977 and February 1979, the regime had killed 2,781 people.[81] The fearsome SAVAK turned out to be an organization manned largely by former military officers who were good at surveillance but too timid to offer the shah any useful analysis. This time there was no General Zahedi or Alam available to save the monarchy.

The shah moved in bewildering directions that only confused his supporters and empowered his enemies. He deployed his army to the streets but ordered them to avoid casualties at all cost. He loosened censorship and then complained about poor press coverage. He promised more liberalization measures at a time when the street was dictating the pace of events. Having spent decades creating a system where only he could issue orders, he was now paralyzed by indecision.

As the shah vacillated, Khomeini steeled himself for confrontation. He denounced the shah as a lackey of America and Israel who had plundered Iran and massacred its people on behalf of his foreign masters. Many chose not to notice that his comments were often a jumble of contradictions. The Imam promised that a religious government's "constitution is Islamic and must conform to the laws of Islam which are the most progressive laws."[82] On gender rights, "Women are free to choose their own activities and destiny as well as their mode of dress within Islamic standards."[83] On the press, "All press is free unless their essays are against the country."[84] On speech, "Freedom of expression is allowed, if it is not detrimental to the nation."[85] On political parties, "All parties will be free in Iran, unless they are against the exigencies of the nation."[86] For every promise there was a hedge.

In the aftermath of Black Friday, strikes began to affect all of Iran's major industries. Khomeini once more took the lead and proclaimed, "From now on it is time for us to close our businesses, not forever, but for the short time it will take to overthrow the ruling oppressor."[87] A once dynamic country went dark. Newspapers stopped publishing, electricity flickered, bazaars shuttered, banks stopped processing transactions, and most importantly, the oil industry ground to a halt. Iran's oil production fell from 5.8 million barrels per day before Black Friday to 2.3 million barrels in November and, by January, output was close to zero.[88] The regime had some success in sporadically jump-starting the oil installations by using military technicians, but in the end it could not cope with the walkout of all the essential personnel. Iran had stopped functioning.

In the midst of these problems, Sharif-Emami was suddenly confronted with Khomeini's expulsion from Iraq. Saddam Hussein's Sunni-dominated government feared that Khomeini's agitation would arouse its own restive Shia population. Suddenly, the Imam and his companions were stranded on Iraq's border with Kuwait, with neither country willing to grant them entry. Khomeini wanted to settle in a Muslim country, but few would take him. At this point his Western-educated aides thought of France. There was already a sizeable community of dissidents there, and Iranians did not need a visa to enter the country. Khomeini grumbled about being among the infidels, but he had no choice. It was now time for the Iranian government to make its move.

President Valéry Giscard d'Estaing did not want to admit Khomeini without consulting the shah. This decision by the Pahlavi government has often been seen as disastrous in light of the access that Khomeini gained to international media. But Sharif-Emami's principal fear was that the Imam would actually return to Iran. He had already been amnestied and could easily have tried to come home. At a time when the prime minister was still engaged in sensitive negotiations with Shariatmadari and Bazargan, the last thing he needed was another crisis. In the end, Sharif-Emami thought it better to have Khomeini in the Parisian suburb of Neauphle-le-Château than in Tehran.

The Iranian government may have assumed that Khomeini would keep quiet during his French exile, but the Imam had other ideas and ultimately gave 132 interviews. The usual practice was for journalists to submit their questions in advance and for Khomeini's advisers to formulate the responses. During the actual interview, Khomeini would typically stick to the script, and no follow-up questions were allowed. That leading members of the press accepted this practice is a discredit to their profession. Meanwhile, telephones and telex machines worked energetically to disseminate Khomeini's messages to Iran. Given the ease of travel, countless Iranian dissidents journeyed to Paris to pay tribute to the leader of the revolution.

In Tehran, Sharif-Emami's delicate and seemingly hopeless negotiations suddenly began to produce results. Bazargan still did not believe that the shah's government could topple. Like most oppositionists, he wanted assurances that the shah's liberalization really meant a return to a constitutional order. For his part, Shariatmadari feared that Iran was coming undone and that a military coup might be on the horizon. Both men sought to save Iran by coming to terms with the shah.

After much wrangling, Bazargan and Shariatmadari offered their terms to the prime minister. Their list included free elections, freedom of the press, legal limits on the shah's powers, formation of independent political parties, release of all political prisoners, greater respect for religion in public affairs (including clerical oversight of parliamentary legislation), the return of Khomeini from exile, and the royal family's withdrawal from all business affairs. After consulting with the shah, Sharif-Emami accepted all demands. Before they could announce a deal, however, Bazargan insisted that he had to go to Paris and obtain Khomeini's consent.

Once presented with the agreement, Khomeini curtly rejected it. Bazargan tried to explain to him the urgency of the situation, stressing that "the world of diplomacy and Qom seminary are different and one cannot prevail just because he is just."[89] But the Imam was not about to call off his Islamist revolt to preserve a constitutional monarchy. The masses in the streets were not clamoring for restraints on the shah's powers—they were demanding an Islamic government. Bazargan and Shariatmadari now had a choice: they could accept the shah's offer or continue the struggle under Khomeini's leadership. To the detriment of Iran, they opted to side with Khomeini.

The other major opposition leader who had sporadic negotiations with the shah about accepting the premiership was the head of the National Front, Karim Sanjabi. Once Bazargan folded, Sanjabi rushed to France to offer his own surrender terms. Unlike Bazargan, whom the Imam treated with respect, Sanjabi was offered no such deference. He was the head of Mossadeq's party, and despite the Islamic Republic's exploitation of the 1953 coup, the Islamists had only contempt for the National Front and its liberalism. After a meeting lasting just a few minutes, Sanjabi made his capitulation clear, telling the assembled press that "the current monarchy, having systematically violated the constitution, having committed acts of cruelty and injustice, having fostered corruption and having been subservient to foreign interests, had no legal and religious foundation and had lost its legitimacy."[90]

All three men would be purged by the triumphant revolutionaries. Bazargan would serve briefly as prime minister before being relegated to the parliament, where he filled his time giving speeches. Shariatmadari's fate was darker; he was defrocked and died while under house arrest. Sanjabi published a revealing memoir, aptly titled *Hopes and Despairs,* and retired to America, a country he so often relished criticizing. Such is the justice the revolution meted out to those who knew better.

The question remains how an exiled cleric achieved such political hegemony. Khomeini was known as courageous and utterly incorruptible. He could afford to be maximalist because, unlike those inside Iran, he did not have to accommodate the government. In the 1970s, when the shah was all powerful, Khomeini was the only important leader calling for his overthrow. He brooked no compromise and attained iconic status in both the seminary and the street—a stature that, paradoxically, he could have obtained only in exile. At the height of his success, the Imam acknowledged this point, musing that "it is more convenient to unveil the Shah's crimes on a worldwide level while living abroad."[91]

Sharif-Emami's premiership reached its inglorious end on November 6, 1978. He had lost control of his liberalization process and made concessions he could not reclaim. Perhaps he should have sensed that the men he was negotiating with could not deliver. But his options were limited, given that he faced a national uprising, a crippled economy, and a bewildered monarch. Like many Persian politicians of his generation, he relied on a conspiracy theory to explain his predicament. His was that SAVAK had undermined his premiership because he had cashiered many of its top officers.[92] Perhaps, given that he settled in New York City, he thought it unseemly to blame the CIA.

THE MESSAGE OF THE REVOLUTION

As Iran teetered on the brink, President Carter spent much of his time at Camp David brokering peace between Israel and Egypt. At Sullivan's urging, he had called the shah after Black Friday and assured him of America's support while urging him to continue his reforms. This was the only time the two leaders spoke during the entire crisis.

As the revolution unfolded, the intelligence community tried to keep up with events. In August 1978, the CIA produced a report that would do much to tarnish its reputation, featuring the memorable phrase, "Iran is not in a revolutionary or even a pre-revolutionary situation."[93] This is certainly damning, but it is not the entire story. Stansfield Turner, director of the CIA, had already commissioned a National Intelligence Estimate, but he decided to shelve it because events were moving so quickly. Still, by September, a draft of the NIE had begun to circulate. The latest assessment noted that "as a result of [the] lifting of constraints, political expression by a wide variety of groups, loyal and disloyal, has mushroomed beyond the ability of the country's enfeebled official institutions to cope." At a time when Carter was pressing the shah to stick to his reforms, the NIE warned, "Even sweeping concessions will not ensure continued calm, however, for there is almost a universal tendency among Iranians, and certainly among the political and religious opposition, to interpret any concessions as signs of weakness that should be exploited rather than as positive elements of political settlement."[94]

In the first half of 1978, most intelligence analysts assumed that a monarch who had weathered so many crises would once more rise to the occasion. The summer brought some signs of hope. The demonstrations had calmed down, and the government was negotiating with the opposition. The shah was talking tough and seemed in command of the situation. The CIA's report claiming that Iran was not in a revolutionary stage was certainly wrong, but not outlandish. All of this changed by the fall. Given that no final NIE was going to be produced, the State Department's Bureau of Intelligence and Research was tasked with crafting an assessment that reflected the judgment of the entire intelligence community. That report, produced in late September, stated that there was a question "of his [the shah's] ability to survive in power over the next 18 to 24 months."[95] In a separate paper reflecting just its own views, INR was even starker: the shah's "reversion to the moods of depression and vacillation he displayed in the early 1950s make it doubtful that he can move to salvage what remains of national unity, unless others intervene on his behalf."[96]

The embassy in Tehran largely affirmed the judgment of the intelligence services. Since the mid-1960s, ambassadors to Iran had feared that talking with opposition leaders would anger the shah, so they had prohibited such contacts. One of Sullivan's first acts was to do away with this unwise policy and free his diplomats to roam the cities, gather information, and establish contact with a variety of Iranians. In one of its most comprehensive surveys up to that time, the embassy observed "a willingness among sizeable numbers who have supported the Shah consistently as Iran's best hope for the future to question whether the Shah should remain."[97]

The stream of alarming reports coming from the bureaucracy finally snapped the Carter White House out of its torpor. A procession of high-ranking Americans journeyed to Tehran to take a look at the shah for themselves. The first to come was Michael Blumenthal, secretary of the treasury, who was taken aback when the shah said to him, "What can I do? No one will listen." Then he plaintively asked Blumenthal, "What is your advice? What does the president suggest I do?" The secretary could only repeat the ritualistic assurance that Washington stood behind the shah in whatever course he chose, but it would not dictate a decision to him.[98]

Next to arrive was Robert Bowie, head of the CIA's National Foreign Assessment Center. Bowie had been a high-ranking State Department official in 1953, so he should presumably have known of the monarch's indecisiveness in times of crisis. When they met, the shah was more distracted than usual and did not seem to be paying much attention to the latest visiting American. Bowie's more important conversation was with Moqaddam, who told him that while the secular politicians might be open to negotiations with the shah, the more important clerical community was under Khomeini's spell. Moqaddam, the head of SAVAK, confessed that so long as the Imam remained the most consequential actor, a compromise was unlikely.[99] Upon his return, Bowie nonetheless recommended that the White House reach out to the moderate elements of the opposition.

As Carter began considering his options, there was a clear division among his top advisers. Vance and the State Department, fearing that a military crackdown would lead only to bloodshed and chaos, persistently pressed for a negotiated solution to the crisis. They somehow convinced themselves that negotiations could produce a coalition government that would preserve the monarchy while granting the revolutionaries a share of the spoils, and that the key to all this was direct talks with Khomeini. Vance could not grasp that the seventy-six-year-old cleric had no interest in sharing power with a humbled monarchy.

Zbigniew Brzezinski remained Carter's most clear-eyed and perceptive aide. As an academic who had studied the Soviet Union, Brzezinski understood how revolutions devour everything in their path. He sensed that the shah could not continue a liberalization policy that was rapidly dissolving what was left of his regime, and he understood better than Vance that Khomeini was not waging his revolution in order to yield power to the moderates. Brzezinski's preferred option was to crack down on the revolution first, then institute reforms that would yield a constitutional government. For him restoring order meant just that, putting an end to the demonstrations and strikes. But Brzezinski failed to see that no one in Tehran was prepared to be his iron fist.

It is often suggested by historians that Carter was caught between these two poles and could not impose order on his bickering aides. He was often told by Vance and Vice President Walter Mondale that in the aftermath of Vietnam, he could not ask another head of state to massacre his people. His entire human rights crusade and his disdain of despots certainly weighed heavily on him. But Carter was made of tougher stuff than his liberal aides. He often sided with Brzezinski over Vance and grew frustrated with diplomats who advised patience. In November, he sent a clear signal to the shah that if he wanted to use force, America would stand by him.

Prior to an NSC meeting, Brzezinski told Carter that "unless the Shah can combine constructive concessions with a firm hand he will be devastated."[100] As he met his assembled aides, Carter essentially accepted this advice, and a cable was dispatched to Sullivan. The message the ambassador was to convey to the Shah was blunt:

On the highest authority and with Cy Vance's concurrence you are instructed to tell the Shah as soon as possible:

1. That the United States supports him without reservation in the present crisis.

2. We have confidence in the Shah's judgment regarding the specific decisions that may be needed concerning the form and composition of government; we also recognize the need for decisive action and leadership to restore order and his own authority . . .

3. That once order and authority are restored we hope that he will resume prudent efforts to promote liberalization and to eradicate corruption.[101]

Brzezinski now called the shah himself. The British government had recently advised the monarch to avoid a military government, and to make it clear that the United States was not following Britain, Brzezinski told the shah that while he did not intend to tell him what to do, Washington would support whatever decisions he made and had complete confidence in his rule. He ended the conversation by telling the shah, "It is a critical situation, in a sense, and concessions alone are likely to produce a more explosive situation."[102] Sullivan then met with the shah and presented the president's message to him. In his memoirs, Brzezinski hints that perhaps the ambassador diluted Carter's assurances. The documentary record belies this claim. At their meeting, it was not Sullivan but the shah who objected to the use of force. He pointedly asked the ambassador, "Why [does] the President [think] a military government would be successful?" After months of pleading with Americans to tell him what to do, the shah now insisted that he "could not see what [the] President could actually do in tangible terms . . . [the] situation was vastly different from 1953, when U.S. assistance had been helpful." He ended the meeting by telling Sullivan that if the army used massive force, Khomeini "would call for a Jihad and there would be a bloodbath. Even some of the military would take their obligations to Islam ahead of their obligations to the Shah."[103]

Since arriving in Tehran, Sullivan had been one of the shah's most reliable supporters. But now he underwent his own conversion and began to consider that the monarchy might collapse. Taking advantage of a long weekend in November, he decided to dispatch a memorandum to Washington titled "Thinking the Unthinkable." Seldom has a diplomatic cable been more misunderstood. The memorandum was an exercise in speculation, and it was certainly replete with misjudgments. Sullivan began by noting that the monarchy was a spent force and that the shah's "support among the general public has become almost invisible." The conflict was now between the military and the religious sector as represented by Khomeini. Given that both wished to avoid a bloodbath, he thought it might be possible to craft a compromise whereby "Khomeini could be expected to return to Iran in triumph and hold a Gandhi-like position in the political constellation." To be fair, Sullivan cautioned that "all this Pollyannaish scenario could come about only if every step along the way turned out well." He concluded his cable by saying, "Our current posture of trusting that the Shah and the military will be able to face down the Khomeini threat is obviously the safe course to pursue at this junction," but should that fail, "we need to think the unthinkable."[104]

As a shrewd diplomat, Sullivan had observed the workings of the Pahlavi state and arrived at the sensible judgment that the shah was not capable of managing the crisis and that his generals were not inclined to crack down and shed blood. The lesson he drew from Sharif-Emami's ill-fated negotiations was that it was no use talking to oppositionists other than Khomeini. It is here that Sullivan's imagination failed him. He underestimated Khomeini's determination to impose an Islamic government on Iran at all costs. As an emissary of a secular republic known for its pragmatism, Sullivan simply could not comprehend revolutionaries who meant what they said.

After Sharif-Emami's resignation, the shah decided to play his last card: a military government. He hoped that a military regime would intimidate the opposition long enough for him to find a suitable civilian to take over and for his liberalization plan to succeed. He had been negotiating with various politicians, including his bête noire, Amini. In his desperation, he had forgotten his many grudges and summoned the ghosts of the past to rescue his monarchy. Few, however, volunteered for such an unenviable reclamation project. They preferred exile in Europe.

The military to which the shah turned was the same institution he had spent decades hollowing out. He had lavished much attention on the military, continuously increasing its budget and adding to the perks enjoyed by the generals, but the price for these rewards was unquestioning acceptance of the shah's mandates. The monarch was not above engaging in petty moves, and he had long encouraged his generals to scheme against each other, causing much distrust in the ranks. The officers leading the various branches of the armed forces thus reported to the shah individually and had little experience working together. Their organization was nothing like the army of 1953 when Zahedi and others were fully capable of stepping in and taking charge.

The shah tapped General Gholam Reza Azhari, chief of staff of the armed forces, to lead the government. Azhari had moved up in the ranks primarily because he rarely created friction. He was typical of the shah's officers: obedient to the monarch, diligent at staff work, and rarely capable of coming up with an idea of his own. He was the wrong man to take over in a crisis, but it is hard to see who in the upper echelons of the regime was better suited. Azhari treated his promotion with all the melancholy that the occasion required. As he left the shah's office with the official proclamation in hand, he was asked by a palace official why he looked so dejected. He could only murmur, "I am ruined . . . His Majesty has appointed me prime minister."[105]

Still, the arrival of the new government and the declaration of martial law made an impression on the opposition. Ten thousand troops were dispatched to man the city's key choke points. Demonstrations that had been raging across the country died down a bit. Iran was still paralyzed by strikes, but for now protests simmered down. And then, on November 5, the shah gave a speech.

The idea of an address to the nation started with the queen and her liberal aides. Perhaps instead of fighting the revolution, the shah could join it. He could reclaim the initiative by somehow separating himself from the Pahlavi state. In his speech the shah stated, "The revolution of the Iranian people cannot fail to have my support as the monarch of Iran and as an Iranian . . . I heard the revolutionary message of you people, the Iranian nation." He promised that "in the future the Iranian government will be divorced from tyranny and oppression, and will be run on the basis of the constitution and social justice."[106] But it was the shah's physical appearance, more than the content of his speech, that shocked the nation. For months, foreign emissaries had been astonished by how diminished he looked, and now the entire nation saw a monarch who was haggard and nearly lachrymose. This was hardly the way to introduce a military government.

Further, the new prime minister soon removed whatever fear the opposition might have had of the armed forces. In one of his first cabinet meetings, Azhari set the stage by telling his ministers that "the majority of people may be devoted to the Shah, but given the recent events I have to confess that they have separated the Shah from the nation."[107] Beyond that untimely confession, his cabinet deliberations were an exercise in indecision. For every problem, the prime minister recommended a committee to study the issue. The one decision that he did make was to arrest many members of the Pahlavi elite, including Hoveyda and Nasiri on charges of corruption. Parsons, who had befriended Hoveyda, told the shah that he had just finished indicting himself. The charge of graft was true of Nasiri but not of Hoveyda, who had diligently kept himself away from all affairs of the state, including its shady side. In a final act of callousness, the shah called Hoveyda to tell him that he would be apprehended for his own protection. Soon, two SAVAK officers were at his door to take him into custody, where he would remain until the mullahs got to him.

In Paris, Khomeini sensed the weakness in the shah's military display and assured his supporters that "these tanks, machine guns, and bayonets are all rusty and nothing can withstand the people's strong will."[108] The Imam called for "strikes, demonstrations and making the strikes as wide as possible."[109] When demonstrators returned to the streets, the army was as reticent as before. The possibility of a military government had always lurked in the background as the shah's last line of defense, an implied threat that was supposed to cause fear. Now it appeared that the military regime had been emasculated too.

Azhari met his most significant challenge in early December, when Iran once more commemorated Ashura, the day of mourning Imam Hossein's martyrdom. The opposition planned to use the occasion to bring millions to the streets across the country. At first the shah's generals contemplated banning all demonstrations, but Azhari had no stomach for a confrontation and instead pretended that a clash with protesters was exactly what the opposition wanted in order to discredit his government. He told his ministers, "Our enemies want us to shed the blood of thousands so they can achieve their objectives."[110] The prime minister was thinking of himself as too clever to fall into this trap, and instead offered the oppositionists an arrangement whereby the army would pull back and secure critical locations such as ministries, and the revolutionaries could roam the streets provided they did not burn down the cities. Khomeini took the deal.

On December 10, millions of Iranians took to the streets, proclaiming Khomeini their leader and the Islamic Republic their preferred form of government. The Imam correctly noted that the marches across the country constituted a referendum on Iran's future. The tight control the revolutionaries exercised over the public showcased their discipline and organizational skills. Khomeini demonstrated that he was the only leader in Iran capable of summoning millions to the streets and dictating their behavior.

Azhari's most notable achievement in office was the demystification of the armed forces. The December protests marked the end of his exhausted premiership. Visiting the prime minister, Sullivan was whisked away to a side office to find Azhari surrounded by medical equipment, the apparent victim of a mild heart attack. The general told the ambassador that "the country is lost because the king cannot make up his mind."[111] His last words to his cabinet were, "I don't know where we are going. We—the government and the clergy—where do we want to take this nation?"[112] Then he boarded a plane to his own exile in America.

THE BAKHTIAR INTERLUDE

The year 1979 began with much bickering. Vance feuded with Brzezinski. Carter contemplated firing his envoy to Iran and scolded mid-level State Department officials about leaks. The shah brooded in his palace about the fecklessness of his ungrateful subjects. Many of the Pahlavi elite either had a medical emergency or urgent business requiring them to immediately leave the country. Khomeini was the only figure in this imbroglio who was free of doubt and uncompromising in his approach.

The shah's most urgent task was to find someone to accept the premiership. Shapour Bakhtiar, a member of the National Front and a former deputy minister of labor in Mossadeq's government, finally stepped forward and accepted the mandate. Bakhtiar was a man of courage and idealism who had fought in the French Resistance during World War II and at times seemed more at home in Paris than in Tehran. He stood for a Mossadeq tradition that the National Front had abandoned in its abject surrender to Khomeini. Bakhtiar was a constitutionalist; he believed in democracy and was prepared to wrestle the revolution away from Khomeini. The two had one thing in common: steely determination. But one had the allegiance of a nation; the other, command of a broken army. It was hardly an even contest. Bakhtiar, however, would not give up his principles as easily as the liberals around him.

The one point on which everyone seemed to agree was that the shah should leave Iran. The new prime minister did not think he could salvage the situation with the monarch lingering around. Vance and Sullivan, too, believed the shah's presence was an obstacle to creating a power-sharing arrangement between the army and the opposition. Brzezinski felt that the shah's vacillation was hamstringing the military and that once he was gone, Bakhtiar and the generals could restore order.

In the end, the person most eager for the shah to leave was the monarch himself. After much pestering, Sullivan assured the shah that he would be welcomed in America and that Walter Annenberg's estate in California was ready for his use. Like most promises made at the time, this offer would soon be withdrawn. The shah seemed to know that the end of his dynasty was at hand, and he had no confidence in his prime minister. In one of their last meetings, the shah confided to Sullivan that "unless Khomeini calls off the strike actions, Bakhtiar does not have a chance."[113] Both men knew that Khomeini was not about to let go of his prey.

On January 16, Mohammad Reza Pahlavi, accompanied by his wife, left Iran.[114] It was a frigid day in Tehran as the shah walked around his palace grounds for the last time, trailed by reporters. He talked about needing rest and hoped that his leaving would calm the revolutionary fires. The Mehrabad Airport, where so many dignitaries had arrived to pay tribute to the monarch, was silenced by strikes. The shah seemed strangely preoccupied with protocol; he hung around the royal pavilion until Bakhtiar was formally approved by the parliament. Once the prime minister arrived at the airport, the transfer of power was complete. An entourage depleted by defections bid the shah farewell and pretended he would soon return. The monarch piloted the airplane himself and went off to an exile that would have its own share of humiliation.

To the extent that Bakhtiar had a strategy, it was to differentiate himself from both the shah and Khomeini. He gave impassioned speeches about democracy and the rule of law; he freed the few remaining political prisoners; and he insisted, as the legitimate ruler of Iran, that he would not be hounded out of office by street protests. He was open to negotiating with Khomeini and even offered to go to Paris as a private citizen, but he would not resign his office as a precondition to such a meeting.

For his part, Khomeini sensed that the end was near, but the revolution still had vulnerabilities. Bakhtiar had to be isolated, and then the armed forces would have to be persuaded to give up the fight. Khomeini now insisted that "collaboration with this usurpatory government in any manner or form is forbidden by religion and a crime under the law."[115] Bakhtiar was already having trouble filling his cabinet, and the few politicians who agreed to join him were either in charge of empty buildings or locked out of the ministries by their own staff. The impression made on the public was that Bakhtiar was a man without authority.

For months, the revolutionaries had battered the army's morale with messages of friendship and solidarity. The "flower campaign" had protestors putting flowers on the tips of soldiers' guns and imploring them not to shoot their brothers. The Imam now sought to decapitate the military by promising the generals immunity should they give up their hopeless mission of defending a monarch who had already fled. "Abandon him," he said of the shah, "and don't think that if you abandon him, we will execute you."[116] Khomeini also sent word to his most trusted aide in Iran, Ayatollah Mohammad Beheshti, to contact the generals and "offer them confidence and assurance that the military will be better than it is."[117] (After the triumph of the revolution, scores of the shah's generals would be summarily executed.)

From Tehran, Sullivan kept up his barrage of cables calling for the administration to craft some compromise between the revolutionaries and the armed forces. He did not think Bakhtiar had a chance and insisted that "our national interests demand that we attempt to structure a modus vivendi between the military and the religious, in order to preempt the Tudeh."[118] It is hard to see why Sullivan thought a dormant political party was poised to assume power. The ambassador went on to stress that it was time to open talks with the exiles in Paris in "an effort to normalize relations with Khomeini and make it clear that Washington did not regard him as an enemy, but rather wanted to become familiar with his views."[119]

Sullivan's advice was at odds with the intelligence community's judgment. Stansfield Turner told the White House, "I emphasize that we have seen no indication of willingness to compromise on . . . [Khomeini's] part and that optimism that an arrangement might be worked out was unjustified."[120] The INR reported, "Khomeini is likely to continue to ignore entreaties from lesser religious leaders and moderate politicians that steps be taken to prevent [the] disintegration of [the] Iranian polity."[121] In championing Sullivan's cause, Vance and Christopher chose to ignore their own analysts.

All of this infuriated Carter, who once again had to be talked out of firing Sullivan by Vance. In the end, the president did authorize reaching out to Khomeini. Warren Zimmerman, an official in the U.S. embassy in France, approached Khomeini's top aide, Ebrahim Yazdi, and the two began a series of desultory talks. But the channel of communication was not without importance: Khomeini used it to issue a direct threat to Carter. On January 27, Yazdi gave Zimmerman a personal message from Khomeini to the president. The message that Zimmerman jotted down was indeed blunt:

> The activities and works of Bakhtiar and the present leaders of the army are not only harmful for [the] Iranians but also are very harmful for the American government and especially for the future of the Americans (Yazdi: That means the Americans in Iran). Those activities may force me to issue new orders in Iran. It is advisable that you recommend to the army (Yazdi: The army as a whole not just the leadership; we draw no distinction between the two) not to follow Bakhtiar and to cease these activities. The continuation of these activities by Bakhtiar and the army leadership may bring great disaster. If Bakhtiar and the present army leadership stop intervening in the affairs (Yazdi: of Iranians), we will quiet down the people and this will not create any harm for the Americans.[122]

Khomeini followed up his private threat with a more subtle public warning to Carter. "You better advise the army not to obey Bakhtiar and stop such measures. The continuation of such measures by Bakhtiar and the commanders of the army may create a gigantic tragedy in Iran."[123] These messages were sent at a time when there were still fifteen thousand Americans in Iran. Although Carter was often accused of weakness and passivity by his critics, he refused to be intimidated by Khomeini. The White House continued to support the Bakhtiar government.

The Iranian military that was subject to so much speculation now began to sort itself out. In early January, General Abbas Gharabaghi, supreme commander of the armed forces, established the Commanders Council, which included the head of all branches of the military as well as the SAVAK, to determine their course of action. The council's first meeting took place a day before the shah left Iran. In that session, General Moqaddam, the head of SAVAK, made it clear that the priority of the military was to "preserve the independence of the country and preserve the armed forces so they can safeguard the nation."[124] Gharabaghi added that the "royal army will not intervene in internal politics."[125] The generals were prepared to acknowledge Bakhtiar as the head of state, but there were clear limits to how far they would go in supporting him. This was an army incapable of killing thousands of its own civilians to sustain the monarchy.

None of this was apparent to Brzezinski, who still thought of the army as his trump card. He feared that the departure of the shah would provoke an exodus of military commanders, foiling his plans for a potential coup. Both Carter and Brzezinski had lost confidence in Sullivan and felt they needed their own emissary to the Iranian army. The man chosen for this mission was General Robert "Dutch" Huyser, the deputy commander in chief of the U.S. European Command.

Huyser arrived in Tehran on January 4 for what he assumed would be a short visit to inspect the military's blueprints and lift their morale. He ended up staying a month, because the Iranian generals had no plans for him to assess. Gharabaghi confessed to him that "they had little experience in planning because the Shah formulated all the plans single-handed."[126] Huyser was shocked that after a full year of revolutionary tumult, the Iranian general staff had not developed any contingency plans. As an American officer, he failed to see that these men had been trained all their lives not to take initiative or assume responsibility. Huyser tried to get them to work together, gain control over key sectors of the economy, clear the docks, and develop means of controlling the crowds. The Iranian generals listened politely but did not implement any of his suggestions.

Sullivan and Huyser now dispatched conflicting assessments of the military. The ambassador, who had been dealing with the generals for a long time, judged the shah's army to be a "paper tiger."[127] Huyser was often frustrated by the Iranian officers but nonetheless assumed that he could whip them into shape and seems to have taken their pledges seriously.[128] In their private deliberations, which Gharabaghi recorded and the Islamic Republic published, the Iranian generals never even mentioned Huyser, or for that matter, America. They bemoaned their predicament, argued with each other, complained about BBC broadcasts, and plotted their own exits. They were in touch with Bazargan and Beheshti and assumed that the Imam would honor their assurances.

Khomeini was still in France but getting restless and wanting to come home. Bakhtiar tried various ploys to keep him out. He suddenly announced that should Khomeini return, the army might stage a coup. This prompted Gharabaghi to threaten to resign, only to be talked out of it by a stern Huyser. Having failed to intimidate Khomeini with talk of a coup, Bakhtiar closed the airport. But given the public clamor and the army's refusal to hold back the crowds, the prime minister had no choice but to acquiesce. On February 1, after fourteen years in exile, Khomeini returned to Tehran.

Millions of Iranians rushed to the streets in a frenzy to welcome him home. His initial speech was at Behesht-e Zahra Cemetery, where he saluted the martyrs of the revolution and sent a blunt message to Bakhtiar: "You are illegal and must go."[129] He then addressed the military: "Members of the armed forces, Islam is better for you than unbelief, and your own nation is better for you than the foreigners. It is for your sake, too, that we are demanding independence, so you should do your part by abandoning this man. Do not think that if you do, we will slaughter you all."[130] He was not above mendacity and dissimulation to ensure the success of his revolution.

Khomeini established his headquarters at the Rafeh School, a religious institution for girls. In a nation littered with the shah's opulent palaces, Khomeini set himself apart from the ancien régime by choosing a modest dwelling. The next step was to establish a provisional government. Bazargan was quickly chosen as the prime minister, because the Imam wanted to reassure the remnants of the Pahlavi state. Bazargan was a man of unimpeachable integrity, but more importantly he was familiar to the generals who were nervously watching all of this. Iran now had two governments, but only one with authority.

Although the revolution's hallmarks were strikes and demonstrations, it had a violent end. Fada'iyan-e Khalq and Mujahedin-e Khalq guerrillas resurfaced, and pious young men who would later form the nucleus of the Revolutionary Guards readied themselves for battle. For months, the revolutionaries had been attacking arms depots and storing weapons in mosques. It is impossible to determine how much of the shah's army was left, but in one of his soliloquies, Gharabaghi estimated that only 55 percent of it was intact.[131] This was still a lot of firepower for an army of 500,000 men. The spark came with an insurrection of air force technicians.

At this point there was much loose talk of a coup, but it was unclear who could have executed it. General Hassan Toufanian, vice minister of war, told Sullivan that if "Khomeini called for Jihad, all senior officers would leave in the same plane." He added that all the generals "had their families out of the country and could leave rapidly."[132] Sullivan—who never had much confidence in the Iranian armed forces—was not surprised.

All this made little impression on Washington. Twenty-five years after the infamous Operation TPAJAX, the United States once more contemplated a coup to salvage the Pahlavi dynasty. On February 11, Huyser was contacted at his headquarters in Stuttgart, Germany, by Chairman of the Joint Chiefs of Staff David Jones, Deputy Secretary of Defense Charles Duncan, and Brzezinski. Duncan asked if Huyser would be willing to return to Tehran and stage a coup. Huyser, who understood that the end was at hand, agreed to do so only if the White House provided him with ten thousand crack American troops. After an awkward silence, the call ended.[133]

Amid this mayhem, Bakhtiar declared that a curfew would begin at 4:30 in the afternoon, a decision he seems to have taken without consulting his military. He had to gain control of his capital from the roaming bands of guerrillas. As the revolutionaries threatened to take over the main arms factory in central Tehran, Bakhtiar implored the commander of the air force, purported hardliner General Amir Hossein Rabii, to "go ahead and bomb; I shall take the responsibility for the consequences."[134] Rabii refused on the ground that bombing the base would cause civilian casualties.

It was now Khomeini's turn. The Imam rejected the advice of some of his aides, who wanted to calm the situation, and instead issued a statement: "As for the declaration of martial law, that is a mere trick. It is contrary to the *shari'a* and people should not pay it the slightest attention."[135] People filled the streets and the atmosphere seemed joyous. But in other parts of the city, pitched battles were taking place as the guerrillas assaulted military bases and distributed weapons to bystanders.

The battle of Tehran was won by the revolutionaries. A more capable army might have been able to regroup, call in reinforcements, and reclaim the capital. But the shah's generals decided to sue for peace and collectively issued a statement declaring their neutrality. So ended 2,500 years of monarchy in Iran.

CHAPTER 9

Republic of Virtue

During the nine months between the rise of the provisional government and the hostage crisis, remarkable changes occurred in Iran. The triumphant clerics dispensed with the old elite, established an array of new institutions, crafted a remarkable constitution, and assaulted the U.S. embassy in breach of all international norms. But the most consequential victim of this period was political moderation. Mehdi Bazargan's government was the last stumbling block for an Islamic regime that would subordinate all authority to clerical fiat. Over the next four decades, Iran would have many intellectuals and politicians who tried to harmonize faith and freedom, but all these reformers could only try to liberalize the Islamic Republic. They could not propose an alternative to it. They worked within the system, while Bazargan stood apart from it. Though the failure of the provisional government was likely inevitable, it still marks an important turning point in the modern history of Iran.

During the last months of his exile, Khomeini had set up a shadowy organization, the Revolutionary Council, to direct events. The council's membership was initially kept secret but it soon revealed itself as the primary seat of power. It included Khomeini's clerical disciples, such as Beheshti, Mohammad-Javad Bahonar, Abdul-Karim Mousavi Ardebili, Akbar Hashemi Rafsanjani, and Ali Khamenei. The council also had non-clerical loyalists such as Abolhassan Banisadr, a French-trained intellectual who spent his time trying to conform economics to Islamic injunctions. Banisadr would become the Islamic

Republic's first president, only to be exiled back to France for challenging the clerical oligarchs. Bazargan himself was a member of the council, but he soon left it to form his government. From the beginning there were two parallel structures of authority, but only one had Khomeini's trust.

Still, the Imam appreciated that at this point he needed the liberals. He distrusted the Left and feared that the remnants of the Pahlavi state might stage a coup with America's support. Bazargan and his cohort were there to assure everyone that the revolution was in steady hands. The prime minister's mandate was to get the economy moving while preparing the ground for a still poorly defined Islamic government. There would be a referendum to legitimize the new order, and a constitution would follow.

Bazargan's most critical mistake was his assumption that he could hold the center. He even differentiated himself from Khomeini, telling a puzzled crowd, "Don't expect me to act in the manner of [Khomeini] who, head down, moves ahead like a bulldozer, crushing rocks, roots and stones in his path. I am a delicate passenger car and must ride on a smooth, asphalted road."[1] A revolution that devoured a 2,500-year-old institution of monarchy had little use for such considerations.

Bazargan's new cabinet comprised skilled professionals drawn mostly from his own Liberation Movement and representatives from the National Front and the Islamic Society of Engineers. These were devout men, and at the onset of the revolution, nearly all of them had been prepared to come to terms with the shah if he adhered to constitutional limits. Bazargan's spokesman, Abbas Amir-Entezam, who would go on to be the Islamic Republic's longest serving political prisoner, captured the spirit of the new government when he said, "The revolution is over. The era of reconstruction has begun."[2]

In some ways, Khomeini's dispositions were more in tune with the times than were the sensibilities of the provisional government. The Imam understood that the masses had risen up for an Islamic government. "The rebellion . . . is not a nationalist rebellion," he said; "this rebellion is a Quranic rebellion; this rebellion is an Islamic rebellion."[3] Soon he and his cohort began extolling the virtues of the lower classes, the oppressed—the *Mostazafin*. In Khomeini's telling, it was not the affluent who had faced the shah's bullets and given up their lives, but those struggling on the margins of the society. They had waged the revolution and they were the essence of the new Iran. Unlike Bazargan, Khomeini had a powerful constituency attuned to his messages of religious empowerment.

As Bazargan tried to form his government, the Islamists began setting up organizations that challenged his authority at every turn. Shortly after the collapse of the monarchy, Khomeini's allies, led by Beheshti, Rafsanjani, and Khamenei, established the Islamic Republican Party (IRP). Its mission was to attack the Left as well as "pseudo clerics," meaning traditional members of the clergy who did not subscribe to Khomeini's theological innovations. As soon as it was established, the IRP claimed to have two million members. It quickly began publishing a daily newspaper and took over the task of appointing Friday prayer leaders throughout the country. This meant that every city had a local mullah propagating the IRP's claims. There was now a political party on the scene with a clear mandate and a nationwide organization.

Khomeini, who seems to have gotten over his previous aversion to clerically dominated parties, warmly embraced the IRP. He looked at the party as an alternative to Bazargan's government, which he had to tolerate while consolidating his revolution. Beheshti recalled that Khomeini would often check on the party's progress and whether it was ready to assume control. At the beginning, Beheshti had to inform his mentor that the "party's government should be a completely independent government and should have a specific program and we have not reached that stage yet."[4] There were still urgent tasks ahead, such as eradicating the old order and crafting a suitable constitution. While this was going on, Bazargan and his provisional government were still useful.

During the revolution, various local committees had been created to coordinate strikes and demonstrations. The so-called komitehs were usually based in mosques, and after the collapse of the monarchy they took on a life of their own. They were accountable to the mullahs and had their own vigilantes. It has been estimated that nearly 300,000 weapons were scattered about the country, giving every mullah a militia to back his claims.[5] The komitehs now took matters into their own hands, looting the businesses of those who had fled or were suspected of ties to the ancien régime. They also settled old scores and many people saw their property confiscated simply because they had succeeded under the old order. Abuse and criminality went under the banner of defending the revolution.

The lawlessness was even more pronounced in the provinces, where local clerics established their own committees and ran them with little deference to the central government. Bazargan understood the danger that the komitehs presented to his rule. He often complained about them, saying they created "instability, terror, uneasiness and fear," but to little effect.[6] After much protest from the government, Khomeini finally agreed to place the committees under the authority of one his confidantes, Ayatollah Mohammad Reza Mahdavi-

Kani, who ensconced himself in one of the shah's barracks and issued decrees. He was not one to object to the komitehs' excesses.

Among Khomeini's more intelligent moves was to create his own Islamist militia. On May 5, the Imam decreed the formation of the Revolutionary Guards. By the fall of 1979, the Guards had grown to an army of eleven thousand and were still adding recruits. The clerics, who distrusted the regular army and were wary of leftist guerrillas with their experience in the armed struggle, understood that they had to shield their revolution from all contenders. Given the regime's celebration of the lower classes, the Guards were comprised of the poor and the pious who believed in their sacred mission. They would soon prove their mettle fighting leftist forces, separatist Kurdish groups, and eventually, Iraq's army. Although at first they had little technical competence, they would grow in both size and sophistication.

From the beginning, the Guards had a taste for money and proved adept at confiscating the land and property of escaping Iranians. The mullahs would also get involved, setting up their own bonyads, or charitable foundations, which took over much of the Pahlavi court's wealth. The bonyads would eventually control large swaths of Iran's economy.

The Guards operated under the watchful eyes of the ayatollahs, with the clerics providing divine sanction and the Guards the muscle. This symbiosis has endured because each party needs the other's unique attributes. There is often speculation that the Guards could simply dispense with the mullahs and set up their own dictatorship. This misses the point that the Guards are not just an army but also a deeply ideological entity that requires at least the veneer of clerical approval. The balance of power between the two sides may change, but the Islamic Republic will likely never be just another autocracy devoid of ideological content.

The apparatus of repression required its own tribunals, which soon became the ghastly face of the new Iran. The revolutionary courts were Khomeini's creation: he used them to destroy the old order by executing as many of its officials as he could get his hands on. The Imam, who seemed to have forgotten his many pledges of amnesty to the shah's generals, now insisted that "the purging of the armed organizations affiliated with the former diabolical regime is among the top priorities of the new government."[7] The continual rhetoric about a possible counter-revolution provided the mullahs with justification for their grisly acts.

To lead the revolutionary courts, Khomeini chose well, tapping the mentally deranged Sadeq Khalkhali. Upon being given this task, Khalkhali claimed to have protested that too much blood would be shed, only to be assured by the Imam that he was the right man for the job. Khomeini's instructions to his protégé were clear: "These individuals are guilty and must be executed."[8] The killings started quickly, with the first wave of executions taking place just three days after the revolution. The justice was swift, and the charge was usually spreading corruption on earth. The judge acted as prosecutor, and there was no defense attorney. Prolonged procedures were not required since the verdict was usually predetermined, and the sentence was carried out shortly after its pronouncement.

The courts and their contrived procedures were nothing but state-sanctioned murder, normally carried out by firing squad. After the execution, the body would be dispatched to the city morgue, but before a makeshift burial could take place, the corpse would be photographed and the pictures of the mutilated body published in the next day's newspapers. In his memoirs, Khalkhali printed before-and-after photos of prominent officials whom he executed.

Khalkhali's most prominent victim was Hoveyda. The former prime minister's trial followed the usual grim pattern. The hearing was held at night, and Hoveyda was awakened to face his tormentors. The charge was the usual spreading corruption on earth and whatever Khalkhali could make up on the spot. The seventeen-point indictment listed accusations such as defiling forests and smuggling heroin. Petitions for clemency poured in from abroad, including from British luminaries, a task that Anthony Parsons, Hoveyda's old friend, must have had a hand in. The attention only energized Khalkhali to speed up the proceedings.

Banisadr and Yazdi also pleaded for a delay of execution, because they had other plans for Hoveyda. The former prime minister had offered to write a complete dossier of the Pahlavi regime's misdeeds, and they were interested in an elaborate show trial that would garner international attention. The best way of discrediting the monarchy, they thought, would be to have its longest-serving prime minister chronicle its crimes in front of the global press. Khalkhali's blood-soaked trials were only convincing many that the new order was indeed mad.

The Imam was less impressed by show trials than by the killings, a function that Khalkhali was performing with joyous exuberance. After delegations of visitors came to his compound, Khomeini made his decision clear: "We try these people according to documents [evidence], but our obligation is that criminals should not be tried. They should be killed."[9] He then assured Khalkhali, "Don't listen to the Bazargans of this world."[10]

Hoveyda's defense was that although he was part of the system, he was not responsible for its many malfeasances. It was a plausible argument, given that he had spent his tenure meticulously shielding himself from affairs of the state. He was not corrupt, a trump card that he wrongly assumed would save him. When he asked for additional time to prepare his defense, Khalkhali responded, "Most of the charges against you are general in nature and need no proof or evidence."[11] After a few hours in which the two men talked past each other, Khalkhali announced his predictable verdict, "You are found to be a corrupter of earth. You are condemned to death."[12] Hoveyda was ushered to the corridor leading to the execution ground, but he never made it there. Hadi Ghaffari, another demented cleric with a love for guns, snuck behind him and shot him twice in the neck. Hoveyda's last words were, "It wasn't supposed to end this way."[13]

The execution of the heads of SAVAK may have been an easy decision. General Nasiri, the longest-serving and notably corrupt head of the secret police, was brutalized, paraded in front of cameras, and quickly executed. But two of SAVAK's three living directors had decent relations with the clerical community. The humane and erudite General Pakravan, who had been head of the organization when Khomeini was exiled in 1964, actually had a good rapport with the ayatollah. The Imam himself noted, "I regarded Pakravan as a reasonable, law-abiding person."[14] This did not save him. When the general asked Khalkhali what spreading corruption on earth meant, the judge merely replied, "What you are guilty of."[15] Pakravan was executed after a trial that lasted just fifteen minutes.

Moqaddam, the last director of SAVAK, had been appointed to the job primarily because of his ties to the clerical order. He seems to have taken seriously the pledges of immunity from the revolutionaries. He had played a pivotal role in the decision by the armed forces to declare its neutrality, and throughout the end stages of the revolution, he was the most reluctant of the shah's generals to use force, betraying the reputation of his own organization. He was not without supporters in Khomeini's camp: Ayatollah Hossein Ali Montazeri described him in his memoirs as a man of integrity.[16] The day after the revolution triumphed, Moqaddam was on his way to Prime Minister Bazargan's office to hand over the files of the old secret police. The two men knew each other and had been in touch during the intervening year. Moqaddam was instead picked up by scruffy men from the komiteh and handed over to Khalkhali. He was soon executed in the usual manner: first a bullet to the back of his neck, then his dead body was riddled with more shots, and finally a picture was taken for the morning newspapers.

In his complaint about the mullahs' latest transgression, Bazargan castigated the trials as "irreligious, inhuman and a disgrace."[17] What he missed was
that Khomeini looked at his instruments of terror as a means of controlling
the revolution and dispensing with his enemies, both real and presumed. The
notion of a transparent judicial process, with evidence, jurors, and defense
attorneys, was to the Imam a Western disease that had infected too many
Iranian minds. He even publicly rebuked his prime minister, attacking him
for believing that "everything should be copied from the West." He ended his
diatribe by scolding Bazargan, "You are weak, mister, you must be strong."[18]

Khalkhali's conduct was not without its comic moments. He soon tried to
destroy Iran's pre-Islamic monuments, but after a public uproar, he had to
settle for Reza Shah's mausoleum. This large edifice, constructed to honor the
founder of the Pahlavi dynasty, was a particular affront to Khalkhali. Yet the
structure did not yield to easy demolition. The site was finally razed with the
help of much dynamite and bulldozers. Khalkhali wanted to put public toi-
lets in its place, but eventually a seminary was built there instead.

Nearly all of the shah's generals who had not fled were put to death. Then
came the ministers, civil servants, and Farrokhroo Parsa, the only female
member of the shah's cabinet. But the courts did not limit themselves to officials of the defunct regime. A sixty-seven-year-old Jewish businessman
named Habib Elghanian was executed after being charged with "treason
through his connections with Israel and Zionism."[19] Scores of Arab and Kurdish separatist leaders, and then the leftists who had cheered when the shah's
officials were put to death, also faced the mullahs' wrath. The trials demonstrated Khomeini's indifference to human life and his determination to safeguard his revolution at all cost.

Later, looking back at this time, both Khalkhali and Khomeini regretted
that they did not go far enough. The hanging judge recalled, "I believe I did
not kill enough and some escaped my clutches. The Shah, Farah [empress],
Ashraf [Pahlavi], Jafar Sharif-Emami, General Gharabaghi, General Hossein
Fardust . . ."[20] Khomeini was similarly contrite for not having been cruel
enough in the initial days of the revolution:

> One of the mistakes we made was that we didn't act in a revolutionary
> fashion. We were patient with these corrupt factions. The revolution-
> ary government, the revolutionary army, the revolutionary guards,
> none of them acted like revolutionaries. We would not have these
> problems today if in the very beginning we had shattered the former

corrupt regime and closed down all these corrupt newspapers and magazines and punished their publishers and banned the corrupt political parties and given their leaders what they deserved and set up gallows in the main squares and cut down all the corrupt people. In the presence of God Almighty and the dear nation of Iran, I apologize for our mistakes.[21]

A REFERENDUM AND A CONSTITUTION

Mehdi Bazargan looked like a man without a friend. Khomeini and his allies were constructing a parallel government with its own tribunals and militia. The Fada'iyan-e Khalq largely maintained its rejectionist stance, protesting everything around it, while the Mujahedin-e Khalq (MEK) and the Tudeh played a more cynical game and would suffer at the hands of the vengeful mullahs. The clerical community itself was fracturing, because the more traditional ayatollahs had qualms about the unfolding order. The Kurds and Arabs were agitating for a measure of autonomy, which was brutally repressed. Violence was increasingly the arbiter of Iran's politics.

The MEK viewed the immediate post-revolutionary period as an ideal time to extend its reach.[22] The group had substantial support among the university students, intelligentsia, and labor, as well as the prestige of having waged an armed struggle against the shah in the early 1970s. During the later stages of the revolution, it had been instrumental in bringing down his regime. The MEK had little patience with the provisional government's moderation and desire for correct relations with the United States. More importantly, its leadership believed that once the Bazargan regime was disposed of, they could wrest power away from the benighted mullahs. For this reason they sided with other groups in their assault on the government. The party's most glaring miscalculation was its perception that it could not just rival Khomeini; it could replace him. The confrontation between the two sides would indeed be vicious, but the Imam was bound to prevail because his power exceeded that of any single group.[23]

The Tudeh, under the leadership of Nureddin Kianouri, also tried to revive itself. Long suspected of being a Russian proxy and having little sway over the Left, the party believed that its path to relevance was an uncritical embrace of Khomeini. The Tudeh's cadre privately scoffed at religion as the opiate of the masses and never thought the mullahs were up to the complex task of governing a nation. The Tudeh's many exiled leaders now returned to Tehran and began their plots.

They were not without sources of strength: the Tudeh Party received generous Soviet assistance and had some appeal among university students. Its plan was to steadily undermine the provisional government and then somehow stage a coup. But like most Marxist ideologues, the Tudeh leaders thought in absurd categories. The provisional government, in their telling, was a capitalist foe, while the mullahs were dismissed as politically naïve. Therefore, to weaken the Bazargan regime, they had to make common cause with the clerical reactionaries. Kianouri described this strategy as "finding out the very center of gravity, that center which moves the society. Then finding access to, or controlling, that center."[24] In this conception, Khomeini and his allies were the center, which the Tudeh would first influence and then dislodge. The party's architects did not calculate that the center could strike back and devour them.

After some hesitation, Shariatmadari entered the political fray and established his own party, the Muslim People's Republican Party (MPRP), which was active in his native Azerbaijan. The Grand Ayatollah stood for the tradition of staying some distance from the seat of power, insisting, "We must simply advise the government when what they do is contrary to Islam . . . It is the duty of the government to govern."[25] The party offered some support to Bazargan, but its most important mission was to illustrate that not all traditional clerics accepted Khomeini's ideas. The two religious leaders met on occasion to hammer out their differences, but to no avail. In one such meeting, Khomeini brought documents from the shah's vaults demonstrating the extent of Shariatmadari's contact with the royal court. The conflict within the priestly class would turn brutal once the Islamic Republic established special tribunals to prosecute errant clerics. One of the ironies of Iran is that the theocracy has abused far more clerics than the shah ever did. One of the most prominent victims was Shariatmadari himself.

Given his history of cooperating with the monarchy, Shariatmadari posed little threat to Khomeini. The cleric who did worry the revolutionaries was one of their own, Ayatollah Taleqani. A close associate of Bazargan and a co-founder of the Liberation Movement, Taleqani had suffered in the shah's prisons and his erudition made him a popular figure on the Left. He was critical of komitehs and was known to be skeptical of Khomeini's religious musings. As the first prayer leader of Tehran, he had warned against a return to "dictatorship and despotism."[26] He was not above complaining about the Imam, albeit with caution. But Taleqani was also in poor health, and his untimely death on September 10, 1979, deprived Bazargan of an indispensable ally.

The arbitrariness of the new regime was highlighted by the referendum it organized in March 1979. The public would be given a choice of voting yes or no to the Islamic Republic. There was no other option. Khomeini had always said that he aimed to establish a religious state and that the many demonstrations during the revolution were a public affirmation of this plan. Bazargan pleaded for adding a Democratic Islamic Republic option to the ballot, but Khomeini angrily rejected the idea. "Don't use the Western term 'democratic.' Those who call for such a thing don't know anything about Islam," the Imam thundered.[27]

In another act of self-abnegation, the National Front, the Tudeh, and Bazargan's Liberation Movement all called for a yes vote. The MEK also accepted the sanctity of the vote. Across the nation, the mosque network that had been so effective during the revolution went to work urging an affirmative response. The actual referendum hardly looked like a real plebiscite. The "yes" ballot was colored green and "no" was red. The ballots would be distributed at the polling centers and the voter had to ask for the color he wanted. The final tally suggested that 98.2 percent of the population supported the regime. Khomeini celebrated the results: "I am declaring today the day of the Islamic Republic of Iran, and I would also like to declare that such a referendum is unprecedented in history—to establish a government of righteousness and to overthrow and bury the monarchy in the rubbish pile of history."[28] It is important to stress that even without such contrived procedures, the majority of the public would probably have endorsed the Islamic Republic. Two months after its triumph, the revolution still had a hold on the popular imagination.

The next task was to write a constitution for the newly christened republic. Khomeini's book *Islamic Government* was a guide to ideology, but it was too imprecise to provide a blueprint for actually operating a government in the late twentieth century. The Imam had mused that all the necessary laws were in the Quran and all needed revenue could come from charitable donations. More flesh had to be added to these bare bones. All claimants to power now focused on crafting Iran's new constitution.

The initial draft, written by Bazargan's allies, was an eclectic document that borrowed from the 1906 constitution as well as France's Fifth Republic with its strong presidency. It provided for a guardian council to ensure that parliamentary legislation conformed to Islamic law, but even that prerogative was circumscribed. The council could review legislation only if it was requested to do so. Such a petition could come from the president, the head of the supreme court, or senior ayatollahs. Beyond this, the document gave the clergy no special privileges. More importantly, it did not feature Khomeini's idea of *velayat-e faqih* (guardianship of the jurist), the notion that in the absence of the Hidden Imam, an esteemed cleric versed in Islamic canons would oversee national affairs.

Khomeini initially accepted the constitution, suggesting only that women be barred from serving as president and judges. Given that he had spent so much time justifying the concept of *velayat-e faqih,* its omission from the draft must have irked him. But the Imam was patient, and he still needed to consolidate his government. There were the shah's officials to execute, leftist militias to disarm, and a provisional government to subvert. All documents could be revised, as indeed Iran's constitution had been in 1989, and Khomeini was confident that his stature would allow him to rule the country whatever the constitutional procedures.

The draft constitution provoked debate from all corners. Newspapers editorialized, lawyers' guilds issued judgments, and clerics made objections. The National Front complained that the presidency was too strong and the parliament too weak. The MEK wanted the armed forces disbanded and peasant and worker groups established to run the country. The Fada'iyan claimed that the constitution did not deal with "dependent capitalism and imperialism." And Kurdish and Arab groups called for greater regional autonomy.[29]

The notion that an assembly would examine the draft and devise the final constitution had been there all along. In his initial order appointing Bazargan to the premiership, Khomeini had instructed him to prepare such a convention, and he later reiterated this promise on several occasions. Once the Islamic Republic came into being, it was natural to believe that an assembly would be convened to ensure that a religious state had the right governing document.

Now, suddenly, came calls for dispensing with the assembly altogether and just submitting the existing constitution to a referendum. Many in Khomeini's camp felt that in the tense political atmosphere, another prolonged debate could benefit those seeking to undermine the revolution. So long as there was no official governing document, the new order would be vulnerable to intrigues of all sorts. In yet another of their miscalculations, the leftists objected to this move and demanded a constitutional convention, which they assumed they would control. In a final act of compromise, it was agreed that an assembly would convene, but its size would be limited to seventy-three men. Delegates would be elected and their final product submitted to a referendum.

Khomeini now decided to reclaim the initiative and called on his followers to join the battle. "The constitution of the Islamic Republic means the constitution of Islam. Don't sit back while foreignized intellectuals, who have no faith in Islam, give their views and write the things they write."[30] The Imam's disciples heeded his summons. Montazeri published many commentaries on the importance of Islam to the constitution, and a stream of editorials and speeches by Khomeini's allies insisted that the Guardian Council should have greater powers and that the president and head of the armed forces must have sufficient knowledge of Islamic law. Most importantly, they insisted that the *velayat-e faqih* be included in the constitution. How could Iran retain an Islamic government without the clerics in a supervisory role?

As the campaign began, Khomeini took to the airways. "We wish to create an Islamic constitution," he said, and for this task no "Westernized jurists were needed but only noble members of the clergy and other knowers of Islam who were not clerics."[31] The mosques and komitehs used their nationwide networks to mobilize the population. Given the government's control of the national media, many parties could not get their messages across. The National Front and some leftist parties called for a boycott, and Shariatmadari demanded that the election be postponed for ten days until all parties had an opportunity to express their views. None of these calls were heeded, and the election gave the Islamic Republican Party the majority of delegates. Montazeri was to chair the assembly, and Beheshti would serve as his deputy. As it turned out, it was Beheshti who dominated the proceedings.

Khomeini's message to the delegates made his preferences clear. "If the Islamic jurists present in the assembly find contradictions to Islam in any of the articles of the preliminary draft or in the adopted amendments, they must declare this openly and not have fear of the uproar this may cause in the press or amongst the Westernized writers."[32] Montazeri and Beheshti took control of the convention and eviscerated the existing draft. It seemed that they had come with their own document, which included many Islamic injunctions.

The new constitution began with a set of ahistorical claims that the theocracy's own record keepers have often refuted. In the preamble, the clergy celebrated their revolution and attributed its success to Khomeini's exalted guidance. In the document's telling, the previous revolts, including the 1953 uprising, failed because they did not enjoy divine approbation. The constitution also asserted that sixty thousand people were killed during the revolution. As we have seen, the actual number of fatalities, according to the Islamic Republic itself, was 2,781, which means the constitution was off by 57,219.[33]

The core of the constitution was the position of *velayat-e faqih*. According to Article 5, "During the absence of his holiness, the Lord of the Age, May

God all mighty hasten his appearance, the sovereignty of the command of God and religious leadership of the community of believers in the Islamic Republic of Iran is the responsibility of the *faqih* who is just, pious, knowledgeable about his era, courageous and a capable and efficient administrator." The powers of the *faqih* were indeed awesome. He would set the overall national course, command the armed forces, declare war and peace, confirm the appointment of leading officials including the president, dismiss officeholders at will, and have the final say on all legislative matters. Khomeini's arcane theological speculation had turned into concrete legal expression.[34]

The amendments pertaining to the *velayat-e faqih* set off a debate among the delegates. One of the few liberals in the assembly, Ezzatollah Sahabi, stressed that the Imam's concept "does not mean that the *faqih* should be involved in day-to-day politics, the dispenser of power and overseer of state affairs." Beheshti batted away all such arguments. "The Islamic government," he answered, "is based on an ideology different from that of a democratic republic." That the Iranian people had voted for an Islamic Republic in a plebiscite, Beheshti believed, meant they wanted "a leader acquainted with Islam." The chamber voted to approve the powers of the *velayat-e faqih*.[35]

But there was more. The shah's legal codes were discarded and the judiciary was turned over to the clergy. The task was to create a "judicial system that is based on Islamic justice and is composed of just judges who are aware of the precise criteria laid down in Islam."[36] Then came the Guardian Council, another clerically dominated body, which had the power to ensure that all legislation was compatible with Islamic law. Moreover, all candidates for public office had to have their credentials approved by the council.

Still, some of the constitution's own provisions undermined its totalitarian spirit. Sovereignty might belong to God, but a series of elected institutions would make their own claims. The president and the parliament may have been subordinated to clerical bodies, but given their popular mandate, they were bound to have a voice. The system could function only with a figure such as Khomeini, who commanded the obedience of all the factions. The passing of the charismatic leader was bound to bring to the surface both personal rivalries and the tensions imbedded in the text.

The unveiling of the constitution, with all of its provocative provisions, caused a national stir. For the Left, a document that granted such sweeping powers to unaccountable bodies smacked of dictatorship in clerical garb. Bazargan and the provisional government were not averse to a religious state, but they thought it should accept the primacy of election-based institutions. Even in the clerical community, the constitution caused a measure of disquiet. Many senior ayatollahs, such as Shariatmadari, were not just skeptical of Khomeini's concept of *velayat-e faqih;* they also worried that the elevation of a single cleric above all others would compromise their standing. The Shia seminary had always resisted hierarchy and allowed the grand ayatollahs to operate with a measure of independence. The ayatollahs collected their own religious dues, subsidized their own schools, and yielded as little as possible to the central authorities. One of the complaints against the shah had been that he had encroached too far into Islam's realm. All these forces could be counted on to resist a document that still had to be ratified in a national referendum. The Imam and his followers needed a crisis to galvanize the population. The U.S. embassy provided a tantalizing target.

AMERICA HELD HOSTAGE

As Iran sorted itself out, the shah traveled from country to country in search of refuge. After his initial stay in Egypt, he went to Morocco, then to the Bahamas, and finally to Mexico. His cancer worsened while his doctors bickered about the best course of treatment. Even though he had been under the care of a French medical team for years, French President Giscard d'Estaing made it known that he was not welcome in France. The shah owned property in Britain, but Prime Minister Thatcher was not eager to host him either. The one thing that his doctors agreed on was that his best option was to seek treatment at New York–Presbyterian Hospital.

Since his exile, President Carter had kept his distance from the shah, even retracting his previous invitation for him to stay in America. But the shah still had powerful friends such as David Rockefeller and Henry Kissinger, who lobbied hard on his behalf.[37] He had been a loyal friend of America for three decades, and the humanitarian case for his admission to the United States was hard to deny. Carter had his premonitions and pointedly asked his aides, "What are you guys going to advise me to do if they overrun our embassy and take our people hostage?"[38] Bruce Laingen, the chargé d'affaires in Tehran, was deputized to assess the Iranian reaction. Sullivan had already slipped out of the country and out of the diplomatic service. Yazdi, who had assumed the post of foreign minister, warned Laingen against opening Pandora's box.

On October 23, 1979, the shah entered the hospital in New York and underwent two surgeries in quick succession, then a round of chemotherapy. Outside the hospital, protesting Iranians jeered and prayed for his quick death. In Tehran, Khomeini and his allies grew both anxious and excited. Given the paranoid nature of Iranian politics and the long shadow of the 1953 coup, some assumed that the diabolical Americans were once more plotting to restore the Pahlavi state. But the monarch's latest misadventure also provided an opportunity to incite the population ahead of the all-important referendum on the constitution.

The provisional government gave Khomeini all the ammunition he needed. On November 1, Bazargan, Yazdi, and defense minister Mostafa Chamran went to Algeria to commemorate its uprising against France. Zbigniew Brzezinski was also there, and the two sides met for an hour. This was not the first encounter between the provisional government and the Carter administration; Yazdi had already met with Vance on the sidelines of the U.N. General Assembly. The thrust of these conversations was that the Iranians complained about lack of delivery of military supplies purchased by the shah and wanted the Americans to acknowledge Iran's revolution. The most consequential result of the gathering was the dispute that arose later about who had actually requested the meeting. Even so, the combination of the meeting in Algiers and the shah's admission to America proved too disturbing for the radicals in Tehran.

November 4 seemed like a typical day at the U.S. embassy. Crowds outside the compound chanted "death to America," while inside, a stream of Iranians petitioned for visas to come to the United States. Suddenly, approximately four hundred students breached the embassy walls and began occupying its various buildings. The initial reports did not unduly alarm Washington, because the embassy had been attacked before: on February 14, a band of leftist students had made their way inside but were quickly evicted by the government. This time, however, things seemed different. What was thought to be a short-lived occupation would last for 444 days.

It has long been assumed by many in the scholarly community that Khomeini did not know about the attack beforehand. Only after the assault took place did the Imam see its political value and exploit it as a means of displacing his rivals. Four decades after the embassy takeover, however, it is possible to construct a circumstantial case suggesting that Khomeini actually instigated the hostage crisis.

In his memoirs, Mahdavi-Kani offers intriguing insights on the event. As the head of the komitehs who were responsible for internal security, shortly after the attack Mahdavi-Kani called Khomeini's son, Ahmad, who acted as his father's chief of staff, to discuss the situation. As he recalled, "The night of the embassy's occupation I contacted Ahmad and asked him what is happening?

Initially, he just laughed and would not answer. I asked him did you know about this? He laughed. Finally, after I insisted, he said, the Imam is satisfied with this and you should not get involved."[39] Ahmad's dismissive attitude toward Mahdavi-Kani's persistent questioning indicates that he had prior knowledge of the event and did not want the security forces to remove the occupiers.

The students' spiritual leader, Ayatollah Mohammad Mousavi-Khoeiniha, played an important and curious role in all this. Mousavi-Khoeiniha was a former student of Khomeini and was known to be close to Ahmad. It is difficult to believe that he was not in touch with the Imam about a plot of such importance. One of the hostage-takers, Habibolah Bitaraf, who would go on to serve as minister of energy, has acknowledged the critical role that Mousavi-Khoeiniha played in the entire saga:

> For us, particularly the students of University of Tehran, the Imam's opinion on this issue was important, and many of our friends said that if the Imam is against this we will not participate in this affair. The opinion of the students was transmitted to Mousavi-Khoeiniha who agreed to take the issue to Imam. If the Imam was against it, his views would be given to us immediately or in two days. Two days passed, Khomeini did not respond but he issued a statement encouraging an attack on America. We, the students, accepted this statement as a positive response.[40]

Just prior to the attack, Khomeini's office did in fact issue a statement: "It is incumbent upon students in the secondary schools and universities and the theology schools to expand their attacks against America and Israel. Thus, America will be forced to return the criminal, deposed Shah."[41] This must have been the signal the students were waiting for before attacking the U.S. compound.

Yet another of the hostage-takers has said that Khomeini had foreknowledge of the event. Mohammad Hashemi-Esfahani, one of the student radicals, stressed that "prior to attacking the U.S. embassy, Ahmad Khomeini, the son of Ruhollah Khomeini, was involved in our operations and he also informed Imam Khomeini."[42] Finally, Bazargan, who became the chief victim of the attack, later recalled, "The whole business with the American embassy was probably due to [Khomeini's] influence."[43]

Still, shortly after the takeover of the embassy, Khomeini kept silent for a few days. He wanted to see how Washington would respond before showing his hand. Had he immediately embraced the attackers, then he would be held responsible for their action. And if Carter suddenly acted tough and issued an ultimatum for the release of the diplomats, Khomeini would have to back down—a retreat that was bound to weaken his standing amid an internal power struggle. As it turned out, the White House issued condemnations but appeared to have no plans for a military response.

Once assured of Carter's reticence, Khomeini went on the offensive. The attack was proving popular as the frenzied public once more rushed to defend the revolution from a nonexistent foreign plot. The militants calling themselves Students Following the Imam's Line began to selectively release embassy records suggesting all sorts of nefarious schemes. Khomeini took to the airways and issued his famous pronouncement, "America can't do a damn thing." The Imam confidently stressed, "The speculation about American military intervention is nonsense. How can America militarily intervene in this country? It is not possible. The whole world is watching. Can America stand up to the world and intervene here? America would not dare."[44]

Mehdi Bazargan understood immediately that the capture of the American diplomats presented his government with the most serious crisis of its tenure. The prime minister, who had no power to free the Americans, insisted that the Revolutionary Council take responsibility. All along, his government had been undermined by the parallel state, and it was time for the actual rulers of Iran to bear the burden created by the mischief of their radical partisans. But the council refused to hold itself accountable. As Khamenei recalled, "We stood firmly, in the face of such actions. Me personally and two of the brothers issued a warning and proclaimed that if the Revolutionary Council took in the hostages we will make our objection public and we shall discuss the issue with the Imam."[45]

On November 6, Bazargan submitted his resignation. The leftist parties that had routinely accused the provisional government of weakness toward the forces of imperialism cheered his departure, having all along assumed that with the government out of the way, they could easily take on the mullahs. This was one of their more catastrophic misjudgments. Khomeini was also happy to see the prime minister go. Bazargan had been important to the success of the revolution, but he was no longer needed and his resignation was quickly accepted.

Amid this national frenzy, the Revolutionary Council took over management of the government. As the Iranians went to the polls to vote on the constitution, Shariatmadari called on his party to boycott the election because it did not "allow a free expression of opinion."[46] The National Front and the

MEK joined the boycott. Khomeini paid little attention to their meanderings. An affirmative vote, he insisted, was necessary to protect the revolution from America. On December 2 and 3, millions of Iranians went to the ballot box and, by the regime's account, voted 99 percent in favor of the constitution. A theocracy with a radical constitution now came into existence.

Ruhollah Khomeini stands as one of the most successful revolutionaries of the twentieth century. He transformed his arcane religious speculations into a governing template and then displaced all of his rivals. The shah died in exile, Shariatmadari died under house arrest, and the leftist forces died in street battles with hardened Islamists. The republic would survive ethnic insurrections and Saddam's invasion. The Bazargan government was the last regime to challenge Khomeini's theocratic absolutism and reject his idea of *velayat-e faqih*. In the coming decades, the Islamic Republic would fracture as competing factions asserted their power, but they would all remain within the parameters drawn by Khomeini. Through the institutions he created and the elite followers he molded, the Imam ensured that his ideology would endure long after his passing. No other twentieth-century revolutionary leader can make this claim. God is indeed great.

Conclusion

THE PAST HAS ANOTHER PATTERN

In the 1940s, Iran looked like a feudal state, but it had real politics. The old order was led by an aristocratic class that owned vast tracts of land and controlled much of the country's trade. Although these landowners resided in urban areas, they kept a close eye on the provinces where most of the population lived. The system did not lack inequalities and exploitations. The peasants saw little profit for all their toil, the elites were incestuous and constantly bickering, and the schemes of the upper class led them to solicit foreign emissaries to try to gain leverage over their rivals. Still, these men believed in the nation's institutions. They believed in a parliament that guarded its prerogatives. They believed in cabinets that were genuinely responsible for national affairs. And they believed in a monarchy that deferred to the constitution and to the traditions of this class.

Iran's nobility was not without its accomplishments or traces of idealism. The Pahlavi dynasty survived the expulsion of its founder because the elite stood behind the young crown prince. Both Britain and Russia considered doing away with the monarchy, only to be dissuaded by Prime Minister Foroughi. During the war years, Iran changed prime ministers so often that the system appeared unstable. But this ever-changing cast of premiers managed to get the great powers to respect Iran's sovereignty, and when Stalin tried to evade his obligations, they compelled him to retreat. Truman helped, but he could not have succeeded without resolute Iranians who refused to be intimidated by the Soviet Union's strongman at the zenith of his power.

The aristocratic class also included idealists like Mohammad Mossadeq. He not only championed the nationalization of oil, but also led a coalition devoted to reforming Iran's politics and society. The National Front had first come together to protest electoral fraud, and it remained focused on clean elections. It soon pressed for universal education, free health care, and an end to corruption. Some within the aristocratic class even appreciated that land reform was inevitable and that industry had to be the mainstay of the economy.

The shah chafed under a system in which his powers were circumscribed by competing institutions. He had no use for parliaments, cabinets, or Persia's statesmen. Democratic accountability was even more distasteful to him than to the clerics who displaced him. He wanted to modernize Iran and believed that only an autocrat could do it. His youthful experience with elite pluralism included the bitter sight of Iran's noblemen conspiring with the Allies to exile his father. He never appreciated that this had been the only way for the Pahlavi dynasty to survive. He drew all the wrong lessons from his father's tragedy and always believed that America and Britain might plot against him too. And he distrusted strong leaders, whatever their commitment to the monarchy. The shah was most comfortable with sycophants and filled his army and bureaucracy with men who could never make a decision or take initiative.

The 1953 coup casts a long shadow over Iran. The oft-repeated slogan that the United States crushed Iran's nascent democracy and ushered in a rigid dictatorship conceals more than it reveals. The Western powers were not blameless. Britain imposed an oil embargo on Iran, and America and the oil giants adhered to it. The less money Mossadeq got, the more despotic he became. He rigged elections, disbanded the parliament, usurped the powers of the monarchy, and showed little respect for the constitution. His inability to resolve the oil stalemate threatened to bankrupt the economy, and his dictatorial tendencies estranged too many power brokers. Mossadeq was a great man who should never have become prime minister. But it was the Iranians who took the essential steps in overthrowing him. The CIA was complicit, but its role has been exaggerated, particularly by its chief agent, Kermit Roosevelt.

The shah often extolled the virtues of dictatorship. His casual remarks about how Stalin and other such monsters were men who got things done unsettled his interlocutors. He would speak contemptuously of Western democratic practices. At first, his advisers and foreign ambassadors dismissed these remarks, or gently reminded him that the system shielded him from much responsibility in a country where things usually went wrong. But the shah was a visionary who wanted to modernize Iran. He dreamed of a nation of factories, sprawling cities, and technological innovations of all sorts, a country that dominated its neighborhood and commanded respect on the international stage. His tragedy was that he believed none of this was possible unless he concentrated all power in his hands.

The shah carried out a relentless assault on the old order. He spent much of his time chipping away at the authority of men and institutions that had served him well. He emasculated the parliament that was once the seat of great decisions, sent prominent politicians into exile (banishments that were sometimes dressed up as diplomatic postings), shuttered the press, and had no use for independent political parties. His infatuation with all things Western alienated a clerical class that had always stood behind the monarchy. He expanded the armed forces but refused to tolerate an independent or even competent officer corps. And he created a secret police that accumulated vast troves of information that it did not know how to use.

The shah was not without his successes and achievements. The White Revolution was the first time in Persia's history that a government took land from the rich and gave it to the poor. The land-reform schemes did not all work well, but even the shah's critics had to admit that the peasants benefited. For the shah, idealism and cynicism were always mixed together, and land reform not only helped the peasants but undermined the aristocracy. Factories sprung up everywhere while migration from the countryside brought a steady stream of people into the cities. None of this was well planned, corruption was everywhere, but everyone seemed to be making money. The shah was also an ironic champion of female emancipation, granting women the right to vote and to participate in public affairs while insisting that they did not measure up to men. Religious minorities, too, enjoyed protections that would soon be countermanded by the Islamic Republic. Iran seemed to be a country on the move.

By the 1970s, the shah was seen as a global statesman and Tehran a crucial stopping place for the world's dignitaries. He was instrumental in increasing oil prices and seemed to be a master of Middle Eastern politics. Unlike his clerical successors, the shah's hegemonic aspirations were practical and limited to the Persian Gulf. He needed clear navigational routes and friendly sheikhdoms. He paid little attention to the Levant and was willing to have good relations with Arab states so long as they did not plot against Iran. He was America's ally and Russia's trading partner. He was happy to sell oil to Israel while censuring it at the United Nations.

The shah's modernization drive changed the face of Iran, dramatically enlarging the professional middle class. The universities kept expanding, and thousands of students went abroad in search of diplomas. These people were to be the shah's technocratic elite, encouraged so long as they kept their political ideas to themselves. It proved an impossible bargain, because many Iranians aspired to live in a nation where elections and institutions mattered. The economic recession of the mid-1970s is sometimes casually blamed for the revolution, but the Iranian people were frustrated with the shah's dictatorship even when the economy was performing well.

Beneath the glitter of the 1970s, Iranians were returning to their religion. The corruption of the ruling elite, the provocative class stratifications that sudden wealth often generates, and the frustration of working in a system that discounted merit led many to reclaim their traditions. In the hands of enterprising clerics and intellectuals, Shia Islam soon became an ideology of dissent. Symbols and rituals of faith were cleverly used to mobilize the public.

America would loom large in the tale of the Pahlavi dynasty, but its influence was never as toxic as its detractors claim. Washington certainly made mistakes, but it may come as a surprise to many that every U.S. president who dealt with the shah since 1941, with the exception of Richard Nixon, urged him to develop his economy and liberalize his politics. Every secretary of defense, including the two who served under Nixon, opposed the shah's reckless arms buildup. He was never America's obedient client, and as his confidence grew, he seldom hesitated to defy Washington.

By the mid-1970s, even the shah sensed that something was wrong in Iran. His cancer focused his mind on succession, and he did not think his young son could manage a system where the monarch made every decision. It was then that the shah launched his ill-advised liberalization program that flung all the doors open. Instead of fielding petitions by moderate politicians for needed reforms, the shah faced demonstrations and strikes. All of his promises crumbled at once. His economy was failing while his liberalization program was empowering the radicals. He had no stomach for a bloody crackdown, and lacked military leaders willing and able to carry one out in his stead.

Still, the revolution would not have succeeded without a man of unusual determination who brooked no compromise. Whenever an opposition leader brought the shah's latest concessions to Ruhollah Khomeini, he rejected them and insisted that the monarchy could retreat further. He was always right. His resolution was matched by the suppleness of his tactics. He was all things to all people. He talked of an Islamic order that promised liberals an inclusive government, the merchants freedom from state intrusion, leftists a non-aligned foreign policy, women real emancipation, and students and intellectuals freedom of thought. Many strands of opposition submitted to Khomeini because he seemed the most capable of leading the revolution to success.

Jimmy Carter did not lose Iran; Khomeini won it. When trouble began, it was natural for Carter to assume that the shah could handle the situation. The monarch had been in power for thirty-seven years and had demonstrated an uncanny ability to survive multiple crises. This was, after all, the imperious shah who often lectured Westerners on how to adjust their society. Washington had not learned the lessons of its own experiences in Iran. The shah was always indecisive in times of crisis and needed others to salvage his fortunes. Until it was too late, Carter and his aides kept assuring themselves that the shah and the army, this time, could maintain control.

But recasting the revolution as an Iranian drama does not absolve the American policymakers of their misjudgments. Iran in the 1970s was a nation in discontent. Its political order was suffocating and its economy was cooling. Intelligence and embassy reports documented the signs of distress and described how the monarchy lacked support in key sectors of society. They noted ferment among the young, gloom among the middle class, and increasing unity between the religious and secular opposition movements. An astute policymaker might still have come to the conclusion that the shah could handle all of this, but no one should have been surprised by how wobbly the regime had become. The tragedy is that these warnings were ignored, and those who issued them were later blamed for the "intelligence failure."

History does not always repeat itself, nor does it necessarily rhyme. The Islamic Republic has now been in power slightly longer than the shah's monarchy. It is a different regime, existing in a different time, yet it is making many of the shah's mistakes. Like the monarchy in its later years, the Islamic Republic is at an impasse, having become a regime that cannot reform itself even when it senses an urgent need for change.

Throughout its four decades in power, the theocracy has generated enterprising intellectuals who have sought to refashion the regime's governing canons. Mohammad Khatami devoted his presidency in the 1990s to harmonizing faith and freedom. He wanted an inclusive national compact that would preserve Iran's Islamic traditions while upholding democratic values. His was the most impressive attempt thus far to modernize the foundations of the republic and make it accountable to both man and God. But Khatami's reforms sparked protests in 1999 from those who felt he had not gone far enough and a backlash from hardliners who thought he went too far. His failure foreclosed the possibility that the Islamic Republic could liberalize itself through its own constitutional provisions. The idea of working within the system to broaden its political parameters is a discredited notion in today's Iran.

Mahmoud Ahmadinejad, who came to power in 2005, was best known for his crass anti-Semitism and nuclear truculence. But in his crude way he tried to make social justice the foundation of the regime's legitimacy. He spoke of income inequality and equitable distribution of wealth. Yet his most important legacies are massive corruption and crackpot schemes that wasted Iran's oil wealth. He ruled in a time of unusually high oil prices, yet left the state nearly bankrupt. After his tenure in power, it is hard for anyone to believe that the Islamic Republic can craft a judicious economic platform that serves all of its citizens.

President Hassan Rouhani is the latest president to try to rescue the economy and end Iran's isolation. He bet his presidency on a nuclear agreement whose benefits were not entirely obvious even before the United States abandoned it. Like his predecessors, he has promised much and delivered little. Rouhani has been a man of the center, and his failure has discredited the pragmatic middle of Iran's politics.

The economic dilemmas of the shah and the clerical oligarchs are eerily similar in their unfulfilled expectations. Neither regime created sufficient jobs and opportunities to meet the demands of its growing constituency. Corruption and provocative class cleavages are their most visible achievements. Today, as in the 1970s, the Iranian people have come to the stark conclusion that their government will never meet their basic economic mandates, and that only those connected to the state will benefit from its largesse.

Like the shah, the Islamic Republic has purged its government of its best and brightest. The imaginative reformers who tried to refashion religion as the basis of democratic rule have long been excised from the body politic. In the lexicon of the hardliners, reform and sedition are one and the same. The more pragmatic elements of the Rouhani government, who thought they could purchase political passivity with a growing economy, stand disillusioned. The peculiarity of Iran's revolutionaries is that they rarely learn from their own revolution. The Iranian people are not about to sell off their political aspirations for financial gain, even if the regime were capable of providing such rewards. And Ahmadinejad proved that those who talk most often of God are usually the most corrupt and incompetent of the regime's elite.

Both the shah and the mullahs embraced priorities that their people found questionable. For the shah, it was a massive arms buildup that drained the treasury. For the clerical rulers, it was and is the pursuit of the most ambitious imperial venture in Iran's modern history. Iran is meddling everywhere in the Middle East: prolonging the civil wars in Syria and Yemen, and training and subsidizing numerous militias, the most successful of which is the lethal Hezbollah. It is pursuing self-defeating confrontational policies toward the conservative Arab monarchies and Israel while undertaking costly nation-building efforts in Iraq and Afghanistan. It is insisting on a hostility toward the United States that blocks its pathway to the global markets. All of these policies are questioned by Persians who cannot understand why their limited resources are being wasted on Arab wars. Imperialism that was supposed to enhance the regime's domestic fortunes is instead tarnishing its tattered legitimacy.

The theme of Iranian history is a populace seeking to emancipate itself from tyranny—first monarchical, now Islamist. Many insist on seeing Iran as an island of autocratic stability, but for the past century it has been locked in a struggle between rulers wishing to sustain their prerogatives and a citizenry seeking freedom. The Islamic Republic has been beset by a succession of protest movements. The first to give up on the regime were the leftists, whose suppression in the early 1980s caused vicious street battles. The students were next, with their riots in 1999. Then came the Green Movement of 2009, when a fraudulent presidential election led to huge protests that discredited the regime with the middle classes. In December 2017 nearly one hundred Iranian cities and towns erupted in protest. The poor were thought to be the regime's last bastion of power, tied to the theocracy by piety and patronage. Yet this time, they too took to the streets with condemnations of their own. Two years later, the poor rebelled again and the regime had to resort to massive violence to regain control of its cities.

The Islamic Republic stands today as a regime without a real constituency, covering itself in an ideology that few believe in. Its security forces look formidable, but so did the shah's army and secret police. If a government has nothing left but its enforcers, it has little true strength. Still, the one lesson of history is that things don't happen because they should. The regime may linger much longer than the Pahlavi state, but if so, it would be wrong to assume that the clerical rulers have achieved the dictatorial success that eluded their predecessor. The only thing that can be said with certainty is that the Iranian masses' search for freedom continues. Should it one day succeed, it will confound another generation of Americans who had assured themselves that, like the shah, the Islamic Republic would endure.

Acknowledgments

This is my fifth book while at the Council on Foreign Relations, and in many ways, the most challenging. I wish to thank Richard Haass and James Lindsay for providing me a sanctuary at the Council. The library staff at CFR was indispensable in terms of dealing with my many arcane requests for books of all sorts, old newspaper clips, and documents from across the country.

Throughout this process I have benefited from the generosity of a number of individuals. Roger Hertog is a philanthropist with unusual intellectual curiosity. I appreciate his support for my work and his criticisms of the book. Paul Singer and his important foundation have been a source of much needed support for many scholarly endeavors, and I am grateful for all they have done for me over the years.

William Frucht has been a model editor—supportive, inquisitive, critical, and patient. Bill and the entire staff of the Yale University Press have done much to improve the manuscript. At every stage of the production, Yale has been exceptional in its professionalism. My agent Andrew Wiley was once more an indispensable source of guidance.

A number of friends read the entire manuscript and offered many helpful suggestions and comments. Marvin Zonis, one of the pioneers of Iranian Studies, spent hours with me on the telephone as we exchanged stories about the shah. His insights are unparalleled, for as they say, he was present at the creation. His tales about meeting both the shah and Ayatollah Ruhollah Khomeini are priceless. Misagh Parsa, who has done much to explain the Iranian revolution, read the entire draft with his usual scholarly care and steered me in the right direction. Greg Craig is a rarity in Washington, a man who has held tight to his ideals long after this sort of a thing has become unfashionable. He not only read the entire book but also helped me better understand the dilemmas that American presidents face in dealing with problematic allies. James West and Zachary Shapiro assisted me in the research process and were most helpful in organizing my path forward.

Throughout the book I have relied on popular usage of names most familiar to the general reader. And as it is customary to acknowledge, I am responsible for all the shortcomings of this book.

Notes

Works frequently cited have been identified by the following abbreviations:

DNSA   Digital National Security Archive
FRUS   *Foreign Relations of the United States*
NARA   National Archives and Records Administration
NSC   National Security Council

1. IRAN UNDER OCCUPATION

1. Cyrus Ghani, *Iran and the Rise of Reza Shah: From Qajar Collapse to Pahlavi Power* (London: I.B. Tauris, 2000).
2. Peter Avery, *Modern Iran* (New York: Praeger, 1967), 210–269.
3. Donald Wilber, *Iran: Past and Present* (Princeton, NJ: Princeton University Press, 1976), 125–332; Amin Saikal: *The Rise and Fall of the Shah* (Princeton, NJ: Princeton University Press, 1980), 11–35.
4. Majid Yazdi, "Patterns of Clerical Political Behavior in Postwar Iran, 1941–1953," *Middle Eastern Studies* 26, no. 3 (Summer 1990): 280–285.
5. Suleyman Seydi, "Intelligence and Counter-Intelligence Activities in Iran during the Second World War," *Middle Eastern Studies* 46, no. 5 (September 2010).
6. Gholam Reza Afkhami, *The Life and Times of the Shah* (Berkeley: University of California Press, 2009), 70.
7. F. Eshraghi, "The Immediate Aftermath of Anglo-Soviet Occupation of Iran in August 1941," *Middle Eastern Studies* 20, no. 3 (July 1984).
8. Nikolay Kozhanov, "The Pretexts and Reasons for the Allied Invasion of Iran in 1941," *Iranian Studies* 45, no. 4 (July 2012): 495.

9. Shaul Bakhash, "Britain and the Abdication of Reza Shah," *Middle Eastern Studies* 52, no. 2 (Spring 2016): 323–327.

10. Shaul Bakhash, " 'Dear Anthony,' 'Dear Leo': Britain's Quixotic Flirtation with Dynastic Change in Iran during World War II," *Iran Nameh* 30, no. 4 (Winter 2016).

11. *Memoirs of Mahmoud Foroughi,* ed. Habib Ladjevardi (Cambridge, MA: Center for Middle East Studies, Harvard University, 2003), 64–65.

12. Fakhreddin Azimi, *Iran: The Crisis of Democracy; From the Exile of Reza Shah to the Fall of Musaddiq* (London: I.B. Tauris, 2009), 35–51.

13. George Lenczowski, *Russia and the West in Iran, 1918–1948: A Study in Big-Power Rivalry* (Ithaca, NY: Cornell University Press, 1949), 175.

14. Rouhollah Ramazani, *Iran's Foreign Policy, 1941–1973: A Study of Foreign Policy in Modernizing Nations* (Charlottesville: University of Virginia Press, 1975), 49.

15. Reader Bullard, *Letters from Tehran: A British Ambassador in World War II Persia* (London: I.B. Tauris, 1991), 82.

16. Afkhami, *Life and Times of the Shah,* 79–80.

17. Marvin Zonis, *Majestic Failure: The Fall of the Shah* (Chicago: University of Chicago Press, 1991), 39.

18. Ibid., 98.

19. Ibid., 151.

20. Ervand Abrahamian, *A History of Modern Iran* (Cambridge, UK: Cambridge University Press, 2008), 97–123.

21. L. P. Elwell-Sutton, "Political Parties in Iran, 1941–1948," *Middle East Journal* 3, no. 1 (January 1949). See also Elwell-Sutton, "The Iranian Press, 1941–1947," *Journal of the British Institute of Persian Studies* 6, no. 1 (1968).

22. Ali M. Ansari, *Modern Iran since 1921: The Pahlavis and After* (London: Longman, 2003), 79.

23. Bullard, *Letters from Tehran,* 89.

24. Sepehr Zabih, *The Communist Movement in Iran* (Berkeley: University of California Press, 1966), 46–123; Ervand Abrahamian, *Iran between Two Revolutions* (Princeton, NJ: Princeton University Press, 1982), 326–419.

25. "Cable from Dimitrov to Stalin, Molotov, Beria, and Malenkov," December 9, 1941, Wilson Center History and Public Policy Program Digital Archive, RGASPI, f. 558. op. 11, d. 66, ll. 43–44, http://digitalarchive.wilsoncenter.org/document/119104.

26. Ibid.

27. Robert Dallek, *Franklin D. Roosevelt and American Foreign Policy, 1932–1945* (Oxford, UK: Oxford University Press, 1979); James MacGregor Burns, *Roosevelt: The Soldier of Freedom* (New York: Harcourt Brace Jovanovich, 1970), 406–414.

28. *FRUS, 1943,* vol. 4: *The Near East and Africa* (Washington, DC: Government Printing Office, 1964), 414.

29. Stephen McFarland, "A Peripheral View of the Origins of the Cold War: The Crisis in Iran, 1941–1947," *Diplomatic History* 4, no. 4 (Fall 1980): 337. See also Hassan Arfa, *Under Five Shahs* (New York: William Morrow, 1965), 297–365.

30. Stephen McFarland, "A Peripheral View of the Origins of the Cold War," 337.

31. *FRUS, 1942,* vol. 4: *The Near East and Africa* (Washington, DC: Government Printing Office), 77.

32. Ibid.

33. *FRUS, 1943,* 4:378.

34. *FRUS, 1942,* 4:259.

35. *FRUS, 1943,* 4:330.

36. Mark Lytle, *The Origins of the Iranian-American Alliance, 1941–1953* (New York: Holmes & Meier, 1987), 49.

37. *FRUS, 1944,* vol. 5: *The Near East, South Asia, and Africa* (Washington, DC: Government Printing Office, 1965), 349.

38. Barry Rubin, *The Great Powers in the Middle East, 1941–1947* (New York: Frank Cass and Company, 1980), 90.

39. Ibid.

40. *FRUS, 1943,* 4:330.

41. Richard Cottam, *Iran and the United States* (Pittsburgh: University of Pittsburgh Press, 1988), 55–66.

42. *FRUS, 1944,* 5:437.

43. Ervand Abrahamian, "Factionalism in Iran: Political Groups in the 14th Parliament (1944–46)," *Middle Eastern Studies* 14, no. 1 (Winter 1978). See also Abrahamian, *Iran between Two Revolutions,* 176–203.

44. Hooshang Tale with Farhad Tale, *Iran in the Claws of the Bear: The Failed Soviet Landgrab of 1946* (New York: iUniverse, Inc., 2007), 13.

45. Azimi, *Iran,* 99–113.

46. Lytle, *Origins of the Iranian-American Alliance,* 90.

47. *New York Times,* October 30, 1944.

48. Ramazani, *Iran's Foreign Policy,* 105.

49. Anthony Eden, *The Reckoning: The Memoirs of Anthony Eden* (Boston: Houghton Mifflin, 1965), 595–596.

50. R. K. Karanjia, *The Mind of a Monarch* (London: George Allen & Unwin, 1977), 84.

2. A CRISIS IN AZERBAIJAN

1. Geoffrey Roberts, "Moscow's Cold War on the Periphery: Soviet Policy in Greece, Iran, and Turkey, 1943–8," *Journal of Contemporary History* 46, no. 1 (January 2011), https://doi.org/10.1177/0022009410383292; Vladislav Zubok, *A Failed Empire: The Soviet Union in the Cold War from Stalin to Gorbachev* (Chapel Hill: University of North Carolina Press, 2007), 29–62.

2. Natalia I. Yegorova, "The Iran Crisis of 1945–46: A View from the Russian Archives," Working Paper 15, Wilson International Center for Scholars, Washington, DC, 1996, https://www.wilsoncenter.org/publication/the-iran-crisis-1945-46-view-the-russian-archives.

3. Fernande Scheid Raine, "Stalin and the Creation of the Azerbaijan Democratic Party in Iran, 1945," *Cold War History* 2, no. 1 (October 2001): 9, https://doi.org/10.1080/713999940.

270 NOTES TO PAGES 32-42

4. Ibid., 11.

5. "Message from Bagirov and Maslennikov to Beria on Arming the Autonomous Movement in Iranian Azerbaijan," October 21, 1945, Wilson Center History and Public Policy Program Digital Archive, GAPPOD, f. 1, op. 89, d. [95], https://digitalarchive. wilsoncenter.org/document/120542.

6. Louise Fawcett, *Iran and the Cold War: The Azerbaijan Crisis of 1946* (Cambridge, UK: Cambridge University Press, 1992), 88.

7. Associated Press, December 25, 1945.

8. Associated Press, December 20, 1945.

9. *FRUS, Conferences at Malta and Yalta, 1945* (Washington, DC: Government Printing Office, 1975), 439–500.

10. *FRUS, 1946*, vol. 7: *The Near East and Africa* (Washington, DC: Government Printing Office, 1969), 293.

11. Fakhreddin Azimi, *Iran: The Crisis of Democracy; From the Exile of Reza Shah to the Fall of Musaddiq* (London: I.B. Tauris, 2009), 142.

12. *New York Times,* December 14, 1945.

13. United Nations, *Official Records of the Security Council,* First Year Series, 1946, supplement no. 1, 17–19.

14. James F. Byrnes, *Speaking Frankly* (New York: Harper and Brothers, 1947), 118–119.

15. *FRUS, 1946,* 7:344.

16. Telegram 861.24591/3–1546, Murray to Secretary of State, March 12, 1946, NARA.

17. Hooshang Tale with Farhad Tale, *Iran in the Claws of the Bear: The Failed Soviet Landgrab of 1946* (New York: iUniverse, Inc., 2007), 87.

18. Ibid.

19. Ibid., 96.

20. Ibid., 97.

21. Hugh Thomas, *Armed Truce: The Beginnings of the Cold War, 1945–46* (London: Hamish Hamilton, 1986), 690.

22. James Forrestal, *The Forrestal Diaries* (New York: Viking Press, 1951), 86–127.

23. Ibid., 236.

24. John Gaddis, *George Kennan: An American Life* (New York: Pantheon, 2011), 218; Walter Hixon, *George Kennan: Cold War Iconoclast* (New York: Oxford University Press, 1989), 25–45.

25. Gaddis, *George Kennan,* 220.

26. Ibid.

27. Ibid., 221.

28. Townsend Hoopes and Douglas Brinkley, *Driven Patriot: The Life and Times of James Forrestal* (New York: Knopf, 1992), 272.

29. Dean Acheson, *Present at the Creation: My Years in the State Department* (New York: W.W. Norton, 1969), 86.

30. Charles Bohlen, *Witness to History, 1929–1969* (New York: W.W. Norton, 1973), 26–29.

31. Memorandum of Conversation by Patterson, August 21, 1947, RG 59, 741.83/8–2147, NARA.

32. Ibid.
33. Fraser Harbutt, *The Iron Curtain: Churchill, America and the Origins of the Cold War* (Oxford, UK: Oxford University Press, 1986), 186.
34. Ibid.
35. Ibid.
36. William Manchester and Paul Reid, *The Last Lion: Winston Spencer Churchill; The Defender of the Realm, 1940–1965* (New York: Little, Brown, 2012), 957–963.
37. Thomas, *Armed Truce,* 705.
38. Arthur M. Schlesinger, *Robert Kennedy and His Times* (Boston: Little, Brown, 1978), 89.
39. Richard Nixon, *Memoirs* (New York: Grosset & Dunlap, 1978), 45.
40. *New York Times,* March 17, 1946.
41. Thomas, *Armed Truce,* 718–719.
42. Ibid.
43. Randall Woods and Howard Jones, *Dawning of the Cold War: The United States' Quest for Order* (Oxford, UK: Oxford University Press, 1991), 98–133; Robert Dallek, *The Lost Peace: Leadership in a Time of Horror and Hope, 1945–1953* (New York: HarperCollins, 2010), 211–241.
44. Richard Pfau, "Containment in Iran, 1946: The Shift to an Active Policy," *Diplomatic History* 1, no. 4 (Fall 1977): 364.
45. Ibid., 365.
46. Arnold Offner, *Another Such Victory: President Truman and the Cold War, 1945–1953* (Stanford, CA: Stanford University Press, 2002), 47–185.
47. Victor Sebestyen, *1946: The Making of the Modern World* (New York: Pantheon, 2014); Kenneth Weisbrode, *The Making of Indecision, 1946: A Tour through the Crucible of Harry Truman's America* (New York: Viking, 2016).
48. Harry S. Truman, *Memoirs: Years of Trial and Hope, 1946–1952* (New York: Doubleday, 1956), 95.
49. Henry Ryan, "A New Look at Churchill's 'Iron Curtain' Speech," *Historical Journal* 22, no. 4 (December 1979): 900.
50. Robert Donovan, *The Presidency of Harry S. Truman, 1945–8: Conflict and Crisis* (New York: W.W. Norton, 1977), 185.
51. "The Reminiscences of Dean Rusk," Iranian-American Foreign Relations Oral History Project, Columbia University, 1987, 3.
52. Fawcett, *Iran and the Cold War,* 167–168.
53. Alexander Nicholas Shaw, "'Strong, United and Independent': The British Foreign Office, Anglo-Iranian Oil Company and the Internationalization of Iranian Politics at the Dawn of the Cold War, 1945–46," *Middle Eastern Studies* 52, no. 3 (Fall 2016), https://doi.org/10.1080/00263206.2015.1124417; Simon Davis, "'A Projected New Trusteeship'? American Internationalism, British Imperialism, and the Reconstruction of Iran, 1938–1947," *Diplomacy and Statecraft* 17, no. 1 (Summer 2006), https://doi.org/10.1080/09592290500533429.
54. Yegorova, "Iran Crisis of 1945–46," 18.

55. "Memo from Atakishiyev, Kerimov, Ibragimov and Gasanov to Bagirov on April 4 meeting with Pishehvari," April 5, 1946, History and Public Policy Program Digital Archive, Cold War International History Project, Woodrow Wilson International Center for Scholars, http://digitalarchive.wilsoncenter.org/document/120538.

56. Gholam Reza Afkhami, *The Life and Times of the Shah* (Berkeley: University of California Press, 2009), 103.

57. "Joseph Stalin to Ja'far Pishehvari, Leader of the Democratic Party of Azerbaijan, May 8, 1946," History and Public Policy Program Digital Archive, Cold War International History Project, Woodrow Wilson International Center for Scholars, http://digitalarchive.wilsoncenter.org/document/117827.

58. Azimi, *Iran*, 172.

59. Ervand Abrahamian, *Iran between Two Revolutions* (Princeton, NJ: Princeton University Press, 1982), 225–242; Afkhami, *Life and Times of the Shah*, 263–317.

60. Mohammad Reza Pahlavi, *Mission for My Country* (New York: Hutchinson, 1961), 103.

61. James Bill and William Roger Louis, eds., *Musaddiq, Iranian Nationalism, and Oil* (Austin: University of Texas Press, 1988), 93.

62. *FRUS, 1949*, vol. 6: *The Near East, South Asia and Africa* (Washington, DC: Government Printing Office, 1977), 576.

3. THE OIL NATIONALIZATION CRISIS

1. William Roger Louis, *The British Empire in the Middle East, 1945–1951: Arab Nationalism, the United States and Postwar Imperialism* (Oxford, UK: Oxford University Press, 1984), 638.

2. Stephen Dorrill, *MI6: Inside the Covert World of Her Majesty's Secret Intelligence Service* (New York: Free Press, 2000), 561.

3. Karim Sanjabi, *Hopes and Despairs: The Political Memoirs of Dr. Karim Sanjabi* (London: Book Distribution Center, 1989), 134.

4. Shahrough Akhavi, *Religion and Politics in Contemporary Iran* (Albany: State University of New York, 1980), 60–91.

5. Gholam Reza Afkhami, *The Life and Times of the Shah* (Berkeley: University of California Press, 2009), 121.

6. Mary Ann Heiss, *Empire and Nationhood: The United States, Great Britain, and Iranian Oil, 1950–1954* (New York: Columbia University Press, 1997), 29.

7. *FRUS, 1950*, vol. 5: *The Near East, South Asia and Africa* (Washington, DC: Government Printing Office, 1978), 589, 618.

8. Fakhreddin Azimi, *Iran: The Crisis of Democracy; From the Exile of Reza Shah to the Fall of Musaddiq* (London: I.B. Tauris, 2009), 236; Fakhreddin Azimi, *The Quest for Democracy in Iran* (Cambridge, MA: Harvard University Press, 2008), 118–224.

9. *Memoirs of Jafar Sharif-Emami*, ed. Habib Ladjevardi, Iranian Oral History Project, Center for Middle Eastern Studies, Harvard University, 1999.

10. *New York Times*, March 9, 1951.

11. Interview with George Middleton, October 15, 1985, Iranian Oral History Project, Center for Middle Eastern Studies, Harvard University, transcript, tape 1, p. 9.

12. Fariborz Mokhtari, "Iran's 1953 Coup Revisited: Internal Dynamics versus External Intrigue," *Middle East Journal* 62, no. 3 (Summer 2008): 468.

13. Christopher de Bellaigue, *Patriot of Persia: Muhammad Mossadegh and a Very British Coup* (London: Bodley Head, 2012), 151–154.

14. Jack Straw, *The English Job: Understanding Iran and Why It Distrusts Britain* (London: Biteback Publishers, 2019), 125.

15. *FRUS, 1952–1954,* supplement to vol. 10: *Iran, 1951–1954* (Washington, DC: Government Printing Office, 2017), 73.

16. Abbas Milani, *The Shah* (New York: Palgrave Macmillan, 2011), 150.

17. Ervand Abrahamian, *Iran between Two Revolutions* (Princeton, NJ: Princeton University Press, 1982), 267.

18. Mohammad Reza Pahlavi, *Mission for My Country* (London: Hutchinson, 1961), 93.

19. Majid Yazdi, "Patterns of Clerical Political Behavior in Postwar Iran, 1941–53," *Middle Eastern Studies* 26, no. 3 (July 1990): 286–287, https://doi.org/10.1080/00263209008700819.

20. Mohammad Hassan Faghfoory, "The Role of the Ulama in Twentieth Century Iran with Particular Reference to Ayatollah Sayyid Abul-Qasim Kashani," Ph.D. diss., University of Wisconsin, 1978.

21. Heiss, *Empire and Nationhood*, 64.

22. H. W. Brands, "The Cairo-Tehran Connection in Anglo-American Rivalry in the Middle East, 1951–1953," *International History Review* 11, no. 3 (August 1989): 438, https://doi.org/10.1080/07075332.1989.9640519.

23. Steve Marsh, "Anglo-American Relations and the Labour Government's 'Scuttle' from Abadan: a 'Declaration of Dependence?,'" *International History Review* 35, no. 4 (Fall 2013): 825, https://doi.org/10.1080/07075332.2013.817462.

24. Bernard Donoughue and G. W. Jones, *Herbert Morrison: Portrait of a Politician* (London: Weidenfeld & Nicolson, 1973), 470–515.

25. Steve Marsh, "Continuity and Change: Reinterpreting the Policies of the Truman and Eisenhower Administrations toward Iran, 1950–1954," *Journal of Cold War Studies* 7, no. 3 (Summer 2005): 83.

26. Ibid., 86.

27. *FRUS, 1952–1954,* vol. 10: *Iran, 1951–1954* (Washington, DC: Government Printing Office, 1989), 60–61.

28. Marsh, "Anglo-American Relations," 834.

29. Clement R. Attlee, *As It Happened* (New York: Viking, 1954), 246.

30. John Gurney, "Ann Katharine Swynford Lambton, 1912–2008," in *Biographical Memoirs of Fellows of the British Academy*, vol. 12 (Oxford, UK: British Academy, 2013), 258.

31. James Goode, *The United States and Iran under the Shadow of Musaddiq* (New York: Palgrave, 1997), 47.

32. Louis, *British Empire*, 662.

33. *New York Times*, May 27, 1951.

34. Artemy Kalinovsky, "The Soviet Union and Mossadeq: A Research Note," *Iranian Studies* 47, no. 3 (March 2014): 405.

35. Vladislav Zubok, "Stalin, Soviet Intelligence, and the Struggle for Iran, 1945–53," *Diplomatic History* (November 2019).
36. *FRUS, 1952–1954*, 10:58.
37. Mostafa Elm, *Oil, Power and Principle: Iran's Oil Nationalization and Its Aftermath* (Syracuse, NY: Syracuse University Press, 1992), 124.
38. *New York Times*, July 12, 1952.
39. "Man of the Year: Challenge of the East," *Time Magazine*, January 7, 1952, http://content.time.com/time/magazine/article/0,9171,815775,00.html.
40. Vernon Walters, *Silent Missions* (Garden City, NY: Doubleday, 1978), 241–263.
41. *FRUS, 1952–1954*, supplement to vol. 10: *Iran*, 130.
42. *FRUS, 1952–1954*, 10:145.
43. *FRUS, 1952–1954*, supplement to vol. 10: *Iran*, 130.
44. Muhammad Musaddiq, *Memoirs*, trans. S. H. Amin and H. Katouzian (London: National Movement of Iran, 1988), 316.
45. Dean Acheson, *Present at the Creation: My Years in the State Department* (New York: W.W. Norton, 1969), 510.
46. *FRUS, 1952–1954*, 10:242.
47. Ibid.
48. George McGhee, *Envoy to the Middle World: Adventures in Diplomacy* (New York: Harper & Row, 1983), 318–345.
49. Ibid., 247.
50. Ibid.
51. Goode, *United States and Iran*, 50.
52. David McLellan, *Dean Acheson: The State Department Years* (New York: Dodd, Mead, 1976), 382–397.
53. Anthony Eden, *Full Circle* (New York: Houghton Mifflin, 1960), 201; Robert Rhodes James, *Anthony Eden: A Biography* (London: Weidenfeld & Nicolson, 1987), 343–394.
54. *FRUS, 1952–1954*, 10:280.
55. Barry Rubin, *Paved with Good Intentions: The American Experience and Iran* (New York: Penguin, 1980), 68.
56. Elm, *Oil, Power and Principle*, 236.
57. *FRUS, 1952–1954*, supplement to vol. 10: *Iran*, 149.
58. *FRUS, 1952–1954*, 10:405.
59. *Kayhan*, July 19, 1952.
60. *New York Times*, July 22, 1953.
61. *FRUS, 1952–1954*, 10:323.
62. Ibid., 10:320.
63. Ibid., 329.
64. "VKP(b) CC Decree, 'Concerning Instructions to Cde. Sadchikov, the Soviet Ambassador in Iran, in Connection with the Iranian Government's Offer to Sell the Soviet Union Oil,'" April 1952, Wilson Center History and Public Policy Program Digital Archive, RGASPI, f. 82, op. 2, d. 1219, l. 98, https://digitalarchive.wilsoncenter.org/document/119164.

65. *FRUS, 1952–1954,* 10:320.
66. Ibid., 10:384–385.
67. Ibid., 10:406.
68. Ibid., 10:341.
69. Ibid., 10:475.

4. THE COUP

1. For important studies on Eisenhower, see William I. Hitchcock, *The Age of Eisenhower: America and the World in the 1950s* (New York: Simon & Schuster, 2018); Jim Newton, *Eisenhower: The White House Years* (New York: Random House, 2011); Blanche Wiesen Cook, *Eisenhower: An Anti-Militarist in the White House* (St. Charles, MO: Forum Press, 1974); John Gaddis, *Strategies of Containment* (Oxford, UK: Oxford University Press, 1983); George Quester, "Was Eisenhower a Genius?," *International Security* 4, no. 2 (Fall 1979); H. W. Brands, "The Age of Vulnerability: Eisenhower and the National Security State," *American Historical Review* 94, no. 4 (October 1989); and Robert Divine, *Eisenhower and the Cold War* (Oxford, UK: Oxford University Press, 1981).

2. Fred I. Greenstein, *The Hidden Hand Presidency: Eisenhower as Leader* (New York: Basic Books, 1982). See also Greenstein, "Eisenhower as an Activist President: A New Look at New Evidence," *Political Science Quarterly* 94 (1979–1980); Richard H. Immerman, "Eisenhower or Dulles: Who Made the Decisions?," *Political Psychology* 1, no. 2 (Autumn 1979); Douglas Kinnard, *President Eisenhower and Strategy Management: A Study in Defense Politics* (Lexington: University Press of Kentucky, 1989).

3. For important studies on John Foster Dulles, see Townsend Hoopes, *The Devil and John Foster Dulles* (Boston: Little, Brown, 1973); Richard Immerman, ed., *John Foster Dulles and the Diplomacy of the Cold War* (Princeton, NJ: Princeton University Press, 1991); John Gaddis, "The Unexpected John Foster Dulles: Nuclear Weapons, Communism and the Russians," in *The United States and the End of the Cold War* (Oxford, UK: Oxford University Press, 1992); Ronald Pruessen, "Beyond the Cold War—Again: 1955 and 1990s," *Political Science Quarterly* 108, no. 1 (Spring 1993).

4. Sherman Adams, *First-Hand Report: The Story of the Eisenhower Administration* (New York: Harper, 1961), 87.

5. Dwight Eisenhower, Oral History, July 20, 1967, Dwight D. Eisenhower Presidential Library, Abilene, KS.

6. Peter Grose, *Gentleman Spy: The Life of Allen Dulles* (New York: Houghton Mifflin, 1994).

7. For the uses of covert action during Eisenhower's tenure, see Kermit Roosevelt, *Countercoup: The Struggle for Control of Iran* (New York: McGraw-Hill, 1979); James Bill, *The Eagle and the Lion: The Tragedy of American-Iranian Relations* (New Haven: Yale University Press, 1988); Andrew Rathmell, *Secret War in the Middle East: The Covert Struggle for Syria, 1949–1961* (London: I.B. Tauris, 2013); Stephen Rabe, *Eisenhower and Latin America: The Foreign Policy of Anti-Communism* (Chapel Hill: University of North Carolina Press, 1988), 38–94; Douglas Little, "Mission Impossible: The CIA and the Cult of Covert Action in the Middle East," *Diplomatic History* 28, no. 5 (November 2004), https://doi.org/10.1111/j.1467-7709.2004.00446.x.

8. *FRUS, 1952–1954,* vol. 2: *National Security Affairs* (Washington, DC: Government Printing Office, 1984), 397.

9. NSC Study, January 7, 1954, Ann Whitman File: DDE Diary (box 13), Dwight D. Eisenhower Presidential Library.

10. Cabinet Meeting, November 6, 1954, Ann Whitman File: Cabinet Series (box 19), Dwight D. Eisenhower Presidential Library.

11. Ray Takeyh, *The Origins of the Eisenhower Doctrine: The US, Britain, and Nasser's Egypt, 1953–1957* (New York: St. Martin's, 2000), 6–7.

12. Barry Rubin, *Paved with Good Intentions: The American Experience and Iran* (New York: Penguin, 1980), 77.

13. Jean Edward Smith, *Eisenhower in War and Peace* (New York: Random House, 2013), 621.

14. Mostafa Elm, *Oil, Power and Principle: Iran's Oil Nationalization and Its Aftermath* (Syracuse, NY: Syracuse University Press, 1992), 279.

15. Smith, *Eisenhower in War and Peace,* 622.

16. *FRUS, 1952–1954,* vol. 10: *Iran, 1951–1954* (Washington, DC: Government Printing Office, 1989), 695.

17. Steve Marsh, "The United States, Iran and Operation 'Ajax': Inverting Interpretative Orthodoxy," *Middle Eastern Studies* 39, no. 3 (July 2003): 23.

18. *FRUS, 1952–1954,* 10:702.

19. Gholam Reza Afkhami, *The Life and Times of the Shah* (Berkeley: University of California Press, 2009), 150.

20. Ibid.

21. Fakhreddin Azimi, *Iran: The Crisis of Democracy; From the Exile of Reza Shah to the Fall of Musaddiq* (London: I.B. Tauris, 2009), 316.

22. *FRUS, 1952–1954,* 10:720.

23. *FRUS, 1952–1954,* 10:323.

24. *FRUS, 1952–1954,* 10:351.

25. Dwight Eisenhower, *Mandate for Change, 1953–1956: The White House Years* (Garden City, NY: Doubleday, 1963), 161.

26. Ibid., 162.

27. Abbas Milani, *The Shah* (New York: Palgrave Macmillan, 2011), 184.

28. *New York Times,* July 7, 1953.

29. Mervyn Roberts, "Analysis of Radio Propaganda in the 1953 Iran Coup," *Iranian Studies* 45, no. 6 (November 2012): 767, https://doi.org/10.1080/00210862.2012.726848.

30. Muhammad Musaddiq, *Memoirs,* trans. S. H. Amin and H. Katouzian (London: National Movement of Iran, 1988), 350–351.

31. Kennett Love, "The American Role in the Pahlavi Restoration," unpublished manuscript, Princeton University Library, 1960, 23.

32. Ibid., 24.

33. *New York Times,* July 14, 1953.

34. *FRUS, 1952–1954,* supplement to vol. 10: *Iran, 1951–1954* (Washington, DC: Government Printing Office, 2017), 555.

35. H. W. Brands, *Inside the Cold War: Loy Henderson and the Rise of the American Empire, 1918–1961* (New York: Oxford University Press, 1991), 280.

36. *FRUS, 1952–1954,* supplement to vol. 10: *Iran,* 499.
37. Artemy Kalinovsky, "The Soviet Union and Mosaddeq: A Research Note," *Iranian Studies* 47, no. 3 (Summer 2014): 415, https://doi.org/10.1080/00210862.2014.880633.
38. Ibid., 414.
39. Ibid., 416.
40. "Notes from Meeting between Iranian Military and Nicolae Ceauşescu, Bucharest," March 13, 1958, Wilson Center History and Public Policy Program Digital Archive, National Central Historical Archives [ANIC], Central Committee of the Romanian Communist Party, Foreign Relations Section, https://digitalarchive.wilsoncenter.org/document/119594.
41. Osamu Miyata, "The Tudeh Network during the Oil Nationalization Period," *Middle Eastern Studies* 23, no. 3 (July 1987); Maziar Behrooz, "Tudeh Factionalism and the 1953 Coup," *International Journal of Middle East Studies* 33, no. 1 (August 2001).
42. Some important books that have recently been published on the coup are Ali Rahnema, *Behind the 1953 Coup in Iran: Thugs, Turncoats, Soldiers and Spooks* (Cambridge, UK: Cambridge University Press, 2015); Ervand Abrahamian, *The Coup: 1953, the CIA, and the Roots of Modern U.S.-Iranian Relations* (New York: New Press, 2013); Darioush Bayandor, *Iran and the CIA: The Fall of Mosaddeq Revisited* (New York: Palgrave, 2010); and Mark Gasiorowski and Malcolm Byrne, eds., *Mohammad Mosaddeq and the 1953 Coup in Iran* (Syracuse, NY: Syracuse University Press, 2004).
43. Mark Gasiorowski, "The CIA's TPBEDAMN Operation and the 1953 Coup in Iran," *Journal of Cold War History* 15, no. 4 (Fall 2013).
44. Donald Wilber, *Regime Change in Iran: Overthrow of Premier Mossadeq of Iran, November 1952–August 1953* (Nottingham, UK: Spokesman, 2006), 23.
45. Ibid., 20; Fariborz Mokhtari, "Iran's 1953 Coup Revisited: Internal Dynamics versus External Intrigue," *Middle East Journal* 62, no. 3 (Summer 2008): 484.
46. Mark Gasiorowski, *U.S. Foreign Policy and the Shah: Building a Client State in Iran* (Ithaca, NY: Cornell University Press, 1991), 72.
47. Wilber, *Regime Change,* 93.
48. Scott Koch, *"ZENDEBAD, SHAH!": The Central Intelligence Agency and the Fall of Iranian Prime Minister Mohammad Mosaddeq, August 1953* (Washington, DC: History Staff, Central Intelligence Agency, June 1998), 29–30.
49. Ashraf Pahlavi, *Faces in a Mirror: Memoirs from Exile* (New York: Prentice Hall, 1980), 139.
50. Wilber, *Regime Change,* 35–36.
51. Ibid., 36–37.
52. Stephen Dorrill, *MI6 : Inside the Covert World of Her Majesty's Secret Intelligence Service* (New York: Free Press, 2000), 589–590.
53. Kalinovsky, "Soviet Union and Mossadeq," 770.
54. *FRUS, 1952–1954,* supplement to vol. 10: *Iran,* 664.
55. Wilber, *Regime Change,* 62.
56. *FRUS, 1952–1954,* supplement to vol. 10: *Iran,* 679.
57. Ibid., 684.
58. *FRUS, 1952–1954,* 10:749.

59. Wilber, *Regime Change,* 45.
60. Siavush Randjbar-Daemi, "Down with the Monarchy: Iran's Republican Moment of August 1953," *Iranian Studies* 50, no. 2 (March 2017): 299.
61. Wilber, *Regime Change,* 47.
62. Randjbar-Daemi, "Down with the Monarchy," 301.
63. *FRUS, 1952–1954,* supplement to vol. 10: *Iran,* 694.
64. Ibid., 784.
65. Ardeshir Zahedi, *The Memoirs of Ardeshir Zahedi,* vol. 1: *From Childhood to the End of My Father's Premiership* (Bethesda, MD: Ibex, 2006), 188.
66. *FRUS, 1952–1954,* supplement to vol. 10: *Iran,* 679.
67. Mehdi Hairi-Yazdi, Iranian Oral History Project, Center for Middle Eastern Studies, Harvard University, tape 2, page 4.
68. *FRUS, 1952–1954,* supplement to vol. 10: *Iran,* 671.
69. Afkhami, *Life and Times of the Shah,* 175.
70. Ardeshir Zahedi, Oral History Archives, Foundation for Iranian Studies, tape 3, slide 1, July 2001.
71. Wilber, *Regime Change,* 62.
72. Richard Helms, Oral History Archives, Foundation for Iranian Studies, tape 1, page 7.
73. Earnest Oney, Oral History Archives, Foundation for Iranian Studies, 27.
74. Two other spooks involved in the coup have also written their memoirs, and both make a better read than Roosevelt's account. See C. M. Woodhouse, *Something Ventured* (London: Granda, 1982); and Sam Falle, *My Lucky Life: In War, Revolution, Peace and Diplomacy* (Sussex, UK: Book Guild Ltd, 1996).
75. Stephen Ambrose, *Eisenhower,* vol. 2: *The President* (New York: Simon & Schuster, 1984), 129.
76. Ervand Abrahamian, "The Crowd in Iranian Politics, 1905–1953," *Past and Present* 41 (December 1968): 190.

5. THE SHAH'S EMERGING AUTOCRACY

1. Marvin Zonis, *Majestic Failure: The Fall of the Shah* (Chicago: University of Chicago Press, 1991), 151.
2. Gholam Reza Afkhami, *The Life and Times of the Shah* (Berkeley: University of California Press, 2009), 184.
3. R. K. Karanjia, *The Mind of a Monarch* (London: George Allen & Unwin, 1977), 157.
4. Andrew Scott Cooper, *The Fall of Heaven: The Pahlavis and the Final Days of Imperial Iran* (New York: Henry Holt, 2016), 81.
5. *FRUS, 1952–1954,* vol. 10: *Iran, 1951–1954* (Washington, DC: Government Printing Office, 1989), 797.
6. Ibid., 799.
7. *FRUS, 1952–1954,* supplement to vol. 10: *Iran, 1951–1954* (Washington, DC: Government Printing Office, 2017), 807.
8. Abbas Milani, *The Shah* (New York: Palgrave Macmillan, 2011), 195.
9. U.S. ambassador in London to Marquess of Salisbury, September 9, 1953, Public Record Office, FO371/104577, EP 1024/10G.

10. Mary Ann Heiss, *Empire and Nationhood: The United States, Great Britain, and Iranian Oil, 1950–1954* (New York: Columbia University Press, 1997), 199.

11. Milani, *Shah*, 194.

12. Mostafa Elm, *Oil, Power and Principle: Iran's Oil Nationalization and Its Aftermath* (Syracuse, NY: Syracuse University Press, 1992), 320.

13. Ibid., 315.

14. Ibid., 318.

15. Afkhami, *Life and Times of the Shah*, 199.

16. Transcript of interview with Ali Amini, Oral History Archives, Foundation for Iranian Studies, 1983, tape 1, page 13.

17. Cooper, *Fall of Heaven*, 81.

18. Homa Katouzian, *The Political Economy of Modern Iran, 1926–1979* (New York: Penguin, 1981), 196.

19. Transcript of interview with Ali Amini, tape 1, page 16.

20. Milani, *Shah*, 201.

21. Fakhreddin Azimi, *The Quest for Democracy in Iran: A Century of Struggle against Authoritarian Rule* (Cambridge, MA: Harvard University Press, 2008), 161.

22. Ibid., 162.

23. Karanjia, *Mind of a Monarch*, 171.

24. *FRUS, 1955–1957*, vol. 12: *Near East Region: Iran and Iraq* (Washington, DC: Government Printing Office, 1991), 737.

25. "Notes from Meeting between Iranian Military and Nicolae Ceauşescu, Bucharest," March 13, 1958, Woodrow Wilson Center History and Public Policy Program Digital Archive, National Central Historical Archives [ANIC], Central Committee of the Romanian Communist Party, Foreign Relations Section, https://digitalarchive.wilsoncenter.org/document/119594.

26. *FRUS, 1955–1957*, 12:879.

27. Milani, *Shah*, 202.

28. Rouhollah Ramazani, *Iran's Foreign Policy, 1941–1973: A Study of Foreign Policy in Modernizing Nations* (Charlottesville: University of Virginia Press, 1975), 260.

29. *FRUS, 1955–1957*, 12:684.

30. Barry Rubin, *Paved with Good Intentions: The American Experience and Iran* (New York: Penguin, 1981), 97.

31. *FRUS, 1955–1957*, 12:748.

32. *FRUS, 1951–1954*, 10:894.

33. *FRUS, 1955–1957*, 12:772.

34. Ibid., 894.

35. Ibid., 903, 905.

36. *New York Times,* January 2, 1957.

37. Ibid.

38. Ibid.

39. Ervand Abrahamian, *Iran between Two Revolutions* (Princeton, NJ: Princeton University Press, 1982), 420.

40. Azimi, *Quest for Democracy in Iran*, 163.

41. *FRUS, 1955–1957*, 12:880.
42. Mark Gasiorowski, "The Qarani Affair and Iranian Politics," *International Journal of Middle Eastern Studies* 25, no. 4 (November 1993), https://doi.org/10.1017/S0020743800059298.
43. *FRUS, 1958–1960*, vol. 12: *Near East Region: Iraq; Iran; Arabian Peninsula* (Washington, DC: Government Printing Office, 1993), 539.
44. Ibid.
45. *Memoirs of Ali Amini*, ed. Habib Ladjevardi, Iranian Oral History Project, Center for Middle Eastern Studies, Harvard University, 1995, 89.
46. Transcript of interview with General Hassan Alavi-Kia, Oral History Archives, Foundation for Iranian Studies, 1983, tape 1, page 583.
47. *FRUS, 1958–1960*, 12:541.
48. Ibid., 12:553.
49. Ibid., 12:582.
50. For an account of the shah's penchant for control, see Khosrow Fatemi, "Leadership by Distrust: The Shah's Modus Operandi," *Middle East Journal* 36, no. 1 (Winter 1982).
51. Transcript of interview with Colonel Gratian Yatsevitch, Oral History Archives, Foundation for Iranian Studies, 1988, tape 1, page 41.
52. *FRUS, 1958–1960*, 12:568.
53. Ibid., 12:591–594.
54. Roham Alvandi, "Flirting with Neutrality: The Shah, Khrushchev, and the Failed 1959 Soviet-Iranian Negotiations," *Iranian Studies* 47, no. 3 (Spring 2014): 435.
55. "Transcript of a CC CPSU Plenum, Evening," June 28, 1957, Wilson Center History and Public Policy Program Digital Archive, Istoricheskii arkhiv 3–6(1993) and 1–2(1994), https://digitalarchive.wilsoncenter.org/document/111990.
56. Alvandi, "Flirting with Neutrality," 425.
57. *FRUS, 1958–1960*, 12:654.
58. Alvandi, "Flirting with Neutrality," 428.
59. *FRUS, 1958–1960*, 12:630.
60. Ibid., 12:628.
61. Ibid., 12:629.
62. Karim Sanjabi, *Hopes and Despairs: The Political Memoirs of Dr. Karim Sanjabi* (London: Nashre Ketab, 1989), 205.
63. *FRUS, 1958–1960*, 12:694.
64. Central Intelligence Agency, *NSC Briefing Paper*, January 13, 1960, https://www.cia.gov/library/readingroom/docs/CIA-RDP79R00890A001200010008-5.pdf.
65. *FRUS, 1958–1960*, 12:478.

6. THE AGE OF REFORM

1. Robert Dallek, *An Unfinished Life: John F. Kennedy, 1917–1963* (New York: Little, Brown, 2003); Dallek, *Camelot's Court: Inside the Kennedy White House* (New York: HarperCollins, 2013); and Richard Aldous, *Schlesinger: The Imperial Historian* (New York: W.W. Norton, 2017).

2. Michael Latham, "Modernization and the Kennedy-Era Alliance for Progress," *Diplomatic History* 22, no. 2 (Spring 1998) and *Modernization as Ideology: American Social Science and "Nation Building" in the Kennedy Era* (Chapel Hill: University of North Carolina Press, 2000); Nils Gilman, *Mandarins of the Future: Modernization Theory in Cold War America* (Baltimore, MD: Johns Hopkins University Press, 2003); and Michael Latham, *The Right Kind of Revolution: Modernization, Development and U.S. Foreign Policy from the Cold War to the Present* (Ithaca, NY: Cornell University Press, 2010).

3. David Milne, *America's Rasputin: Walt Rostow and the Vietnam War* (New York: Hill and Wang, 2009); Kimber Charles Pearce, *Rostow, Kennedy and the Rhetoric of Foreign Aid* (East Lansing: Michigan State University Press, 2001).

4. For a biography of Komer, see Frank Leith Jones, *Blowtorch: Robert Komer, Vietnam, and American Cold War Strategy* (Annapolis, MD: Naval Institute Press, 2013).

5. For studies of the Kennedy administration's approach to Iran, see David Collier, *Democracy and the Nature of American Influence in Iran, 1941–1979* (Syracuse, NY: Syracuse University Press, 2017), 186–229; David Collier, "To Prevent a Revolution: John F. Kennedy and the Promotion of Democracy in Iran," *Diplomacy & Statecraft* 24, no. 3 (Summer 2013); Ben Offiler, *US Foreign Policy and the Modernization of Iran: Kennedy, Johnson, Nixon and the Shah* (New York: Palgrave Macmillan, 2015), 13–69; April Summitt, "Perspectives on Power: John F. Kennedy and U.S.-Middle East Relations," Ph.D. diss., Western Michigan University, 2002, 58–66; James Goode, "Reforming Iran during the Kennedy Years," *Diplomatic History* 15, no. 1 (Winter 1991).

6. "The Reminiscences of Dean Rusk: Oral History, 1986," transcript, Iranian-American Relations Project, Columbia Center for Oral History, New York, p. 25.

7. William O. Douglas, *The Court Years, 1939–1975: The Autobiography of William O. Douglas* (New York: Random House, 1980), 303.

8. Andrew Scott Cooper, *The Oil Kings: How the U.S., Iran, and Saudi Arabia Changed the Balance of Power in the Middle East* (New York: Simon & Schuster, 2011), 23.

9. Randall Woods, *Fulbright: A Biography* (Cambridge, UK: Cambridge University Press, 1995), 312.

10. Gholam Reza Afkhami, *The Life and Times of the Shah* (Berkeley: University of California Press, 2009), 216.

11. *FRUS, 1961–1963*, vol. 17: *Near East: 1961–1962* (Washington, DC: Government Printing Office, 1994), 33.

12. Ibid., 17:55.

13. *Washington Post*, December 23, 1984.

14. Arthur Schlesinger Jr., *A Thousand Days: John F. Kennedy in the White House* (New York: Houghton Mifflin, 1965), 363.

15. "A Review of Problems in Iran and Recommendations for the National Security Council," May 15, 1961, NARA.

16. Asadollah Alam, *The Shah and I: The Confidential Diary of Iran's Royal Court, 1969–77* (London: I.B. Tauris, 1991), 384.

17. Mohammad Reza Pahlavi, *Answer to History* (New York: Stein and Day, 1980), 22.

18. Ali Amini, Oral History Archives, Foundation for Iranian Studies, January 1983, 19.

19. *FRUS, 1961–1963*, 17:118.

20. Afkhami, *Life and Times of the Shah*, 218.

21. Kenneth Pollack, *The Persian Puzzle: The Conflict between Iran and America* (New York: Random House, 2004), 85.

22. *New York Times*, June 9, 1961.

23. Ibid., May 6, 1962.

24. Barry Rubin, *Paved with Good Intentions: The American Experience and Iran* (New York: Penguin, 1981), 106.

25. On land reform, see Eric Hooglund, *Land and Revolution in Iran, 1960–1980* (Austin: University of Texas Press, 1982), 36–100; Keith McLachlan, *The Neglected Garden: The Politics and Ecology of Agriculture in Iran* (London: I.B. Tauris, 1990); Afsaneh Najmabadi, *Land Reform and Social Change in Iran* (Salt Lake City: University of Utah Press, 1987), 59–203; M. A. Katouzian, "Land Reform in Iran: A Case Study in the Political Economy of Social Engineering," *Journal of Peasant Studies* 1, no. 2 (Spring 1974); Homa Katouzian, *The Political Economy of Modern Iran, 1926–1979* (New York: Palgrave Macmillan, 1981), 188–313.

26. Abbas Amanat, *Iran: A Modern History* (New Haven: Yale University Press, 2017), 579; Charles Issawi, "Iran's Economic Upsurge," *Middle East Journal* 21, no. 4 (Autumn 1967): 454–455.

27. *Time Magazine*, June 6, 1961.

28. *FRUS, 1961–1963*, 17:58.

29. Karim Sanjabi, *Hopes and Despairs: The Political Memoirs of Dr. Karim Sanjabi* (London: Nashre Ketab, 1989), 213.

30. Homa Katouzian, *Mossadeq and the Struggle for Power in Iran* (London: I.B. Tauris, 1999), 227–256; Fakhreddin Azimi, *The Quest for Democracy in Iran: A Century of Struggle against Authoritarian Rule* (Cambridge, MA: Harvard University Press, 2008), 157–201.

31. James Bill, *The Eagle and the Lion: The Tragedy of American-Iranian Relations* (New Haven: Yale University Press, 1988), 146–147.

32. *FRUS, 1961–1963*, 17:202.

33. Ibid., 17:119.

34. Central Intelligence Agency, *NSC Briefing Paper*, January 13, 1960, https://www.cia.gov/library/readingroom/docs/CIA-RDP79R00890A001200010008-5.pdf.

35. Abbas Milani, *The Shah* (New York: St. Martin's, 2011), 271.

36. *FRUS, 1961–1963*, 17:510.

37. Ibid., 17:430–431.

38. Stephen McGlinchey, *U.S. Arms Policies towards the Shah's Iran* (London: Routledge, 2014), 22–38; Stephanie Cronin, *Armies and State-Building in the Modern Middle East: Politics, Nationalism and Military Reform* (London: I.B. Tauris, 2014), 133–205.

39. Matthew Shannon, *Losing Hearts and Minds: American-Iranian Relations and International Education during the Cold War* (Ithaca, NY: Cornell University Press, 2017), 43–93; Afshin Matin-Asgari, *Iranian Student Opposition to the Shah* (Costa

Mesa, CA: Mazda Publishers, 2002), 40–78; Lawrence Brammer, "Problems of Iranian University Students," *Middle East Journal* 18, no. 4 (Autumn 1964); James Bill, "The Politics of Student Alienation: The Case of Iran," *Iranian Studies* 2, no. 1 (Winter 1969).

40. *FRUS, 1961–1963*, 17:593.

41. Victor Nemchenok, "In Search of Stability amid Chaos: U.S. Policy toward Iran, 1961–63," *Cold War History* 10, no. 3 (August 2010): 356.

42. *FRUS, 1961–1963*, 17:593.

43. Ibid., 17:532.

44. Ibid., 17:593.

45. Ibid., 17:595.

46. 87 Cong. Rec. 108, part 2 (daily edition, April 2–24, 1962).

47. Milani, *Shah*, 286.

48. *FRUS, 1961–1963*, 17:609.

49. *FRUS, 1961–1963*, vol. 18: *Near and Middle East, 1962–1963* (Washington, DC: Government Printing Office, 1995), 11.

50. Amini, Oral History Archives, January 1983, 25.

51. Ministry of Information of Iran, *Dr. Ali Amini: The Official SAVAK Document* (Tehran: Center for Study of Historical Documents of the Ministry of Information, 2000).

52. Afkhami, *Life and Times of the Shah*, 227.

53. Roland Popp, "Benign Intervention? The Kennedy Administration's Push for Reform in Iran," in *John F. Kennedy and the* "Thousand Days," ed. Manfred Berg and Andreas Etges (Heidelberg: University of Heidelberg, 2007), 213. See also Popp, "An Application of Modernization Theory during the Cold War? The Case of Pahlavi Iran," *International History Review* 30, no. 1 (Winter 2008).

54. *FRUS, 1961–1963*, 18:22.

55. Bill, *Eagle and the Lion*, 141.

56. *FRUS, 1961–1963*, 18:72.

57. Andrew Scott Cooper, *The Fall of Heaven: The Pahlavis and the Final Days of Imperial Iran* (New York: Henry Holt, 2016), 107.

58. Ali M. Ansari, "The Myth of the White Revolution: Mohammad Reza Shah, 'Modernization,' and the Consolidation of Power," *Middle Eastern Studies* 37, no. 3 (July 2001); Rouhollah Ramazani, "Iran's White Revolution: A Study in Political Development," *Middle East Journal* 5, no. 2 (April 1974).

59. Mohammad Gholi Majd, "Small Landowners and Land Distribution in Iran, 1962–71," *International Journal of Middle East Studies* 32, no. 1 (February 2000): 126.

60. Yann Richard, *Iran: A Social and Political History since the Qajars* (Cambridge, UK: Cambridge University Press, 2019), 245.

61. For clerical politics, see William Floor, "The Revolutionary Character of the Iranian Ulama: Wishful Thinking or Reality?," *International Journal of Middle East Studies* 12, no. 4 (December 1980); Hamid Algar, "The Oppositional Role of the Ulama in Twentieth Century Iran," in *Scholars, Saints, and Sufis: Muslim Religious Institutions since 1500*, ed. Nikki Keddie (Berkeley: University of California Press,

1972); Misagh Parsa, "Mosque of Last Resort: State Reform and Social Contract in the Early 1960s," in *A Century of Revolution: Social Movements in Iran,* ed. John Foran (Minneapolis: University of Minnesota Press, 1982); Shahrough Akhavi, *Religion and Politics in Contemporary Iran* (Albany: State University of New York Press, 1980), 91–117.

62. Hussein Ali Montazeri, *The Complete Memoirs of Ayatollah Hussein Ali Montazeri* (Spånga, Sweden: N.p., 2001), 104.

63. Baqer Moin, *Khomeini: Life of the Ayatollah* (New York: St. Martin's, 1999), 88.

64. *U.S. News and World Report,* February 11, 1963.

65. Moin, *Khomeini,* 83.

66. Cooper, *Fall of Heaven,* 112.

67. Moin, *Khomeini,* 104.

68. Marvin Zonis, *Majestic Failure: The Fall of the Shah* (Chicago: University of Chicago Press, 1991), 136.

69. Amanat, *Iran,* 597.

70. Alam, *Shah and I,* 279–280.

71. *FRUS, 1961–1963,* 18:571.

72. Ibid., 18:610.

73. April Summitt, "For a White Revolution: John F. Kennedy and the Shah of Iran," *Middle East Journal* 58, no. 4 (Autumn 2004): 572.

74. Yann Richard, *Iran: A Social and Political History since the Qajars* (Cambridge, UK: Cambridge University Press, 2019), 252.

75. Abbas Milani, *The Persian Sphinx: Amir Abbas Hoveyda and the Riddle of the Iranian Revolution* (Washington, DC: Mage, 2000), 154.

76. Amanat, *Iran,* 599.

77. Moin, *Khomeini,* 121–122.

78. Afkhami, *Life and Times of the Shah,* 249.

7. MASTER OF THE UNIVERSE

1. *The Soviet Union in the Middle East,* ed. Adeed Dawisha and Karen Dawisha (New York: Holmes & Meier, 1982), 24–45, 124–134; Roy Allison, *The Soviet Union and the Strategy of Non-Alignment in the Third World* (Cambridge, UK: Cambridge University Press, 1988), 126–180.

2. *New York Times,* December 21, 1965.

3. Andrew L. Johns, "The Johnson Administration, the Shah of Iran, and the Changing Pattern of U.S.-Iranian Relations, 1965–1967: 'Tired of Being Treated Like a Schoolboy,' " *Journal of Cold War Studies* 9, no. 2 (Spring 2007): 72.

4. Ibid., 83. See also Claudia Castiglioni, "No Longer a Client, Not Yet a Partner: The U.S.-Iranian Alliance in the Johnson Years," *Cold War Studies* 15, no. 4 (Fall 2015).

5. Stephen McGlinchey, *US Arms Policies towards the Shah's Iran* (London: Routledge, 2014), 45.

6. Stephen McGlinchey, "Lyndon B. Johnson and Arms Credit Sales to Iran, 1964–1968," *Middle East Journal* 67, no. 2 (Spring 2013): 232.

7. "The Reminiscences of Armin Meyer," Iranian-American Foreign Relations Oral History Project, Columbia University, 1987, 26.

8. *FRUS, 1964–1968,* vol. 22: *Iran* (Washington, DC: Government Printing Office, 1999), 366.

9. John Darwin, *Britain and Decolonisation: The Retreat from Empire in the Post-War World* (New York: Palgrave, 1988), 292.

10. William Roger Louis, *Ends of British Imperialism: The Scramble for Empire, Suez and Decolonization* (London: I.B. Tauris, 2006), 877–907; Simon C. Smith, "Britain's Decision to Withdraw from the Persian Gulf: A Pattern Not a Puzzle," *Journal of Imperial and Commonwealth History* 44, no. 2 (Winter 2015); F. Gregory Gause, "British and American Policies in the Persian Gulf, 1968–1973," *Review of International Studies* 11, no. 4 (October 1985).

11. Darwin, *Britain and Decolonisation,* 295.

12. Jeremy Fielding, "Coping with Decline: US Policy toward British Defense Reviews of 1966," *Diplomatic History* 23, no. 4 (Fall 1999): 639; W. Taylor Fain, *American Ascendance and British Retreat in the Persian Gulf Region* (New York: Palgrave Macmillan, 2008), 141–201.

13. Fielding, "Coping with Decline," 639.

14. Kevin Boyle, "The Price of Peace: Vietnam, the Pound, and the Crisis of the American Empire," *Diplomatic History* 27, no. 1 (January 2003).

15. Shahram Chubin and Sepehr Zabih, *The Foreign Relations of Iran: A Developing State in a Zone of Great-Power Conflict* (Berkeley: University of California Press, 1974), 250.

16. *FRUS, 1964–1968,* 22:493.

17. Rouhollah Ramazani, *Iran's Foreign Policy, 1941–1973: A Study of Foreign Policy in Modernizing Nations* (Charlottesville: University of Virginia Press, 1975), 349.

18. George Lenczowski, "The Oil-Producing Countries," *Daedalus* 104, no. 4 (Fall 1975). See also Lenczowski, *Iran under the Pahlavis* (Stanford, CA: Hoover Institution Press, 1978), 201–248.

19. Barry Rubin, *Paved with Good Intentions: The American Experience and Iran* (New York: Penguin, 1981), 131.

20. Gholam Reza Afkhami, *The Life and Times of the Shah* (Berkeley: University of California Press, 2009) 271.

21. *New York Times,* January 24, 1973.

22. Rudiger Graf, "Making Use of the 'Oil Weapon': Western Industrialized Countries and Arab Petropolitics in 1973–1974," *Diplomatic History* 36, no. 1 (January 2012); Ian Smart, "Oil, the Super Powers and the Middle East," *International Affairs* 53 (January 1977); Daniel Yergin, *The Prize: The Epic Quest For Oil, Money and Power* (New York: Simon & Schuster, 1990), 561–745.

23. Andrew Scott Cooper, *Oil Kings: How the U.S., Iran, and Saudi Arabia Changed the Balance of Power in the Middle East* (New York: Simon & Schuster, 2011), 146.

24. Richard M. Nixon, "Asia after Viet Nam," *Foreign Affairs* (October 1967): 114.

25. Fredrik Logevall and Andrew Preston, eds., *Nixon in the World: American Foreign Relations, 1969–1977* (Oxford, UK: Oxford University Press, 2008); William Bundy, *A Tangled Web: The Making of Foreign Policy in the Nixon Presidency* (New York: Hill

and Wang, 1998), 428–473; Dan Caldwell, "The Legitimation of the Nixon-Kissinger Grand Design and Grand Strategy," *Diplomatic History* 33, no. 4 (September 2009); Jeffrey Kimball, "The Nixon Doctrine: A Saga of Misunderstanding," *Presidential Studies Quarterly* 36, no. 1 (February 2006). See also Ben Offiler, *US Foreign Policy and the Modernization of Iran: Kennedy, Johnson, Nixon, and the Shah* (New York: Palgrave Macmillan, 2015), 154, 165.

26. "National Security Decision Memorandum (NSDM) 92," November 7, 1970, in *FRUS, 1969–1976*, vol. E-4: *Documents on Iran and Iraq, 1969–1972* (Washington, DC: Government Printing Office, 2006).

27. Douglas Little, *American Orientalism: The United States and the Middle East since 1945* (Chapel Hill: University of North Carolina Press, 2002), 144.

28. Cooper, *Oil Kings,* 39.

29. "The Reminiscences of Douglas MacArthur II," Iranian-American Foreign Relations Oral History Project, 1985, Columbia University, 43.

30. Asadollah Alam, *The Shah and I: The Confidential Diary of Iran's Royal Court, 1969–1977* (London: I.B. Tauris, 2008), 390.

31. "Memorandum from Henry Kissinger to Joseph Farland," July 5, 1972, in *FRUS, 1969–1976,* vol. E-4.

32. Arash Reisinezhad, *The Shah of Iran, the Iraqi Kurds, and the Lebanese Shia* (New York: Palgrave Macmillan, 2019), 163; Roham Alvandi, *Nixon, Kissinger, and the Shah* (Oxford, UK: Oxford University Press, 2016), 63; both quoting Asadollah Alam's diaries, *Yad'dashtha'ye 'Alam Virayish va muqaddamah az Ali Naqi Alikhani,* vol. 2 (Bethesda, MD: Iranbooks, 1993), 260.

33. "The Reminiscences of James Schlesinger," Iranian-American Foreign Relations Oral History Project, Columbia University, 1991, 15.

34. Sepehr Zabih, "Iran's Policy toward the Persian Gulf," *International Journal of Middle East Studies* 7, no. 3 (July 1976); Rouhollah Ramazani, "Iran's Changing Foreign Policy: A Preliminary Discussion," *Middle East Journal* 24, no. 4 (Autumn 1970).

35. Rouhollah Ramazani, *The Persian Gulf: Iran's Role* (Charlottesville: University of Virginia Press, 1972), 46.

36. Denis Wright, Oral History Archives, Foundation for Iranian Studies, 1986, 31.

37. Roham Alvandi, "Muhammad Reza Pahlavi and the Bahrain Question, 1968–1970," *British Journal of Middle Eastern Studies* 37, no. 2 (July 2010): 168.

38. Ibid., 169.

39. Ramazani, *Iran's Foreign Policy,* 416.

40. James F. Goode, "Assisting Our Brothers, Defending Ourselves: The Iranian Intervention in Oman, 1972–1975," *Iranian Studies* 47, no. 3 (Fall 2014): 447.

41. *FRUS, 1969–1976,* vol. 27: *Iran; Iraq, 1973–1976* (Washington, DC: Government Printing Office, 2012), 102.

42. Ibid.

43. James Bill, *The Eagle and the Lion: The Tragedy of American-Iranian Relations* (New Haven: Yale University Press, 1988), 207.

44. Reisinezhad, *Shah of Iran,* 165.

45. Roham Alvandi, *Nixon, Kissinger, and the Shah* (Oxford, UK: Oxford University Press, 2014), 114.

46. Asadollah Alam, *The Shah and I: The Confidential Diary of Iran's Royal Court, 1969–77* (London: I.B. Tauris, 1991), 417.

47. Central Intelligence Agency, *The President's Daily Brief,* March 8, 1975, https://www.cia.gov/library/readingroom/docs/DOC_0006014740.pdf.

48. *FRUS, 1969–1976*, 27:755.

49. William Burr, "A Brief History of U.S.-Iranian Nuclear Negotiations," *Bulletin of Atomic Scientists* 65, no. 1 (January 2009).

50. Alvandi, *Nixon, Kissinger, and the Shah*, 130.

51. Afkhami, *Life and Times of the Shah*, 346.

52. Abbas Milani, *Eminent Persians: The Men and Women Who Made Modern Iran*, vol. 1 (Syracuse, NY: Syracuse University Press, 2008), 134–139.

53. Akbar Etemad, Oral History Archives, Foundation for Iranian Studies, 1982, 104.

54. David Patrikarakos, *Nuclear Iran: The Birth of an Atomic State* (London: I.B. Tauris, 2012), 59.

55. *New York Times*, September 23, 1975.

56. Ibid., October 2, 1975.

57. Afkhami, *Life and Times of the Shah*, 354.

58. Hal Brands, "Rethinking Nonproliferation: LBJ, the Gilpatric Committee, and U.S. National Security Policy," *Journal of Cold War Studies* 8, no. 2 (Spring 2006): 99.

59. *FRUS, 1969–1976*, 27:347.

60. Maziar Bahari, "The Shah's Plan Was to Build Bombs," *New Statesman*, September 15, 2008, https://www.newstatesman.com/asia/2008/09/iran-nuclear-shah-west.

61. *FRUS, 1969–1976*, 27:473.

62. Jacob Darwin Hamblin, "The Nuclearization of Iran in the Seventies," *Diplomatic History* 38, no. 5 (November 2014): 1118.

63. Alvandi, *Nixon, Kissinger, and the Shah*, 153.

8. THE REVOLUTION

1. Michael Axworthy, *Revolutionary Iran: A History of the Islamic Republic* (Oxford, UK: Oxford University Press, 2013), 77.

2. Marvin Zonis, "Political Elites and Political Cynicism in Iran," *Comparative Political Studies* (October 1968): 354. See also Zonis, *The Political Elite of Iran* (Princeton, NJ: Princeton University Press, 1971).

3. James Bill, *The Politics of Iran: Groups, Classes, and Modernization* (Columbus, OH: Charles E. Merrill, 1972), 88.

4. Asadollah Alam, *The Shah and I: The Confidential Diary of Iran's Royal Court, 1969–77* (London: I.B. Tauris, 1991), 315.

5. Ibid., 461.

6. Michael Metrinko, Oral History Archives, Foundation for Iranian Studies, June 4, 1988, 55.

7. For important studies on the performance of the intelligence community during the revolution, see Robert Jervis, *Why Intelligence Fails: Lessons from the Iranian Revolution and the Iraq War* (Ithaca, NY: Cornell University Press, 2010); Uri Bar-Joseph, "Forecasting a Hurricane: Israeli and American Estimations of the Khomeini Revolution," *Journal of Strategic Studies* (2013).

8. National Intelligence Estimate no. 34–69, January 10, 1969, *FRUS, 1969–1976*, vol. E-4: *Documents on Iran and Iraq, 1969–1972* (Washington, DC: Government Printing Office, 2006).

9. Situation Report, February 28, 1972, *FRUS, 1969–1976*, vol. E-4.

10. Memorandum from the Director of the Central Intelligence (Helms) to the President's Assistant for National Security Affairs (Kissinger), May 8, 1972, *FRUS, 1969–1976*, vol. E-4.

11. *FRUS, 1969–1976*, vol. 27: *Iran; Iraq, 1973–1976* (Washington, DC: Government Printing Office, 2012), 120–121.

12. Ray Takeyh and Reuel Gerecht, "Be Careful What You Revolt For," *National Review*, March 11, 2019.

13. Anthony Parsons, *The Pride and the Fall: Iran, 1974–1979* (London: Jonathan Cape, 1984), 56.

14. Takeyh and Gerecht, "Be Careful."

15. Ruhollah Khomeini, *Islamic Government* (Tehran: Institute for Compilation and Publication of Imam Khomeini's Works, 1975), 7.

16. *New York Times*, December 30, 1978.

17. Charles Kurzman, "The Qum Protests and the Coming of the Iranian Revolution," *Social Science History* (Fall 2003).

18. *New York Times*, June 11, 1975.

19. Intelligence Report: Centers of Power in Iran, Central Intelligence Agency, May 1972, *FRUS, 1969–1976*, vol. E-4.

20. *FRUS, 1969–1976*, 27:352.

21. Ibid., 27:487.

22. "Selecting a New Leader for Shi'ite Islam," Embassy to Department of State, July 7, 1979, *FRUS, 1969–1976*, vol. E-4.

23. *The Islamic Revolution According to SAVAK Documents*, vol. 1 (Tehran: Historical Documentation Center, Ministry of Information, 1997), 262.

24. *Sahifeh-Ye Imam: An Anthology of Imam' Khomeini's Speeches, Messages, Interviews, Decrees, Religious Permissions, and Letters*, vol. 4: *October 14–November 16, 1978* (Tehran: Institute for Compilation and Publication of Imam Khomeini's Works, 2008), 148.

25. Ibid., 233.

26. Farah Pahlavi, *An Enduring Love: My Life with the Shah; A Memoir* (New York: Miramax Books, 2004), 241–295.

27. James Buchan, *Days of God: The Revolution in Iran and Its Consequences* (London: John Murray, 2012), 191.

28. Abbas Milani, *The Shah* (New York: Palgrave Macmillan, 2011), 380.

29. Alam, *Shah and I*, 422.

30. Darioush Bayandor, *The Shah, the Islamic Revolution, and the United States* (New York: Palgrave Macmillan, 2019), 97.

31. Alam, *Shah and I*, 535.

32. Ibid., 464.

33. Ibid., 538.

34. Misagh Parsa, *Social Origins of the Iranian Revolution* (New Brunswick, NJ: Rutgers University Press, 1989), 92–93.

35. Ibid., 103.

36. Gholam Reza Afkhami, *The Life and Times of the Shah* (Berkeley: University of California Press, 2009), 447.

37. Ibid.

38. Ervand Abrahamian, *Iran between Two Revolutions* (Princeton, NJ: Princeton University Press, 1982), 502.

39. *Sahifeh-Ye Imam: An Anthology of Imam' Khomeini's Speeches, Messages, Interviews, Decrees, Religious Permissions, and Letters*, vol. 3: *October 8, 1978–October 13, 1978* (Tehran: Institute for Compilation and Publication of Imam Khomeini's Works, 2008), 267.

40. Baqer Moin, *Khomeini: Life of the Ayatollah* (New York: St. Martin's, 1999), 185.

41. Ibid.

42. Gary Sick, *All Fall Down: America's Tragic Encounter with Iran* (New York: Random House, 1985).

43. Richard Sale, "Carter and Iran: From Idealism to Disaster," *Washington Quarterly* 3, no. 4 (Summer 1980): 76.

44. Barry Rubin, *Paved with Good Intentions: The American Experience and Iran* (New York: Penguin, 1980), 194.

45. Hamilton Jordan, *Crisis: The Last Year of the Carter Presidency* (New York: G.P. Putnam's Sons, 1982), 89.

46. Jimmy Carter, *Keeping Faith: Memoirs of a President* (Fayetteville: University of Arkansas Press, 1995), 445.

47. Alam, *Shah and I*, 540.

48. David Collier, *Democracy and the Nature of American Influence in Iran, 1941–1979* (Syracuse, NY: Syracuse University Press, 2017), 272.

49. "Tehran, Iran, Toasts of the President and the Shah at a State Dinner," December 31, 1977, archives of the American Presidency Project, UC Santa Barbara, https://www.presidency.ucsb.edu/documents/tehran-iran-toasts-the-president-and-the-shah-state-dinner.

50. Mohammad Reza Pahlavi, *Answer to History* (New York: Stein and Day, 1980), 152.

51. Jimmy Carter, Oral History, Presidential Oral Histories, Miller Center, University of Virginia, 1982, 16.

52. Abbas Amanat, *Iran: A Modern History* (New Haven: Yale University Press, 2017), 714.

53. Moin, *Khomeini*, 185, 186.

54. Ibid., 186–187.

55. Said Amir Arjomand, *The Turban for the Crown: The Islamic Revolution in Iran* (Oxford, UK: Oxford University Press, 1988), 91–134. *Sahifeh-Ye Imam: An Anthology of Imam Khomeini's Speeches, Messages, Interviews, Decrees, Religious Permissions, and*

Letters, vol. 5: *November 17, 1978–January 28, 1979* (Tehran: Institute for Compilation and Publication of Imam Khomeini's Works, 2008), 404.

56. Buchan, *Days of God,* 203.
57. Ervand Abrahamian, "Structural Causes of the Iranian Revolution," *MERIP Reports* (May 1980): 24.
58. "Human Rights Discussion with the Shah," Cable from Sullivan to State Department, March 28, 1978, NARA.
59. Afkhami, *Life and Times of the Shah,* 454.
60. "Uncertain Political Mood: Religious Developments, Tougher Royal Line on Demonstrations," Cable from Sullivan to the State Department, January 28, 1978, DNSA.
61. Ibid.
62. Michael Donovan, "National Intelligence and the Iranian Revolution," *Intelligence and National Security* (Winter 1997): 144, 148.
63. "We are Engaged in a Real Psychological War: Transcript of the Discussion of Military Commanders on August 14 and August 21, 1978," Tehran, Center for Documents of the Islamic Revolution, 1997, 28.
64. Rubin, *Paved with Good Intentions,* 206.
65. "Rumors of Shah's Health," Cable from Embassy to the State Department, July 26, 1978, NARA.
66. Afkhami, *Life and Times of the Shah,* 457.
67. *Sahifeh-Ye Imam,* 3:489.
68. *The Islamic Revolution According to SAVAK Documents,* vol. 9 (Tehran: Historical Documentation Center, Ministry of Information, 2002), 265–276.
69. Buchan, *Days of God,* 214.
70. Joseph Kraft, "A Letter from Iran," *New Yorker,* December 18, 1978, 33.
71. "Meeting with Hoveyda," Cable from Sullivan to the State Department, August 31, 1978, NARA.
72. "Audience with the Shah," Cable from Sullivan to the State Department, August 28, 1978, NARA.
73. Parsons, *Pride and the Fall,* 71.
74. Ibid.
75. Kraft, "Letter from Iran," 2.
76. Afkhami, *Life and Times of the Shah,* 461.
77. Houchang Nahavandi, *The Last Shah of Iran: Fatal Countdown of a Great Patriot Betrayed by the Free World,* trans. Steve Reed (New York: Aquilion, 2005), 200.
78. William Sullivan, *Mission to Iran: The Last U.S. Ambassador* (New York: W.W. Norton, 1981), 157.
79. "Zahedi's Call on Acting Secretary," Cable from the State Department to the Embassy, September 15, 1978, NARA.
80. The most important study on the shah's complex psychological makeup is Marvin Zonis, *Majestic Failure: The Fall of the Shah* (Chicago: University of Chicago Press, 1991).
81. Ervand Abrahamian, *A History of Modern Iran* (Cambridge, UK: Cambridge University Press, 2008), 161.

82. *Sahifeh-Ye Imam*, 3:541.

83. *Sahifeh-Ye Imam*, 4:231.

84. *Sahifeh-Ye Imam*, 5:405.

85. Ibid., 5:505.

86. Ibid., 5:522.

87. Charles Kurzman, *The Unthinkable Revolution in Iran* (Cambridge, MA: Harvard University Press, 2004), 78–79.

88. *Worldwide Crude Oil and Gas Production 77* (February 26, 1979): 166; *Worldwide Crude Oil and Gas Production 77* (March 26, 1979): 204.

89. Mehdi Bazargan, *Six Decades of Service and Opposition*, vol. 2 (Tehran: RASA Publications, 1996), 256.

90. Bayandor, *The Shah, the Islamic Revolution, and the United States*, 235.

91. *Sahifeh-Ye Imam*, 4:228.

92. "Meeting with the Prime Minister," Cable from Sullivan to the State Department, October 29, 1978, NARA.

93. "Iran after the Shah: An Intelligence Assessment," August 31, 1978, Central Intelligence Agency, CIA Reading Room: CIA-RDP80T00634A000900100001–6.

94. Draft of the NIE [National Intelligence Estimate], September 1978, Central Intelligence Agency, CIA Reading Room: CIA-RDP80T00634A000900100002–7.

95. "The Evolution of the U.S.-Iranian Relationship: A Brief Survey of U.S.-Iranian Relations, 1941–1979," September 28, 1979, DNSA.

96. Briefing Memorandum, "The Gathering Crisis in Iran," Bureau of Intelligence and Research (INR), Department of State, November 2, 1978, DNSA.

97. "Looking Ahead: Shifting Attitudes of Iranian Public," Cable from Sullivan to the State Department, October 28, 1978, NARA.

98. W. Michael Blumenthal, *From Exile to Washington: A Memoir of Leadership in the Twentieth Century* (New York: Overlook Press, 2013), 357.

99. Ibrahim Yazdi, *Final Attempts in the Last Days: Untold Stories of the Islamic Revolution of Iran* (Tehran: Qalam, 2000), 407–414.

100. Zbigniew Brzezinski, *Power and Principle: Memoirs of the National Security Advisor, 1977–1981* (New York: Farrar, Straus & Giroux, 1983), 362.

101. Ibid., 364.

102. Ibid., 365.

103. "Audience with the Shah," Cable from Sullivan to the State Department, November 4, 1978, NARA.

104. "Thinking the Unthinkable," Cable from Sullivan to the State Department, November 9, 1978, NARA.

105. Afkhami, *Life and Times of the Shah*, 481.

106. Bulletin, CIA Operation Center, November 6, 1978, CIA Reading Room, CIA-RDP8-IB00401R002000120006-4.

107. *Documents on Azhari and Bakhtiar Governments* (Tehran: Office of the President, Division of Research and Documents, Office of Communications and Information, 2013), 17.

108. *Sahifeh-Ye Imam*, 4:337.

109. Ibid., 4:364.
110. *Documents on Azhari and Bakhtiar Governments,* 89.
111. Sullivan, *Mission to Iran,* 212.
112. *Documents on Azhari and Bakhtiar Governments,* 169.
113. "Decision on Khomeini," Sullivan to State Department, January 11, 1979, NARA.
114. For the shah's final days in Iran, see Andrew Scott Cooper, *The Fall of Heaven: The Pahlavis and the Final Days of Imperial Iran* (New York: Henry Holt, 2016), 201–260, 279–481.
115. *Islam and Revolution: The Writings and Declarations of Imam Khomeini,* trans. and annot. Hamid Algar (Berkeley, CA: Mizan Press, 1981), 247.
116. Amanat, *Iran,* 735.
117. Yazdi, *Final Attempts,* 318.
118. Sullivan, *Mission to Iran,* 233.
119. Javier Gil Guerrero, *The Carter Administration and the Fall of Iran's Pahlavi Dynasty: US-Iran Relations on the Brink of the 1979 Revolution* (New York: Palgrave Macmillan, 2016), 177.
120. Morning Meeting, January 29, 1979, Central Intelligence Agency, CIA Reading Room, https://www.cia.gov/library/readingroom/docs/CIA-RDP81B00493R000100070002-4.pdf.
121. Briefing Memorandum, "Gathering Crisis in Iran."
122. "Message to USG from Khomeini," Cable from Warren Zimmerman to Vance, January 27, 1979, NARA.
123. *Sahifeh-Ye Imam,* 5:530.
124. *We Will Melt Like Snow: Minutes of the Debates of the Council of Commanders of the Armed Forces, January–February 1979* (Tehran: Nashr-e Ney, 1986), 61.
125. Ibid., 88.
126. General Robert E. Huyser, *Mission to Tehran: The Fall of the Shah and the Rise of Khomeini; Recounted by the U.S. General Who Was Secretly Sent at the Last Minute to Prevent It* (New York: Harper & Row, 1986), 48.
127. Cyrus Vance, *Hard Choices: Critical Years in America's Foreign Policy* (New York: Simon & Schuster, 1983), 338.
128. Huyser, *Mission to Tehran,* 170.
129. *Islam and Revolution,* 256.
130. Ibid., 260.
131. *We Will Melt Like Snow,* 175.
132. "Toufanian/Von Marbod," Conversation Cable from Sullivan to Vance, February 9, 1979, NARA.
133. Huyser, *Mission to Tehran,* 283–284.
134. Bayandor, *The Shah, the Islamic Revolution, and the United States,* 388.
135. *Islam and Revolution,* 261.

9. REPUBLIC OF VIRTUE

1. Shaul Bakhash, *The Reign of the Ayatollahs: Iran and the Islamic Revolution* (New York: Basic Books, 1984), 54.

2. Ibid., 55.

3. Mohsen Milani, *The Making of Iran's Islamic Revolution: From Monarchy to the Islamic Republic* (Boulder, CO: Westview, 1988), 141.

4. Cheryl Benard and Zalmay Khalilzad, *The Government of God: Iran's Islamic Republic* (New York: Columbia University Press, 1984), 109.

5. H. E. Chehabi, *Iranian Politics and Religious Modernism: The Liberation Movement of Iran under the Shah and Khomeini* (Ithaca, NY: Cornell University Press, 1990), 258.

6. Bakhash, *Reign of the Ayatollahs,* 57.

7. Gregory Rose, "The Post-Revolutionary Purge of Iran's Armed Forces: A Revisionist Assessment," *Iranian Studies* 17, nos. 2/3 (Spring–Summer 1984): 154.

8. Sadeq Khalkhali, *Memoirs of Ayatollah Khalkhali,* vol. 3 (Tehran: N.p., 2001), 11.

9. James Buchan, *Days of God: The Revolution in Iran and Its Consequences* (London: John Murray, 2012), 301.

10. Ibid.

11. Abbas Milani, *The Persian Sphinx: Amir Abbas Hoveyda and the Riddle of the Iranian Revolution* (Washington, DC: Mage, 2000), 318.

12. Buchan, *Days of God,* 301–302.

13. Milani, *Persian Sphinx,* 339.

14. Khalkahli, *Memoirs,* 393.

15. Buchan, *Days of God,* 296.

16. Hussein Ali Montazeri, *Memoirs of Ayatollah Montazeri* (Los Angeles: Ketab Books, 2000), 230–231.

17. *New York Times,* April 7, 1979.

18. *Washington Post,* March 9, 1979.

19. *New York Times,* May 9, 1979.

20. Khalkhali, *Memoirs,* 12.

21. International Campaign for Human Rights in Iran, "Recording on 1988 Prison Massacre Exposes Early Fissure in the Islamic Republic of Iran," August 30, 2016, http://www.payvand.com/news/16/aug/1169.html.

22. Ervand Abrahamian, *Radical Islam: The Iranian Mojahedin* (London: I.B. Tauris, 1989), 186–206; Maziar Behrooz, *Rebels with a Cause: The Failure of the Left in Iran* (London: I.B. Tauris, 1999), 95–135.

23. Ervand Abrahamian, *Tortured Confessions: Prisons and Public Recantations in Modern Iran* (Berkeley: University of California Press, 1999), 146–154, 209–229.

24. Mohsen Milani, "Harvest of Shame: Tudeh and the Bazargan Government," *Middle Eastern Studies* 29, no. 2 (April 1993): 311.

25. Dilip Hiro, *Iran under the Ayatollahs* (New York: Routledge & Kegan Paul, 1985), 117.

26. *New York Times,* April 19, 1979.

27. Ervand Abrahamian, *A History of Modern Iran* (Cambridge, UK: Cambridge University Press, 2008), 163.

28. *New York Times,* April 2, 1979.

29. Milani, *Making of Iran's Islamic Revolution,* 154–155.

30. Bakhash, *Reign of the Ayatollahs,* 78.

31. Asghar Schirazi, *The Constitution of Iran: Politics and State in the Islamic Republic,* trans. John O'Kane (London: I.B. Tauris, 1998), 30.

32. Ibid., 33.
33. Constitution of the Islamic Republic of Iran, available at https://www.wipo.int/edocs/lexdocs/laws/en/ir/ir001en.pdf.
34. Ibid.
35. Said Saffari, "The Legitimation of the Clergy's Right to Rule in the Iranian Constitution of 1979," *British Journal of Middle Eastern Studies* 20, no. 1 (Winter 1993): 71, 73.
36. Constitution of the Islamic Republic of Iran.
37. David D. Kirkpatrick, "How a Chase Bank Chairman Helped the Deposed Shah of Iran Enter the U.S.," *New York Times*, December 29, 2019, https://www.nytimes.com/2019/12/29/world/middleeast/shah-iran-chase-papers.html.
38. Jimmy Carter, *Keeping Faith: Memoirs of a President* (New York: Bantam, 1982), 455.
39. Muhammad Reza Mahdavi-Kani, *Memoirs of Ayatollah Mahdavi-Kani* (Tehran: Center for Documents of the Islamic Revolution, 2007), 218–219.
40. Ray Takeyh, "The Ayatollah and the US Embassy: Khomeini's Role in the 1979 Hostage Crisis," *Weekly Standard*, February 2, 2015.
41. Kenneth Pollack, *The Persian Puzzle: The Conflict between Iran and America* (New York: Random House, 2004), 154.
42. Takeyh, "Ayatollah and the US Embassy."
43. Chehabi, *Iranian Politics and Religious Modernism*, 276.
44. Baqer Moin, *Khomeini: Life of the Ayatollah* (New York: St. Martin's, 1999), 227.
45. *Jomhouri-e Eslami*, March 17, 1981.
46. *New York Times*, August 8, 1979.

Index

The term "shah" in the index refers to Mohammad Reza Pahlavi.

Zahedi, Fazlollah: in AIOC negotiations, 122–123; American support for, 120; anti-Mossadeq coalition and 1953 coup and, 3, 73, 85–86, 95–97, 104–106, 108, 110, 113–114; Association of Retired Officers and, 95, 97; background of, 96–97; Henderson and, 119; military joining in opposition to Mossadeq, 93, 231;

Mossadeq dismissing as minister of the interior, 73, 96; Nixon and, 180; ouster of, 124, 125, 129; as prime minister, 109, 110, 114, 131, 204; religious coalition and, 94; shah's relationship with, 99, 119–121, 136

Zimmerman, Warren, 236

Zonis, Marvin, 196; *Majestic Failure*, 164

Printed and bound by CPI Group (UK) Ltd, Croydon, CR0 4YY

26/03/2025

14648094-0001